Modern Japanese Culture

The Insider View

Leith Morton

OXFORD
UNIVERSITY PRESS

OXFORD

UNIVERSITY PRESS

253 Normanby Road, South Melbourne, Victoria 3205, Australia

Oxford University Press is a department of the University of Oxford.
It furthers the University's objective of excellence in research, scholarship,
and education by publishing worldwide in

Oxford New York

Auckland Bangkok Buenos Aires Cape Town Chennai
Dar es Salaam Delhi Hong Kong Istanbul Karachi Kolkata
Kuala Lumpur Madrid Melbourne Mexico City Mumbai Nairobi
São Paulo Shanghai Taipei Tokyo Toronto

OXFORD is a trade mark of Oxford University Press
in the UK and in certain other countries

National Library of Australia
Cataloguing-in-Publication data:

Morton, Leith.
    Modern Japanese culture: the insider view.

    Bibliography.
    Includes index.
    ISBN 0 19 554089 1.

    1. Japan—Civilisation—21st century. 2. Japan—
    Intellectual life—21st century. I. Title.

    952.05

Edited by Anne Mulvaney
Proofread by Liz Filleul
Text and cover design by Racheal Stines
Typeset by Racheal Stines
Indexed by Neale Towart
Printed through Bookpac Production Services, Singapore

CONTENTS

ACKNOWLEDGMENTS

The author wishes to thank the many people and institutions that provided assistance in the writing of this book. In particular, my thanks are extended to the University of Newcastle, especially the Department of Modern Languages, which provided a secure environment during the writing and editing of the manuscript. The author's gratitude is especially extended to Carrol Doble, one-time Modern Languages secretary, for typing assistance; and also to his wife Sachiko for the same during the final revisions of the manuscript. Research assistance also came from the Tokyo Metropolitan Institute of Technology (Tokyo Kagaku Gijutsu Daigaku) in 1996–97 and from the International Research Center for Japanese Studies (Nichibunken) in Kyoto in 1996 and 2000, which allowed the author to carry out research in Japan. Special thanks must be extended to Professor Nozomu Kawamura whose early collaboration and support was of immense assistance in the writing of the book. Thanks must also go to my editor at Oxford University Press, Jill Henry, for her continued support and encouragement.

A note on names

Japanese names will follow the Japanese order of surname followed by personal name, except for Japanese authors writing in English who follow the English convention.

Introduction

Everything passes behind my back,
Blown by the hard wind.
Memory, emotion, psychology, God, Kwannon,
Something like music, even something like an image.

Anzai Hitoshi, 'Winter in M Harbour' (Anzai, 1988: 30–1)

There are, in theory, as many possible accounts of the culture of a particular people as the sum total of all individuals who have been counted as belonging to that people. In fact, there is no reason to restrict such a set of possible accounts only to members of the people being described; it could extend to anyone who has even attempted to compose such an account.

In the case of Japan, a glance at all the past accounts of the culture of that nation and its inhabitants would seem to partially justify such a viewpoint, as even with the reading that I can claim to have done, opinions have differed radically about the nature of Japan, and its culture, since they first began to be recorded. Their observations confirm the fundamental conceptual difficulty of describing a culture from either inside or outside, as both terms cover such a large range of possible responses that the task of generalisation may seem at best an illusion.

The division of Japanese writers on culture into the categories of insider and outsider is useful for a number of reasons: it is essentially neutral, and so does not make implicit value judgments in the way that the political categorisations of 'left' and 'right' or the categorisations of 'nationalist' and 'ultra-nationalist' do. Nor do the terms insider and outsider connote domains of meaning so strictly defined that this might prevent, for instance, a thinker from falling into both categories simultaneously, depending upon the particular topic under discussion. But this conceptualisation also retains a central core of meaning that is both easy to understand and has a long and venerable history as a means for classifying and comprehending different viewpoints. Under the rubrics of 'emic' and 'etic'—originally derived from the field of linguistics—this categorisation has become a fundamental methodology utilised by a wide variety of social scientists in their analysis of social, cultural, and historical phenomena. Thus, its all-round utility makes it an ideal tool for classifying Japanese cultural and intellectual discourse.

Philosophers such as Willard Quine have argued that insider viewpoints cannot be translated into understanding that outsiders can take as an accurate and true representation of their views (Quine, 1960: 243; Feleppa, 1988: 32–50). This viewpoint has also been echoed in the writings of important Japanese thinkers like Yanagita Kunio. But such reservations also apply, by extension, to insider attempts to convey understanding to other insiders. Other thinkers, for example Hans-Georg Gadamer, admit these fundamental difficulties but conclude that the insider and outsider viewpoint (construed in this case as self and other) can create a hermeneutic horizon that allows for meaningful dialogue (Gadamer, 1994: 358–62).

What do I mean by insider and outsider accounts when discussing modern Japanese culture? By insider accounts of culture, at the simplest level, I mean explanations of cultural phenomena by people who are writing inside the culture being described, who have been raised inside that culture; in this specific case, writers whose language and social and cultural background are explicitly Japanese. But in this book I mean something else as well. This study will focus on Japanese thinkers and writers who predominantly adopt a nativist approach, rather than those who adopt a universalist approach to discourse. So, outsider here not only conveys the meaning of investigators working outside the perspective of a Japanese background (such as myself), but also thinkers who conceive of their formulation of culture as not belonging to an insider scheme of reference but interpret cultural phenomena in a universal light.

Put very broadly, the universalists accept the notion of universal values or at least common paradigms in areas of debate concerning culture. The nativists often dispute the very possibility of a universalist paradigm (thus explaining perhaps why postmodern theory is so popular in Japan), contending that cultural, social, political, and philosophic realities are essentially so different that paradigms can rarely cross cultural or linguistic barriers. This is a gross simplification, of course, with opinions spread across the whole spectrum (many intellectuals are universalist in some areas but nativist in others), but nativist sentiment has historically been fed by continuing resentments concerning what such thinkers see as the Western bias inherent in 'value-free' philosophical and conceptual paradigms. However, it is important to note that many Western critics also challenge such notions, as seen in the examples of Quine and Gadamer quoted above.

My view is that, to date, accounts of Japanese culture in English have more often been written from an outsider perspective or based upon such a perspective, rather than focusing on insider views. There are very good reasons for this. Japanese intellectuals who publish in English find it easier to adopt the approach to discourse more commonly found in the English-speaking world which is, as naturally applies to a culture that purports to be truly international, much more centred in a universal frame of reference than a predominantly local viewpoint. Also, when outsiders such as myself attempt accounts of Japanese culture (whether by translation or original analysis), we find it easier to synthesise and comprehend writers who take positions similar to our own general theoretical orientation, which is overwhelmingly universalist. This study takes a different path by its specific concentration on insider theorists of culture, but because it is attempting to open a dialogue with such thinkers (as outlined by Gadamer in his hermeneutics), it quite naturally adopts a comparative approach.

This book will also offer detailed factual descriptions of various expressions of Japanese culture like literature and cinema that, while based more on insider interpretations than otherwise, will nonetheless encompass all the major aspects of that particular cultural phenomenon. There is no bias at work here that seeks to exclude anything significant in our discussion of modern Japanese culture. Nevertheless, the limitations of time and space make it impossible to be absolutely comprehensive. Modern Japanese art, for instance, is not covered in this book.

But, there are numerous accounts of modern Japanese art available to English-language readers and, of late, increasing opportunities for people in English-speaking countries to view exhibitions of modern art, thus providing a more than adequate array of sources for those seeking information on this topic.

It is not possible to paint a picture that will encompass the whole of the culture of modern Japan, if defined in such a way as to exclude virtually nothing from our critical eye. As is commonly recognised, it is manifestly impossible to 'freeze' a living, changing culture in all its bewildering complexity to provide a perfect photograph of that culture. This study will, instead, focus on certain moments in the life, history, and thought of modern Japan in order to build up a description of the culture of that society, which will answer some questions that are now being asked about its present state. The illumination cast by this analysis will also serve to highlight the vast areas that still remain unknown. But this, I hope, will point to other questions that need to be asked, and this process of questioning will also shed its own kind of illumination on Japan.

Consequently the general framework in which this study works is that of identifying and utilising the insights arising from insider discourse, and by explicit comparisons with insights deriving from outside that frame of reference, arrive at a synthesis that will reflect my views on the issues I have chosen to write about. My analysis will not attempt to consider all the major insider figures, as it is essentially an introductory study. Rather, by selecting several of the most influential Japanese thinkers, and discussing their approaches to Japanese culture, this book will draw a picture that will give readers a broad overview of the main features of modern cultural discourse in Japan, and a general outline of contemporary Japanese culture. Explanations of these phenomena will engage in a dialogue with several of these major thinkers, which is, at times, critical and, I hope, original and stimulating. Thus, the chapters may be read more easily as interpretative essays rather than attempts to create a definitive account of the culture of modern Japan.

The map thus traced of modern Japan will inevitably, therefore, be contentious and contingent. But this contentiousness is, I believe, inherent in the very nature of interpretation. The Japan that will be described here is but one of several possible versions of Japan. Contemporary Japan is not a fixed entity; it is a constantly changing complex, composed of over one hundred million individual Japanese living and working together in a myriad different environments. The moments that we will be focusing upon, the thinkers that we will be foregrounding and discussing, will only illuminate parts of this constant hive of activity. This book can only suggest some of the underlying patterns that various thinkers have identified as applicable to the evolution of culture in Japan.

This book is an attempt to map certain patterns but it will not provide the final word as I believe that this is not humanly possible. Totalising narratives or explanatory metaphors that seek to characterise whole societies with two or three conceptual formulae are doomed to failure. By highlighting agreements and disagreements with insider accounts of Japanese culture, I wish to clearly demonstrate my belief that conceptual schema are contingent and, at best, only partial maps of a complex of interactions that cannot, in the final analysis, ever all be forced onto any single map of Japan.

The Japan that this book seeks to characterise is, however, not a Japan dichotomised into two entirely separate worldviews: one from outside and one from inside. On the contrary, insider views of Japan make constant use of outsider viewpoints. I will cite not only Japanese thinkers on Japan, but several Western thinkers, not just for their insights into Japanese culture but, as with Japanese thinkers, for insights into culture in general. My viewpoint, then, despite my use of the insider frame, will be determinately comparative and internationalist.

My aim is not to argue that Japan is a cultural isolate, incomprehensible outside the frames of reference constructed within Japan by its native intellectuals, but to assert that understanding is only possible if Japan is viewed from as large and multifaceted a perspective as possible. Naturally, I will be quite selective in my use of the various perspectives utilised here but this should not obscure the fact that no society can be completely understood, grasped or conceptualised from any one, or even from any group, of competing perspectives. Discussions of the cultural patterns that these thinkers have used to characterise Japan are inevitably partial, and contingent as they attempt to map something that is constantly in a state of change.

Hence, to sum up, the approach of this book will be synthetic, syncretic—in short, overtly interpretative. I will be sifting and sorting, in a quite critical and open manner, the insights of many other thinkers and scholars without whose massive labours this study would not have been possible. The cognitive maps that these thinkers have imposed upon Japan may be viewed, therefore, simply as working models deriving from the data they have used as their base, and the particular historical and intellectual context in which they are working. In no sense will this book adopt these cognitive maps as a complete explanation of how Japan should be studied or as a theory that permits us to make definite statements about the material reality of Japan. These insights by the several thinkers that we discuss deserve our respect and attention, but they do not provide any final answers. Nor does this book attempt to provide any final answers. Rather, the approach will be to question old hypotheses and propose new ones, as well as to introduce many of these hypotheses to English-language readers.

Chapter one examines in more detail the notions of insider and outsider discourse in both Japan and the West. It attempts to problematise our own conceptual frame, and to seek the origins of such discourse in modern Japanese thought by a close reading of two volumes on this topic by the psychologist Minami Hiroshi. Minami is widely acknowledged as an authority on insider discourse, and his studies cover an impressively wide array of Japanese writers on culture, who are subjected to a comprehensive and scholarly analysis. However, my analysis is not confined to Minami or to the works he identifies as significant in the evolution of Japanese ethnocentric discourse, or 'Nihonjinron'; rather, we will investigate a wide range of thinkers over a large number of areas of intellectual enquiry. The purpose is both to probe the unexamined assumptions behind much writing of this kind in Japan and also to attempt an evaluation of some of the key modern thinkers in this area.

Some of the thinkers whose views are interrogated here include the philosophers Nishida Kitarō and Kuki Shūzō and the psychologist Kawai Hayao. But readings of such figures are juxtaposed against and explicitly compared with readings of major Western thinkers on the same topics, such as Quine and Richard Rorty. Thus this chapter deliberately seeks out a number of insider theorists in addition to those studied by Minami, while devoting considerable attention to the dual structure I identify as fundamental to Japanese insider discourse. Naturally, such comparisons are not attempts at systematic analysis but instead highlight specific points of interest, which are treated only insofar as they illuminate the general concerns addressed here.

Chapter two does engage, on the other hand, in a detailed and rigorous analysis of one of the major writers on culture in Japan—indeed, in the eyes of many Japanese, the major theoretician of culture of modern Japan: Yanagita Kunio. This chapter attempts to historicise the most important attempts made by Japanese critics to characterise Yanagita's system of ethnology, which he called 'minzokugaku', by comparing a number of contending views of Yanagita held by various contemporary thinkers. We also examine the image of Yanagita in the West, constructed comparatively recently by a small number of mainly American commentators.

The heart of the chapter is a detailed analysis of four of Yanagita's major works—two on Okinawa—which he took as the basic template of Japanese culture, and two seminal works on methodology that enshrine the main principles of his system. I engage in a close reading of these four works, something rarely attempted outside Japan, in order to both comprehend and critique his achievement. It is also worth noting that none of these works have been translated into English; therefore, much detail is provided for readers who do not have access to the Japanese texts. In addition, I try to construct a detailed context covering the reception of Yanagita's works in Japan, and also discussing their significance, so that the hermeneutic horizon, so to speak, is made visible and transparent. Yanagita's project has had a profound influence on Japanese ways of conceptualising, and thinking about society and culture; this influence is demonstrated by citing various thinkers in connection with several ideas proposed by Yanagita.

Chapter three focuses on one of Yanagita's most prominent successors in contemporary Japan: Yoshimoto Takaaki. After introducing Yoshimoto's life and work, I engage in a close reading of three of Yoshimoto's major works. These works are among the most significant that Yoshimoto wrote, both in terms of their impact on contemporary Japanese conceptualisations of culture, and for their importance in Yoshimoto's own evolution as a thinker. Two of the books date from the 1960s, while the last work examined was written in 1984. I examine Yoshimoto as an insider thinker who drew heavily from outsider perspectives (like his predecessor Yanagita) in his formulation of basic theories about culture. None of Yoshimoto's works are available in English, so this chapter goes to some length to describe and summarise these examples of his oeuvre, as well as furnishing a context summarising the reception in Japan of these works, and also the critical response to them. Without such a context, it is extremely difficult for non-Japanese readers to gain any real understanding of Yoshimoto's achievements.

Thus, the chapter attempts to historicise Yoshimoto's writings by reading them in the context of debates within Japan, and also by seeking out Yoshimoto's debts to his peers in the West. This is the first time such a task has been attempted in detail in English-language writings on Japan, and thus the analysis draws almost exclusively from Japanese insider sources for evaluation of Yoshimoto's novel forays into such new areas of cultural discourse as manga (comics) and advertising copy.

Chapter four provides a snapshot of modern Japanese literature through an analysis of selected postwar novelists and poets. I scrutinise postwar fiction by establishing the particular historical and aesthetic context in which the novelists Mishima Yukio and Ōe Kenzaburō are located by using literary critics, such as Oketani Hideaki and Karatani Kōjin, who have been prominent in establishing insider discourse on modern Japanese writing. The critic Kokai Eiji has been equally influential in laying the foundations for scholarship on postwar poetry, and so his work provides the basis for much of the poetry analysis. Reactions to the war, and, later, to the 1960s debate over the renewal of the US-Japan Security Treaty inform many of the works written by the postwar generation of writers.

I argue that contemporary fiction and poetry, while still drawing inspiration from 1960s issues, have moved in a different direction to this postwar generation. Again, the literary context is a product of insider discourse by such critics as Hasumi Shigehiko, but outsider discourse in the form of feminist poetics and 'language' poetry has also influenced contemporary Japanese writers, as I demonstrate. Major contemporary novelists such as Murakami Haruki and Yoshimoto Banana are clearly writing for an international as well as a domestic audience, thus showing how, in practice, contemporary culture is very much a hybrid phenomenon. While many of the works of contemporary writers are available in English translation, an even larger number remain untranslated, so this chapter also provides basic information on these as yet untranslated novels and poems. Nevertheless, most of the major works by these writers (with the partial exception of poetry) have been translated into English, thus enabling readers to make their own judgments on the works discussed. But the interpretative frames, the literary and cultural contexts, that have given birth to these works are, as yet, little known to English-language readers, so this study breaks new ground in its description of this context.

The fifth and final chapter deals with mass culture. I concentrate on postwar television, cinema and manga, again focusing on representative figures. Yoshimoto Takaaki, who introduced television and manga as topics of serious intellectual discourse for many Japanese intellectuals, is an important guide. The chapter also pays attention to a number of important artists whose work crosses boundaries, such as the TV personality, actor, and movie director Kitano Takeshi and the comic artist and animator Tezuka Osamu. The difficulty of 'freezing' contemporary cultural phenomena such as TV and cinema to produce a coherent description is apparent here, as these media are constantly changing. Thus, I have turned to a number of recent studies by contemporary cultural critics, such as Yomota Inuhiko and Ishiko Jun, to make sense of the mass of data currently available. I have also looked at some recent journalism to try to obtain the latest information and statistics.

I also consider the impact of contemporary intellectual currents on mass culture, which, as is the case with literature, is a hybrid of many influences. The specific topic chosen to illustrate this hybridity is women's manga, with a number of works by the contemporary woman manga artist and novelist Uchida Shungicu (b.1948) subjected to a close reading. Uchida is a controversial but extremely popular author in contemporary Japan. Her themes, however, are not always entirely original, as I demonstrate with some comparisons to earlier women writers, such as the poet Itō Hiromi who came to prominence in the 1980s.

The epilogue reflects on several of the ideas and themes that emerge as common to many of the cultural phenomena explored in the book.

1

Interpreting Culture
in Modern Japan

'Sometimes I copied, sometimes I rewrote, I erased names, sometimes a person's name, sometimes a shapeless dream-fragment
from a single tale (naturally nobody's in particular), sometimes I
transcribed whole texts perfectly...'

Asabuki Ryōji, from '20' (Asabuki, 1988: 46)

This chapter will trace ways of seeing and interpreting cultural patterns
by an examination of indigenous discourses of culture in the modern
era, focusing initially upon Western perspectives on culture, next examining dual systems in Japanese thought identified by various Western
scholars writing on Japan, then shifting to two books by the psychologist Minami Hiroshi (b.1914), which summarise and contextualise most
of the major thinkers on these matters in modern Japan. Minami, as
noted earlier, is acknowledged in Japan as an authority in this field, so his
investigation of insider discourse is a useful introduction to the major
figures who have shaped the debate on culture in modern Japan.

From time to time, we shall pause in our reading of Minami to scrutinise some of these writers (and their books) more closely, and also
examine some works not discussed by Minami in order to present a
more complete picture of insider discourse on culture. By singling out
some studies for a more sustained analysis, I seek to draw a sharper outline

of their contribution to insider discourse, and also to supplement and enrich Minami's opinions with a contrasting outsider viewpoint. Consequently, such an intensive analysis will provide a more detailed description of these seminal works than given by Minami. Finally, we will investigate the very notion of 'culture' and introduce some recent writers on culture in Japan who explicitly attempt to explore cross-cultural comparisons.

Western perspectives on cultural communication

First, however, we need to make some general remarks about the notion of culture, and its interpretation from an explicitly outsider perspective, namely, from that of Western thought. I have already noted both the advantages and the limitations of an outsider/insider dichotomy, of the kind advocated by Kenneth Pike in his famous 'etic/emic' distinction (Pike, 1954). But such limitations do not invalidate the basic problems raised by philosophers, cultural anthropologists, and linguists who have attempted to conceptualise the interpretation of cultures different from one's own. The notion that languages incorporate worldviews is undoubtedly quite old but, for modern thinkers in the West, the most important advocate of this idea was the philosopher Wilhelm von Humboldt (1767–1835).

George Steiner has argued that, intellectually, there is an unbroken line from Humboldt, via the anthropologist Franz Boas (1858–1942) and the linguist and anthropologist Edward Sapir (1884–1939), to the 'ethno-linguistics' of Benjamin Lee Whorf (1897–1941) (Steiner, 1975: 85). Humboldt's emphasis on language as worldview is undoubtedly linked to the German critic Johann Gottfried Herder's (1744–1803) nationalistic celebration of the German soul 'organically rooted in the topography, customs, and communities of the local native [i.e. German] tradition', as the historian Simon Schama puts it (Schama, 1995: 102–3). Since both Herder and Humboldt, and later Boas, Sapir, and Whorf forge links between ethnicity, language, culture, and national identity, it is not altogether surprising that by 1929 Sapir was able to write: 'No two languages are ever sufficiently similar to be considered as representing the same social reality. The worlds in which different societies live are distinct worlds, not merely the same world with different labels attached' (Steiner, 1975: 87).

Thirty odd years later, Whorf conflated this claim into: 'Every language is a vast pattern-system, different from others, in which are culturally ordained the forms and categories by which the personality not only communicates, but also analyses nature, nurtures or neglects types of relationship and phenomena, channels his reasoning, and builds the house of his consciousness' (Quoted Steiner, 1975: 89.) The problem here is, as many commentators have objected, that this would imply great difficulties in any interlinguistic or intercultural communication but such communication is commonplace and ubiquitous, occurring at many levels of linguistic and social interaction.

Perhaps the most sceptical thinker in the West about the possibility of intercultural communication is the American philosopher Willard Van Orman Quine (b. 1908) who argues in his 1960 book *Word and Object* that: 'an alien language may well fail to share, by any universal standard, the object-positing pattern of our own' (Quine, 1960: 243). In other words, that material reality, as commonly understood, is fundamentally different in different languages. Quine's thesis arises from his argument concerning the indeterminacy of meaning, in his own words, 'manuals for translating one language into another can be set up in divergent ways, all compatible with the totality of speech dispositions, yet incompatible with one another' (Quine, 1960: 27).

Quine is chiefly interesting in advancing a radically sceptical and physicalistic view of how humans know reality and relate this to language. It is no accident that he begins his account with a discussion of George Berkeley (1685–1753), the philosopher of how ideas are manifested, as Berkeley's position is radically undermined by Quine's indeterminacy thesis. Quine is always pragmatic, however, and, with his notion of 'semantic ascent', leaves a way out for meaningful conceptual discussion between different languages (Quine, 1960: 271 ff).

The original impulse behind the ethno-linguists' work was to avoid an ethnocentric approach to the study of culture. These thinkers wished to understand culture from the perspective of its indigenous makers, to somehow grasp the insider understanding of cultural phenomena without contaminating this by their own outsider perspective. This explains earlier theorists' anxieties about imposing their own value system on the peoples they studied and also provides the motive for the attempts of thinkers such as Victor Turner (b.1920), Clifford Geertz (b.1926), and Nelson Goodman (b.1906) to evolve such conceptual tools as 'symbolic anthropology' (Turner, Geertz) and 'worldmaking' (Goodman) to avoid the traps of subjectivity (Feleppa, 1988: 100–4, 192–200) and to arrive at a more objective characterisation of another culture.

As explained earlier, while sharing many of the reservations expressed by the thinkers cited above about the possibility of any objective or comprehensive account of culture, I intend to open a dialogue with various Western and Japanese commentators on culture, believing that such a dialogue, explicitly open and comparative, is both possible and useful. There are many commentators who endorse this view, such as the German philosopher Hans-Georg Gadamer (1900–2002). Gadamer has argued in his 1960 book *Wahrheit und Methode* (Truth and Method) that the hermeneutic method (Gadamer's own theory of interpretation) or 'horizon' as he calls it, outlines a rationale for dialogue in which: 'the dialectic of question and answer always precedes the dialectic of interpretation. It is what determines understanding as an event' (Gadamer, 1994: 472). This dialectical methodology thus determines that: 'the true locus of hermeneutics is this in-between' (Gadamer, 1994: 295).

In a sense, then, Gadamer advocates a continual interrogation of the other's position, at the same time as a continual questioning of one's own, as a means to move towards an understanding of insiders by outsiders. Gadamer gives credit to Humboldt for his insight that a language view is a worldview but argues that 'in the same way as with perception we can speak of the "linguistic shadings" that the world undergoes in different language worlds…each one potentially contains every other one within it—i.e. each worldview can be extended into every other. It can understand and comprehend, from within itself, the "view" of the world presented in another language' (Gadamer, 1994: 448).

Hermeneutics thus acknowledges the insight that 'etic' and 'emic', insider and outsider distinctions, while sharply differentiated in theory, are not so clear-cut in actual practice. This approach to describing Japanese culture, where insider and outsider views are engaged in a continual dialogue, is the basic methodology employed in this study. Quine's scepticism concerning the inscrutability of reference acknowledges the pragmatic reality that, as Gadamer notes, the difference between self and other can be found in any characterisation of the subject to itself (Feleppa, 1988: 33–4). In this sense, the insights gained from a hermeneutic viewpoint reflect the basic realities of communication within societies, let alone between societies. Nevertheless, as we have seen, the duality of self and other, or insider and outsider, or universal and particular is a dichotomy common to much Western writing on culture in the twentieth century, and earlier. Precisely the same statement can be made of the Japanese discourse on culture.

Dual systems in Japanese thought

Just as Herder and Humboldt constructed their discourses on language and culture against the background of a protean German nationalism, and the emergence of an 'authentic' German identity, so Japanese discourses on culture and language have done likewise. David Pollack in his 1986 study *The Fracture of Meaning* argues that the major Japanese thinker of the eighteenth century, Motoori Noringa (1730–1801), in his important essay on the problem of good and evil, *Naobi no Mitama* (The Power of Rectification, 1771), had a political objective as his ultimate aim in defining what was truly Japanese as against what was not, that is, what was Chinese (Pollack, 1986: 50–2). In other words, the dichotomy of self and other, in this case Japan and China, is invoked for a specifically political purpose, that of the construction of national identity. Indeed, Pollack's whole book is devoted to exploring China as the fateful other to Japan; as Pollack notes, 'China was Japan's walls, the very terms by which Japan defined its own existence' (Pollack, 1986: 4). Motoori was by no means unique in his construction of this 'dual system'.

In this chapter, we will focus on the modern discourse on culture, rather than, as Pollack has done, exploring its origins in the distant past. But the centrality of China to the evolution of a Japan-centred discourse is evident in the modern period as well. Stefan Tanaka has traced in his 1993 book *Japan's Orient* how Japanese historians in the nineteenth and twentieth centuries constructed a national history that was at first located in a universal historical narrative, the 'world history' invented by the West, but which eventually became independent of the Western frame, and defined the world in its own terms. As Tanaka notes, Western 'universal' history, though 'built on a scientific epistemology that pretends to be objective and universal' is actually that of 'Western nation-states, international and domestic politics, and a male elite…these histories were about the writer's own nation' (Tanaka, 1993: 34).

In a similar fashion, Japanese constructions of history in the late-nineteenth century by historians like Taguchi Ukichi (1855–1905) in his *Nihon Kaika Shōshi* (Brief History of Civilisation in Japan) place Japan into a universal order of progress (Tanaka, 1993: 36–7). Soon, however, modifications of the Western 'universal' narrative begin to appear. By 1889, the historian Miyata Yonekichi (1860–1929) was exploring the importance of ancient Japanese myths and legends (paralleling Herder a century or more before), and calling for the study of the past through language, arguing that 'Language expressed thought, but at the same time, thought produced language' (Quoted Tanaka, 1993: 52). The rewriting of a Japanese world history along different lines to the West eventually resulted in the subject of Tanaka's study, 'Tōyōshi' or the history of the Orient but, as Tanaka observes, the Western Orient and the Japanese Orient 'were not...the same orient' (Tanaka, 1993: 107). China, not the Middle East, was the centre of the Japanese Orient.

Tanaka documents the development of the Japanese conception of 'Oriental History', Japan's version of world history, to the point where there arose the need to 'create a Japanese origin', and this eventually 'became the imperial system' (Tanaka, 1993: 112). The narrative of 'Tōyōshi' thus emerges as a parallel but different world history to those created by the West, as much a product of ideological and political debates within Japan as, for example, Nazi rewritings of European history become a triumphant progress of the Aryan race. In both examples, we see insider narratives emerge to explicitly challenge a universal outsider narrative history.

Naturally the various schools of historical interpretation catalogued by Tanaka paint a more diverse and complex picture than can be summarised here. Individual historical texts, whether interpretative or documentary, can be read in manifold ways, and these readings are, in many cases, adaptable to quite different ends, some of which compete or contend with one another. For example, one of the key figures in Tanaka's discussion of the emergence of the 'Orient' in Japanese historical discourse is the historian Shiratori Kurakichi (1865–1942). Shiratori redefined the concept of democracy in Confucian terms, Tanaka argues, so that 'it fit Japan and China, unconstrained by definitions from the West' (Tanaka, 1993: 144). But Shiratori's complex view of the Emperor, a view based in his rewriting of Confucian doctrine, was adapted by other thinkers to become 'completely identified with Japan' (Tanaka, 1993: 148).

The prehistorian Gina Barnes, in her 1990 discussion of the 'idea of prehistory' in Japan, traces disparities and complexities similar to those identified by Tanaka. As she concludes: 'the retention of native patterns of thought within modern Japanese archaeology reveals how differently archaeological terms can be conceptualised within different modern societies...the idea of prehistory in Japan had, and has, its own special character' (Barnes, 1990: 939). This 'special character' encompasses various kinds of narrative reminiscent of the categories Tanaka enumerates: Imperialist chronologies, multi-channelled antiquarian narratives, Neo-Confucianism, and so on. These various traditions of native archaeology were all profoundly influenced by the Western narrative of archaeology introduced into Japan by Edward S. Morse (1838–1925) in the 1870s, but what results is a complex amalgam: native traditions are absorbed and reconceptualised into a new discourse, as Barnes points out. This is but one example of how an insider reading of cultural history—in this case archaeology—absorbed outsider influence, not so much as a means of constructing a universal discourse but rather to create an indigenous or insider version of archaeology.

In his 1994 book *Dreams of Difference*, Kevin Michael Doak argues that Yasuda Yojūrō (1910–81), the chief theoretician of the Japan Romantic School, which had a major influence on cultural debate in Japan during the 1930s and 1940s, had elaborated a dual system in which Japan is perceived as the harbinger of modernity, an ironic vision of universality, as against the West where 'the universality of freedom was replaced by the universality of the English currency, language and culture' (Doak, 1994: 6). In other words, a Japanese insider notion of what is universal replaces a Western outsider view. Yasuda's logic was shot through with paradox and contradiction; he argued (in Doak's words) that 'it was precisely in ancient Japanese traditions that the best archetype of universality might be found' (Doak, 1994: 9). But, eventually, Yasuda succumbed to the lure of cultural exceptionalism and nationalism, and began to pursue an idealistic notion of Japanese ethnicity where the individual only has significance as a member of this larger national collectivity: a view that clearly has racist and ultra-nationalist overtones.

A powerful critique of this model of Japanese culture, observes Doak, was proposed by the cultural critic Kobayashi Hideo (1902–83), who situated identity 'in a social tradition that resists the model of society derived from Western theories' (Doak, 1994: 114). Kobayashi insisted upon a new vision of culture that accommodated a 'multiplicity of individual perspectives' which, in turn, results in a new social tradition, but one derived from Japanese realities, not imported outsider realities. This perspective also resulted in a paradox whereby, in seeking to avoid Western-derived theories of universalism, Japanese intellectuals were forced to retreat to a notion of culture that focuses on the individual self but which can only be realised 'by constantly deferring any fixed definition of the self' (Doak, 1994: 114). Such complicated and circular exercises in logic were an inevitable result of the efforts of Japanese intellectuals to seek out a 'dual system' of cultural discourse that attempts to avoid the trap of simply replicating the Western dichotomy of the universal as against the particular, but which instead produces quite explicit insider and outsider discourses.

In a later article, 'Ethnic Nationalism and Romanticism in Early Twentieth-Century Japan', Doak expands his analysis to include the debate over the Japanese nation that was also taking place in the 1930s and 1940s. Working from the exchange of polemic on the Japan Romantic School between the philosopher Miki Kiyoshi (1897–1945) and the literary critic Kamei Katsuichirō (1907–66), Doak argues that Miki saw the difference between 'Western knowledge' and 'Japanese knowledge' as merely a variant in a topos of a universal space. But Kamei and the Japan Romantic School rejected the 'monolithic conflation of state and nation' (Doak, 1996: 89), which therefore led Yasuda to try to 'transcend the simplistic opposition of West (universal) versus East (particular) by reaffirming that culture carried with it a universal value' (Doak, 1996: 12). We see here a restatement of the attempt by Japanese romantics to evade the boundaries of dual systems altogether, but the notion of culture having a universal value is itself complicit with European romanticism, and therefore offers no real solution to this dilemma, which is, in reality, a fruitless search to construct a discourse that will transcend such boundaries.

The paradigm of dual systems can be found in areas of cultural discourse other than the purely humanistic. The anthropologist Emiko Ohnuki-Tierney has argued in two relatively recent books, *Illness and Culture in Contemporary Japan* (1984) and *The Monkey as Mirror* (1987), that Japanese concepts and behaviour regarding health and illness (Ohnuki-Tierney, 1984: 1) are culturally patterned, that Japanese culture, to a large degree, constructs or shapes even biological or physical phenomena like disease. This is a dual system that lays claim to the most material realm of human activity, the body—not merely the individual bodies of the Japanese but also the collective body of Japanese medicine.

In *The Monkey as Mirror*, Ohnuki-Tierney argues that stranger-deities, gods who visited Japan from 'the other side of the sea' (Ohnuki-Tierney, 1987: 129), represent 'the semiotic other for the Japanese self' and constitute the basic model by which the Japanese interpret and classify their universe (Ohnuki-Tierney, 1987: 144). The notion of 'stranger-deities' specifically originates in the idea of the 'marebito' (visitors, stranger-gods) that was first conceptualised by Orikuchi Shinobu (1887–1953), one of the major Japanese thinkers of the twentieth century. However, as we will see in the next chapter, Yanagita Kunio also had a role to play in constructing or rediscovering the 'land of eternal summer' across the sea whence the gods came. Indeed, Ohnuki-Tierney frequently uses ideas and themes that originate in Yanagita, such as in her discussion of the 'sacred' and 'secular' in the Japanese ethos (Ohnuki-Tierney, 1987: 137–44).

Ohnuki-Tierney argues in her 1984 study that dual systems are the very essence of Japanese culture, asserting that such systems make up 'a conceptual structure that has been central to Japanese culture from earliest time to the present. This conceptual structure is characterised by a dominant system of meaning, purity: impurity, whose concrete manifestations are expressed in the spatial idioms of in: out: above: below' (Ohnuki-Tierney, 1984: 46–7). In relation to her own investigations, Ohnuki-Tierney advances several reasons why insiders, 'native anthropologists', are advantaged over outsiders, though such logic itself serves as a perfect demonstration of the dual system that we have been discussing (Ohnuki-Tierney, 1984: 17–18).

Among scholars both in Japan and the West, the practice of documenting dual systems of thinking in various areas of intellectual or cultural enquiry has resulted in what is almost a new branch of scholarship: 'Nihonjinron' or the study of ethnocentric discourse in Japan. My discussion in this chapter, and indeed in this book as a whole, cannot be subsumed beneath this heading, as I am essentially conducting a dialogue, touching on specific points across a large spectrum of Japanese society and culture. Nevertheless, a brief glance at some of the more influential theorists of the Nihonjinron discourse will help to illuminate some of the habits of thought commonly found among Japanese attempts to theorise 'self' and 'other' and will provide a short summary of major Japanese insider conceptualisations of culture.

Insider discourse in modern Japan: Watsuji and Kuki

One of the most prominent contemporary historians of the Nihonjinron phenomenon is the psychologist Minami Hiroshi. Following is a description of two books specifically written on the topic by Minami over the last two decades which summarise and discuss most of the major Nihonjinron theorists of the twentieth century from an insider perspective. While Minami will be our guide to this phenomenon, his account is supplemented by close scrutiny of particular texts in an attempt to go beyond the limits of his analytic boundaries. In addition, a number of texts not discussed by Minami will also be investigated with a view to broadening and deepening our account of insider discourse.

The first book is Minami's 1980 study *Nihonjinron no Keifu* (The Genealogy of Nihonjinron), in which he analyses in thematic fashion several major currents of thinking, and several major thinkers, whose combined output has substantially created the modern ethnocentric discourse on Japan. The first chapter discusses the precursors of the debate, commencing with the seventeenth-century Neo-Confucian philosopher Arai Hakuseki (1657–1725) and concluding with the leading nineteenth-century populariser of things Western, Fukuzawa Yukichi (1834–1901). Minami's chief interest is in Fukuzawa.

Two of the most significant achievements of Fukuzawa, observes Minami, lay in valuing human contacts as the chief spiritual gain from Japan's encounter with the West, and in proposing the notion of public opinion (Minami, 1980: 24). As a result of this, Fukuzawa 'wiped away the feudalistic mentality which still remains within the Japanese today, and conceived of a method to totally transform the character of the Japanese people' (Minami, 1980: 41). It is fascinating that the psychologist Minami highlights these achievements as a change in the psychology of the Japanese (would Fukuzawa himself have conceived of them in those terms?), although Fukuzawa is also placed firmly into the contemporary historical context.

The chief subject of the second chapter is the philosopher Watsuji Tetsurō's (1889–1960) famous 1935 book *Fūdo* (Climate and Culture;

hereafter *Climate*). Minami traces the lineage of a discourse linking climate and temperament from Seki Motohira's 1701 gazetteer on the subject, through works by nativist scholars such as Ban Nobutomo (1773–1864) and Hirata Atsutane (1776–1843), to such Meiji nationalist writers as Miyake Setsurei (1860–1945) and Shiga Shigetaka (1863–1927). As this is not his purpose, Minami does not note the parallel history of the Western discourse on climate and character that can be found as far back as the writings of the Roman poet Lucretius (c.98–55 BC), and, most famously in Montesquieu (1689–1755) and Herder. After locating *Climate* in the context of its times—the distinctly anti-Marxist tone of the book, Minami argues, is a revolt against the contemporary dominance of left-wing ideology—Minami summarises the impact upon its contemporary heirs and critics, like the ethnographer Umesao Tadao's (b.1920) notion of 'ecological history' and the geographer Suzuki Hideo's revisionist critique of the book (Minami, 1980: 56–7, 68–71).

Let us pause a little in our reading of Minami to take a closer look at *Climate*. The book itself is divided into five chapters. The first chapter discusses the fundamental theory of climate from the perspective of sense perception and intentionality. Watsuji argues that we 'do not feel a sensation of "coldness" but directly experience the chill of outdoors'. Therefore, he argues, 'cold as something felt as intentional experience is not "something subjective" but is "something objective"' (Watsuji, 1935: 9). He describes the relationship between ourselves and cold as characterised by intentionality, what Martin Heidegger calls the 'ex-sistere' (Watsuji, 1935: 9).

He notes next that experience is shared in common, thus it is relational ('aidagara') (Watsuji, 1935: 10). This effects a shift in perception of climate away from individual subjectivity to relational sociality. He links form in human social life (e.g. the shapes of roofs) to climate, as elemental forms are shaped by this fundamental relationship (Watsuji, 1935: 12–15). Climate is a phenomenon expressed in religion, art, and literature; thus it is clearly different from the object of natural science (Watsuji, 1935: 13). Our humanity—our construction of time and space—is expressed in the historicity of the principle of climate (Watsuji, 1935: 15).

Watsuji further connects the issue of climate to the split between the body and the mind which is effected by the division between anthropology and philosophy. This results in the recovery of the subjective in the relationship between climate and the body. As he puts it, 'the opportunity for subjective human existence to objectify itself exists in [the phenomenon of] climate' (Watsuji, 1935: 18). Thus, the forms of climate define the forms of self-understanding (Watsuji, 1935: 22).

We can conclude from this broad conceptualisation of 'climate' that Watsuji is interpreting this notion as a fundamental hermeneutic strategy for reconciling the subjective and the objective, for grounding subjective experience in its relations to social and cultural expression. In this specific case, Watsuji is attempting to outline the contours of Japanese identity. So in chapter two, he examines three types of environment as case studies of the effects of climate on social institutions etc. Chapter three considers the special characteristics of monsoon climate as it applies to China and Japan. Chapter four discusses the relationship between art and culture. Watsuji answers a question posed forty years previously by the German philosopher Wilhelm Dilthey (1833–1911) as to how the creative force is manifested in differing ethnic groups and periods by focusing on time and place. Aesthetic questions relating to place (whether Japan or Europe) are inevitably bound up with climate, argues Watsuji (Watsuji, 1935: 170–204). The final chapter (not included in the 1956 English translation by Geoffrey Bownas) analyses Herder, Georg Hegel (1770–1831) and later writers such as Karl Marx (1818–83) and the German geographer Friedrich Ratzel (1844–1904) on climate.

Climate, at times, is understood by Watsuji to refer to the totality of the various kinds of Japanese experience. This is clear from Watsuji's musings on the unusual nature of Japanese culture where he discusses such issues as Japanese houses and the apolitical (meaning here a lack of public solidarity) nature of the Japanese people (Watsuji, 1935: 156–69). His discussion of art demonstrates his comparative methodology, containing a broad-ranging analysis of European art and its traditions and forms (Watsuji, 1935: 170–204).

Climate is similar to the philosopher Kuki Shūzō's (1888–1941) 1930 study *'Iki' no Kōzō* (The Structure of 'Iki'), which attempts to construct another, similar insider discourse on culture, also explicitly comparing and contrasting insider and outsider views in the same way as Watsuji. I will examine *The Structure of 'Iki'* presently but it is fascinating to note that in the introduction to *Climate*, Watsuji wrote that the book was inspired by his reading of Heidegger's *Sein und Zeit* (Being and Time, 1927) in Berlin in the summer of 1927, the text being based on lectures Watsuji gave during 1928 and 1929. As we shall see, Heidegger also influenced Kuki's book, which was published in magazine form a few months after Watsuji's lectures. In a sense, this betrays the outsider origins of the notion of using climate as a conceptual frame to ground social and cultural phenomena, to construct an ethnic hermeneutic to mediate between subjective experience and objective reality. But the volume is no less pioneering as a result, and it exercised a profound influence on Watsuji's contemporaries.

Minami's third chapter focuses on aesthetics, beginning with Watsuji's famous 1919 study *Koji Junrei* (A Pilgrimage to Ancient Temples) but devoting most attention to the highly influential *Structure of 'Iki'*, with various excursions to earlier writers on aesthetics, including Motoori Norinaga and the poet Kitamura Tōkoku (1868–94) (Minami, 1980: 78–108). Minami argues that in the conclusion to *The Structure of 'Iki'*, Kuki 'expanded the problem of aesthetics to include the Japanese character as an expression of national character, and finally arrived at the mythology of nationalism, which was quite unlike him' (Minami, 1980: 107). The last comment by Minami directly contrasts Kuki's explicit silence on the 'Japanese character' in his wartime writings with Watsuji's positive exaltation of the Japanese spirit in his works written at the same time.

In his introduction to John Clark's 1997 English translation of *The Structure of 'Iki'*, the philosopher Hajimu Nakano notes that Kuki 'took something Japanese as his subject and constructed an aesthetics which theorised it using Western methods. Consequently, Kuki's relationality appeared...as subject vs method, and as Japan vs the West.' Kuki himself wrote in *The Structure of 'Iki'* that (in John Clark's translation): '...the study of *iki* can only be constituted as the hermeneutics of ethnic being' and this leads to Kuki's characterisation of 'iki' as 'the kind of individually particular ethnic specificity which nominalism advocates. We must...dare a reverse transformation of Plato's epistemology' (Kuki, 1997: 118, 121). So, in his book, Kuki was seeking to reconstitute the universal logic of Western epistemology along his own hermeneutic lines: the very epitome of a dual system, and a project as ambitious as it was controversial. We will now examine Kuki's study in a little more detail.

The book is divided into four chapters plus an introduction and conclusion. In the introduction, Kuki defines 'meaning, or language' (imi mata wa gengo) as 'nothing but the self-manifestation of the past and present mode of being of a people, and the self-unfolding of a specific culture endowed with history' (Kuki, 1997: 28; Kuki, 1979: 12). This view is remarkably close to Herder's notion of 'worldview' touched upon earlier. Thus, 'iki', the chic, refined aesthetic quality Kuki is seeking to define, must first be analysed intensionally. The first chapter does this by examining the notion of coquetry (bitai), and relates this to Japanese culture by arguing that coquetry embodies 'iki' as it reflects the 'religious anti-realism' of Japan, that is, it possesses an aesthetic authority denied to Western cultures which have as their foundation an absolute religious authority (Kuki, 1997: 46).

Chapter two, on the extensional structure of iki, defines the meaning of iki by contrasting opposing aesthetic categories like 'showy–subdued' and 'chic–conventional', using examples from eighteenth- and nineteenth-century fiction and drama. The next chapter, on the natural expression of iki, seeks to analyse iki through physical gestures and expressions. Chapter four examines iki as artistic expression, namely, as design, architecture, and music. In the conclusion, Kuki indicates explicitly how his study is an attempt to construe understanding through ethnic specificity, as noted above. Kuki defines what is at stake: 'the problem [is] whether or not iki as a phenomenon of consciousness exists in Western culture' (Kuki, 1997: 118). Kuki's answer is in the negative. Kuki even maintains that if iki 'may be manifested in Western culture as a specific individual experience', then 'it has quite a different significance from the form of ethnic iki manifested in the public sphere' (Kuki, 1997: 120).

The only way for non-Japanese to appreciate the significance of iki as 'ethnic value' is via the Japanese language. But whether it is possible for non-Japanese to experience the 'individually particular ethnic specificity' of iki is problematic, although it is interesting to note that ethnicity is seen as virtually identical with language. The points Kuki makes in this most influential study are important not merely for understanding specifically Japanese notions of love and eros but also for cultural communication in general. Kuki refutes Plato's notion of Ideas (what he describes as 'Platonic Realism') to argue for a nominalist position, or, put another way, he rejects the notion of outsider understanding in favour of an insider view of cultural discourse. The political or ideological context of Kuki's argument is apparent in his remarks that this analysis is necessary so as 'not [to consign] our spiritual culture to oblivion' (Kuki, 1997: 121).

Kuki may well have influenced the German philosopher Martin Heidegger (1889–1976) (the two exchanged views in a famous published dialogue) and this connection has led recent critics like Karatani Kōjin (b.1941) to brand both of the philosophers as 'typical ideologue[s] of nineteenth-century imperialism' (Karatani, 1989: 267). But the contribution of both philosophers to problems of communication can be evaluated more positively, and many commentators have done so, notwithstanding Heidegger's open embrace of Hitler in the 1930s. In Kuki's case, the observation that he is attempting to synthesise the self (interpreted as the notion of 'iki') from within a system of thought irredeemably 'other' leads us to the fundamental contradiction (of which, no doubt, Kuki was well aware) that his success in grasping 'iki' as 'the self-unfolding of our [Japanese] ethnic being' (Kuki, 1997: 121) is vitiated precisely by virtue of the logic of the 'other'. Namely, Kuki's discourse itself is an attempt to read an insider culture from another insider position; such a move, of course, constitutes the essence of outsider discourse. A more favourable affirmation of the discourse Kuki is seeking to undermine could scarcely be imagined.

The same contradiction can be observed in Quine's indeterminacy thesis. The philosopher William P. Alston teases out this contradiction in his comments on indeterminacy: 'Quine requires that any fact about a language be available to an investigator who approaches the language purely as a spectator…. Being *au courant* with the social form in question is to count as nothing, epistemically. It gives one no edge in principle over the non-participant investigator' (Alston, 1987: 67). This is the logical conclusion of the proposition that languages are radically indeterminate. But, as Alston notes, 'we can critically examine a certain method of hypothesis testing, or a certain practice of belief formation, only by using some other practice to do so, a practice that either has not itself passed a critical scrutiny or has done so by our use of still another practice…unless we argue in a circle…we can't carry out an injunction to use no method that has not survived a critical scrutiny' (Alston, 1986: 67–8). This leads inescapably to the conclusion that there must exist insider and outsider perspectives.

It is clear that both Kuki and Quine are impaled on the horns of the same dilemma, but the very act of conceptualising the problem in their respective books has created many possibilities of fruitful cross-cultural comparison, in the same way that Kuki and Heidegger established a fruitful dialogue on the issues. Minami's analysis of Kuki does not go as far as the above reflections but his sympathetic reading of Kuki is exemplified by his comment that 'Kuki's aesthetics were indisputably linked to a strong desire to place a clear distance between himself and militarism' (Minami, 1980: 107–8).

In chapter four of his book Minami delves further into the origins of the notion of the 'Japanese character'. He dates the evolution of this idea in modern times back to the enlightenment thinker Nishi Amane's (1829–97) article *Kokuminkifūron* (National Character), published in 1875, in which Nishi states that the Japanese national character is ideally suited to a monarchy, and by this statement criticises the national tendency to servility (Minami, 1980: 110–11). Also in 1875, Fukuzawa Yukichi published his *Bunmeiron no Gairyaku* (An Outline of A Theory of Civilisation) in which he made his famous declaration that in Japan 'there exists a government but not a nation' (Quoted Minami, 1980: 114). Minami characterises both these early theorists of the Japanese character as progressive, in that they were attempting to create a sense of independence and pride in the Japanese people in the face of the superior technology and advanced democracies of the West.

A more nationalist bias is adduced to the Japanese character by Miyake Setsurei's two volumes *Shin Zen Bi Nihonjin* (The True Good Beautiful Japanese) and *Gi Aku Shū Nihonjin* (The False Evil Ugly Japanese) published in 1891 (Minami, 1980: 117–20). After citing various participants in the debate over the national character in the mass circulation journal *Taiyō* (The Sun), such as Kanbe Masao (1877–1959) and Toda Kaiichi (1872–1924) in the 1890s and early 1900s, Minami finds a precocious version of the psychiatrist Doi Takeo's (b.1920) 'amae' (dependence) thesis in *Nihon Kokuminsei no Kenkyū* (Studies in the Japanese National Character, 1914) by the educationalist Noda Yoshio, who put forward the social–Darwinian thesis that 'war was, in the final analysis, a struggle of national character' (Quoted Minami, 1980: 132) and also argued that the Japanese are emotional by nature, 'eschewing rationality' (Quoted Minami, 1980: 134).

The latter idea Minami sees as a precursor to Doi's famous 1971 book *Amae' no Kōzō* (The Anatomy of 'Dependence'), which argued for 'dependence' being the major constituent of Japanese interpersonal relations. Minami cites nationalist and socialist thinkers on the topic before ending the chapter with a sustained exposition of the ideas of the sociologist Nakane Chie (b.1926) as put forward in her famous 1967 study *Tate Shakai no Ningen Kankei* (Japanese Society), where she emphasised the 'vertical' nature of Japanese interpersonal relations (Nakane, 1970). The last chapter compares Doi and Nakane to foreign commentators on Japanese society, including the American anthropologist Ruth Benedict and the English sociologist Ronald Dore.

Maruyama Masao and the internationalisation of Japanese culture

By far the longest chapter of Minami's 1980 book is the chapter on national character, so perhaps it is not unexpected that Minami begins his 1994 study *Nihonjinron—Meiji kara Konnichi made* (Discourses on the Japanese—From Meiji to Today) with an introduction on national character studies. This work is much longer and more detailed than *The Genealogy of Nihonjinron*, with a rich collection of data (more than 300 individual studies are cited), although Minami notes in the foreword that he has chosen from among well over a thousand works only studies with a unique perspective (Minami, 1994: vi).

The book is roughly divided into two halves: the first treats ethnocentric discourses chronologically from the Meiji era to the post-World War II occupation era; the second treats works written since then to the present day. Many more studies are referred to than in the 1980 book but, generally speaking, this results in a less detailed and less opinionated analysis of individual thinkers. For example, Minami's discussion of Kuki Shūzō's *The Structure of 'Iki'* is more factual, shorter, and less sympathetic than in the earlier book (Minami, 1994: 116). In addition, more attention is paid to fascist writers than in the first book (Minami, 1994: 137–87).

What is substantially new about the 1994 book is the second half, which introduces a large range of contemporary examples of Japanese ethnocentric discourse. Summarising the overall trends in ethnocentric discourse during this period, Minami categorises the period from 1960 to 1973 as focusing on human relationships, from 1974 to 1985 as the era of mass or collective psychology studies, and from 1986 to 1994 as concentrating on life psychology (Minami, 1994: 216). Four or five authors appear often among those writers cited in the periods from 1960 to 1985. As well as the frequently cited Nakane Chie and Doi Takeo, we find the political scientist Maruyama Masao (1914–96), the Jungian psychoanalyst Kawai Hayao (b.1928) and the sociologist Hamaguchi Eshun (b.1931) appearing prominently.

Minami highlights Maruyama's characterisation of Japanese society and culture as an 'octopus-trap' pattern rather than a 'bamboo whisk' pattern (as in the case of Europe); this famous trope first appeared in Maruyama's 1961 book *Nihon no Shisō* (Japanese Thought) (Minami, 1994: 218). The difference between the two is that Japan absorbed European culture in the late nineteenth century—a time when knowledge was being compartmentalised into various subdivisions and specialities—and thus failed to preserve the essential unity of the body of knowledge itself. European culture, like a bamboo whisk, has many bristles but is still connected together by the handle, unlike the Japanese octopus-trap pattern where culture and learning is fragmented and independent. We will subject Maruyama's study to closer scrutiny.

Maruyama's book is divided into four parts. The first part begins with a preface lamenting the poverty of comprehensive histories of Japanese thought written in Japan—although Maruyama allows that there exists a native tradition of Confucian or Buddhist histories (Maruyama, 1961: 2). Maruyama contrasts this to the richness of postwar Western intellectual histories, especially those published in the USA. Essentially, the Japanese studies are too narrow compared to their Western equivalents and too prone to a binary division of traditional versus imported modes of discourse (Maruyama, 1961: 8). We see here that Maruyama is adopting a 'universalist' frame, and is stating his intention to write a meta-discourse (a study of studies), which will seek to problematise and transcend these limiting categories.

In the remaining four chapters of part one, Maruyama subjects the notions of 'tradition' and 'ideology' to critical scrutiny by examining the nationalist Confucian school of scholarship exemplified by Motoori Norinaga, then subjects the wartime idea of 'national polity' (kokutai) to analysis, and finally considers these notions in relation to modernity (Maruyama, 1961: 11–66).

Part two is a study of modern Japanese thought and literature. In his preface to this part, Maruyama explains that his interest in this issue arose from a debate about the relationship between science and literature in 1937, a debate sparked by the philosopher Tosaka Jun's (1900–45) attack on the notion of 'fukkō' (revival) that had been taken up in contemporary literary circles. Maruyama read into this debate the issue of politics and its relationship to literature (Maruyama, 1961: 68–70). This part traces a history of the impact of political doctrines, especially Marxism, on literary debates. Maruyama focuses his history mainly on the 1920s and 1930s, when proletarian literature was at its peak. He criticises the totalising power of the Marxist dialectic as a methodology for reading and writing literature, while acknowledging its explanatory power (Maruyama, 1961: 70–119). Part three focuses on what 'thought' should be, beginning with a discussion of images that act as a lubricant between oneself and one's environment (Maruyama, 1961: 124–5). Maruyama stresses the power of images to create a new reality. This is where his famous trope of the Western bamboo whisk and the Japanese octopus trap comes into play, which leads to a comparison between inward (i.e. Japanese) and outward-looking (i.e. international) perspectives (Maruyama, 1961: 126–47).

Maruyama's discussion of the power of mass communication, especially commercial broadcasting, in creating common perspectives, and thus obscuring the barrier between private and public, is reminiscent of some of Yoshimoto Takaaki's writings on the same subjects some years later, as we will discover in chapter three of this book. But Maruyama's view of the role of the imagination in creating a variety of plural images is generally positive (Maruyama, 1961: 145–51). The final section, part four, deals with moving from thought to action, concentrating on the need to protect and enhance the freedoms inherent in Japanese civil society. Maruyama stresses the importance of citizen's groups in strengthening democracy, and democratic values (Maruyama, 1961: 154–79).

In his postscript, Maruyama notes that the four parts of the volume were published separately between 1957 and 1959. There is a polemical air to some of the discussions which perhaps betrays the Cold War background to Maruyama's advocacy of a non-Marxist intellectual perspective. It is noteworthy that in the period preceding the publication of the book, Maruyama was at the centre of the political debate in Japan over the re-signing of the US–Japan Security Treaty: in reality, a debate over the future of Japan–US relations. Maruyama's views ran contrary to those of Yoshimoto Takaaki, who was seen at the time as a kind of spokesman for the Japanese New Left (Yoshimoto argued for Japanese independence from US military protection). Maruyama's deliberate adoption of a 'universalist' perspective in this volume can thus be read as a counter-argument to Yoshimoto's insider views as expressed in numerous publications produced at that time, as we shall see in chapter three. The categories of outsider and insider are especially helpful in this regard, as both thinkers would have been characterised by many as belonging to the 'left', despite their political differences.

To return to Maruyama's metaphor of bamboo whisk and octopus trap, we see that this trope captured the sense of 'dual system' perfectly, with the West represented as a unitary 'other' but Japan as a fragmented 'self' (Maruyama, 1961: 129–30). Minami summarises Maruyama's view of history as explained in his 1972 article 'Rekishi Ishiki no Kosō' (The 'Ancient Stratum' of Historical Consciousness) where Maruyama defines the 'basso obstinato' that underlies the Japanese historical consciousness as an 'ancient stratum'. Maruyama explains this ancient stratum as a sense of continuity where historical upheavals (revolution etc.) are interpreted as emerging naturally, as creating no real discontinuity with the past. Such a viewpoint conceives of history as an expression of the present—a 'continuous present'—and is deeply rooted in Japanese myth and legend (Minami, 1994: 227–8). It is remarkable how closely Maruyama's perspective resembles that of Yanagita Kunio, as we shall later demonstrate.

Kawai Hayao: insider as outsider

Minami discusses three books by Kawai Hayao. The first, *Bosei Shakai Nihon no Byōri* (The Pathology of Japan, a Maternal Society), was published in 1976 and analyses Japanese society from a Jungian perspective. Kawai argues that Japan is, at heart, a maternal society governed by the maternal principle, which enfolds all within itself, thus smothering conflict. This leads Kawai to contrast the modern West, which takes as given various fundamental differences in ability between individuals, with modern Japan which seeks to minimise such differences, and develops a conception of self with no clear barrier against the 'other'. Thus Japanese society is constructed upon a model of 'eternal adolescence', a psycho-social model close to Doi Takeo's vision of a Japan built upon patterns of 'dependence' (Minami, 1994: 237–8).

Another important study published in 1976 but not treated by Minami is Kawai's *Kage no Genshōgaku* (The Phenomenology of Shadows), which we will subject to closer examination. This book is written in an orthodox Jungian frame, with the central concern of the study being Jung's notion of the shadow, often likened to a doppelgänger, or double. Kawai begins the first chapter, on shadows, by discussing the German romantic poet Adalbert von Chamisso's (1781–1838) story *Peter Schlemihls wundersame Geschichte* (1816) about a character who has sold his shadow to the devil. By investigating the significance of shadows through an examination of folklore (via James Frazer's *Golden Bough*), and stories told by Australian aborigines (among other sources), Kawai explores the dichotomies of light and dark, mind and body, conscious and unconscious, and good and evil (Kawai, 1987: 10–23).

This enquiry then turns to the process of ego formation and the world of images. At this point, Kawai introduces Jung's notion of 'shadow', and discusses its significance in relation to the unconscious. In summary, in this first chapter, Kawai connects an outsider discourse— Jung's theory of shadow—to traditional Japanese notions of disease, which visualise illness as a shadow. The underlying metaphor is of the shadow being the spirit or soul (Kawai, 1987: 10–67).

In the second chapter, on illness, Kawai further explores the traditional Japanese belief that if one is separated from one's shadow, then one dies. The figure of the doppelgänger is connected to this discourse by a discussion of tales featuring doppelgängers by such authors as Fyodor Dostoevsky (1821–81) and E.T.A. Hoffman (1776–1822). Kawai next turns to multiple personality disorder in an attempt to probe the origins of various psychological problems (Kawai, 1987: 68–125).

Chapter three investigates the world of darkness—night—or, in another guise, the underworld. Kawai relates the dreams of patients suffering from depersonalisation to the invasion of shadows into such persons' psyches. Here Kawai is citing the research of the psychiatrist Kimura Bin. Kawai's chief concern is with shadows invisible to sight but which can be perceived by the other senses. Such experiences are symptomatic of a variety of disorders that he investigates (Kawai, 1987: 142–63). He then turns to visions and representations of hell in

Buddhism and Christianity, again using dream therapies to elicit from patients descriptions of the descent into hell (Kawai, 1987: 163–83).

The next chapter extends the notion of paradise that Kawai finds in shadows to the figure of the clown (dōke) or fool. He refers to the work of the sociologist Yamaguchi Masao, who will be discussed shortly, in developing this figure as an expression of social anomie. In addition to Yamaguchi's elaboration of this thesis, Kawai utilises the research of W. Willeford on the figure of the fool, thus demonstrating how this whole volume juxtaposes quite explicitly insider and outsider perspectives (Kawai, 1987: 186–249).

The last chapter, chapter five, discusses how we can come to terms with our shadows by examining, among other works, the fiction of the South African writer Laurens van der Post (1906–1996). Kawai demonstrated in chapter four that shadows are manifested positively as trickster figures but negatively as strangers in our psychic lives. Thus, we can conclude that Kawai is conducting a dialogue between the two worlds of the ego and its shadow (Kawai, 1987: 260). His objective is to enlighten Japanese readers about the benefits of Jung's symbolic system in order to assist them with their psychic health.

The book demonstrates how Japanese culture—in this particular instance the culture of psychological medicine—can be constructed on the basis of a dialogue with insider and outsider discourse. It can be argued here that Kawai, as a student of Carl Jung (1875–1961), primarily conceives his role as interpreting outsider theory to the Japanese but, as we have seen, this is too simplistic a reading of Kawai's book, which essentially conducts a dialogue between two different discourses: one Western and one Japanese.

Kawai's 1982 study *Mukashibanashi to Nihonjin no Kokoro* (Folktales and the Japanese Mind) expands the thesis of *The Pathology of Japan* with Kawai using narrative and folk tales as his source. Western narratives have the sense of an ending but Japanese narratives do not: only by focusing on reader response can an 'ending' occur. Kawai argues that the image of woman in old tales and narratives is decisive; only by reading these narratives seeking for woman (if she is 'lost' from the narrative), reading with a 'woman's eye' rather than a 'man's eye', can the whole meaning be grasped. The Japanese ego is thus expressed in the image of the female: a psycho-social reality that patriarchal authority, in the form of the dominant order, seeks constantly to conceal (Minami, 1994: 247–8).

At the same time, Kawai published a collection of essays entitled *Chūkū Kōzō—Nihon no Shinsō* (The Deep Layer of Japan as Empty Centre), which also corrected his 1976 book by stating that Japan is a maternal society only in comparison with the West. If one compares Japan to Asian societies, which are even more maternal in orientation, then Japan is properly categorised as a society balanced between the male and female principles. From an analysis of Japanese mythohistory as revealed in ancient texts like the *Kojiki* (Record of Ancient Matters), Kawai proposes the thesis of the 'empty centre' where a power vacuum exists at the centre of the Japanese mythohistorical universe; gods at the centre lack power, and struggles for authority occur at the periphery. Kawai argues that such a model explains the continued existence of the Imperial 'system' (Minami, 1994: 248–9).

Kawai has written and edited a very large number of studies but, unlike most of the authors examined in this chapter, Kawai has also written a number of books in English. So, in a sense, both in his theoretical approach and his target audience, Kawai is a truly international thinker, simultaneously straddling both the categories of insider and outsider, balancing one view against the other while working in an explicitly outsider context of Jungian thought. Undoubtedly Kawai's attempt to read Japanese culture from an outsider perspective has had an influence on his English-language studies. These volumes are not treated by Minami, so it is appropriate that we briefly consider here Kawai's English-language approach to culture.

In his latest English-language volume to date, *Dreams, Myths and Fairy Tales in Japan* (1995), Kawai uses Jung to investigate the meaning and significance of several archetypal Japanese tales. His introduction to this study provides an illuminating insight into the dilemma faced by thinkers such as Kawai in straddling these two categories of insider and outsider. Kawai notes that in his youth, he was 'strongly attracted to Western culture', and as a result of World War II, he 'came to hate the irrational…Japanese attitude toward life.' But after studying in the West, he realised that 'European consciousness is not "the best"…for everybody' (Kawai, 1995: 10). Kawai further observes that 'until recently I had thought in terms of integrating [the West and Japan], or of finding a third way somewhere between them. But nowadays I think it is impossible' (Kawai, 1995: 11). His hope now is just for Western readers 'to see their own way of life from a different angle' (Kawai, 1995: 11)—in other words, he is opening a dialogue, seeing if intercultural communication, at least, is possible.

The dilemma that modern Japanese face, and which is described by Kawai is not new. The same problem has plagued Japanese intellectuals for most of the twentieth century, as noted earlier in this chapter. The retreat from Western culture is an idea most famously publicised by the poet Hagiwara Sakutarō (1886–1942) in 'Nihon e no Kaiki' (Return to Japan), an essay he wrote in 1937, and which was republished in book form in an essay collection of the same name the following year. We will examine this essay here as it puts the dilemma of Kawai and, as we shall see shortly, Umehara Takeshi (b.1925) into a useful historical perspective.

Hagiwara begins the essay by stating the problem: 'Until only recently, the West has been our homeland. Just like Urashima Tarō in ancient times who sought the homeland of his spirit, and pictured it as an undersea palace over the sea, so we pictured our homeland as the image of the West across the sea' (Hagiwara, 1984: 485). He then goes on to argue that this was inevitable: 'Since the Meiji era Japan has, with almost superhuman determination, desperately studied Western civilisa-tion…forced to do this for its own protection from the danger of inva-sion by white people' (Hagiwara, 1984: 486). He does not attempt to gloss over the extent of Japanese obsession with Western culture: 'Without our infatuation with Western culture, how could we have studied so intently?' (Hagiwara, 1984: 486) He then cites the writer Lafcadio Hearn's (1850–1904) prediction that Japan, without this infat-uation, would have soon ended up in armed conflict with the West.

However, writes Hagiwara, in the most frequently quoted section of the essay, this has had the effect of virtually destroying Japanese culture: 'But we have travelled abroad for too long. When we returned home the vestiges of the past had already disappeared; the eaves had decayed, the garden had fallen to ruin, no trace of anything Japanese has survived, everything has been lost…' (Hagiwara, 1984: 487). The poet's message is not to despair, for the very fact of being Japanese means that things can change. But, for the present, this has resulted in the situation where: 'Now, most of us who criticise or are concerned with things Japanese are strangely enough a group of "outsiders" or "strangers." Superficial observers claim that this phenomenon represents the failure of intellec-tuals, it signals "a cowardly retreat" from our struggle' (Hagiwara, 1984: 488). Hagiwara denies that this is so. In fact, he argues, the desert of the present presages a bright future: 'The reality is nothingness. In Japan today nothing exists. We have lost our entire culture. But we intellectuals fighting amid the emptiness are struggling towards the construction of the future' (Hagiwara, 1984: 489).

Finally, Hagiwara urges a return to Japan but, in a fascinating coda to the essay, he does so by demanding that this be accomplished away from the ranting of the ultra-nationalists: 'Those who issue ultra-nationalist commands to us in loud voices—leave us in peace for a time!' (Hagiwara, 1984: 489) Here he distinguishes his kind of nationalism from the more strident jingoism of the times. Nevertheless, as the critic Isoda Kōichi has argued in reference to this essay, this does not mean Hagiwara was entirely free from patriotic outpourings. Isoda cites a poem Hagiwara wrote celebrating the fall of Nanking as evidence (Isoda, 1983: 204). But, as Isoda notes, Hagiwara's plea to return to Japan does not involve a wholesale rejection of Western values; rather the focus is upon resuscitating Japanese culture.

Read in the context of the dilemma outlined above relating to latter-day intellectuals like Kawai, Hagiwara's essay actually sketches out the trajectory that some of these thinkers were to take: a retreat or about-face from outsider culture to insider culture but undertaken, initially, as outsiders since Japanese culture could only be reconstructed from the aftermath of its encounter with the West. The difference clearly lies in the fact that Hagiwara's return to Japan involved a near-absolute absorption in Japanese culture, explicitly re-creating that culture from a new 'inside', whereas contemporary thinkers like Kawai openly seek for others and, by implication, for themselves 'to see their own way of life from a different angle' (Kawai, 1995: 11): a plainly comparative perspective that is free from xenophobic overtones.

Culture as collectivity

The first book by the social psychologist Hamaguchi Eshun that Minami treats is *Nihon Rashisa no Sai Hakken* (The Re-Discovery of Japaneseness), published in 1977. Hamaguchi evolved a new perspective to replace the old categories of 'group' and 'individual' to characterise Japanese society. His concept is the 'contextual' or 'man-in-nexus' which, he argues, arises from the traditional focus of Japanese society on how human beings cooperate in shared contexts of mutual support.

Hence, in the Japanese case, the individual ego lives within a group, as part of a shared context, and therefore evades Western categorisation, which seeks to limit psycho-social categorisation to Western systems of social formation (Minami, 1994: 242–3; Hamaguchi, 1985: 289–321).

One feature of Hamaguchi's study that we need to consider further here is Hamaguchi's own evaluation of many of the writers on Japan considered above. After briefly reviewing the theses proposed by Watsuji Tetsurō, Ruth Benedict, Kimura Bin, Doi Takeo, and the philosopher Nakamura Hajime (b.1912) among others (Hamaguchi also examines critically Minami's work on the Japanese ego), Hamaguchi argues that: 'Conceptualisations of individual Japanese phenomena [by these authors] can only be expressed as a unique morphology.' This leads Hamaguchi to ask: 'Why cannot these phenomena be put into a general paradigm?' (Hamaguchi, 1998: 299) He is seeking to convert insider nativist paradigms of culture, such as those examined above, into an outsider frame.

The general hypothesis that Hamaguchi arrives at is that Japan is an 'outside-in' society; a culture formed from a socialisation process that reverses the ego formation mechanism of Western societies, which are 'inside-out' (Hamaguchi, 1998: 311–16). The details and nature of how this process takes place need not concern us here. What is significant in Hamaguchi's thesis is that he has created a universal morphology of culture that can be used to classify all human societies: an explicit example of an outsider discourse, but produced by reflection upon, and out of the process of, insider discourse. This is made clear in the preface where Hamaguchi writes that his study is 'an internal investigation, an emic study of culture as K. Pike advocated' (Hamaguchi, 1998: 6). However, what is fascinating is that Hamaguchi approaches his emic investigation from an etic perspective (to restate the point made above), as his scholarly base is in 'psycho-anthropology', a very new field (Hamaguchi, 1998: 329). Hamaguchi noted in the postscript to the expanded paperback edition of *The Re-Discovery of Japaneseness* (the edition used here) that it was this book which gave him 'citizenship' (shiminken) in the Japanese scholarly world (Hamaguchi, 1998: 330).

The second book, *Nihonteki Shūdanshugi—Sono Shinka wo Tou* (Japanese Collectivism—Questioning its True Worth), is edited by Hamaguchi and Kumon Shinpei and was published in 1982. In this volume Hamaguchi develops his earlier hypothesis further to the point where it can encompass whole social systems. He argues for the notion of humans cooperating collectively on the basis of a 'shared autonomy' or a 'participatory identity' which is contrasted to the Western notion of 'individual autonomy' or, simply, the 'individual'. Thus the notion of 'man-in nexus' defines the Japanese self within a contextual identity (Minami, 1994: 249–50). The implicit background into which Hamaguchi's conceptualisation is embedded is clearly that of the Japanese industrial enterprise, but this necessarily historicises his argument, and considering the changed industrial landscape in Japan since the book was written, perhaps renders it less than persuasive.

Minami contrasts the general nature of those examples of ethnocentric discourse produced between 1960 and 1985 with the much more specific and detailed studies that characterise the period from 1986 to 1994. Minami identifies the 1970s as the starting point for the explosion of 'Nihonjinron' publications (Minami, 1994: 277). This decade is often seen as a turning point, a time when the material prosperity achieved by Japan's rapid postwar economic growth became a matter of public discussion and reflection, and not only because of the 'oil-shock' suffered by Japan later in the decade. Some pundits saw the 1970s as marking the end of the postwar era, and later commentators looked back to the end of the decade and the beginning of the 1980s as signalling a transition from a 'modern' to a 'postmodern' culture. Among the large number of studies described by Minami, a few important thinkers stand out.

The agricultural economist Iinuma Jirō (b.1918) inherited the tradition of Watsuji Tetsurō with two books written during the seventies exploring the link between climate and temperament. Iinuma's 1970 study *Fūdo to Rekishi* (Climate and History) commences with an attack on Watsuji and outlines his project of taking up the links between climate and social development. Iinuma argued, writes Minami, that Watsuji's view of the influence of climate was too static. Iinuma's notion of climate focuses on human responses to changes in the environment: this he carries over into the political sphere, criticising the Imperial institution as unnatural (Minami, 1994: 279–80). Iinuma's 1979 study *Rekishi no Naka no Fūdo* (Climate in History) attempts to expand upon the earlier book by investigating the Imperial institution over the course of history. Iinuma examines the manipulation of the Imperial institution by the 'bakufu' (military government) in the seventeenth and eighteenth centuries, emphasising the deliberate linkage made by the political elite between agricultural religious practices and the Emperor (Minami, 1994: 280).

In his 1991 book *Tennōsei to Kirisutosha* (The Imperial System and Christians), Iinuma takes up the Imperial institution once again, arguing that 'Since the Meiji era the fundamental ideology of the Imperial system, which has been made the basis of the unity of state and people, is ethnic egoism…emphasising this leaves Japan with no future' (Quoted Minami, 1994: 389). Iinuma raises the role of Christianity as providing a possible oppositional basis to 'ethnic egoism'. In one sense, Iinuma's critique of ethnocentrism can be read as a reaction to and revision of a 'dual system' inherited from thinkers like Yanagita Kunio, his revision accomplished by the deliberate importation of a foreign religious doctrine into an indigenous realm of politico-religious debate.

The same kind of criticism, namely, the construction of a Christian critique of the Imperial ideology, has been the subject of several books by the intellectual historian Takeda Kiyoko (1917–94), who has concentrated on tracing the sources of an indigenous tradition of resistance, often by arguing the case for a 'dual system' of Christian discourse in Japan. Takeda reconstructs a tradition of indigenous Christian discourse that may well be characterised by Western Christian thinkers as heterodox or even apostate but which exists as an alternate vision of ethical, social, and moral responsibility. Minami cites Takeda's 1978 study *Tennōkan no Sōkoku—1945 Nen Zengo* (Rival Views of the Emperor Around 1945), but more reflective of the concerns outlined above is her 1976 study, *Seitō to Itan no 'Aida'—Nihon Shisōshi Kenkyū Shiron* ('Between' Orthodoxy and Heterodoxy—A Study of Japanese Intellectual History), which questions the notions of universalism and particularism by examining Meiji Japanese thinkers as well as Asian interpretations of Christian thought (Minami, 1994: 385; Takeda, 1976: 116–28).

Japanese religiosity

Another major figure in the debate over Japanese indigenous systems is the philosopher Umehara Takeshi. Umehara is the author of a vast number of philosophical, philological, and historical studies in literature, myth, and culture, as well as several original creative works. Minami chooses three seminal studies for discussion: the first is the 1967 volume

Bi to Shūkyō no Hakken—Sōzōteki Nihon Bunka Ron (The Discovery of Beauty and Religion—On Creative Japanese Culture) in which Umehara argues that the Japanese people are unique in their ability to forget their religiosity. The 'National Learning' scholars in the seventeenth century, and later, encouraged this trait which protected Japan against Western invasion, and enabled Japan to quickly absorb Western culture. The eighteenth-century scholar Hirata Atsutane changed the traditional worship of nature into a veneration of humans, thus anthropomorphising the gods. The notion of the source of political authority (i.e. the Emperor) in the nation being simultaneously a god was born at this time. Umehara traces how traditional religious beliefs became first Confucian, then Samurai ethics, then were anthropomorphised and finally, in the Meiji era, resulted in state Shintō (Minami, 1994: 314).

Umehara also analyses the Japanese aesthetic sensibility by a close reading of the preface to the famous tenth-century poetry collection, the *Kokinshū*. He identifies sadness, as manifested in the many poems of separation and mourning, as the major tone. Why this was so is partially explained by the quest for transience exemplified by the poetry in this collection, a quest which was strongly associated with Buddhist beliefs. Finally, Umehara argues that purity as an expression of traditional religious values, and as the highest aesthetic value, became inextricably associated with Emperor worship and militarism via the vehicle of state Shintō (Minami, 1994: 315).

The second study chosen by Minami is Umehara's 1985 book *Nihon no Shinsō Bunka—Buna Tai ni Ikita Hitobito no Sekaikan* (Japan's Deep Layer Culture—The Worldview of People who Lived in the Beechwood Zone). Umehara argues that glossy-leaf forests are numerous in western Japan but there are few prehistoric Jōmon sites, and indeed, western Japan was a relatively unpopulated area. Jōmon culture flourished in eastern Japan where glossy-leaf forests are rare. To develop a hypothesis relating to Jōmon culture therefore requires that attention is paid to deciduous broad-leafed forest environments where Japanese beechwood and oak trees grow.

Umehara also hypothesises that when Buddhism was brought to Japan early in the sixth century, the belief of the Mahayana tradition of Buddhism that all living creatures could become Buddhas, rather than a chosen few as taught by Hinayana (or Theravada) precepts, was current. That not only humans but also animals and plants could achieve

Buddhahood became the basis of a traditional mode of thinking. But, Umehara argues, this worldview where humans are part of a natural ecological system was lost and replaced by an anthropocentric perspective (Minami, 1994: 28). The similarities between Umehara's argument and the Gaia hypothesis—that the Earth functions as a single organism as proposed by James Lovelock in the 1970s—hardly need to be stressed; yet again we find another example of a dual system, underlining in this case the intellectual links between the rise of the ecology movement in the West and environmentalists in Japan.

The last book by Umehara that is analysed by Minami is the 1989 volume *Nihonjin no 'Ano Yo' Kan* (The View of the Japanese 'Other World'). This book elaborates upon the ideas expressed in the two earlier works to describe the prehistoric Japanese conception of the 'other world', the land to which we go after death. Umehara finds four common elements in Japanese views of the other world: firstly, the other world and this world do not differ much, that is, there is no distinction between heaven and hell, and no judgment in the afterlife. Secondly, after humans die, they leave their fleshly bodies to become gods in the other world. Thirdly, all living creatures possess souls, and all become gods after death. Fourthly, after a time in the other world, all the spirits of the dead are reborn in an eternal cycle in this world. This conception of the other world was lost with the growth of urban centres but still survives in traditional agricultural cultures (Minami, 1994: 343–4).

From Minami's description of these three studies, it is obvious that one of Umehara's major interests is Buddhism and its role in shaping Japanese culture. Umehara's 1980 study *Kūkai no Shisō ni Tsuite* (On the Thought of Kūkai) is typical of many volumes he has written on this theme (though it is not mentioned by Minami). It is characteristic of Umehara's opus that this volume itself is a revised edition of a text that originally appeared as part of a three-volume set on esoteric Buddhism (Umehara, 1980: 6). Let us examine this volume in more detail.

Kūkai (774–835) was the founder of Shingon or Esoteric Buddhism, an immensely influential school of Buddhist thought, which had its headquarters on Mt Kōya in western Japan. Kūkai wrote in a Japanese version of medieval or classical Chinese and so his works are impossible for modern Japanese to read unaided. Umehara begins his study by discussing what he calls the 'two faces' of Kūkai—his achievements as a theorist and as a man of action. He emphasises how all-encompassing

Kūkai's achievements were. Kūkai's extensive collected works include treatises on a huge range of topics—his *Bunkyōhifuron* (The Secret Treasure House of the Mirrors of Poetry), for instance, occupies a position in Japanese poetics analogous to that in Western poetics occupied by Aristotle's *Rhetoric*, and, as Umehara notes, this work has no religious overtones whatsoever, being written purely for literary purposes (Umehara, 1980: 7–11).

Umehara argues that Kūkai's message transcends language and it is this dimension of his achievements that is impossible for modern people to grasp. This is especially the case now as the type of Esoteric Buddhism that Kūkai advocated is seen as akin to the practice of magic by modern Japanese intellectuals, and this accounts for his recent unpopularity (Umehara, 1980: 11–20). But, at this point, Umehara related his own doubts about the study of Western philosophy that he had pursued for over thirty years—these doubts led him to return to the study of Japanese thought (Umehara, 1980: 20–2). Here we see the outsider in the process of becoming an insider: the same intellectual crisis experienced by Kawai. And this change in direction took place as there was a resurgence of interest in Kūkai in Japan.

Umehara gives a brief biography of Kūkai, explaining the significance of the many sutras and other important texts Kūkai brought back to Japan after his period of study in China (Umehara, 1980: 24–40). He then explains the principal doctrines of Esoteric Buddhism as preached by Kūkai, noting especially how Esoteric Buddhism in some senses repudiates doctrines taught by the historical Buddha Gautama, instead focusing on the cosmic Vairocana Buddha (Umehara, 1980: 40–50). Umehara divides Kūkai's writings into two categories: the first expresses the special intellectual features of Shingon teaching—including such works as *Benken Mitsu Nikyōron* (The Difference Between Exoteric and Esoteric Buddhism) and *Shōji Jissō Gi* (The Meanings of Sound, Word and Reality)—and the second expresses the Shingon view of Buddhism as a whole. This latter category of works Umehara compares to the Hegelian dialectic; the most famous example being Kūkai's *Hizō Hōyaku* (The Precious Key to the Secret Treasures) (Umehara, 1980: 50–4).

In the remainder of the book, Umehara summarises and analyses three representative works of Kūkai: his *Sokushin Jōbutsu Gi* (Attaining Enlightenment in this Very Existence), *The Meanings of Sound, Word and Reality* and *Unji Gi* (The Meanings of the Word Hūm) (Umehara, 1980:

62–118). Arguably, Kūkai can also be regarded as a kind of insider theorist, since it was his exposition of Esoteric Buddhism that proved most congenial to Shintō, the native expression of Japanese religious belief. Indeed, eventually a fusion of the imported religion Buddhism and the native Shintō emerged, and this synthesis—a classic syncresis of religious traditions—owed much to Kūkai's teaching (Hakeda, 1972: 8–9). The nativist emphasis, or at least, the impact of Kūkai on Japanese religious and intellectual traditions, provides a clue to why Umehara should have been attracted to this particular Buddhist thinker: both men can be described as working within intellectual traditions that attempted to ground outsider views (Buddhism for Kūkai; Western philosophy for Umehara) in an insider frame.

In another recent exposition of Japanese culture, the 1991 two-volume study *Ama to Tennō* (Women Divers and the Emperor), not discussed by Minami, Umehara argues that the legend that Emperor Shōmu's (701–56) mother was a woman diver's daughter is true. This has large-scale ramifications for the advocacy of Buddhism in Japan by Emperor Shōmu and his daughter Empress Kōken (718–70) at a critical time for the spread of the Buddhist faith in an alien environment (Umehara, 1991). Perhaps the most interesting issue raised by Umehara is in the question of the 'Imperial system' (tennōsei), the investigation of which is the chief reason Umehara embarked upon this work (Umehara, 1991(2): 254).

Umehara's conclusion is that the Imperial system was first constructed on the basis that the emperor should be female. He also argues that the notion of the emperor being divine originated in the reign of Emperor Temmu (622–86), the fortieth emperor according to tradition. Consequently, writes Umehara, Temmu's successor Empress Jitō (645–702) was the first emperor in the true sense of the word, that is, in the associations (including divinity) attached to the office of 'tennō' (emperor) for much of Japanese history (Umehara, 1991(2): 255–7).

Umehara's concerns in this book range far and wide, and cover the role of Buddhism in the early Japanese state, the role of women, and especially empresses and Imperial princesses, in the formation of Japanese identity. What Umehara is trying to accomplish is to trace the fundamental pattern of Imperial rule from its earliest template. The cliché that emperors reign but do not rule, expressed in the modern era as the idea of the Emperor as symbolic (arising from the postwar constitution), originates according to Umehara's thesis in the arrangements relating to Imperial succession constructed by the courtier Fujiwara Fubito (659–720) and later implemented after Empress Kōken attempted to have her lover, a monk called Dōkyō, made emperor (Umehara, 1991(2): 257–349). This fundamental pattern, Umehara argues, has had major implications for the evolution of Japanese culture. Certainly, it has had important implications for the postwar debate on the legitimacy or otherwise of the Imperial institution, which may well be the debate with which Umehara is principally concerned here. But this fascination with origins is not confined to Umehara and, as we will see later, such an interest owes much to the work of Yanagita Kunio.

The emphasis upon the prehistoric Jōmon culture as the source for traditional Japanese beliefs and culture is much in evidence among the thinkers cited by Minami. The anthropologist Hanihara Kazurō (b.1927) in two books discussed by Minami—Hanihara's edited 1985 collection *Jōmonjin no Chie* (The Wisdom of the Jōmon People) and his edited 1990 volume *Nihonjin Shin Kigen Ron* (A New Study of the Origins of the Japanese)—raises the issue of the reclassification of ethnic groups on the periphery like the Ainu and the Okinawans as early immigrants into the Japanese archipelago from the Asian continent. This, in turn, sets up a contrast between an early stratum of Japanese culture and a later stratum, which immediately becomes dominant, brought to Japan by a more technologically advanced group of immigrants. The latter group is associated with rice cultivation and with the more sophisticated continental civilisations of China and Korea (Minami, 1994: 283–4).

The Jōmon boom has recently inspired a major series of poetical, dramatic, and scholarly works by the poet Soh Sakon (b.1919), for which he was awarded an important literary prize, with titles in the Jōmon series including such works as *Nihonbi—Jōmon no Keifu* (Japanese Beauty—The Genealogy of Jōmon, 1991), *Jōmon Rentō* (Jōmon Linked Prayer, 1992), *Shin Jōmon* (New Jōmon, 1993), *Fuji no Hana* (Wisteria Flowers, 1994), *Jōmon no Kyōgen—Hisui* (Jōmon Kyōgen—Jade, 1994) and *Hyōchūka* (Frozen Flowers, 1995). Soh's use of Jōmon motifs and themes is partially a rewriting of history, an extended requiem for the souls of those killed in World War II, as well as a personal exploration of a potent symbol of loss. Soh links the Jōmon figurines, found in some tombs dating from early in Japan's past, to the religious beliefs which inspired them. These beliefs and their expressions he then connects, as metaphor or symbols, to the war dead. The personal connection is made manifest in the fact that the poet's own mother was killed during an air raid in 1945.

We see a paradoxical but characteristic mixture of regret and hope in Soh's poem 'Matsuri' (Festivals) from the book *Jōmon Rentō*. In this poem, Soh contrasts the numinous and the human in the ritual of festival, seeing both qualities as interrelated but also attempting to conjure up an imagined Jōmon sense of community in both the spiritual and local sense, as we can see in these extracts from the 14-stanza poem.

> ......
> Festivals
> Call back the departed dead
> Festivals
> Burn the past in the flames of the future
> Festivals
> Exchange this world for that
> Festivals are
> When god becomes an infant
> Such a thing
> Is impossible for humans
> ......
> Fill up your cup with *sake*
> For God within you
> Allow God within you
> To dance
>
> *Soh, 1992: 118–19*

The Jōmon period as the source of Okinawan culture is explored by the novelist Shimao Toshio (1917–86) in the three famous essays he wrote in 1970: 'Yaponeshia to Ryūkyū Ko' (Yaponesia and the Ryūkyū Archipelago), 'Ryūkyū Ko Kara' (From the Ryūkyū Archipelago), and 'Kaiki no Sōnen: Yaponeshia' (The Idea of Return: Yaponesia). Like Soh's Jōmon series, this exploration is both personal and political. It was at the edge of the Okinawan island group that Shimao escaped death as a Kamikaze pilot; this climactic event is one of the sources of the alternative vision of Japan that he constructs in his essays, a vision of a Japan with Asian and Pacific links (thus the coining of the word 'Yaponesia' in 1961, although it did not enter popular use until the 1970s), a radical 'self' which has Imperial Japan as its opposite 'other' (cf. Clarke, 1985: 7–21; Gabriel, 1996: 205–20). Shimao's yearning for an alternative self has him, in the first essay cited above, even declaring: 'I regret not having been born in Okinawa' (Shimao, 1970: 266).

Western views of Japanese ethnocentric discourse

Neither Soh nor Shimao are mentioned in Minami's 1994 book, which demonstrates both the limitations and the achievement of studies of this kind. How does one select from the thousands upon thousands of works published over the last four or five decades in Japan (or even earlier, as with the works discussed in Minami's 1980 volume) which contribute to a lengthy and venerable debate over culture? The use of the ethnocentric frame—the Nihonjinron concept—clearly has advantages as it presents readers with a neat, clearly defined category. But the very amorphousness of any kind of book labelled 'ethnocentric'—is it not the case that most, if not all literature on the culture of any society could fall under the same heading?—makes it hard to define boundaries or to mark limits.

Clearly, there are themes common to the 300-odd works that Minami selects for comment out of the thousands he has read. Some of these themes are: an obsession with origins, specifically the origin of particular religious, linguistic, social, or political formations; a concern with national identity or, to use an older phrase, national character; an equally strong concern with the Imperial institution; a deep interest in interpersonal relations, kinship systems and parent–child relations; a fascination with various conceptions and expressions of the numinous; a profound love of aesthetic questions and the artistic products which flow from this; a constant quest to comprehend the present in political, geographic, economic, and historical terms; and a recurring need to rewrite and rethink history.

To compound the problem of how to choose reliable guides to Japanese culture, and the problem of how to conceptualise particular moments in intellectual history, the thought remains that even these themes seem hardly confined to Japanese discourse or to define a unique Japanese discourse. Minami has, as he notes in his 1994 foreword, evaluated these works and only discussed books that are original and significant. Ultimately such evaluations are always subjective, and so, for purposes of comparison, we shall briefly glance at a few other guides to culture in contemporary Japan.

Western guides mentioned by Minami include the Australian sociologists Ross Mouer and Yoshio Sugimoto, who in a number of books in both Japanese and English have attempted to problematise and contextualise 'Nihonjinron' discourse. Mouer and Sugimoto generally take such publications to task for a lack of cross-cultural comparisons, as well as a lack of hard data, and have sought to develop a comparative methodology themselves (Sugimoto and Mouer, 1989: 13–14). However, the philosophical problems associated with the conceptualisation of 'self' and 'other' referred to at the outset of this chapter indicate that such a task is fraught with difficulty and far from complete.

The problems associated with where one draws the line at data collection and categorisation or analysis are notoriously difficult to resolve. Inevitably, claims that challenge Western 'universal' systems are answered by overt or implicit or, in some cases, disguised appeals to other universals, which turn out, more often than not, to be the same systems under attack in the first place. And, rarely is a systematic defence of this 'universal' paradigm provided. A highly self-conscious form of contextualisation of the kind employed by various thinkers, like Stefan Tanaka or, at times, Yanagita Kunio, seems to answer some of the difficulties, but not all, as we shall see later.

Peter N. Dale's 1986 study *The Myth of Japanese Uniqueness* has been criticised on the grounds that the target of his attack—fascism, or imperialist totalitarianism, as the hidden or not-so-hidden agenda behind many Nihonjinron studies—is 'routinely produced in his own methodology which takes unproblematically the given of the Western universal project which claims "epistemological privilege"', a claim accepted but not argued by Dale (Marshall, 1989: 266–72). Gadamerian hermeneutics offers one way to read texts without assuming such privileges, to engage in a dialogue where both self and other are under construction, where the very possibility of empathy is continually doubted and interrogated but continually invoked. Or, reading Japanese ethnocentric literature as part of the dual structure of colonial and postcolonial discourse—especially complicated by Japan's dual role as coloniser (of prewar Korea and Taiwan) and colonised (the US occupation serving as erstwhile colonial power)—is yet another way to structure the analysis without falling victim to ethnocentric bias.

Even the pragmatics of the American philosopher Richard Rorty (b.1931) allows insights from an 'emic' perspective. As Rorty argues: 'For us pragmatists…there is no such thing as an intrinsically privileged context' (Rorty, 1991: 96). Here Rorty denies the possibility of the object of enquiry having its own context, whether intellectual, cultural, or ideological, that it is outside the 'web of beliefs', in a state of disembodied objectivity, and thus he takes issue with anthropologists like Clifford Geertz (and, by implication, critics like Peter Dale) who dislike ethnocentrism (Rorty, 1991: 96). This argument may yet well be vulnerable to a strong dose of Quinian scepticism but it still avoids the trap into which Dale has fallen.

Nevertheless, Dale's combative analysis is, at times, a thoughtful and revealing one of the 'dual system' of German and Japanese ethnocentric discourse. As Dale demonstrates in his analysis of Kuki's *The Structure of 'Iki'*, the links between Heidegger, the phenomenologist thinker Edmund Husserl (1859–1938), and Kuki create a complex discourse that has transparent political links to nationalist ideology in the specific historical context of the rise of fascism in Germany and Japan (Dale, 1986: 68–76). Dale also argues an even more persuasive case for the connections between Watsuji Tetsurō and Heidegger, where Watsuji's reading of Heidegger in *Fūdo* glosses over antinomies evident in Heidegger's own writings to create a narrative even more blatant in its advocacy of statist ethics (Dale, 1986: 216–18).

The personal links existing between many Japanese and German philosophers because of the program of study many Japanese thinkers undertook in Germany in the prewar period is well documented in Michiko Yusa's 1998 study 'Philosophy and Inflation'. The major figure among these philosophers and one of the central figures of the dual system of a philosophy based in Japanese tradition—primarily the Buddhist tradition—but also constructed along Western lines is Nishida Kitarō (1870–1945).

Nishida Kitarō and a universal culture

Nishida's position on culture is complex, and in recent years has been hotly debated by commentators in the West, inevitably as part of an attempt to understand his political views (Yusa, 1991: 203–9; Lavelle, 1994: 139–65; Arisaka, 1996: 81–105; Suzuki, 1997: 87–105). But, in one major respect, Nishida's attitude towards Japanese culture seems to have changed little throughout his career: namely, his view that Western culture is not universal but if Eastern, especially Japanese, culture were considered as part of a larger paradigm of culture, then, a true universal culture may emerge. For instance, in his 1917 essay 'Nihonteki to iu Koto ni Tsuite' (On Being Japanese) he wrote: 'We are increasingly developing a unique culture, but, at the same time as it is becoming increasingly Japanese, we wish to ensure that this culture is made part of world culture…we do not even remotely consider that Japanese culture is isolated, we believe that it is to be esteemed as part of a world culture' (Nishida, 1970: 444).

The same sentiments are repeated in his famous 1938 lecture (later published in book form in 1940) 'Nihon Bunka no Mondai' (The Problem of Japanese Culture): 'Until now Westerners believed that their culture was the most excellent among all human cultures…other peoples in the Orient were backward and so if they were to develop they had to arrive at the same point as [the West].… I do not believe this.… I believe that the Orient is fundamentally different. It can add to this [Western culture] and create a human culture which will express a perfect humanity' (Quoted Ueyama, 1970: 78). Clearly, in respect of culture, Nishida is an opponent of a dual system; he identifies a 'world culture', a 'human culture' that incorporates both East and West.

Suzuki Sadami in his 1997 study 'The Problem of Japanese Culture' argues that if this text is contextualised in the light of wartime politics, then, it is simultaneously affirming the 'meaning of the imperial family…[as] a way of establishing a philosophical base for Japanese culture' and also expressing 'a resistance to imperialist expansion in and domination of other countries by Japan' (Suzuki, 1997: 90). This contradiction is resolved in the fact that Nishida's vision of the Imperial way was, according to Suzuki, a profoundly idealised, peaceful conception (Suzuki, 1997: 92–3). Suzuki focuses on the political implications of this essay, especially stressing Nishida's declaration: 'With the imperial family as the centre, our national culture has been living and developing for thousands of years' (Quoted Suzuki, 1997: 89). Hiromatsu Wataru underlines the same sentence in his 1989 book *Kindai no Chōkoku Ron: Shōwa Shisōshi e no Shikaku* (A Study of 'Overcoming the Modern: A View of Shōwa Intellectual History') to make the same point (Hiromatsu, 1989: 207–22).

Oketani Hideaki in his massive intellectual history of modern Japan, first published in 1992, evinces a similar ambiguity to Hiromatsu in regard to this text, arguing that, while Nishida's explanation of ways by which Japan could forge an alternative path to Western imperialism opened up the possibility of resistance to military rule, it was also complicit with it by its particular conceptualisation of the Imperial way (Oketani, 1996: 429). However, the philosopher Ueda Shizuteru in his intellectual biography of Nishida, first published in 1995, contextualises Nishida's essay in a much more favourable way.

Ueda notes the differences between the 1938 lecture and the 1940 book, which is three times as long. He argues that the addition of phrases like 'Imperial Way' (which hardly occur at all in the essay), in the expansion of the essay into the book, can be explained by Nishida's attempt to define Imperial way as the opposite of the ultra-nationalist expansionist ideology. He supports his view with references to several other addresses by Nishida which criticise the path Japan's leaders were taking, and also by the fact that Nishida himself was attacked by the ultra-nationalists as a result of the book (Ueda, 1996: 193–200). The debate over 'culture' symbolised by this controversy demonstrates how the question of culture has always had political and social implications.

Tessa Morris-Suzuki in two recent interesting articles has argued against conceptions of culture and civilisation commonly found among many of the Japanese thinkers cited earlier in this chapter. Rather, like Herder's attack on culture in 1791, where he denounced the assumption that culture or civilisation was a unilinear process, arguing instead for cultures in the plural representing the specific and variable cultures of different social and economic groups, Morris-Suzuki advocates the replacement of culture by contending 'dimensions of identity' or the replacement of 'civilisation' by the 'histor[ies] of small societies' (Herder quoted by Williams, 1985: 89; Morris-Suzuki, 1993: 546; Morris-Suzuki, 1995: 776). The rationale behind her critique lies essentially in what she perceives as the manipulation of the notion of culture by various Japanese thinkers to 'use the category "Japanese culture" as a means of escaping the grasp of the modern western worldview', a struggle Morris-Suzuki sees as self-defeating because of basic flaws in the notions of 'culture' or 'society' that such thinkers espouse (Morris-Suzuki, 1995: 773).

In essence, this is not a radical challenge to the notion of culture, as some idea of 'Japanese culture', no matter how different or radical, underlies the very categories Morris-Suzuki seeks to deconstruct. In this respect Morris-Suzuki's viewpoint has affinities with critics of culture like the ethnographer James Clifford who replaces culture with 'some set of relations that preserves the concept's differential and relativist functions and that avoids the positing of cosmopolitan essences and human common denominators' (Clifford, 1988: 274–5). In other words, culture under another name.

Some thinkers argue that if we are to retain the notion of culture, then it must be modified to reflect the diversity of experiences that cultures encompass. For instance, Arati Rao and Carol Nagengast insist upon the necessity of conceptualising culture but maintain that culture is an evolving process. Yuriko Moto summarises their approach as follows: 'It is necessary to acknowledge change, complexity and interpretive privilege in cultural formation in order to avoid reductionism, essentialism and rhetorical rigidity' (Moto, 2002: 54). Thus, to critique culture does not mean to abandon the idea altogether. Rather, if we follow the general thrust of Rao and Nagengast, we can point to specific issues that can be debated on their own merits, thereby acknowledging the complexity and diversity inherent in the notion of culture.

Also, adopting an insider/outsider frame permits debate on fundamental questions of culture without prejudicing the discussion by appealing to any fixed criteria. Quine's scepticism, despite his own retreat to practicalities in the application of the indeterminacy thesis, Rorty's radical pragmatism—where he can argue, 'Once we dump the idea that the aim of enquiry is to represent objects and substitute the view that enquiry aims at making beliefs and desires coherent...'—and Gadamer's like-minded self-critical hermeneutics all provide a much more searching critique of such matters while also furnishing a means of approaching Japanese writers on culture (as with Rorty) or opening a dialogue with them (as with Gadamer) without substituting yet another predetermined version of culture (Rorty, 1991: 106).

Cross-cultural interpretations

The anthropologist Aoki Tamotsu (b.1938), together with thinkers like the historian Amino Yoshihiko (b.1928), is one of the writers on culture

Morris-Suzuki singles out for praise, observing that the notion of the escape from culture that Aoki proposes in his 1988 study was a useful challenge to established notions of culture in Japan (Morris-Suzuki, 1995: 775). Since then, Aoki has written a more detailed study of Japanese culture with his book *'Nihon Bunka Ron no Hen'yō—Sengo Nihon' no Bunka to Aidentitii* (The Transformation of Studies of Japanese Culture—Culture and Identity in Postwar Japan), first published in 1990. In this book, Aoki places great stress on studies of Japanese culture by foreigners, emphasising the importance of Ruth Benedict's formulation of Japan as a 'shame culture' in opposition to the 'guilt culture' that characterises Western society in her famous 1948 study *The Chrysanthemum and the Sword: Patterns of Japanese Culture* (Aoki, 1990: 30–53, 81–154 *passim*).

Aoki argues that this book had an enormous impact in Japan and in his generally negative evaluation of Peter N. Dale's 1986 study—Aoki states that Dale's viewpoint is clearly biased and his use of words like 'fascist' to describe the vast bulk of Nihonjinron scholars is problematic—laments that fact that Dale's challenge was never taken up and seriously addressed by Japanese authors, in contrast to the reception given to Benedict's work (Aoki, 1990: 134–7, 186–7). He also regrets that Japanese-language studies of Japanese culture which compare Japan and the West rarely reveal the depth of research into 'the West' or 'Europe' that Dale displayed in his research into Japanese sources on Japan (Aoki, 1990: 136). Aoki praises Benedict, agreeing with Clifford Geertz's comment that her book should be read in the same light as Jonathan Swift's *Gulliver's Travels*: when we look into the face of the other we see our own face reflected there (Aoki, 1990: 154–5).

Aoki is extremely well read in Western cultural theory, and frequently applies it to Japanese culture. This kind of cross-cultural reflection has become increasingly common over the past two decades among Japanese theorists on culture; this being, as I have argued, essentially a continuation of a tradition that began long ago with Japan's adaptation of cultural and philosophic discourse from China and, over the last two centuries, from the West. In other words, this is a continuation of the 'dual structure' in cultural discourse proposed earlier. In a sense, this trend represents an unambiguous attempt to compare and contrast outsider and insider views of culture in an attempt at a cross-cultural dialogue, exactly the same kind of dialogue this study is attempting. As we will soon see, Yanagita Kunio made extensive use of Western social and cultural theorists in his writing, as did his major successor, the thinker Yoshimoto Takaaki (b.1924).

The sociologist Yamamoto Tetsuji (b.1948) has written several books discussing the ideas of Western theorists like Michel Foucault (1926–84), Pierre Bourdieu (1930–2002) and Ivan Illich (1926–2002). His writings include his 1987 book *Discourse no Seijigaku: Foucault, Bourdieu, Illich* (The Politics of Discourse: Foucault, Bourdieu, Illich) and his 1988 book *Chōryōiki no Shikō e* (Towards Transdisciplinal Thinking: Theories of Contemporary Pratique). Like Yoshimoto and Yanagita, Yamamoto's perspective argues for a rewriting of 'universal' systems to accommodate non-Western realities. Yamamoto claims that the absorption of post-modernist theorists like Foucault and Bourdieu into Japanese discourse has been strongly opposed by Japanese Marxist thinkers who Yamamoto charges with 'closed off exclusiveness' (Yamamoto, 1989: 35).

Another major voice advocating a diverse range of Western and non-Western theoretical perspectives is the anthropologist Yamaguchi Masao (b.1931). In common with many recent Japanese theorists, Yamaguchi has spent long periods studying and working abroad. After spending two years doing fieldwork in Nigeria, Yamaguchi has lectured in countries as diverse as Mexico, France, and the USA. Like many of his generation, Yamaguchi also publishes extensively in languages other than Japanese. The anthropologist Imafuku Ryūta (b.1955) cites two elements central to Yamaguchi's work: the figure of the 'trickster' and the influence of semiotics (Imafuku, 1987: 93–108).

Yamaguchi himself has frequently published on the fool or trickster from his 1975 books *Dōke no Minzokugaku* (Folklore of the Fool) and *Dōketeki Sekai* (The World of the Fool) to his 1984 study *Bunka to Shikake* (Culture and Trick). Yamaguchi has a vast corpus of writing devoted to cultural studies but it is noticeable that he often utilises the work of non-Western theorists, such as his 1988 study '"Center" and "Periphery" in Japanese Culture' which draws heavily on Tartu semiot-icians like Uspenski and Toporov. Yamaguchi here argues that marginal-ity belongs to 'otherness' and therefore that only by knowing those who dwell on the margins of society can we know ourselves (Yamaguchi, 1988: 199–219).

Many contemporary Japanese cultural theorists utilise 'dialogic' frames to analyse discourse, whether cleaving to Barthes-style semiotics or to more traditional Hegelian-Heideggerian or Gadamerian dialectics, such as the philosopher Sasaki Kenichi's (b.1943) prize-winning study *Serifu no Kōzō* (The Structure of Dialogue), first published in 1982. Sasaki uses theatre, like the plays of Harold Pinter, as his starting point to construct a theory of dialogue. Dialogue is also a feature of the cultural studies scholar Inaga Shigemi (b.1957), who has published a series of articles in English examining the assassination of Igarashi Hitoshi, the Japanese translator of Salman Rushdie's *The Satanic Verses*. Inaga is attempting to situate Igarashi 'as one of the "particular points in the geometrical locus of Islamic intellectual history"' (Inaga, 1992: 334). Inaga's 1997 study *Kaiga no Tasogare: Edouaru Mane Botsugo no Tōsō* (Inaga's French title: La Crépuscule de la peinture: la lutte posthume d'Édouard Manet) continues his project of situating art and literature firmly in the context of comparative cultural poetics.

The cross-cultural nature of Inaga's poetics are made transparent in his 2001 English-language article on Laurens van der Post and the relationship between motifs drawn from Noh theatre and van der Post's novels, in particular *The Seed and the Sower* (1963) (Inaga, 2001: 130). At the same time, Inaga is examining the ethics of the postwar Tokyo International War Tribunal, which were questioned by van der Post, himself a former POW in Java during World War II. Inaga's writings show an unmistakable fascination with cross-cultural conflicts over values, and value systems, both in his theoretical and textual studies, and so can stand for this trend in cultural discourse which is currently being taken up by a variety of younger Japanese writers.

Before leaving this topic altogether, we should mention the trend towards scientific investigations of Japanese culture using the tools of recent technology, such as DNA analysis. This trend has been closely associated with Hanihara Kazurō and is abundantly demonstrated in his 1993 edited volume *Nihonjin to Nihon Bunka no Keisei* (The Formation of the Japanese and Japanese Culture), where experts from various branches of science use the latest scientific tools to examine the question of the 'origins' of Japanese culture. Recent studies like Omoto Kiichi's 1996 book *Bunshijinruigaku to Nihonjin no Kigen* (Genetic Anthropology and the Origins of the Japanese) focus on DNA testing as a means to trace the genetic trail of the earliest immigrants to Japan.

This has given studies in this area a major boost but it is fascinating how the trajectory of such scholarship is often determined by earlier, foundational studies. The recent 'Sundaland' thesis, which proposes a common starting point for Asian migration from the ancient (now mostly submerged) archipelago called 'Sundaland', arose from the research of scientists like Hanihara but irresistibly recalls Yanagita Kunio's famous 1961 book *Kaijō no Michi* (The Ocean Road), which argued for a sea route from the south for immigrants to Japan. Yanagita was the major figure in attempts by twentieth-century Japanese intellectuals to define or redefine just what is Japanese culture, and who are the Japanese. It is, therefore, appropriate that in the next chapter we examine his scholarship in the context of this question.

2

Yanagita Kunio and the Origins of Culture

From a nameless distant isle
A single coconut drifts closer
Departing the shores of your homeland
Month after month you drifted on the waves
....

Pillowing my head on the beach
Journeying on a water-journey all alone

Shimazaki Tōson, from 'Coconut' (Shimazaki, 1991: 132)

This chapter begins with a brief examination of Yanagita Kunio's *Tōno Monogatari* (The Legends of Tōno, 1910), the only one of Yanagita's major works to be translated into English (two other works are available in English but both are minor studies). Then, it tracks Yanagita's career as a bureaucrat, focusing on his writings on agro-politics, followed by a description of Yanagita's 'new science'—his highly influential insider paradigm of culture.

The remainder of the chapter is taken up with case studies of four of Yanagita's most important works. They are described in great detail, as no English translations have yet been published of these studies. Much attention is also paid to the reception of these works by Yanagita's contemporaries, and also to critical readings of these four works by some of the major authorities on Yanagita in Japan. Without such a detailed hermeneutic context, it is extremely difficult for non-Japanese readers to grasp the meaning and significance of Yanagita's unmatched contribution to insider discourse in twentieth-century Japan.

The legends of Tōno

Yanagita Kunio began his career as an author by writing poetry, and the literary significance of his writing has often been emphasised by commentators. The famous novelist Mishima Yukio (1925–70) claimed that with the publication of *The Legends of Tōno* Yanagita had created a new kind of realistic literature, one constructed by language while rooted in fact (Mishima, 1970: 45). But, as Ronald Morse, the translator of *The Legends of Tōno* into English, has noted, 'the work never satisfied [Yanagita's] literary friends'. And it was not until the 1930s, two decades after the book's initial publication, that it actually appeared commercially (Morse, 1975: 23–4). However, before his career as the most distinguished modern advocate of an insider view of Japan began, Yanagita enjoyed great success as a bureaucrat.

Yanagita was appointed as an official of the Ministry of Agriculture and Commerce in 1900 when he was twenty-six, and served for nineteen years, mainly working in the area of agricultural policy until his resignation in 1919 at the age of forty-five. While a bureaucrat Yanagita turned to agro-politics, and wrote several studies on agricultural policy, including *Nōseigaku* (Agricultural Policy, 1902), *Nōgyō Seisakugaku* (The Study of Agricultural Policy, 1902), *Nihon Sandō Shiryaku* (A Short History of Agricultural Policy, 1903) and *Jidai to Nōsei* (The Present Age and Agricultural Policy, 1910). Yanagita's resignation from the post of Secretary General of the House of Peers (the upper house of the prewar Japanese parliament) is generally assumed to have been the result of a clash with a senior political figure, a member of the Tokugawa family (Yoneyama, 1988: 37). It is noteworthy that this post was one of the highest it was possible for an official to attain.

Some commentators have read much into the resignation, with the scholar Murai Osamu, for one, arguing that this was the climactic event of Yanagita's life as it indicated his complicity in the colonial annexation of Korea by Japan in August 1910, and that with the rise of the independence movement in Korea in 1919, and the apparent failure of Japanese colonial policy towards Korea, Yanagita's resignation was inevitable. Murai thus discounts the clash with his superiors as a cause of the resignation but, unfortunately, he offers no documentary evidence whatever to sustain his claim and cites no evidence that clearly links Yanagita's activities as a bureaucrat to these political events (Murai, 1995: 21–43).

The significance of *The Legends of Tōno* is much debated by Japanese scholars and, as with all of Yanagita's vast corpus of writing (a recent collected works—by no means complete—comes to 32 volumes), has generated a large secondary literature. Several Western commentators have seen the work as constituting a social imaginary, a nostalgic and idealised conception of the countryside as a kind of utopia or lost arcadia (Harootunian, 1990: 105–7; Ivy, 1995: 59–60). On the other hand, Tada Michitarō has argued that Yanagita's work brought about a kind of 'counter-consciousness' among Japanese intellectuals. This claim is echoed by J. Victor Koschmann who (following Tsurumi Kazuko) argues that *The Legends of Tōno* was a criticism of the 1890 Imperial Rescript on Education, and thus that Yanagita's writing constituted a 'conservative counter-utopia' directly subversive of modern Japan and the bureaucratic order (Tada, 1988: 112; Koschmann, 1988: 162–3). Yet, however it is interpreted, this work is nonetheless seen by virtually all Japanese commentators on modern culture as a supremely important text both for Yanagita's own work, and for the reconceptualisation of Japan that Yanagita created.

The Legends of Tōno is made up of 113 tales, all quite short, and told with no particular sequential logic other than the thematic focus on witchcraft, gods, apparitions, demons, death of various kinds, families, and incomprehensible events occurring within the life of the peasantry. The lack of narratorial focus is stressed by Yanagita, who wrote in the introduction that the tales were 'present day facts' told to him by a local informant (Yanagita, 1910: 9–11). In the introduction, Yanagita cautions against comparing these tales with older tales and legends collected in various well-known compilations of such stories issued in the past (some of these collections having since become part of the classical literary canon). It is nonetheless striking how resemblances can be found between the Tōno stories and older tales. For example, tale 69 about a woman who makes love to a horse (the horse is subsequently killed by the girl's father) is quite similar to an old story from the ninth-century tale-collection *Nihon Ryōiki* telling the story of a maiden who falls in love with a snake (Yanagita, 1910: 41–2; Izumo, 1996: 120–2).

The grotesque and quite horrifying nature of the tales Yanagita tells do not readily create the impression of a rural utopia, unless 'utopia' is interpreted in a quite paradoxical and perverse way to indicate a retreat from an Imperial narrative of rural order and uniformity—in other words, reading the work as a counter-story of diversity to official homogeneous modernisationist narratives, and also as a retreat from an idealised countryside where poverty and ignorance are disappearing. A simpler but perhaps more convincing reading is that the tales suggest the rural backwaters of Japan are marked by both adversity and superstition, from which the cruel extremes described in the stories emerge.

The Tōno tales can also be read as a counter-attack on the literature of Japanese Naturalism, the dominant school at the time, which generally avoided discussing the social reality of the times in favour of concentrating on the anguish of individuals (Nakamura, 1958: 82; 1954: 121). This reading may well account for the Naturalist novelist Tayama Katai's less than enthusiastic reception of the book (Quoted Morse, 1975: 23–4). For Japanese readers in general the work came to be seen as a watershed in a re-evaluation and reconsideration of the very essence of the Japanese nation. Yanagita's stress upon the premodern and pre-Western origins of Japanese culture was the beginning of an entirely new way of thinking about Japan, of imagining how a modern Japan may differ from its European rivals.

Eradicating famine

A reading of *The Legends of Tōno* stressing the hardships of rural Japan dovetails neatly with the bulk of Yanagita's writings on agro-politics, which start from his expressed desire to 'eradicate famine' (Quoted Tsunazawa, 1976: 187). It is generally acknowledged that the bulk of Yanagita's writings on agro-politics stem from this urge to alleviate rural poverty, a task in which he took a practical interest as a working bureaucrat. The most detailed English-language study of Yanagita's policy recommendations and the various books he wrote on agro-politics is Minoru Kawada's (translated) 1993 study *The Origin of Ethnography in Japan: Yanagita Kunio and His Times*. Kawada argues that Yanagita's ultimate vision was 'a thorough transformation of all tenant farmers into small-scale independent farmers'. Such a view envisaged Japan's zaibatsu capitalism (that is, capitalism dominated by giant financial cliques) being changed by a slow, gradual process of reform into a decentralised, more democratic version of capitalism that would ensure the autonomy of Japan's regional economy, and the survival of agriculture as 'the anchor of [the] nation' (Kawada, 1993: 22, 38–9, 70–1).

While not advocating violent or radical change, Yanagita nonetheless challenged the existing view of the state; as Kawada notes, his conception of 'social and economic reform…conflicted at many points with mainstream…policy of the time' (Kawada, 1993: 77). Eventually, observes Kawada, Yanagita came to pin his hopes on 'the creation of a proletarian party which would have the capacity to mobilise not only the limited number of…working class and tenant farmers but also landed farmers and the urban middle class' (Kawada, 1993: 95).

Yanagita's views concerning the efficacy of state-sponsored reforms to bring about the changes he believed necessary to ensure the survival of rural Japan eventually altered under the impact of the rapid urbanisation and industrialisation of the country. The American historian H. D. Harootunian describes the central tenet of Yanagita's reformist program as 'unevenness on the political–economical level', that is a fundamental alienation of the farmer from his land, or the producer from the means of production, brought about by the accumulation of capital in the cities which led to deforestation and starvation (Harootunian, 1998: 147–9). This persuaded Yanagita to move to a conception of the common people or 'jōmin' which was rooted in culture, a model free from contemporary economic and political constraints, one, argues the sociologist Mitsuru Hashimoto, that 'reconstituted the invisible [jōmin] as a tradition that had survived into the present…"jōmin", found everywhere and nowhere, were the bearers of Japanese indigenous culture, because only through them did the unseen culture reveal itself' (Hashimoto, 1998: 143).

This shift from agro-politics to culture, or to 'minzokugaku'— Yanagita translated this word as folklore studies, but Harootunian translates it as 'nativist ethnology'—is Yanagita's most significant achievement. For the school of ethnology that Yanagita invented was the major 'dual system' for most Japanese thinkers of the twentieth century, and exercised a profound influence over Japanese discourse on society, politics, and culture; in short, on what constituted 'Japan' and what it is to be Japanese. It is the very epitome of an insider construction of Japan.

Originally, two different schools of sociology existed in Japan; one was an official state-sponsored school that supported the state ideology located primarily in the Imperial universities; the other was liberal, based on theories imported from the USA and Europe, which sought to analyse civil society independent from the state (Kawamura, 1990: 63–74). Yanagita was aloof from both schools, being sceptical of both statist ideology and imported theories. He explained the motive behind his shift from agro-politics into nativist ethnology in his 1948 postscript to *Jidai to Nōsei* (The Present Age and Agricultural Policy), first published in 1910: 'After the First World War, I realised I was mistaken, the world had utterly changed and the discipline of agro-politics [I had pursued] until then had become totally useless. I quit my post as a government official…' (Yanagita, 1948: 226). This disillusion with agro-politics ended his 'pre-ethnology' period of writing which continued from the 1890s to the 1920s, according to the intellectual historian Akasaka Norio (b.1953) in his 1994 book *Yanagita Kunio no Yomikata—Mō Hitotsu no Minzokugaku wa Kanō ka?* (A Reading of Yanagita Kunio—Is Another Ethnology Possible?).

During this early phase of his career, in addition to his writings on agro-politics, Yanagita outlined a theory of the origins of the Japanese which was to change over time but is originally rooted in the notion that the original inhabitants of Japan were mountain people. As he writes in 'Sanjin Gaiden Shiryō' (Sources for a Biography of the Mountain People), first published in 1913: 'I believe that the mountain people are the descendants of the first inhabitants of this island country, who flourished long ago. To a great degree their culture has retrogressed. Not one book exists documenting their history from the present to three thousand years back into the past. I, a minor scholar, who is their mortal enemy, intend [to write] this today when it is believed this tribe is almost entirely extinct. Just this alone renders them a people truly to be pitied' (Yanagita, 1913: 385).

Akasaka traces the development of Yanagita's search for the origins of the Japanese from this early conceptualisation of the mountain people, who have retreated into the margins and live outside village society, through *The Legends of Tōno*, 'Kijiya Monogatari' (Tales of Wood-Cutters, 1911), '"Itaka" oyobi "Sanka"' ('Shamans' And 'Sanka', 1911), *Miko Kō* (A Study of Shrine Maidens, 1913) and *Kebōzu* (Long-Haired Priests, 1914). In these books Yanagita outlines an elaboration of his schema in which not only early versions of the mountain people appear, but such marginalised groups are enlarged to encompass all who are transient or floating, including shamans, shrine maidens, itinerant entertainers (dancers, drummers etc.) and also the 'eta' or 'untouchable' caste associated with activities and trades involving leather and blood-letting (taboo activities, according to traditional Japanese religious beliefs) (Akasaka, 1994: 118–36).

By 1917, Yanagita's thesis in 'Yamabito Kō' (A Study of Mountain People) has as its starting point 'the unchallenged theory that the people of Japan are a mixture of many races…half the mountain people descend to the lowland and mix with the common people, the rest go into the mountains where they remain and are called "mountain people"' (Yanagita: 1917: 236–42). Thus the marginalised people, the transients, also have blood connections to the people of the villages or the lowland people, as Yanagita also calls them, as can be seen with the example of the untouchable caste.

Yanagita wrote various articles on the untouchable class in an attempt to ameliorate their living conditions by helping them assimilate into the majority (Nagaike, 1994: 4: 519–35). His argument linking the untouchable class and other transients to the Imperial family is praised by Akasaka, who sees such a theory as radical and challenging, an attempt to counter the official mythohistory promulgated by the state (Akasaka, 1994: 128–36). Naturally, Akasaka and also critics like Yoshimoto Takaaki, who are generally favourable to Yanagita, have their criticisms of a conceptualisation such as this, focusing in particular upon the total lack of historicity in Yanagita's account. Yoshimoto in his brilliant analysis of Yanagita's system, published as *[Teihon] Yanagita Kunio Ron* (A Definitive Study of Yanagita Kunio) in 1995, argues that Yanagita's indifference to conventional questions of historiography—his failure to link his theory with archaeological evidence for instance—renders some aspects of his theory nothing more than 'preposterous errors' (Yoshimoto, 1995b: 45).

Despite Akasaka's high praise of Yanagita's recovery and conceptualisation of peoples on the margin, he is greatly disappointed by Yanagita's failure to pursue this theory after 1920, and by Yanagita's subsequent shift of focus to the 'rice-producing people' or the 'common people' who become the centre of his later work. To put it another way, Yanagita shifts his attention from the periphery to the centre, and turns his critical eye away from the mountain people to the people of Okinawa. Shortly, I will investigate four case studies in detail, four of Yanagita's major works, including the two seminal books he wrote on Okinawa. But, first, we will specifically examine his methodology and his system.

Yanagita's new science

Akasaka argues that the works discussed to this point all precede those writings of Yanagita which establish his indigenous system of nativist ethnology, or his new science. However, once Yanagita turned his attention to the 'fixed' category of the rice-producing people, whose origins and culture he pursues from the 1920s to his death in 1962, Akasaka contends that he eliminates or excludes the diversity, the concern with the margin which was such a prominent feature hitherto. This results in the birth of 'nativist ethnology', which then becomes the template for virtually all Yanagita's successors who try to create an indigenous discourse on culture, whether they follow him or oppose him, so powerful is his influence (Akasaka, 1994). As a consequence, Yanagita's system became the major system of insider discourse constructed in Japan in the twentieth century.

Nagaike Kenji, in his commentary on these early works, cites the famous critic and ethnographer Tanigawa Ken'ichi's (b.1921) opinion that it was at this time that 'Yanagita abandoned the perspective which saw the social history of the peoples of the Japanese archipelago as a compound culture of heterogeneous elements' (Nagaike, 1990: 515–16). Tanigawa's view echoes the judgment of his generation on Yanagita: namely, that an opportunity to radically alter the Japanese conception of 'self' and 'other' in terms of national identity was lost at a crucial juncture. In the context of Japanese politico-cultural discourse from the late 1960s onwards, such a critique inevitably implies the loss of an alternative path to the Imperial narrative, the dark road down which Japan was led in the 1930s and 1940s.

However, this is not a judgment shared by Yoshimoto, who also, despite his criticisms of Yanagita, argues that the methodology Yanagita invented is genuinely innovative. This is the most difficult aspect of Yoshimoto's analysis but it is perhaps the most perceptive conceptualisation of Yanagita's methodology to appear to date. Yoshimoto claims that Yanagita demonstrates that custom, the essential feature of experience (possibly similar to H.D. Harootunian's notion of 'repetition' or 'doubling' or 'fold'), can only be differentiated within the 'collective imaginary' or illusion of community that Yanagita constructs (Harootunian, 1998: 152). Further, using the metaphor of a 'speculum' or 'interior endoscope,' Yoshimoto argues that this doubled perspective, seeing internally and externally simultaneously, enables the reader to genuinely establish differences—indeed to differentiate between the self as experiencing subject and the self as observer of the experiencing subject (Yoshimoto, 1995b: 18–31).

As a method of binding endogenous and exogenous logic together—what Yoshimoto describes early in his analysis as the 'poetics of paradox'—this is primarily a linguistic or rhetorical technique (Yoshimoto, 1995b: 24–5, 274). It is at this level of language that Yoshimoto's insight is so powerful, as I will show in my examination of specific texts, but Yoshimoto also argues for the importance of Yanagita's work as cultural history, asserting that Yanagita establishes an original and valuable morphology of cultural exchange by clearly demonstrating the existence of ethnic variations within a 'one-people' model and by evaluating Yanagita's notion of the 'common people' (jōmin) as more useful a concept for endogenous analysis than 'class', which has relevance only for Japanese society from feudal times onwards (Yoshimoto, 1995b: 70–85; 304–5). He also argues that Yanagita's agro-politics is still a useful tool for economic and political analysis (a view shared by Minoru Kawada), far more so than Marxist economics, favoured by some of Yoshimoto's contemporaries (Yoshimoto, 1995b: 304–5). Here we see the continuing significance of Yanagita's work.

It is well known that Yanagita drew upon various Western writers on folklore and anthropology to establish his singular discourse. Minoru Kawada in his extensive examination of Yanagita's Western sources stresses the importance of three major Western thinkers: the British anthropologist James George Frazer (1854–1941), especially his famous study of mythology and folklore *The Golden Bough* (1890); the English folklorist Sir George Laurence Gomme (1853–1916); and, despite the fact that his name does not appear often in Yanagita's writings, the Polish anthropologist Bronislaw Malinowski (1884–1942), especially his 1922 pioneer study *Argonauts of the Western Pacific* (Kawada, 1993: 108–31).

Kawada compares these writers to Yanagita and concludes that while various approaches pioneered by these writers were taken up by

Yanagita, in certain essential areas there were radical differences (Kawada, 1993: 127–31). It is worth noting here that the major difference in approach was, in many cases, the Western neo-colonialist or colonialist bias that was clearly repudiated by Yanagita, and the overt advocacy of an 'etic' or 'outsider' approach, which he rejected equally vehemently.

The sociologist Tsurumi Kazuko (b.1918) in her study of Yanagita, originally published in 1969, compares him to the French thinker Claude Lévi-Strauss (b.1908) and comments that Lévi-Strauss discovered the primitive outside Europe, in other words, outside himself, while Yanagita discovered the primitive inside Japan, that is, inside himself (Tsurumi, 1969: 155). Tsurumi also claims that Yanagita invented a homological (defined as assuming an identification of the self with the other) social science in contrast to the exclusively heterological (assuming a separation of the self from the other) social science hitherto existing in Japan (Tsurumi, 1976: 153). Finally, Tsurumi argues that Yanagita's revolutionary study of emotion, and his stress on the notion of emotion in constructing a conceptual vocabulary to deal with culture, represented a genuine insight into cultural discourse, and one that could be applied usefully to other societies (despite Yanagita's own particularistic or ethnocentric tendencies), a view shared by many Japanese commentators (Tsurumi, 1969: 153–61).

Yanagita's turning to the notion of the 'common people', his wartime and postwar stress on ancestor worship, and his increasing emphasis on the people or 'folk' as having a common origin (which becomes evident in the 1930s and 1940s) incline several critics to view him as having compromised his original impulses as a result of the pressures of the times: namely, the growth in nationalist sentiment in intellectual circles. As noted earlier, Akasaka interprets these trends in Yanagita's thinking as evidence of the influence of a politically inspired conservatism, but harsher critics like Murai Osamu characterise Yanagita's work as colonialist and imperialist and charge him with unambiguous connections to Japanese fascism and Nazi doctrines (Akasaka, 1994: 198, 214; Murai, 1995: 48–51). Owing to a lack of hard evidence for such charges, few commentators go to the extremes of Murai, while some like Akasaka specifically single him out for criticism (Akasaka, 1994: 114).

Western critics range from the recent critique of Yanagita's view of women as essentially conservative by Mariko Asano Tamanoi to the viewpoint expressed by Marilyn Ivy and H.D. Harootunian that Yanagita's Japan is an exercise in nostalgia that creates an idealised Japan that never was (Tamanoi, 1996: 59–86; Ivy, 1995; Harootunian, 1998). The difficulty with such a perspective is that Yanagita's corpus is so huge and diverse that, while nostalgic elements are undeniable in various aspects of his work, as a conceptual tool or paradigm, nostalgia cannot hope to characterise anything but a limited part of his oeuvre. In arriving at this thesis, such commentators often draw upon Benedict Anderson's notion of the 'imagined community' to describe Yanagita's work. But Anderson posits 'three fundamental cultural conceptions' that societies must lose before one can imagine a nation, and two of the three manifestly cannot apply in the case of Yanagita's Japan: neither the idea that language offered privileged access to ontological truth, nor the notion that society is naturally organised under monarchs was lost in Yanagita's time. Therefore, strictly speaking, Anderson's model is inappropriate to Yanagita (Anderson, 1983: 40).

It is fascinating how several commentators on Yanagita draw a dividing line between his early and late writings, with a concern with the margins being the distinguishing mark of the early works while a focus on the centre denotes his late works. This paradigmatic shift resembles the line commentators draw between the young Marx with his focus on alienation, to the late Marx with his emphasis on capital, although it is worth noting that numerous commentators reject such a clear-cut division, arguing, like Leszek Kolakowski, that there is an essential unity of thought in Marx's writing (Kolakowski, 1981: 416). So, too, we may agree with Yoshimoto Takaaki that the central theme of Yanagita's writings was the question of origins, and that this theme ripened throughout his life (Yoshimoto, 1995b: 32–3).

This argument, nevertheless, allows for several other themes to branch off from the main trunk: the role of the common people; notions of the state, family and Imperial institution; ethnicity and conceptualisations of the numinous; material culture and its influence on folkways; oral tradition and its role in defining 'self'. The list could go on but it is clear that the Promethean nature of Yanagita's vast project or system— the entity he defined as minzokugaku—encourages both thinking and action and profoundly shaped the intellectual life of twentieth-century Japan, and its conception of culture. Precisely what this project entails will be the subject of the four case studies to follow. The volumes subjected to critical scrutiny here are among Yanagita's most important studies, and so they will be described in some detail as none have yet been translated into English, nor are there any substantial commentaries on these works yet available in English.

Finally, I need to stress that, in the brief description of Yanagita offered to this point, I have largely ignored his philological writings and the etymological, historical and religious studies which make up a significant portion of his writing as a whole.

Case Study One: South Sea Notes (1925)

After Yanagita's retirement from twenty years of government service, he eventually decided to accept a position on the staff of the *Asahi* newspaper, enticed by the offer of a three-year floating assignment as a travel writer. The first major trip he undertook for the newspaper was to Okinawa. He left Kagoshima on 3 January 1921 to travel by ship to Naha, the capital of the island of Okinawa, itself by far the largest and most populous of the large group of islands generally called Okinawa. Yanagita spent two weeks on the island of Okinawa and then travelled to various of the other islands in the group. He arrived back in Kagoshima on 15 February. This six-week trip had a decisive effect on his writing and was the chief reason for the shift in his focus from the mountain people to the peoples of Okinawa in his search for the origins of the Japanese (Fukuda, 1994: 690–1).

Kainan Shōki (South Sea Notes) was published in April 1925. It consisted of five separate essays, the largest being the first (two-thirds of the whole book) from which the title of the book was taken. The first essay had been serialised in 1921, as were the second and third, which were written at about the same time. The fourth essay, called 'Ajimasa no Shima' (The Island of Betel-Nut Palms), was a lecture that Yanagita gave at a middle school in Kurume in Kyūshū on 21 February 1921, that is, immediately after his return from the Okinawa trip. The last essay was written directly before his Okinawa journey (Fukuda, 1994: 690–1). The book is essentially a travel chronicle, relating in some detail and in the style of a personal diary, the places Yanagita journeyed to during those six weeks. As with much of Yanagita's early writing, the book falls easily into the category of literature or *belle-lettres*. It is worth recalling Akasaka's comment that Yanagita was not an ethnologist, but a writer whose work gave birth to the nativist discipline of ethnology (Akasaka, 1994: 13–14).

The first essay, entitled *Kainan Shōki*, is divided into twenty-nine chapters (although chapters nineteen and twenty-one are divided into two parts) preceded by a preface. In the preface Yanagita explains that he 'seeks to explore the universal principles and laws undergirding the life of the islands, large and small, near and far, of southern Japan; not taking as a standard the historical prejudice [against Okinawa] which has developed in such a short time in the course of the century' (Yanagita, 1925: 302). He notes the fundamental contribution of the native Okinawan scholar Ifa Fuyu (1876–1947) to understanding the ancient Okinawa song-text, the *Omorosōshi*, which is the 'jewel' of Okinawa, and which Yanagita uses as a key source. He dedicates the book to Basil Hall Chamberlain (1850–1935), the pioneer English philologist who was a long-time friend of Japan, and to the new discipline of minzokugaku (Yanagita, 1925: 302-3).

Yanagita begins his exposition with a discussion of the various terms for sweet potato one finds all over Japan, and this leads to various reflections on the social significance of the sweet potato as a crop useful for planting in areas not suitable for rice. This line of speculation in turn leads to the topic of the process of settlement of small islands. Yanagita's masterly rhetorical technique then returns to material culture with an exposition of the role of chopsticks as a marker for rice or sweet potato micro-economies (Yanagita, 1925: 304–7). This first chapter is a classic demonstration of Yanagita's characteristic technique of moving effortlessly from etymology, to material culture, to anthropological or historical speculation, and then, back to material culture again.

Chapters one to eight each dwell on various places, legends, local topographies, customs, and the etymologies of local dialects in Yanagita's journey southwards to the tip of Kyūshū. In chapter three, he discusses the 'Yuriwaka' legend, disagreeing with the famous scholar Tsubouchi Shōyō's (1859–1935) thesis that this is a retelling of the tale of Ulysses, but it is noticeable that this scholarly reflection is bracketed by an account of the difficulties of the lives of the island fisherfolk. Yanagita deals with the tragic realities of whole families disappearing at sea, retelling actual incidents of such losses. In this respect, he always returns to the particular, as he focuses on the ecologies, trade-histories and customs of the tiny islands off the Kyūshū coast.

The last place on the Japanese mainland Yanagita visits is Sata where he takes up the theme of chapter six, in which he discussed the various names for the betel-nut palm. In Sata, Yanagita describes the large number of fern palms and betel-nut palms that grow in that vicinity. The extensive area covered by these palms leads Yanagita to the thought that the seeds may have been carried there by large birds. Yanagita's description of Tajiri, near Sata, ends chapter seven in a characteristic burst of lyricism: 'Only the sound of the waves can be heard on New Year's Eve in Tajiri. The moonlight slides onto the verandahs where the doors are open and a gentle breeze shakes the paper panels of the sliding doors' (Yanagita, 1925: 307–31).

Chapter eight finds Yanagita arriving at Amami-Ōshima, the first island which has affinities to Okinawan, as opposed to mainland Japanese culture. Yanagita locates this cultural divide in various local customs relating to women's appearance, and women's work. His exposition includes much discussion of tattoo-lore, as tattooing was a custom commonly practised by older Okinawa women. The next four chapters focus on Amami-Ōshima. Interspersed with Yanagita's accounts of customs, local history, and so on, are often passages of great lyrical beauty describing the physical conditions of the islands, like the passage on Tajiri quoted above, reminiscent of the travel diaries of poets in previous centuries who developed a similar style, mixing poetry and prose (Yanagita, 1925: 331–4, 335–46).

In chapter thirteen, having arrived on the main island of Okinawa, Yanagita raises the question of the relationship between the Royal House of Okinawa (located in Shuri) and religion. In the previous chapter, Yanagita had discussed the political history of Okinawa, chronicling the loss of the religio-political authority of the Royal House of Shō with the military annexation of Okinawa in 1609 by the Satsuma domain in Kyūshū. The mystical connection between the royal family and the high-priestess of the state religion who is called Kikoe Ōkimi is explained in the context of the history of the various kings of Okinawa.

This leads Yanagita to a consideration of 'yuta', the female shamans of Okinawa, and to the belief in the return of the Nirai gods from islands far across the sea. Yanagita notes the importance of 'yuta', remarking that, 'Without the power of these gentle women who are so sensitive to the feelings of the [Okinawan] people; words alone would never suffice to convey Okinawan hopes and expectations for the future and

even their sorrows and suffering which will be soon lost to memory'
(Yanagita, 1925: 342–50).

Chapters fourteen to eighteen focus on aspects of Okinawan history,
land use and social custom. Yanagita discusses the role that boats play in
facilitating contact between the various islands of Okinawa. This leads
into an analysis of myths relating to the origin of boats, centring on the
notion that boats were originally driven by the power of the gods.
Chapter fifteen discusses Okinawan land-use patterns, where Yanagita
raises the issue of barriers constructed in residential areas to keep out
wild animals. Thence the discussion shifts to philology and the various
native Okinawan terms for wild boar, next to the significance of pork
as a ceremonial food. Finally, the chain of argument is closed with the
assertion that wild boars were brought to Okinawa by boat from the
north. Again, this is a characteristic strategy of argument that creates a
natural logic of rhetoric linking various aspects of Okinawan life and
culture (Yanagita, 1925: 351–60).

Chapter seventeen takes up something Yanagita read in an Okinawan
newspaper: the fact that visitors bring tōfu as a gift to the prostitutes
convalescing in the prostitutes' hospital in Naha. This leads him into an
analysis of tōfu in Okinawa as an article of aesthetic rather than gusta-
tory significance. Chapter eighteen discusses slavery or indentured servi-
tude as a system of organising labour in Okinawa and this perspective
permits Yanagita to draw some provocative conclusions about rural
poverty (Yanagita, 1925: 360–6).

In a sense, the core of the book is reached in chapters nineteen to
twenty-three of this first essay. The two parts of chapter nineteen focus,
first, on the range of written source materials in Japanese (dating mainly
from the eighteenth century) that describe Okinawa, and secondly on
the Okinawan language itself. Yanagita demonstrates that eighteenth-
century documents portray Okinawa as a weird, exotic land, citing the
novelist Takizawa Bakin's (1767–1848) book *Yumiharizuki* (Crescent
Moon, 1806–10) and the dramatist Chikamatsu Monzaemon's
(1653–1725), famous play *Kokusenya* (The Battles of Coxinga, 1715) as
evidence. He also traces cultural borrowings in Okinawan literature
from the mainland, noting the large range of citations of classical
Japanese poetry in the dialect dictionary *Konkōkenshi* (1711) compiled
by the court official Shikina Seimei (1651–1715). Yanagita also comments on how the native folk religion was more popular in these early

times than Buddhism, although the chief means by which culture was disseminated was travelling monks (Yanagita, 1925: 366–9).

In the second part of this chapter, Yanagita discusses the various Okinawan dialects—this issue he links to the debate over whether Okinawa should adopt the standard language used on the mainland. Since, for Yanagita, words and their etymology is central to his method, it is not surprising that he supports dialect usage. But he also laments the colonisation of Okinawan dialects by mainland usage, and notes that the dialects may lose the battle against standard Japanese because of the lack of a single, common Okinawan standard language.

In chapter nineteen, Yanagita coins his famous description of Okinawa as a 'storehouse of words'—thus providing clues to the origins of Japanese words and, indirectly, to the Japanese themselves—and obliquely criticises the official policy of enforcing mainland usage on the Okinawans, commenting: 'We cannot but be saddened by this huge mistake of forgetting one's origins' (Yanagita, 1925: 371). Yanagita continued to contribute to the debate over language and by 1940 his defence of Okinawa dialects had sparked a revival of interest among Okinawans themselves in their own culture (Clarke, 1997: 202).

Chapter twenty retells a tale which Yanagita titles 'The Fart of Kudaka', claiming that it occupies a splendid place in the history of Japanese fartology. The story is of two sisters from Kudaka Island, one of whom went to serve the king in Shuri. In time, she fell pregnant to the king but was expelled from court for emitting a loud fart. Back in Kudaka, she gave birth to a boy who subsequently journeyed to Shuri to present a golden melon to the king. If the melon is given to a girl who has never farted, the prince told the king, its seeds will flourish everywhere. The king replied that such a woman does not exist whereupon the prince revealed his identity. All was forgiven and the prince's mother returned to court. Yanagita commented that the story was apparently over 400 years old. Yanagita's retelling of this tale is not merely an exercise in nostalgia, a glimpse of a simpler, earthier Japan, but a powerful criticism of poverty and the arbitrary exercise of power (Yanagita, 1925: 372–4).

The first half of chapter twenty-one is a vital part, where Yanagita continues his tales of various Okinawan legends and stories. He recounts the legend of the eternal kingdom of everlasting summer across the sea. From this land coconuts floated across to Okinawa. The islanders used them as gourds to fill with liquor. Another story concerns cowrie shells, which the Okinawans believed were more beautiful than jade or damask, but they were ignorant of the fact that cowrie shells were used for money on the China coast. Yanagita relates these tales to the inter-island trade conducted in the tidal shallows. These facts eventually develop into the major thesis of Yanagita's 1961 book *Kaijō no Michi* (The Ocean Road).

It is noticeable that Yanagita links the Okinawans' cultivation of the tidal ecology to poverty. In chapter twenty-two he discusses inter-island trade in abaca cloth, and recounts how the intellectual class of Okinawa exploited the poor fisherfolk, especially the women, of whom it is said the only way they could improve their lives was to bear a child who became an official (Yanagita, 1925: 376–84).

From chapter twenty-three to the final chapter, twenty-nine, Yanagita focuses on religion, telling the stories of the oven god, the three-character pillars which ward off evil demons, and, in chapter twenty-five, analysing stories of a Yaeyama island patriot. The purpose of this exposition is to identify the underlying religious struggle between two female lines that eventually results in the unification of two strands of belief into the fundamental Okinawan religion of Kikoe Ōkimi. He links musical artefacts like the Okinawan shamisen (a kind of lute) to the cultural diversity of the Okinawan islands, before describing in chapter twenty-seven the Akamata/Kuromata religious festival found in Ishigaki island which is, in turn, traced back to the archaic belief in the gods who come from across the sea, from the land of eternal summer. This interweaving of material culture, philology, legends, and religion into an unbroken cloth revealing the fundamental pattern of the origins of Japanese culture, as well as emphasising the importance of Okinawa as a basic template for Japanese culture itself, emerges effortlessly from Yanagita's fluid style which is always rooted in the concrete particularity of his journey (Yanagita, 1925: 387–407).

With the final chapter of the first essay, over two-thirds of the *South Sea Notes* are completed. The two major pieces among the remaining four essays are 'Yonaguni no Onnatachi' (The Women of Yonaguni) and 'The Island of Betel-Nut Palms', originally published in 1921 and 1924 respectively. The latter is of more significance for the development of his theory of origins, so here we will deal solely with this essay.

'The Island of Betel-Nut Palms' documents Yanagita's fascination with betel-nut palms, which were used in ancient Japan to make fans and sedge hats as well as other artefacts; they were also dyed in various colours and were even used in Heian (now Kyoto), the capital of Japan during the cultural peak of the eighth and ninth centuries. Yanagita had heard of the legend of an island of betel-nut palms and, knowing that no palms remained on the mainland, theorised that this island lay somewhere in Okinawa. Fans made of these palms were valuable trade items in antiquity and Yanagita had earlier hypothesised that seabirds had brought palm seeds from various islands south of Japan to the mainland. However, during his Okinawa journey, he was unable to verify the existence of this island so he reverted to the theory of mainland origins. The palm also had connections to sacred Shintō ceremonies and occupied the most sacred religious sites in Okinawa. These religious connections suggested to Yanagita that the Japanese people themselves may have originated in Okinawa. Thus the betel-nut palm led Yanagita to the southern theory of Japanese origins (Yanagita, 1925: 483–517).

Naturally, other links in this complex chain that eventually led Yanagita to write *The Ocean Road* exist. In 1927 Yanagita wrote his famous *Kagyū Kō* (A Study of the [Word for] Snail), which is the first demonstration of his 'contiguity' thesis wherein cultures spread out from the centre, like ripples on a pond (Yanagita was studying the various dialect words for 'snail'). Thus the cultures most on the periphery preserve the oldest features. The contiguity thesis was a vital link in the chain allowing Yanagita to draw the discrete features of mainland and Okinawan culture together to create a single pattern, built upon the two assumptions that Okinawan and mainland Japanese culture are, at their root, the same culture, and that ancient cultural features lost on the mainland are preserved in Okinawa. This thesis eventually became the source of the alternative vision of Japan championed in the 1970s by such writers as Shimao Toshio, discussed in the previous chapter.

Akasaka Norio notes that in Yanagita's 1910 essay 'Shima-jima no Hanashi—Sono ni' (Island Tales: 2), Yanagita believed enormous differences existed between mainland and Okinawan culture, but after his trip he came to stress the similarities. In this respect, there is no denying the great impact the trip had upon him (Akasaka, 1994: 172, 178–81). Akasaka also observes that the whole of *South Sea Notes* is permeated by beautiful, gentle tales but we have seen that sometimes these tales clearly serve the purpose of criticising various social ills (Akasaka, 1994: 177).

The literary style of the work undoubtedly attempts to allow the reader to see through Okinawan eyes, especially with the frequent use of poetry and song.

In *South Sea Notes* this technique works to counter mainland prejudices against Okinawans as racially inferior (and establishes Yanagita's reputation as a travel writer) but it is not yet a fully reasoned argument of origins; a number of decades had to pass before this small seed blossomed into the rich harvest of *The Ocean Road*. Nevertheless, this work was crucial in establishing Yanagita's credentials as an ethnographer, and as the architect of a radically new theory of who the Japanese are. By looking to Okinawa—an area of Japan many of Yanagita's contemporaries saw as exotic at best, and primitive at worst—Yanagita constructed a narrative of national identity and culture that was not found in the West, or the modernised (i.e. Westernised) cities of Japan.

Case Study Two: A Study of Popular Oral Transmission (1934)

Minkan Denshō Ron (A Study of Popular Oral Transmission) was published in August 1934, being based on lectures given by Yanagita at his home every Thursday afternoon from 14 September 1933. Only the introduction, the first chapter and the first half of the second chapter were actually written by Yanagita. The rest of the book was written by one of Yanagita's followers, Gotō Kōzen, who used the lecture notes as a base, but also took extracts from various books by Yanagita to create a complete text. Gotō was the amanuensis at the Thursday talks but clear errors in oral transcription do occur in the text from time to time. Young intellectuals were the main audience at the lectures, and for this reason the commentator Fukuda Ajio describes the book as being written for 'insiders'. Fukuda also argues that, as a consequence, social utility, or the desire to reform society, was not the chief motivation; rather, the book was aimed at a scholarly audience (Fukuda, 1996: 640–2).

The book is divided into ten chapters and an introduction. The introduction consists of twenty-eight short statements which read like a basic list of principles that define Yanagita's science of minzokugaku. The statements combine the extravagant and the visionary: Yanagita calls his method 'the science of tomorrow', and asserts that it encompasses virtually all 'human cultural history'. He notes that 'the way to make social science into "science", can only be the accumulation and organisation of empirical fact' (Yanagita, 1934: 247–9). Empirical fact cannot be limited to written records: Yanagita comments that 'Learning which does not rely upon written records is called anthropology. The study of popular oral transmission is, naturally, included within this. Terms like cultural anthropology or social anthropology arise, in effect, from this perspective [of popular oral transmission]'(Yanagita, 1934: 250).

However, neither cultural nor social anthropology coincide exactly with Yanagita's new science. The study of oral tradition has its base in archaeology and approaches the relationship between mythology and the history of religion. Yanagita argues for the systematisation of learning, and supports the need for classification of social phenomena, in his case using Japan as a base, thus adding to classificatory schema developed for Europe. He proposes three areas of classification: first, the external forms of life (ethnography); second, understanding life, investigation using 'ears and eyes', based on linguistic knowledge, and including 'from names to tales, all the linguistic arts contained therein'; third, life-consciousness, the mysteries of the heart, the psychological reality of the Japanese which is generally unavailable to foreigners (Yanagita, 1934: 247–54).

Chapter one is titled 'The Ethnology of One People' and Yanagita begins perversely by arguing that his new science of 'minzokugaku' (which I translate here as 'ethnology') is at too premature a stage to be fully utilised in Japan. Rather than 'ethnology', the appropriate description of what can succeed in Japan is 'minkan denshōron' or popular oral transmission, which he defines as having almost the same meaning as the French study of 'Les Traditions Populaires' or the English 'Folk-Lore' (Yanagita, 1934: 257). Yanagita does not favour either of the two Japanese words 'minzokugaku' (the second character differs in the two words, despite the same pronunciation), both of which he translates collectively as 'ethnology', because of their failure as yet to realise his overarching vision of this new science.

After a brief history of anthropology in Europe and Japan, Yanagita identifies the major weakness of this branch of learning: anthropology is divided into two kinds, the anthropology of one country, and the anthropology of the world. These two conceptions of anthropology are in conflict. Frazer, by inventing the term 'social anthropology', sought to establish a world discipline but failed. Yanagita's 'popular oral transmission' first established the ethnology of one country (Japan), and on this basis, attempted to create a world ethnology but has encountered many difficulties. We can see here Yanagita conceptualising a larger version of the 'emit/etic' conflict referred to earlier in our discussion of dual systems (Yanagita, 1934: 255–69).

In chapter one, Yanagita lays down the principles of his methodology which, he argues, is not a subjective or selective approach to study. Instead, his system establishes generalisations based on a large body of evidence, comparing similarities and dissimilarities within a vast pool of data, in other words, his preferred method is explicitly comparative. Yanagita subjects contemporary schools of anthropology to severe criticism, discussing issues of subjectivity, source selection and so on.

One of Yanagita's consistent themes is the need to deal with material culture, everyday life, rather than an undue reliance upon written records, and so he also criticises history for its reliance on written records. Japan, he asserts, is a special case in that the past can be found in the present, unlike other countries where the past is buried and unrecognisable in the present. The stress on Japan also finds expression in other ways: 'Moreover, as far as most new Japanese scholarship is concerned, it must be said that it is just an irritating imitation, merely following in the footsteps white people have made' (Yanagita, 1934: 277).

In this statement, we find a clear sense of frustration at the domination of Japanese scholarship by Western paradigms, as well as a contempt for existing Japanese efforts at social analysis. Yanagita contends that the schools of anthropology conceptualised by the developed nations of the West have been only partially understood and imitated in Japan, while on the other hand, his new system is entirely appropriate to Japan, unlike Western-inspired models. He differentiates Japan from England and France, since in Japan, folklore studies can be applied at a more comprehensive and sophisticated level because of the fact that Japan, in contradistinction to the West, still retains the past in the living practices of the present (Yanagita, 1934: 269–79).

Chapter two further extends the argument proposed in the earlier chapter. Yanagita strives to differentiate between ethnography, ethnology, and folklore (he uses the English words) and to describe their relationship to his project of minzokugaku. His purpose is to establish folklore studies in Japan on a proper footing. He criticises ethnographic research based too narrowly on limited evidence, noting that 'the investigations of visitors are limited, we need to attend to the fact that there is much that is not possible [for them]' (Yanagita, 1934: 285). Here Yanagita distinguishes between ethnography as an 'etic' approach, and 'folklore' (his English translation for 'minkan denshō' or 'popular oral transmission') as an 'emic' approach. Ethnography is the older model but, due to the influence of folklore studies, has begun to use modern comparative methods. He criticises the 'etic' ethnographic approach: 'No matter how they try not to make mistakes, observations by people from other ethnic groups will never match reflections by members of the same ethnic group [as those being observed]' (Yanagita, 1934: 285).

Yanagita seems to draw a distinction between self-aware folklore and other-aware ethnography. He observes that E.B. Tylor (1832–1917) started the study of ancient culture in Britain with a rich largesse of ethnographic journals, and this discipline is now called 'anthropology'. But in Japan, the Japanese word 'jinruigaku', the usual translation of anthropology, basically means zoology. However, Yanagita's system, while its original incarnation as folklore was inspired by social Darwinian theories of evolutionary progress, now seeks to discover past customs remaining in the present. This is possible in developing countries like Japan, but impossible in the developed countries of the West (Yanagita, 1934: 280–8).

Yanagita criticises current stereotypes of culture as something fixed and unchanging. He cites the Edo period in Japan, which from outside appeared unchanging but to insiders was in a state of constant change. He praises various Western pioneers for their innovative approach to ethnology, scholars such as Frazer, the philologist Wilhelm Bleek (1827–75) and E.V. Evans-Pritchard (1902–73). Returning to methodology, he castigates collecting for collection's sake, and advocates 'limiting the object of research to a defined area', which means, in practice, avoiding the unusual, weird, or wonderful (Yanagita, 1934: 293).

Shifting to a discussion of such pioneer Japanese scholars as Tsuboi Shōgorō (1863–1913), a professor of Tokyo University, Yanagita asserts that Japanese anthropologists borrowed 'white anthropology'—which originated in the study of exotic, alien cultures—to use in their analyses of Japan, which resulted in their patronising, neo-colonialist attitudes towards rural communities in Japan. However, the results of this pioneer research were useful, and Japanese pioneers could not be blamed for their mind-set which was inherent in white anthropology. He again contrasts 'emic' folklore, which studies whole societies, and 'etic' ethnology, which studies chance encounters with alien ethnic groups. His vision of his own project becomes clear: 'As the study of individual societies expands and spreads to all countries, so international comparisons become possible; the results can be applied to any ethnic group and so the dawn of world ethnology (minzokugaku) becomes visible' (Yanagita, 1934: 288–99).

Chapter three begins with a critique of archaeology for its assumption that knowing prehistory constitutes knowledge. In a similar vein, Yanagita discusses the limitations of history: village history is rarely a history of individual families about whom we know little. History also fails the common people about whom it is mostly silent. For example, Japanese food implements are made of perishable materials so knowledge of this aspect of material culture lies outside archaeology. Yanagita's system tears down the barriers between archaeology and popular oral tradition, it overturns the prejudice against material artefacts in common use, and thus creates a new kind of history. Yanagita's intention is for 'anthropology and archaeology to act in concert to advance the research of living culture' (Yanagita, 1934: 308).

He links his new science to the Scottish polymath Andrew Lang's (1844–1912) investigation of social phenomena in advanced countries. Yanagita states that the purpose of his 'survey research—the investigation of our own country—is to ascertain the history outside history, to fill the spaces left in history' (Yanagita, 1934: 312). He derides the worship of origins, the rush to investigate antiquity; culture, for Yanagita, is a mixture of new and old. Citing his early book *Nochi no Karikotoba no Ki* (A Record of Later Hunting Terms, 1909), Yanagita argues that 'in respect of social phenomena or cultural phenomena…common features exist' (Yanagita, 1934: 316).

His argument is that material phenomena produce definable effects, and the classification of common causes is what his research strives towards. Different cultural and historical phenomena are reactions to particular sets of circumstances, thus past experience is inherited in the human unconscious and, in the right circumstances, is communicated to the consciousness of the present. This truth that the past exists in the present, whether as psychological phenomena or as material circumstance, is not recognised by conventional history.

The material limitations of conventional history especially in relation to the chance recording of facts (determined by how fate deals with the elites who wrote history) can be overcome by data drawn from the present. This allows us to cross-section phenomena, to compare and to contextualise experience. This is one of the fundamental hermeneutic and analytic tools of Yanagita's new science, a methodology he calls 'multi-layered' analysis, and which he likens to a diorama or three-dimensional montage or photograph (Yanagita, 1934: 301–20).

Fukuda Ajio in his commentary on this book notes that this famous statement of Yanagita's methodology is mentioned in this work alone (Fukuda, 1996: 642). The full quotation defining this technique, which Yanagita terms 'jūshutsu risshōhō' or 'double proof', reads: 'contemporary life, cut horizontally into sections, reveals in every region that there are hundreds of differences in material phenomena. If we collect and arrange these phenomena, even if their origins are not understood, we will find it easy to speculate about the process of change' (Yanagita, 1934: 318). This technique may well be what Yoshimoto Takaaki is referring to when he writes of Yanagita's subtle double perspective on experience that simultaneously denies its own double nature, thus inducing in the reader a sense of déja-vu: allowing the reader to experience Yanagita's description with an innocent eye while also disclosing the gaps that inevitably accompany the consciousness of an observing self (Yoshimoto, 1995b: 17–23).

Chapter four discusses the significance of 'kyōdo kenkyū' or local studies. In Yanagita's system, this phrase signifies the study of village life, the collective or communal life of the local community. He begins with the statement that 'the basis of the discipline of popular oral tradition is surveys' (Yanagita, 1934: 322). Surveying is another fundamental element in Yanagita's system but precisely on what basis should surveys be conducted or exactly how Yanagita conducted his own surveys are matters of fierce debate in Japan. Yanagita here stresses that surveys should be conducted at the lowest, most basic level by the people themselves, that is by insiders, not outsiders. However, he also underlines the need to see all data as units which go together to make up a larger picture; in other words, contextualisation and historicisation are a necessary part of this process. Thus both direct observation and comparison are vital techniques.

Observing how a revolution is taking place in scholarship, with more emphasis being placed on low culture (zoku) at the expense of high culture (ga), Yanagita emphasises how the 'low culture' of the countryside should be the object of study rather than the 'high culture' of the cities.

This argument is placed within the context of the need to rediscover the Japanese peasantry: 'Our study of village life can be described as an attempt to foster self-consciousness among the peasantry' (Yanagita, 1934: 330). The shift of population away from the countryside to the cities due to rapid urbanisation and industrialisation provides the historical context for Yanagita's concern for the fate of the peasantry.

Yanagita further defines the nature of his 'emic' analysis: 'One essential point in regard to the study of local communities in Japan is that Japan is fundamentally different from foreign countries and one cannot draw any conclusions about the study of our land using foreign paradigms' (Yanagita, 1934: 334). His nationalistic emphasis is clear in statements like: 'Moreover, it must be noted that the fact that only one ethnic group is spread throughout Japan means our country is exceptional' (Yanagita, 1934: 334).

This emphasis notwithstanding, Yanagita stresses how great regional variations in culture, language and customs are between different parts of the country, opposing a uniform approach to social analysis. After noting how important his trip to Okinawa was, as it revealed to him the fact that Okinawa was a repository of ancient Japanese customs and linguistic practices, Yanagita stresses that, while in the early phase of community studies the local must remain the focus, the ultimate aim of his project is not to be antiquarian or contingent but to create a universal, scientific system (Yanagita, 1934: 321–40).

Chapter five focuses on the classification of knowledge. Yanagita argues that the existing written sources are often biased and partial, yet popular oral tradition can broaden the traditional bibliographic base by including children's poetry and collections of farmers' writings, in other words, by including population groups formerly excluded from elite conceptions of written data. Furthermore, he continues, 'Learning containing much data arising from races other than the white race is never understood simply by looking at data written in the language of the white race' (Yanagita, 1934: 346).

Each people must establish its own bibliographic data bases, as Western libraries are inadequate for non-Western data: 'Foreigners often state their views as universals but they mean by this only the small area they are familiar with; when discussing phenomena outside these areas, their knowledge is useless' (Yanagita 1934: 346). Studies of popular oral tradition are based upon traces of the Japanese past—language, customs, psychological perceptions—that exist in the present or that can be inferred from the present. Yanagita lists a large variety of non-traditional written records, including aristocratic diaries, Buddhist sermons, miscellaneous writings, and literature, but warns that scholars should not allow a fascination with books to misdirect their enquiries (Yanagita, 1934: 341–58).

Chapter six divides the classification of data into three categories: travellers' tales or phenomena one sees; accidental knowledge or phenomena one hears; and community studies or phenomena one feels. This threefold division into the categories of the eyes, ears, and heart is one of Yanagita's most celebrated dictums. The first category, writes Yanagita, corresponds to the English phrase 'social technology' or 'ethnography' (Yanagita, 1934: 371–2). In chapter seven, Yanagita expounds in some detail about material life which also corresponds to this first category of classification. Material life, based upon the concrete particularities of the lives of the 'common people', includes things like funerals, food, and so on. Yanagita cites one of the major discoveries of his system: the dual dichotomy of the 'sacred' (hare) and 'secular' (ke), which he sees as a vital means of classification.

Using this dichotomy, Yanagita can classify relationships in a new and meaningful way. Thus he examines marriage and prostitution in this light, the old calendars which divide time into sacred and secular periods and many other phenomena including art, flower-arranging, fireworks, even make-up which during festivals takes on ritualistic significance. At the end of the chapter, Yanagita turns to games and sports, also in the light of this dichotomy, and finally discusses childhood, which in his view is an equally contingent phenomenon, and differs from era to era (Yanagita, 1934: 387–414). There is no doubt that the broadening of the category of culture that Yanagita undertakes here was of vital importance for the future study of culture in Japan. Moreover, Yanagita's stress on phenomena like make-up and sports, only recently accorded the status of objects worthy of inclusion in the category of culture in the West, is not only pioneering but, in some respects, quite revolutionary.

In chapter eight, Yanagita argues that language is fundamental to his project. This is especially the case for Japan, as compared to countries like Britain. The study of language itself—linguistics, dialectology, etymology—reveals the past which survives into the present.

Yanagita contends that language possesses a special 'flavour' that cannot be comprehended by outsiders. From this it follows that the cultural interaction between the individual and the group, which he terms 'the art of listening', expresses deep structures which cannot be abstracted or internationalised. Presumably, Yanagita is here referring to the deep structure of a culture which is assimilated by individuals in the process of socialisation, primarily through linguistic interaction. The discussion concludes with an attempt to classify myths (Yanagita, 1934: 415–64).

Chapter nine simply expands and elaborates upon the classification of myths and legends (Yanagita, 1934: 452–78). The final chapter, chapter ten, reiterates Yanagita's division of phenomena into material and non-material culture. His fundamental premise is that the ancients had a completely different worldview from the present. In order to understand non-material culture, we need to investigate the psychology of the worldview we have inherited from the ancients. Andrew Lang was the first thinker to grasp this essential point. Yanagita's new science, which he here identifies with folklore studies, is vital for studying folk psychology. He argues that it is impossible to study people in an objective way because of the impossibility of objectifying subjectivity, thus his system focuses on description. The description of taboos, omens, curses, and so on form a schematic upon which knowledge can be organised.

Yanagita then looks at certain key concepts: death and the afterlife (the division between Asian and Western viewpoints), and the Japanese stress on blood-ties, especially in relation to the family shrine, and hence, a notion of the family as the afterlife. This specific concept is fundamental to Asian thought; without an understanding of blood-ties and the family, the Asian experience is incomprehensible. Yanagita urges an end to deductive logic, that a new methodology is necessary, and this he calls the inductive method, later defining it as 'double proof', namely, the multi-layered method of logic he outlined in chapter three (Yanagita, 1934: 489). Finally, he concludes the book with a demonstration of the universal nature of the numinous as held by antiquity (Yanagita, 1934: 479–506). Yanagita's remarkable innovations are clear for all to see—he is constructing a cultural system specific to Asia but which has universal implications. His book is truly one of the crowning glories of Japanese insider discourse.

In 1947 in his essay 'Gendai Kagaku to iu Koto' (What is Known as 'Modern Science'), Yanagita criticised *A Study of Popular Oral Transmission*, claiming that it was a failure as there were too many errors in transcription. He also noted that much that should have been said in the book was not stated, in particular that the reason why Japan should not imitate the ethnology of other societies is that all countries have unique features but Japan has an exceptionally large number (Yanagita, 1947: 569). Fukuda Ajio interprets the use of the word 'failure' by Yanagita as a reaction to the overemphasis on the connection between Yanagita's system and anthropology. But, as the book was originally conceived as 'insider discourse', a set of lectures directed towards specialists and followers familiar with Yanagita's project, perhaps his emphasis was less apparent to its initial audience than it appeared a decade or so later to Yanagita himself. In any case, it is frequently cited by critics and readers as one of the fundamental texts in the system often called in Japan 'Yanagita gaku' or Yanagitaology.

I will shortly demonstrate how *A Study of Popular Oral Transmission* shares much in common with Yanagita's *Kyōdō Seikatsu no Kenkyū Hō* (Studies in Communal Life, 1935), which incorporates material from lectures delivered before the publication of the earlier book. However, the impact of this work in Japan has been quite remarkable. Yanagita's emphasis on comparative techniques, and the explicit attempt at distancing his system from related Western disciplines, has identified this work as a fundamental landmark of Japanese intellectual history. Both Yanagita's nationalism, as well as his attempt to construct a universal discourse based upon the very particular reality of Japan, can be discerned in this book.

The era in which it was published undoubtedly had an effect upon the marked anti-colonialist rhetoric evident in the early chapters yet there is no reason to doubt that these were beliefs that Yanagita genuinely held. The tension between his efforts to stress regional traditions of culture as against a larger paradigm of a national Japanese culture can also be clearly glimpsed in the work, and perhaps this tension too is to some extent a product of the decade in which it was published. Nevertheless, the continuing appeal of the ideas expressed in the book attest to its contemporary significance as an attempt to construct an indigenous social science, as innovative as it was contentious, albeit one built on theoretical foundations developed in the West.

Case Study Three: Studies in Communal Life (1935)

The composition of *Studies in Communal Life* has an even more complicated history than *A Study of Popular Oral Transmission*, although its publication as a single volume was in August 1935. The introduction was a lecture by Yanagita given in 1931, and the first half of the book, consisting of chapters one to six, was a lecture series also delivered by Yanagita in 1931 and published as a pamphlet under the title of 'Kyōdoshi Kenkyū no Hōhō' (The Methodology of Researching Local History) in 1932. The second half of the book, consisting of chapters seven and eight, is slightly larger in length than the first half and was written by a follower of Yanagita called Kobayashi Masakuma who from November 1932 to March 1933 took notes on the 1932 pamphlet in a series of question and answer sessions held with Yanagita at his home. Together with Kobayashi's transcription of an additional lecture or two given at Tokyo University by Yanagita, these notes form the basis of chapters seven and eight.

Thus the book is a patchwork made up of several lectures stitched together (and including oral transcription) to make a single volume, virtually the same technique as that used in the composition of the previous two case studies, and a technique applying to much of Yanagita's published output (Fukuda, 1996: 632–5). We should also note that some of this material (and much of the material included in *A Study of Popular Oral Transmission*) was not included in the 1952 *Teihon Yanagita Kunio Zenshū* (Standard Works of Yanagita Kunio), although it was published earlier, including, naturally, the original volume with this title.

The title can be translated a number of ways. As we have noted earlier, 'kyōdo' can mean local or village but essentially signifies the collective or communal life of the community. Fukuda comments that the book itself is quite different from what a narrow reading of the title might suggest; it is, in fact, a guide to Yanagita's whole system. But Yanagita had not yet settled on 'minzokugaku' as the key term to denote his project, consequently, at this time he used phrases like 'communal life' or 'local studies' to mean his new science. This was certainly the case when the text was aimed at the general public, rather than specialists (Fukuda, 1996: 632).

In a journal article published in 1935, Yanagita explained the origins and purpose of this book: 'it is, generally speaking, an introductory book for people who are not specialists in this area' (Quoted Fukuda, 1996: 633). Thus, the book is written for 'outsiders'. In the second chapter, Yanagita expands on his purpose: 'our research, in the final analysis, must serve society. In other words, our present knowledge serves to lead people's lives into future happiness, to question modern uncertainties and to solve them by drawing on past knowledge.... It would be easier if collecting materials for this purpose, in short, accurately noting and recording things not yet understood, was to be mere surface comprehension, but to understand the inner workings of the minds of local people cannot mean to watch and listen from outside; in the end, the only way to accomplish this is to attend to the self-consciousness of the people themselves. In other words, the collection of data is at the same time a reflection of the inner selves of the local people' (Yanagita, 1935: 30–1).

The book is divided into eight chapters but, as explained above, chapters one to six constitute the first half of the work. This half begins with an introduction which, like the introduction to *A Study of Popular Oral Transmission*, is a statement of principles: 'The first principle of community research is, briefly speaking, to know the past history of the people'. By people, Yanagita makes it clear that he means the 'common people', here expressed by the word 'heimin', and he adds that 'actual written records of the common people are exceedingly rare' (Yanagita, 1935: 10). His exposition of principle is, he writes, a form of self-reflection. But his aim is to discover whether a general law exists that can make sense of our enormously varied individual experiences. To do this, knowledge of the past, even as recent as a mere two centuries ago, is essential.

This leads Yanagita to a restatement of the message of the earlier book: that the past lives in the present. 'Irrespective of what we were later taught by China and America, the traces [of the past] arose, each and every one of them, in our country or they have been here all along' (Yanagita, 1935: 14). The living present as manifest in the people and their language can be used to read the past: 'habits of food, clothing, habitation, from rituals to manners...the actions of people we see today are new but, fundamentally, originate in patterns from the past' (Yanagita, 1935: 15). Thus the 'hope' of his new science is to uncover the undocumented life of the people (Yanagita, 1935: 9–17).

Chapter two discusses the paucity of written sources for the life of the people, thus Yanagita's emphasis on local history. County records are one possible source but the multiplicity of individual sources makes synthesis difficult. As literacy is a relatively recent phenomenon, records of day-to-day details are rare. The bias of the elites who wrote history also presents a problem, and here Yanagita expresses a strong dissatisfaction with the methodology and achievements of history.

In addition to recent scholarship broadening the historical data base, Yanagita's method proposes even more radical solutions to these problems: oral records, interviews, an archaeology of the present. His major hypothesis is: 'Japanese people, having Japanese faces and bone structure, speaking Japanese and living in Japanese-style homes...must have some special characteristic in their lives which still survives in some form' (Yanagita, 1935: 27). Nevertheless, he acknowledges his debt to Western models, especially British folklore studies (Yanagita, 1935: 18–32).

However, in chapter three, Yanagita notes that folklore does not describe his project in its entirety. This leads him, in the next chapter, to conduct a brief survey of overseas ethnological studies. The centre of these studies is London but Britain has lost its old culture through modernisation. In France, the situation is close to that existing in Japan. After noting the different words used to denote 'kyōdo kenkyū' in French and English ('ethnographie' and 'folklore'), Yanagita moves on to Germany where a distinction is made between the study of one's own folklore, and that of other countries. The purposes of the two kinds of research are different. As Yanagita notes, 'One glance at how we Japanese gather and record our oral tradition as a stage in learning about our ancestors' lives...and how white people publish accounts of the lives of the Swahili or Eskimos will show how different they are' (Yanagita, 1935: 54).

Generally speaking, overseas ethnology amounts to a mere fascination with the exotic. When they move past this stage into learning foreign languages, and collecting data in these languages, Yanagita comments, 'there are many [such scholars] who brush the skin but omit the essence' (Yanagita, 1935: 54). He continues: 'the degree differs but even within the same country, those who come from far away cannot completely absorb things [in the same way as natives]. Even so, if they carefully calm their minds, and as if born in that land, listen sympathetically, then understanding is not beyond them. But travellers only possess the psychology of travellers' (Yanagita, 1935: 55–6).

Finally, Yanagita makes an oblique comment on his predecessors in Japan: 'Formerly, the study of ethnology in Japan was established by white men who, with their colleagues abroad, brought with them an attitude derived from the study of red, black and brown societies. The various community studies that we have been advocating for some time have practically nothing in common with this' (Yanagita, 1935: 57–8). The stress here is on an indigenous, insider system which can replace earlier colonial discourses because of its scientific and ethical superiority. Yanagita is making a powerful claim that is a clear challenge to the whole notion of outsider ethnology. Appropriately enough, he concludes chapter four with some remarks on how the ancient seventh-century reciter of genealogies Hieda no Are, and the famous scribe who recorded his utterances, Ō no Yasumaro (d.723), in their methodology, anticipated the brothers Grimm in Germany (Yanagita, 1935: 33–59).

Chapter five traces a history of ethnological studies in Japan. Apart from the references in the previous chapter, no other mention of ancient forebears appear. Yanagita locates the birth of ethnological research in Japan in Motoori Norinaga's *Tamakatsuma* (1795–1812), a kind of literary encyclopaedia in fifteen volumes. Yanagita also cites other Edo-period thinkers like the Confucianist Matsuzaki Kōdō and the famous nativist scholar Hirata Atsutane as predecessors. The first Edo-era collector of tales, which could be designated as ethnographic notes along the lines of the brothers Grimm, was Hirokata Yashiro who began a project to collect notes on customs known as the *Shokoku Fūzoku Toijō* (Queries Concerning Customs in Various Provinces).

Assisted by other scholars like Ishihara Masaakira (1759–1821) and Nakayama Nobuna (1787–1836), the only replies this project elicited appeared to be the *Akita Fūzoku Toijō Kotae* (A Reply on Akita Customs) compiled by Naka Seihō. Yanagita listed other similar works including Murase Kōtei's (1747–1818) *Geien Nisshō* (Art Almanac) and later books by Takizawa Bakin, like *Gendō Hōgen* (Occult Ramblings, 1818–20) and *Enseki Zasshi* (Forgotten Jewels, 1811). He finds Kitamura Intei's *Kyūshōran* (A Manual on Fun) most notable as, unlike the other texts listed, it was organised on a schematic basis (Yanagita, 1935: 60–76).

Chapter six has a title much cited by Yanagita specialists—'Aratanaru Kokugaku' (New National Learning)—as indicative of the nationalistic aims of Yanagita's project but it can also be interpreted to mean a new synthesis of Japanese culture. In this chapter Yanagita outlines the broad contours of his new science. He begins by raising the problems (along the lines of the original synthesis by Motoori Norinaga) associated with evaluation, the need for comparisons to establish a basis of discussion.

In Yanagita's case, Okinawan culture is the chief instrument of comparison, the standard against which Japanese culture may be compared and conceptualised, as he writes: 'the discovery of Okinawa is an event of monumental importance' (Yanagita, 1935: 80). By this he means that the discovery of Okinawan culture by mainland intellectuals provides a means to study ancient Japan; comparisons with Okinawa dialects create a taxonomy of ancient Japanese; Okinawan religion, its ceremonies, the role of women all provide information about the origins of mainland religion; the same logic can be applied to land tenure, the family, and so on. The importance, indeed, the centrality of Okinawa to Yanagita's new science is here clearly revealed.

Next Yanagita discusses maps of cultural influence using the notion of distance as his barometer. His view of Japan is that it is largely unknown: 'Today most of Japan is an unknown frontier' (Yanagita, 1935: 81). While noting that in Europe old tales and stories easily cross national barriers, Yanagita stresses that in Japan this is not the case: 'Japan is an island nation and so, we believe, has a unique tradition' (Yanagita, 1935: 85). Nevertheless, comparison of tales and stories (both within and outside Japan) is the only way to proceed, to establish who the people are. The reason why surveys and the collecting of folktales is so important is because language is the instrument that encodes culture. The same can be said of ancient Japanese religion, and both must be subjected to a form of scientific or historical analysis.

The overarching purpose of such analysis is to solve the problems of the present. Yanagita argues: 'the social system cannot be divided up, as we were taught at school, into separate categories of law, morality and religion' (Yanagita, 1935: 90). Yanagita's holistic vision of a new science which unites conventional social-scientific categories into one coherent system is still in the process of evolution. At this early stage, rather than creating a 'world ethnology', Yanagita 'seeks to establish hypotheses without too much dispute based on what we now know of our own country' (Yanagita, 1935: 93–4). Or, in other words, the first imperative is to know oneself (Yanagita, 1935: 77–95).

Chapter seven, beginning the second half of the book, is a classification of ethnological resources divided into three parts: material culture, linguistic arts, and mental phenomena. Chapter eight is a ten-page conclusion. The first part of chapter seven devoted to material culture constitutes two-thirds of the chapter, thus leaving little room for detailed explanations of Yanagita's other two categories. *A Study of Popular Oral Transmission* actually provides a more detailed explanation of the last category but, as Fukuda Ajio observes, the whole of chapter seven serves as a relatively simple history of the concrete achievements of Yanagita's methodology (Fukuda, 1996: 636–7).

Yanagita's exposition of material culture is divided into nineteen subsections which include such basic categories as food, clothing, transport, villages, labour, marriage, and taboos. The dichotomy of the sacred and the secular makes an early appearance as the major conceptual division into which clothing can be placed. This conceptual axis, which many Japanese commentators still use as a fundamental tool of ethnological analysis, was introduced by Yanagita in his massive 1931 study *Meiji Taishōshi Sesō Hen* (A History of the Meiji and Taishō Eras: Social Affairs) but is developed further in this chapter. Yanagita's writings during the 1930s make frequent use of this dichotomy, and, in the same way, often utilise the notion of the 'jōmin' or common people. But until chapter seven of *Studies in the Communal Life* the meaning of 'jōmin' was left largely undefined.

The famous passage defining 'jōmin' is found in the subsection entitled 'The Village' and reads as follows: 'The first structural unit making up the village is the villagers and this group can be subdivided into two. The first is the "jōmin", that is, the ordinary peasant farmer, who is located in the middle range of the second subgroup that I will mention next; the "jōmin" make up the majority of villagers' (Yanagita, 1935: 150). Yanagita then goes on to define the second subgroup as consisting of, at the upper level, the farm families with a name or proper lineage, in other words, those who can be classified as belonging to the ruling class; the lower level can still be found today but 'they are not farmers, from long ago they possessed occupations or crafts and can be lumped together in one group' (Yanagita, 1935: 150). The passage continues: 'For example, [such people were] priests, blacksmiths, coopers; they live for a short time in a village and then shift elsewhere, they are a floating population…not the "jōmin"' (Yanagita: 1935: 150).

A continuing controversy has developed around this passage, based on the fact that the word 'jōmin' does not occur once in the first half of the book. In explanation, Fukuda quotes the political scientist Kamishima Jirō (b.1918) who, after noting that the word 'commoner' (heimin) appears frequently in the first half of the book, but not at all in the second half, remarked that: 'The words "commoner" (heimin) and "common people" (jōmin) have the same meaning so it may well be that Yanagita was forced to substitute one for the other as part of his accommodation with the "fascist times"' (Quoted Fukuda, 1996: 639).

Here Kamishima sees the replacement of the ideologically loaded 'heimin'—a word long associated with the left—by a neologism of Yanagita's invention as a manoeuvre to avoid criticism from the dominant fascist right. Fukuda interprets this differently, arguing that the first half of the book was originally a lecture series for the general public, while the second half was aimed at a specialist audience of scholars, thus the more common 'heimin' was utilised in the general lectures and the technical term 'jōmin' used for Yanagita's scholarly audience (Fukuda, 1996: 639). This controversy is far from over, with Yanagita's complex, and, at times, contradictory use of the word 'jōmin' ensuring that the debate will continue for many years yet.

The second part of chapter seven examining the linguistic arts is a brief but concise examination of neologisms, new expressions, proverbs, riddles, chants, children's language, folk songs, and folk tales. In addition to citing ancient source collections of such linguistic phenomena, Yanagita uses language as a means to discover the past in the present. He nominates his own study of the word 'snail' (*Kagyūkō*, 1927) as paradigmatic of his purpose (Yanagita, 1935: 190–213).

The third part of chapter seven, on mental phenomena, is also relatively short but important as Yanagita focuses on the heart of his methodology. Yanagita begins by classifying societies into those that are absorbing the new culture of the modern world, and those that have already done so, essentially a division between the West and the rest. Japan is located between these two poles: 'On the one hand China, India and Japan are absorbing a new culture, while at the same time they still cling to old ways of thinking' (Yanagita, 1935: 214). With the possible exceptions of Bulgaria and Yugoslavia, no Western countries have this problem of trying to absorb the new and the old simultaneously. This is why Yanagita had to devise a means of investigation different from those employed in the West, and why this task is of the utmost importance. Here Yanagita virtually defines the necessity of an insider approach to culture; as we have seen in the previous chapter, this argument is still put today. Yanagita's overwhelming importance as an architect of the modern Japanese discourse on culture is no more clearly revealed than in this passage.

As yet, mass phenomena and mass psychology are underdeveloped fields of study: a new epistemology is the first step. Yanagita assesses the role of relative, historical values in determining right and wrong, and such historical moralities are all circumscribed under the heading of 'knowledge': 'For those who share the same way of life (eg. primitives), knowledge is naturally shared but there are many instances in which they have no consciousness of this' (Yanagita, 1935: 220). To illustrate his point, Yanagita uses the example of colour. The ancient Japanese, he argues, were able to distinguish between thirty or fifty types of red but they possessed only a few words for 'red'. They had no need to use such a large number of shades of red so they had no names for them (here Yanagita notes that currently numbers are used to distinguish these shades). But these colours existed as concepts, and the ancients could see these colours under extreme psychological conditions like dizziness or madness. The ancient Japanese had a vision of a multicoloured paradise but this is not reflected in existing records prompting some present-day Japanese to assert that their colour perception was limited. Yanagita does not accept this. The same logic he applies to abstract concepts like gratitude or happiness (Yanagita, 1935: 214–24).

Yanagita summarises his argument by noting that material culture and the language arts arose as mass products of society, not as the results of an individual intuition or sagacity. He then proceeds to an examination of knowledge which he divides into the two categories of critical and deductive, citing the French thinker Lucien Lévy-Bruhl (1857–1939), author of *La Mentalité Primitive* (Paris, 1922) and also Sir James Frazer, among other thinkers on this subject. The question of white ethnology and its characterisation of the 'other' is raised once more. Yanagita is particularly interested in comparing the roles of omens and the laws of causation in his attempt to theorise an 'emic' system of understanding culture (Yanagita, 1935: 225–31).

The conclusion reiterates his aim: 'The single purpose of our discipline is, in short, to clearly determine what parts of our contemporary life have arisen in this new age, how much is a product of our present intellectual state and how much is a product of our unconscious' (Yanagita, 1935: 243–4). His final remarks restate his method: 'In the final analysis, knowing the facts does not end in the knowledge gained solely from just knowing, if knowledge does not become critical or deductive, then scholarship is meaningless' (Yanagita, 1935: 244).

This conclusion does not do justice to Yanagita's achievement, which is to construct the framework of a new way of seeing culture—from inside—that explicitly repudiates an outsider perspective as unscientific and unsuited to Japan due to its colonial bias, or, in Yanagita's words 'white ethnology'. In fact, Yanagita goes further than this, by attempting to formulate a new kind of epistemology, of seeing and knowing. While he drew upon a variety of insider and outsider sources for this epistemology, it is unquestionably his own synthesis, and it is still a remarkable achievement, even viewed from the perspective of nearly seventy years later. The influence that Yanagita's 'new science' as expounded in these two volumes had on later Japanese thought was immense. It was probably greater than any other one individual modern Japanese thinker. But we have yet to explore his magnum opus *The Ocean Road*, the product of almost all his remaining years.

Case Study Four: *The Ocean Road* (1961)

The Ocean Road was published in July 1961, a year or so before Yanagita's death at the age of eighty-five. This book was undoubtedly the major work of Yanagita's last years, and indeed, it is generally considered to be the most important study that he embarked upon in the postwar era. It consists of eight separate essays, all but one published between 1950 and 1955, but all written by Yanagita himself. The commentator Fukuda Ajio argues that, in addition to being the culmination of Yanagita's life-long obsession with Okinawa and the question of Japanese origins, this book represents an attempt to restore Okinawa to its rightful place in the intellectual consciousness of Japan (Fukuda, 1994: 698).

With the signing of the San Francisco Peace Treaty in 1951, and the virtual annexation of Okinawa by the USA given legal force by article 3 of the Peace Treaty which stated: 'the United States will have the right to exercise all and any powers of administration, legislation and jurisdiction over the territory and inhabitants of [Okinawa]', Okinawa slipped out of the Japanese consciousness (Quoted Taira, 1997: 158). But Yanagita was determined to right this wrong, and this he achieved with *The Ocean Road*, which was clearly part of the process that eventually led to the reversion of Okinawa to Japan in 1972.

The Ocean Road, despite continuing criticism of Yanagita's main arguments, is central to the contemporary Japanese evocation of a sense of being Okinawan, mentioned by Okinawans themselves as playing such a role in developing their own sense of ethnic or national consciousness. We can see evidence of this, for example, in the Okinawa poet Chikako Ichihara's 1985 poem 'U Tō Danshō' (U Island Literary Fragments) where she describes Yanagita's book as 'that great novel of the south' (Ichihara, 1985: 55).

The book begins with a brief introduction in which Yanagita discusses his desire to solve the problem of how the Japanese people came to Japan. He dismisses the conventional explanation that the Japanese took a north-south route, travelling down from the north of Japan south through the various islands of the archipelago, and instead proposes a west-east route. As evidence for his view, he cites such matters as ship manufacture, tidal currents, trade routes: these facts are fundamental to his thesis. The first essay, from which the title for the book is taken, then begins with a philological discussion of the names for winds. This topic connects with winds as an aspect of seafaring, and Yanagita develops this theme from exotic names (of dugongs and sealions) to etymology.

The implication is that such speculation uncovers a history not documented, unable to be documented. We can reconstruct the past from songs and tales through our imagination. Topographical links to the sea and its history prompt Yanagita to recall some lines from a famous poem by Shimazaki Tōson (1872–1943) on a coconut washing ashore (cited at the beginning of this chapter). The coconut, asserts Yanagita, is not native to Japan, thus the word for coconut in Japanese is perceived as an item of exotica, and coconut wood is valued for its rarity. Through the distribution of articles manufactured from coconuts, certain hypotheses can be made about the tidal currents upon which coconuts drifted ashore (Yanagita, 1961: 9–39).

With this hypothesis as his starting point, Yanagita explores the relationship between population movements by sea, as charted along the lines outlined earlier, and also expressions of religiosity. Such connections have been neglected by scholars enquiring into the question of Japanese origins, observes Yanagita. Unlike coconuts, people do not drift along currents randomly, therefore, any investigation of the arrival of primitive peoples onto the Japanese archipelago must begin from the psychology of such travellers. Logically, these early seafarers would be reluctant to travel long distances, instead long journeys would emerge gradually from short island hops, moving from familiar shore to less familiar shore.

The reason why early Japanese were impelled to make such journeys is trade in cowrie shells. Along the China coast, cowrie shells were much sought after as trade objects, even serving as a means of exchange. Yanagita's view is that Miyakojima island in Okinawa was where travellers drifted from China due to the rare cowrie shells found on that island which were celebrated in legend and song. Yanagita cites various evidence to prove his hypothesis. Historical accounts of the importance of Miyakojima in Sino-Japanese trade relations, legends, and religious practices confirm the significance of cowrie shells on Miyakojima. He concludes: 'That finding cowrie shells…is one key source in the search for Japanese origins may sound like an unreliable dream or romance but, in all honesty, to this very day I have not heard a more likely explanation (Yanagita, 1961: 52–3). We recall here Yanagita's early expression of this hypothesis in *South Sea Notes*.

To this argument, Yanagita adds an addendum to the effect that rice, in all likelihood, was not imported into Japan from China between the Jōmon and Yayoi eras, as commonly believed. He contests the north-south theory of migration and argues that people must have arrived in Japan earlier than this. Rice is such a fundamental element in Japanese culture that it is inconceivable that it was introduced into Japan as late as the Jōmon period. Furthermore, his study of the tides convinces him that people travel from smaller to larger islands, leading him to the view that rice must have been introduced to the mainland from Okinawa (Yanagita, 1961: 39–58).

The next essay begins with a focus on the relations between the southern islands of Japan, and again takes as its source old stories and tales, in other words, folklore. Yanagita identifies a common myth or legend of the palace of the underwater dragon-king; but in the Okinawan myths, as opposed to versions of the story in other Asian cultures, the dragon changes into a princess. The etymology of the word for dragon-palace leads Yanagita to the Okinawan legend of Niruya— the land across the sea, yet in certain sources like the *Omorosōshi*, the ancient song-text, the land is under the sea. Some similarities exist with mainland mythology but Yanagita argues that the historical narrative underpinning the myths accounts for significant differences in detail. A merging of various myths of origin, based on the Niruya kingdom, can be found in stories of the gods of fire and lightning who come together in the figure of Nira, the life-giver. This god is, in his origins, a uniquely Okinawan deity (Yanagita, 1961: 58–83).

Yanagita then retells a myth he came across in the writings of Ifa Fuyu about mice that were sent into the land of humans from their homeland across the sea. In other words, the mice originated in Niruya. Yanagita then traces other god-myths, and religious beliefs associated with the sea, from their Okinawan origins, and compares them with mainland beliefs. The notion of the land under the sea is altered under the influence of continental systems of thought like Taoism and Ying-Yang. But the core idea of visitors from across the sea remains in Okinawa, as Yanagita comments: 'The dividing line between gods and men has a special significance for the religions of the southern islands and if we pay particular attention, then we can find faint traces of these beliefs also remaining in the northern areas of Honshū' (Yanagita, 1961: 90).

Here Yanagita asserts that the Niruya–Kanaya core of religious beliefs is the most ancient stratum of Japanese religiosity and that the introduction of a new religion based on the sun god did not sweep this older thread away. The religion worshipping the sun god easily turned into a worldview revering heaven but this began late in Okinawa and never became completely separated from its Niruya–Kanaya (land across or under the sea) core. The implications of this line of reasoning for an Okinawan origin for the most fundamental Japanese religious beliefs, and thus for the origin of the Japanese people themselves, is that it overturns the traditional view that the Imperial family, putatively descended from the sun goddess, is the fundamental religious base upon which the Japanese nation is constructed.

Taking his cue once again from Ifa Fuyu, Yanagita then elaborates on the connections between the word 'root' (ne) and various folktales, and these beliefs he also links to the land across the sea. Yanagita concludes that the old religion lost its power, both in Okinawa and on the mainland, and remained only in appearance. This trend was triggered by the growth of cities. The other world remains within this world in Okinawan religious belief, although it has been influenced by Buddhist notions. Yanagita's conclusion to the essay is that legends of an island where the sun rises express a belief in a utopian other world, and this was said to be in the East. He is describing how myth has fashioned the notion of the ocean road—the journey across the sea to Japan (Yanagita, 1961: 83–108).

This essay has affinities with much of the writing explored in the previous chapter. Umehara Takeshi's ruminations about the 'other world' clearly owe much to Yanagita's fascinating speculations about god myths, strata, or layers of conflicting and contradictory religious traditions and the amalgam with Buddhism that resulted. Similarly, Emiko Ohnuki-Tierney's construction of a fundamental Japanese conception of religiosity is undeniably influenced by ideas of the kind Yanagita is exploring above, notwithstanding the importance of Orikuchi Shinobu's notion of 'marebito' (visitor), which, obviously, influenced Yanagita also. The relationship between Yanagita and Orikuchi was complex and even today is much debated. One view holds that Yanagita could not accept Orikuchi's conceptualisation of 'marebito' but this viewpoint appears to be contradicted by the evidence of *The Ocean Road*, as demonstrated earlier.

The critic Kajiki Gō has recently argued that Orikuchi's insight was itself the product of Yanagita's speculations on Okinawa in *South Sea Notes* but that Yanagita, for a variety of reasons, was not able to explore this insight further until *The Ocean Road*. The sequence, according to Kajiki, is that Yanagita creates the germ of the idea of 'visitor gods' in 1925 with the publication of *South Sea Notes*, this idea then becomes the centre of Orikuchi's work, and despite his public statements to the contrary, Yanagita is finally spurred on by Orikuchi's development of the concept to elaborate fully upon it in the essay just discussed (Kajiki, 1989: 41–2, 43–8).

The third essay is quite short and begins with two quotations from a Kashima folk song that refer to 'Miroku's boat' or the boat in the future, in other words, to heaven. 'Miroku' is the Bodhisattva Maitreya or the 'benevolent' one who will appear in the world as the next Buddha millions of years in the future. Yanagita's essay is constructed around the question of how did this Buddhist belief come to Japan? Various links are explored—the second year of the Miroku era is 1507, a contemporary belief in the imminent appearance of Miroku is associated with a chiliastic movement to reform the world (yonaoshi). Yanagita then connects these links to ritual dances and to religious ceremonies in the Yaeyama islands, which, in turn, lead back to the 'pure land' of Nirai (or Niruya) across the sea (Yanagita, 1961: 109–23).

The fourth essay takes up some threads left dangling in the previous essays and draws them together to make up one seamless argument. Yanagita begins with 'Mimiraku' island, mentioned in Japan's oldest verse collection, the *Manyōshū*. Similar references to similar terms in other ancient texts convinces Yanagita that this word refers to a cape whence people left for the continent or, more pertinently, where people left the continent to cross to Japan. The word also carries associations of a meeting place for the dead and so creates a link to 'ne no kuni', the land of roots, which he investigated in the second essay. Yanagita argues that 'Niruya' represents a late morphological evolution of ne, thus, rather than implying an underground land (a Japanese version of Hades), in Okinawa the term denotes the land across the sea. This hypothesis is confirmed by Okinawan religious rites celebrating the Nirai spirits returning from other islands (Yanagita, 1961: 124–34).

The second link in the claim of Yanagita's intricate argument is provided by one Okinawan belief that in ancient times rice came from Niira island as a gift from the gods. After discussing various Okinawa myths and legends about the origin of rice, Yanagita expresses his agreement with Ifa Fuyu's conclusion that, in general, stories from a variety of Okinawa islands all hold that rice came from Nirai Kanai, which Yanagita asserts is the same place as the land of roots, a paradise in the south. Yanagita summarises his argument thus: in the etymology of 'miroku' or 'mimiraku' we find the Okinawa myth of Niruya Kanaya, the land of roots, the homeland across the sea where the gods commune and whence rice came. To this chain of beliefs, Yanagita adds Miroku's boat, which came from abroad bearing gifts (Yanagita, 1961: 134–55).

The fifth essay returns to the thread concerning mice. Yanagita interprets the myth of the 'pure land' (heaven) reserved for mice or rats as an anthropomorphic familiarisation of Nirai Kanai. In this reading, animals are mistakenly substituted for humans. The connection between the other world and the underground derives from this association between mice and the pure land, Yanagita speculates, because of the link between mice or, more likely, rats, and death. Thus the land of roots becomes the land of the dead. The folk traditions would have the mice in the pure land leading humans from the underground to the root-land, the promised land (Yanagita, 1961: 157–209). Yanagita does not need to hint at the fascinating parallel between European folklore—the tale of the Pied Piper of Hamelin—and this example of Japanese folk tradition.

The sixth essay begins with a philological examination of 'tsushiya', a word found in various songs from the *Omorosōshi*. Yanagita believes that this word signifies 'takaragai', literally 'treasure-shell', but which actually means cowrie shell. These shells were abundant in ancient Okinawa, and were probably exported to the mainland as treasure. Here, we see Yanagita developing lines of thought that he had first given voice to in *South Sea Notes*. From the idea that cowrie-shell necklaces were probably in common use, Yanagita raises the matter of another ancient seed which is also likely to have been used as beads in a necklace. The medieval Japanese word for this seed is 'zuzudama', the scientific name is Coix Lachyrma Jobi L. or 'Job's Tears' in English.

These seeds were probably used as substitutes for cowrie shells because of the latter's value, and were most likely used as a kind of rosary bead. Yanagita comments on the significance of the trade in such objects thus: 'Trade in these southern islands which were the birth place of countless beautiful "treasure shells" must be linked to the struggle for supremacy in the ancient cultural world' (Yanagita, 1961: 218). This essay directly links to the next, which takes up the theme of 'Job's Tears' once again. This leads Yanagita to an important point, one of the central theses in his system which seeks to recover the past from the imagination, and the present:

If you will permit me a detailed consideration of the dispersion and provenance of one small plant, something arising out of my own personal history, then you may discover in this an important law of human development. This is the point I wish to explain. The reason why, first of all, our ancestors chose a bead as a neck adornment was perhaps because it complemented our bodies or delighted the eye, or that it was inspired by the need to express the feeling of affection for the way it sparkled so beautifully. This is a difficult matter to decide. But, in any case, there is no doubt that it was confined to the products of nature found on land nearby. As this plant spread to island after island, conditions gradually changed and so people searched even further, and it may be that they learned of objects even more lovely and scarce, deep in the mountains or in the lands beyond the great sea. It was progress for them to desire these objects as their very own. In some of the large islands of Japan, from thousands of underground sites, there have been found objects thought to be various kinds of rare, beautiful jewels threaded through to wear around the neck. For people to gather these objects from far away and collect them in one spot inspires our admiration at the energy of human will. To see this as simply the way of life in ancient times, and to understand this as a decline as they threaded inferior beads made out of bamboo from some isolated island or Job's Tears or shells or nuts; to despise these objects from their pathetic appearance—this is not the correct way to view ancient history. It is a harmful kind of cultural history as far as the future of our nation is concerned.

Yanagita, 1961: 237–8.

Here Yanagita argues for an understanding of the past on its own terms, while nevertheless suggesting how the study of one small aspect of material culture can enrich and deepen our understanding of much larger cultural phenomena.

The eighth and final essay continues the theme of the search for the origins of the Japanese, which Yanagita was again locating in the specific incidence of the history of one small plant, although in this case, the plant changed to rice. Once more, he commences with philology, with an investigation of the Japanese word 'name' which is linked to the harvest festival celebrating the harvesting of new rice. Yanagita argues that while the vocabulary and specific practices of rice harvesting differ according to the region, rice-harvesting ceremonies seem remarkably similar throughout Japan. Developing his thesis on the assumption that the ceremonies were all basically the same, Yanagita traces this ritual to Okinawa. He links the ritual with the universal myth of Ceres, the grain-mother, by finding etymological connections between various words for rice and for 'birth' or 'maternity room' (ubuya) (Yanagita, 1961: 248–89).

The brief conclusion to his book is a reiteration of the main links in this chain of causation that he has traced, and which, in his view, defines the southern route by which the Japanese came from China to Japan (Yanagita, 1961: 290–6). The detail of Yanagita's argument appears tedious but in fact is of vital importance in demonstrating his characteristic methodology of proceeding from philology (language and etymology) to material culture and then to folk tradition and finally to history (not necessarily in that order). This methodology has been much criticised by Japanese intellectuals, as we saw earlier in this chapter. Yet, despite its obvious shortcomings, it has stimulated generations of

Japanese thinkers and writers to emulate it or surpass it. It stands as a monument to a different kind of discourse, an insider discourse that openly and deliberately seeks a methodology different from those hitherto used to characterise Japanese culture, and, as noted earlier, it has been immensely influential.

Furthermore, the various arguments that Yanagita addresses in *The Ocean Road* ought not to obscure the key political points he was making. He is constructing an alternative vision of the sources of Japanese religio-political authority; a vision that places that authority in Okinawa, a region ethnically and linguistically remote from mainland Japan. This vision is clearly behind the 'Yaponesia' thesis that emerges not long after the publication of Yanagita's book. It is linked also to a re-visioning of Japanese culture that we find in the writing of key 1960s authors like Ōe Kenzaburō, who will be investigated in chapter four. In other words, the crucial political watershed of the early 1960s—the struggle against the renewal of the US–Japan Security Treaty, a debate over the future of Japan—also informs and enhances the significance of Yanagita's book. And these same political nuances underlie and accentuate the direct political struggle to establish the importance of Okinawa to Japan proper, which led to the reversion of Okinawa back to Japan a decade or so later.

Reflections

Irrespective of whether one accepts Yanagita's thesis of the origins of the Japanese (and, until recently, it has not generally been accepted in Japan), there is no doubt that it has had an enormous impact on the postwar obsession with the question of national identity. Indigenous discourses of culture often, in fact almost always, focus on the question of origins. Although this may seem a fairly logical thing to do—after all, the question of who we are must be answered in some respects by the knowledge of where we came from—it is virtually certain that without Yanagita's lifelong engagement with this issue, this would not be so to the extent that it has been. Why Yanagita became fascinated with the problem is probably due to his concern with the fate of traditional society which arose, in some measure, from his service as a bureaucrat working in the field of agro-politics; and due to his interest in questions of identity, which also probably arose from his experience as a government adviser on colonial policy. However, biography does not explain everything.

One other reason, both for Yanagita's interest in the question of origins, and also for the same interest expressed by people since, for the concentration on this particular issue, lies in its explanatory power. As we have seen in *The Ocean Road*, Yanagita is able to bundle together a diverse range of historical, literary, linguistic, political, moral, and scientific concerns into one single issue. By investigating the origins of the Japanese, Yanagita is able to pass judgment on a whole mass of related questions; he is able to range far and wide, and to make explicit comments on political questions, most obviously the question of Okinawa's reversion to Japanese sovereignty from American occupation.

Furthermore, as Yoshimoto Takaaki points out, Yanagita also explored theoretical issues, most notably the problem of subjectivity: how can one separate one's own perception from the events one is perceiving? This is one of the most vexed questions, and one of the most hotly debated issues, in twentieth-century thought. The specific context for Yanagita was this issue of insider/outsider, emic/etic discourse, and the means by which he addressed the problem was through language and philology. Precisely the same methodology was adopted by twentieth-century thinkers in the West to deal with the same problem.

Yanagita's 'reading' of ethnology, and, (implicitly) epistemology, by using language as a focus, has had a continuing influence on Japanese writers on identity and nationhood. In Japan it has undoubtedly skewed a debate towards history and society that in the West has tended to drift towards language (Wittgenstein, Quine). It is no coincidence that many of the thinkers prominent in indigenous debates on culture and identity cited in the previous chapter would define themselves as working in the area of ethnology, anthropology, or sociology more than in linguistics or philosophy.

It is difficult for non-Japanese to grasp the significance of Yanagita's achievements in laying the foundation of how modern Japanese culture is constructed and understood in twentieth-century Japan. This is because no equivalent giant exists who has exerted a comparable influence over the formation of the notion of culture in the English-speaking world. Thus, this chapter has explicitly framed Yanagita's achievements through the evaluations of his Japanese contemporaries and successors.

In a study published in 2001 entitled *Yanagita Kunio no Minzokugaku* (Yanagita's Ethnology) summarising his views on Yanagita, Tanigawa Ken'ichi, who has succeeded Yanagita in being the chief advocate of a nativist ethnology in Japan, described *The Ocean Road* as being Yanagita's once-in-a-lifetime parting gift for the Japanese who will live in the twenty-first century. He explicitly linked this praise of Yanagita's last major work to its relevance to both the ongoing political and economic difficulties suffered by the people of Okinawa and to the perennial spiritual issue of death and the afterlife. In other words, Tanigawa saw the book as being of continuing significance in a local, political sense, and also in a universal sense of grappling with an issue that has occupied humanity since the beginning of history (Tanigawa, 2001: i–ii).

Tanigawa also summed up the enduring significance of Yanagita for Japan in the following way: 'Using the yardstick of macro cultures like the Greek, Hebrew and Chinese cultures to judge Japanese culture, Japanese were wont to lose confidence. This gave birth to a tendency to worship imported culture, at the same time, by comparison with imported culture, a climate where our own culture was despised came about. This became the norm for Japanese intellectuals and is still so today. In contrast, Yanagita asserted that a different measure was necessary to evaluate Japanese culture....To create such a measure, we could not rely upon the culture of the rulers or the intelligentsia who were under the marked influence of imported culture. Yanagita believed that we have no option but to seek out the deep structures of the culture of the common people as transmitted from antiquity.... He sought to solve the problem of how to escape from the dilemma of imitating imported culture, how to achieve autonomy of thought' (Tanigawa, 2001: 224–5).

Lest this recent assessment of Yanagita's influence on culture be thought of as simply a case of special pleading, or yet another resurgence of conservative nationalism, then Tanigawa's following coda to these remarks should give us pause: 'The idea at the root of Yanagita's ethnology is how can the Japanese deepen their self-awareness as Japanese without imitating foreign cultures? This is a completely different matter from the prewar Emperor-based view of history. Since such a historical perspective rests on a closed view of the world, as a consequence it cannot grasp a correct view of the international situation, nor can it avoid the mistaken ideal of leadership that steered Japan to defeat [in World War II]….In this respect, the views of such chauvinists are no different from the understanding of Japanese culture held by followers of the West. Both just find fault with the deep structures of the culture of Japan, and wallow in the shallows. The mood of gloom enveloping Yanagita throughout the wartime era was finally lifted by Japan's defeat. His challenge to the Japanese to awaken, his scholarship that demanded pride in itself, his creation of an indigenous discourse (kokugaku): these factors aimed at a new start for a new age' (Tanigawa, 2001: 229–30).

This reading of Yanagita by an exceedingly distinguished student of Yanagita's writings, who has been renowned at times for his criticisms of his master, can stand for the judgment of his generation. Tanigawa invested Yanagita with an epoch-making importance as a thinker and creator of the modern Japanese discourse on culture for the postwar generation of Japanese. Moreover, he argues for an ongoing significance for Yanagita's writings for Japan in the twenty-first century. No more powerful or eloquent a statement can be found to illustrate the central role this thinker has played in the formation of an insider discourse on culture for twentieth-century Japan.

This is not to imply that Tanigawa's assessment is entirely free from partisan considerations. We can object to Tanigawa overlooking how important outsider theorists were for Yanagita's 'new science', and also to the oversimplifications involved in the notion of the culture of the common people. Further, while Tanigawa is careful to distance himself from chauvinistic rhetoric, nonetheless we may judge his tone as somewhat one-dimensional in his unproblematic embrace of the notion of a unitary 'Japan'.

However, Tanigawa was making the point that Yanagita's 'new indigenous discourse' (shinkokugaku) was diametrically opposed to its predecessor, that is, the 'National Learning' of eighteenth-century thinkers like Motoori Norinaga which dominated Japanese culture until the Meiji era (Tanigawa, 2001: 232). Tanigawa's definition of culture is unutterably insider as this was the mode of discourse Yanagita endeavoured to create in the face of the overwhelming, monolithic outsider discourse of the West. Tanigawa's comments sketch out something of the enormous, and unparalleled, contribution Yanagita made to the evolution of an insider culture for modern Japan.

Yoshimoto Takaaki, like Yanagita, also uses ethnology, anthropology, and sociology as a springboard for excursions into almost every field of cultural discourse. In this respect, as in others, Yoshimoto may be Yanagita's true heir. Yoshimoto's writings on culture form the subject of the next chapter.

Yoshimoto Takaaki and Contemporary Culture

We, having lost our flesh, survive on will alone
We emerge from November graves as ghosts
....

To sever our chains, we harbour rebellion
Our skies at last begin to speak
Beneath our skies at last there will be strife
....

Will our humiliation and despair be unearthed?
....

Our corpses will be flogged no doubt
By the difference between rebellion and complicity

Yoshimoto Takaaki, from 'From Despair to Brutality'
(Yoshimoto, 1986: 41–2)

This chapter first briefly outlines the highlights of Yoshimoto Takaaki's career as a political activist before describing his major theoretical treatises. After a short summary of his other significant publications on culture, the rest of the chapter is devoted to a detailed analysis of three of the most important and influential works that he has written. None of these books has been translated into English and so, in addition to a detailed summary of their contents, the chapter provides much information on the reception accorded these works in Japan in an attempt to describe the intellectual, historical, and cultural context to which they belong.

Yoshimoto as a hero of the New Left

Yoshimoto Takaaki, like Yanagita Kunio, made his mark on the literary world first as a poet, and, unlike Yanagita, is still considered one of the major postwar poets. Born in Tokyo in 1924, Yoshimoto is the third son of a shipwright who managed a small boat yard at the time of his son's birth. He was educated at a technical middle school in Tokyo, graduating in 1941 at the age of seventeen. He then shifted to Yonezawa technical high school in northeastern Yamagata prefecture where he began to compose essays and poetry. After his graduation in 1944 at the age of nineteen, he returned to Tokyo to enrol in the electrical and chemical engineering department at Tokyo Kōgyō Daigaku (Tokyo Institute of Technology). In 1945 he was mobilised for war work and sent to a Nihon Carbide Company factory in Toyama prefecture. After returning to Tokyo, Yoshimoto graduated from university in 1947.

After graduation, Yoshimoto worked at a variety of jobs, finally finding employment with the Tōyō Ink Company in 1950 until resigning in 1956 at the age of thirty-one. He was married in the same year. However, by this time Yoshimoto had become known more for his writing than for any other activities. In 1952, with the support of a number of friends, his first important volume of poetry *Koyūji to no Taiwa* (A dialogue with Intrinsic Time) was published. Yoshimoto had already established something of a reputation as a critic of postwar poetry.

In the sole biographical study in English of Yoshimoto to date (a 1998 German study exists by Reinhold Ophüls-Kashima), the American scholar Lawrence Olson charts Yoshimoto's journey from writing to political activism through the 1950s and 1960s (Olson, 1992: 79–112). As Olson notes, the movement opposing the signing of the revised Security Treaty between the US and Japan was the platform that provided Yoshimoto with a brush with fame. Yoshimoto became actively involved with the Zengakuren student movement, being arrested in a student demonstration in 1960, and wrote several articles in an attempt to theorise the movement as a whole, which he saw primarily as an expression of the people's will. At this point in time, he was hailed by some as the leader of the Japanese 'New Left', and, as we shall discover shortly, some of his writings have affinities with some Western New Left thinkers, especially those linked to the prewar Frankfurt school of critical aesthetics like Theodor Adorno (1903–63) and Herbert Marcuse (1898–1979).

Yoshimoto's polemics against various intellectuals, most notably his debate with the leading postwar intellectual Maruyama Masao over democracy and what constitutes Japaneseness (and Japanese nationalism), made him a hero among the younger generation, and especially among students. Yoshimoto criticised both the left and the right and his development of concepts like 'independence' (jiritsu) allowed him to play a leading role among the political theorists of the day (Olson, 1992: 79–112). Something of the perverse complexity of Yoshimoto's position is revealed by his poem 'Zetsobō kara Kakoku e' (From Despair to Brutality), cited at the beginning of the chapter, which relates the feelings of self-disgust he experienced as a result of the occupation and defeat. But by the end of the 1960s he had turned back to writing once again, with a series of critiques on society and culture that have continued to the present day.

This chapter will focus on a small number of Yoshimoto's writings which are generally recognised as among the most acclaimed studies he has written. Yoshimoto's enormous productivity (a continuing phenomenon) limits severely any attempt to characterise his thought as a whole, and also restricts consideration of all but a few of his cultural critiques. Yoshimoto has written well over 100 individual volumes of cultural, social, literary, economic, historical, and political criticism. In fact, depending upon the source consulted and the method of calculation, his output is closer to 200 separate volumes, especially when his published lectures and joint publications with other authors are included.

However, to divide up his critiques into a number of categories is somewhat misleading as Yoshimoto's great strength as a critic is to combine the various categories of human experience together into one seamless critical methodology. In this he resembles Yanagita Kunio, and it is not an exaggeration to say that he, like Yanagita, is in some sense attempting to create a new human science. But there is no doubt his chief focus is upon society and culture.

The majority of Yoshimoto's books were first published in essay form—the longer volumes were written mostly as serialised essays—and so, often in his career, an essay, whether included in a later volume or not, achieved a great deal of fame. His first major critical publication was indeed an essay—his 'Machū Sho Shiron' or 'Draft Essay on the Book of Matthew'—first published in 1954 but later included in his first major book of criticism *Geijutsu teki Teikō to Zasetsu* (Artistic Resistance and Frustration, 1959).

Following a parallel but ultimately different path to the American literary critic Edmund Wilson in his famous series of articles on the Dead Sea Scrolls in the *New Yorker* from 1951 to 1954, Yoshimoto argued that Jesus Christ was an invention of Matthew, a hero created by the apostle to embody Jewish myths about the leader of an oppressed people (Shanks, 1998: 15; Olson, 1992: 87; Yoshimoto, 1969: 42–106). Yoshimoto's focus was on the trauma suffered by the early Christians, and Jesus's attempts to oppose the existing social order. However, it is a simple matter to transpose the tribulations endured by the alienated sect Jesus led with the sufferings of postwar Japanese, and therefore to see how Yoshimoto's immediate surroundings clearly played a major role in the essay's composition.

The same volume in which this essay is included also contains some of Yoshimoto's earliest essays on the 'apostasy' (tenkō) of radical left-wing writers during the 1930s. Yoshimoto attacked the prewar left over their quick about-face from being idealistic opponents of the regime to becoming spokesmen for the militarists. This criticism of the Left Yoshimoto also extended to communist writers both during and after the war, who he castigated for their adherence to ideological dogmas (Yoshimoto, 1969: 109–73; Yoshimoto, 1972b: 5–28).

In *Jōjō no Ronri* (The Logic of Lyricism, 1959), Yoshimoto published a scathing criticism of modernist and avant-garde poets who, after the war's end, deliberately concealed their wartime collaborationist activities with the militarists (Yoshimoto, 1970: 38–119, 317–44). At this juncture, it is worth noting that in Yoshimoto's *Zenchosakushū* (Collected Writings, 1968–78), the various essays that are collected in his individual volumes published to that point in time have all been rearranged and, in many cases, have been subjected to much rewriting and re-editing. Wherever possible, this chapter refers to the latest rewritten versions.

Yoshimoto's major theoretical treatises

During the 1960s and 1970s, Yoshimoto wrote some of the theoretical works that have come to be recognised by commentators as among his most important books, and have subsequently been acclaimed by many critics.

The volume that encapsulates much of the fiery polemic that Yoshimoto engaged in during the demonstrations against the re-signing of the Security Treaty, and established his reputation as a leader of the New Left, is his *Gisei no Shūen* (The Death of the Sham System) published in 1962. Yoshimoto lashes out in the title essay at what he sees as the sham democracy pursued by thinkers like Maruyama Masao; in the end he condemns both the communists and 'progressive' intellectuals like Maruyama. In this essay, and others included in the volume, Yoshimoto argued his thesis of a true, participatory democracy to be brought about by his idealised, independent 'people' (shimin or shomin) (Yoshimoto, 1972b: 47–71). Yoshimoto expanded on these political ideas in volumes like *Maruyama Masao Ron* (On Maruyama Masao, 1963), *Mosha to Kagami* (Imitations and Mirrors, 1964), *Jiritsu no Shisōteki Kyoten* (The Intellectual Base of Independence, 1966), *Kaaru Marukusu* (Karl Marx, 1966), *Jōkyō Eno Hatsugen* (Proposals on the State of Affairs, 1968) and *Jōkyō* (The State of Affairs, 1970).

During the 1960s and early 1970s, three books stood out among Yoshimoto's writings, first, because they were not overtly political in content, and second, because they addressed some of the major intellectual issues of the day, not merely for Japan but for the West also. The main emphasis of these works was on the interaction or relationship between culture and society. The first of these three volumes is *Gengo ni Totte Bi to wa Nanika* (What is Beauty in Respect of Language?) published in book form in 1965. This work will be analysed in more detail later but it is fascinating how Yoshimoto, while trying to establish an indigenous mode of discourse, if not a methodology unique to himself, does so quite consciously utilising a 'dual system' of the type identified in earlier chapters.

Yoshimoto cites a vast range of Japanese and non-Japanese thinkers and writers in this book but is transparently positioning himself as an insider who borrows freely from outsider perspectives. His approach is more sophisticated in its open embrace of this paradox of dual perspectives than such earlier thinkers as Yanagita Kunio, since he is opening a dialogue with Western writers on culture without withholding the possibility of a two-way exchange. However, due to the tyranny of language, and the lack of translations of Yoshimoto's work, his attempts at dialogue have not yet been joined by Western thinkers.

The irony is that Yoshimoto's text focuses on language as the key hermeneutic strategy in representing being or consciousness at almost the same time as such an emphasis was occurring in Western mainstream thought with a revived interest in such seminal thinkers on language as the Swiss linguist Ferdinand de Saussure (1857–1913), and the emergence of a younger generation of like-minded French intellectuals represented by Jacques Derrida (b.1930), and a revival of interest in the influential German thinker, Martin Heidegger (1889–1976), who wrote much on language.

The next instalment in what some critics have called a 'trilogy'— indeed Yoshimoto himself in a lecture on 'language as thought' in 1978 stated unequivocally that all three works formed part of a linked chain—was his *Kyōdō Gensō Ron* (On Collective Imaginaries) published in 1968, which will also be discussed in more detail later (Yoshimoto, 1995: 10). This book represents a shift in emphasis from language to society, and is much closer to the kind of enquiry conducted by Yanagita in his 1961 volume *The Ocean Road*, discussed in some detail in the previous chapter.

The fact that Yoshimoto's book was written in the decade immediately following the publication of Yanagita's book, when the debate over the origins of the Japanese, and Japanese culture, was at fever pitch, might hint at a connection between the two, or, at the very least, that Yoshimoto was inspired by Yanagita. This proposition seems entirely plausible, although it is noticeable how many Japanese commentators on the book compare it to the classic study *Les mots et les choses* (The Order of Things, 1966) by the French thinker Michel Foucault (1926–84) rather than any Japanese works. Nakata Hitoshi, the translator of *On Collective Imaginaries* into French (only available on CD-Rom), has even co-authored a book with Yoshimoto basically comparing Yoshimoto's writings to those of Foucault, with a detailed comparison of the two books (Nakata, 1999).

The final volume in the trilogy is *Shinteki Genshōron Josetsu* (An Introduction to Mental Imaginaries) published in 1971, which will not be discussed later. This book concentrates on the mind, on individual and collective psychological structures, and so cites Western thinkers on the same topic such as Sigmund Freud (1856–1939) and Karl Jaspers (1883–1969) extensively. Drawing much more on ideas and methodologies first articulated in *What is Beauty in Respect of Language?* than *On Collective Imaginaries*, Yoshimoto probes the nature of human consciousness, broadly adopting an approach with parallels to Western phenomenonologists working in the hermeneutic tradition of such philosophers as Heidegger and Maurice Merlau-Ponty (1908–61).

This short summary of Yoshimoto's three major theoretical treatises leaves many questions to be answered in the more detailed analyses to follow but one observation needs to be made: despite *Mental Imaginaries* drawing more on Western thinkers than the previous two books, which cite far more Japanese sources, it too is written very much within the context of contemporary Japanese culture. Literally thousands of Japanese literary and intellectual texts are cited in these three books (*Beauty* was published in two volumes), which collectively represent one of the most sustained attempts by a contemporary Japanese thinker to contemplate some of the most fundamental and profound issues facing humanity.

As noted earlier, Yoshimoto conceives of many of these problems as cultural in nature, although 'culture' here covers an extremely wide area. Nevertheless, the contemporary philosopher Yamamoto Tetsuji (discussed in chapter two) has argued that Yoshimoto, especially in these three great works, has not merely established the fundamental basis of postwar Japanese thought but has also gone beyond this to become a major world thinker. Yamamoto is not alone among contemporary Japanese commentators in holding this view (Yamamoto, 1996: 102).

Criticisms of these major works has largely centred around the difficulty that one writer inevitably encounters when trying to cover vast areas of modern thought. It is simply impossible for any one person, no matter how well read (and Yoshimoto's prodigious reading is legendary), or no matter how brilliant he or she may be, to be able to read every important study of the fundamental issues in human or cultural discourse. We shall examine these criticisms in more detail later but one other comment sometimes made about these three works is how Yoshimoto's hatred of Marxism (his anti-Marxist polemic is so strong that only such a word can convey the ferocity of his attacks) leads him, paradoxically, to rely even more upon Marxian categories of thought.

Yoshimoto's writings 1975–2000

Yoshimoto further extended the theoretical structures he had outlined in his 'trilogy' to encompass a large variety of literary, intellectual, and cultural problems in such books as *Haiboku no Kōzō* (The Structure of Defeat, 1992) and *Shiteki Ken'kon* (Poetic Universe, 1974). His 1975 volume *Shomotsu no Kaitaigaku* (An Anatomy of Reading) was his first extended foray into a detailed analysis of major contemporary Western thinkers. The authors he chose to study were: the French novelist Georges Bataille (1897–1962), the French novelist and critic Maurice Blanchot (b.1907), the French novelist and dramatist Jean Genet (1910–86), the French poet Lautréamont (1846–70), the French poet and anthropologist Michel Leiris (b.1901), the American novelist Henry Miller (1891–1980), the French philosopher Gaston Bachelard (1884–1962), the German poet Friedrich Hölderlin (1770–1843) and the Swiss psychiatrist Carl Gustav Jung (1875–1961).

In his previous books, Yoshimoto had discussed many of the major European thinkers and writers, either in part, or in an extended form as part of a larger argument. Moreover, Yoshimoto's detailed analysis of major Japanese writers and texts in previous works far exceeds in quantity his treatment of their Western counterparts. Nevertheless, his choice of writers, for what started out as a serialised set of book reviews treated 'in a somewhat universalised fashion…in a light-hearted way' (Yoshimoto, 1981: 357), is quite revealing, if only because it discloses his liking for writers whose poetics are compact, difficult, and visionary. In his postscript to the volume, Yoshimoto confesses to a lack of knowledge of Western languages and admits that this created a number of problems as he could know the original texts only in translation. He also reveals his reliance on specialists (Yoshimoto, 1981: 357). Yet his treatments of these writers and texts is pitched at a very high level indeed, and his deeply insightful analyses have impressed many readers.

From the mid-1970s, Yoshimoto's writing displays a clear bias towards Japanese literature, with the publication of a large number of studies of Japanese writers, both ancient and modern. His philosophical explorations do not cease but seem to take second place to more directly cultural interests. A book which blends the political and the literary is the 1975 volume *Isshiki Kakumei Uchū* (Consciousness Revolution Universe), which Yoshimoto co-wrote in dialogue form with the novelist Haniya Yutaka (1909–97).

Books written during this period which have a clear focus on culture and literature include his 1976 volume *Saigo no Shinran* (The Last Shinran), a study of the great Buddhist philosopher and religious reformer Shinran (1173–1262); his 1977 work *Shoki Kayō Ron* (A study of Ancient Song-Poetry); his 1978 book (revised and reissued in 1983)

Sengoshiron (A Study of Postwar Poetry), where he castigated contemporary Japanese poets for their solipsistic reliance on language games and their obsession with language as the major theme of their poems; his 1979 critique of postwar Japanese literature *Bungaku no Sengo* (Literature Postwar), co-written as a dialogue with the poet Ayukawa Nobuo (1920–86); the 1981 volume *Kotoba to iu Shisō* (The Philosophy Known as Language); his 1981 book *Shi no Dokkai* (Interpreting Poetry); and his 1982 work *Genji Monogatari Ron* (A Study of *The Tale of Genji*).

In the 1980s Yoshimoto, while not neglecting literature and culture, seemed to return to more intellectual interests. His 1982 volume *Kūkyo to Shite no Shudai* (Subject as Absence) yokes literature and social analysis together but his book *'Hankaku' Iron* (A Contrary View of 'Anti-Nuclear'), published in the same year, takes up the gauntlet of political polemic once again with a measured critique of contemporary social and cultural trends. Other works written during the decade which take a similar approach include: *Shin no Kōzō* (The Structure of Belief, 1983), a study of Japanese Buddhism and Buddhist thinkers; *Masu Imēji Ron* (On Mass Images, 1984), which will be discussed in detail later; *Inton no Kōzō: Ryōkan Ron* (The Structure of Seclusion: On Ryōkan, 1985), a study of the poet and priest Ryōkan (1758–1831); *Shi no Isōgaku* (A Topology of Death, 1985); and *Hai Imēji Ron 1* (On High Images 1, 1989). This last volume was the first of a trilogy titled *Hai Imēji Ron I, II, III*, with the other two published in 1990 and 1994 respectively.

These latter three volumes were the beginning of a major new theoretical series in the 1990s in which Yoshimoto expanded his familiar mix of social, cultural, and literary criticism to include fashion, architecture, cinema, and photography in volume one, economics, mathematics, spatial topography, dialectology in volume two and, in the final volume, more intensive studies of economics and literature. This last trend was emphasised by his 1995 work *Chōshihonshungi* (Super Capitalism), in which Yoshimoto not only probed contemporary Japanese consumer capitalism but explored the links between the economic superstructure and the gas attack on the Tokyo subways by the Aum sect.

In the same decade, Yoshimoto published his *Teihon Yanagita Kunio Ron* (A Complete Study of Yanagita Kunio) volume in 1995, and books on the novelist Shimao Toshio and Ryōkan in 1990 and 1992 respectively. Also in 1992, he collected various essays on contemporary political topics together into one volume entitled *Dai Jōkyō Ron* (The Great State of Affairs). I do not have the space to describe all the important books from among the myriad studies Yoshimoto published in the mid 1990s, but a number of important works deserve mention: his two 1994 volumes *Hichi E* (Towards Anti-Knowledge) and *Jōkyō E* (Towards the State of Affairs), and also *Bokei Ron* (On Matrices), published in 1995.

Yoshimoto returned to the problems raised by religious extremism in the form of the Aum sect in his 1996 volume *Seikimatsu Nyūsu o Kaidokusuru* (Decoding the End-of-the-World News). Here again Yoshimoto's social critique was linked to consumer capitalism. The rise of the Aum sect was the subject of many books during this period, so it is not surprising that Yoshimoto returned to the topic once more in his 1997 book *Daishinsai Aum Go Shisō no Genzō* (Kobe Earthquake After Aum Intellectual Developments).

From the latter half of the 1990s, Yoshimoto also began to publish a series of volumes which were, in part, intellectual autobiographies. The first of these was *Waga 'Tenkō'* (My 'Apostasy', 1997), a personal account of the 1960s movement opposing the re-signing of the Japan-US Security Treaty. This volume was followed in 1999 by *Shōnen* (Youth), a study of the problems of youth with much autobiographical reference. Next was *Haikei no Kioku* (Memories of My Environment, 1999), which was also explicitly autobiographical. However, in addition to autobiography, Yoshimoto also found time for literary and cultural critiques like *[Ketteiban] Shinran* ([Definitive Edition] Shinran, 1999), another augmented study of Shinran, and also his *Shasei no Monogatari* (Tales of Picture-Realism, 2000), a study of various classical Japanese poets, and some modern poets writing traditional verse.

Clearly, Yoshimoto Takaaki's oeuvre is still very much a work in progress. This brief summary of a few of his most significant studies only confirms that many decades will pass before any definitive judgments can be made on this writer, little known outside Japan but surely one of the most important cultural critics of the last fifty years or so. Because none of Yoshimoto's corpus is available in English, the discussion of his three major volumes which follows summarises in some detail the content of these fundamental studies. At the same time, the critical context and reception that these works provoked is subjected to close scrutiny. It is my contention that without a substantial exposition and analysis of both the books and their context it is impossible to understand or appreciate Yoshimoto's contribution to modern Japanese cultural discourse.

The turn to language

In the nearly forty years since Yoshimoto's *What is Beauty in Respect of Language* was published, critical opinion has come to agree that this is one of the most important works ever written by him, and indeed, some commentators regard it as his most significant work. It was originally serialised in the *Shikō* (Test) magazine from September 1961 to June 1965, exactly coinciding with the peak of Yoshimoto's career as a political activist. The commentator Kawakami Haruo has outlined a prehistory of publications preceding the *Shikō* articles; notably, an article published in November 1959 in the journal *Gendai Hihyō* (Modern Criticism) where Yoshimoto declares (as part of a diatribe against the socialist realist school of literary criticism) that there is 'a unique construction of art as language' (Quoted Yoshimoto, 1972: 627).

In a newspaper dialogue published in September 1960, Yoshimoto also discussed his plan to investigate the 'progress from a framework of expression to a framework of cognition' in intellectual or cultural discourse (Yoshimoto, 1972: 627). The scholar Nomura Seiichi further cites an important article entitled 'Gengo no Bigaku to wa Nanika: Tokieda Biron e no Ichi Chūi' (What is the Poetics of Language? A Note on Tokieda Aesthetics) published in March 1960 in which Yoshimoto takes up the aesthetics of the famous linguist Tokieda Motoki (1900–67) (Nomura, 1985: 104). Thus these 'trial' pieces resulted in the *Shikō* series of articles which were then collected and published with minor corrections as two volumes in May and October 1965. This two-volume text was later republished as volume six of the *Collected Writings* in 1972, again with minor changes and corrections. The latest edition of the text is another two-volume set published in 1990 but with substantial revisions designed to make it easier to read. This set has been used as the basic text here.

In the introduction to the 1990 revised edition, Yoshimoto wrote first, that the revisions were done to make the text easier for contemporary readers to grasp, and second, that the study itself was inspired by the desire to create a new theory of literature, and to overcome or go beyond Marxist theories of literature rooted in the doctrine of socialist realism

(Yoshimoto, 1990: 7–8). The revisions point to one feature of Yoshimoto's style which is often criticised: his use of neologisms to express the difficult, and often quite original ideas he wishes to advance.

By inventing his own private critical or technical vocabulary, Yoshimoto sometimes conceals his borrowings from other thinkers, but more importantly, this stylistic mannerism makes it difficult for him to open a dialogue with other thinkers as there is no shared vocabulary in common. Usually Yoshimoto's coinages are taken from scientific or technical jargon but recombined or used in ways unique to himself. Yoshimoto's justification for his style is that he needs to create a new critical vocabulary to properly convey his new ideas.

The first volume of *Beauty* (for the sake of convenience this shorthand title will be used hereafter) is divided into four chapters, but the fourth chapter is almost as long as the first three chapters. This is because the first three chapters (especially the first two) are concerned with constructing Yoshimoto's theory of language, while chapter four applies this theory to the history of modern Japanese prose. Chapter three focuses on phonology and troping, using examples drawn from modern Japanese poetry.

In his introduction, Yoshimoto cites approvingly from the French poet Paul Valéry's (1871–1945) theory of language—he contrasts Valéry's emphasis on the freedom inherent in language with the doctrine of socialist realism, which sees language as a tool for political ends. Thus, argues Yoshimoto, it is not difficult to criticise Marxist theories of language held by such thinkers as the famous Hungarian theorist Georg Lukâcs (1885–1971). This does not prevent Yoshimoto from criticising Lukâcs several times in the book. Another target of criticism is Soviet aesthetics or literary theory which Yoshimoto associates with the 'proletarian' literary movement popular in Japan during the 1930s (Yoshimoto, 1990: 10–17).

Here again we see evidence of the impact of the times on Yoshimoto, as the cold war confrontation between the USA and the Soviet Union formed the background against which his own opposition to the re-signing of the US–Japan Peace Treaty took place. While attempting to establish a political space where Japan could be free of both Soviet and US influence, Yoshimoto also struggled against the dominance of old-fashioned Marxism (as against his revisionist reading of Marx) in Japanese intellectual circles.

Yoshimoto begins from the premise that literature is primarily a linguistic act and in his description of the essence of language (chapter one) proceeds to discuss the origins of language, which he sees as deriving from representations through sounds as the symbolic expression of self-consciousness. Hence Yoshimoto argues that language is self-expression (jiko hyōshutsu). He cites Freud and the German philosopher Ernst Cassirer (1874–1945) as the chief sources for his linkage between individual or subjective self-consciousness and language. Yoshimoto makes a famous distinction between two functions of language: as self-expression and as referent (shijibutsu). This distinction he takes from the celebrated study *The Meaning of Meaning* (eighth revised edition 1946) by the British linguistic philosophers C.K. Ogden (1889–1957) and I.A. Richards (1893–1979). This distinction forms the basis of Yoshimoto's theory of language, and, as his argument proceeds, it is built into a complex set of contradictions or oppositions, as, for example between 'jiko hyōshutsu' (self-expression) and 'shiji hyōshutsu' (referential expression). The similarity of his argument to the Hegelian dialectic is no accident, as shall be argued later (Yoshimoto, 1990: 29–48).

Cassirer's assertion in his most famous study (often cited by Yoshimoto), *The Philosophy of Symbolic Forms* (Vol 1, 1955), that: 'All language as such is "representation"; it represents a specific "meaning" by a sensuous "sign"', could easily be read as a statement by Yoshimoto, so frequently does this viewpoint appear (Cassirer, 1955(1): 125). In the latter half of chapter one, Yoshimoto analyses phonology, using the work of such distinguished Japanese linguists as Tokieda Motoki and Miura Tsutomu (1911–89) as the basis for his discussion. Yoshimoto stresses how reality is objectivised as language or symbol to the subjective self, using examples from classical Japanese poetry to prove his case (Yoshimoto, 1990: 48–60).

In chapter two, entitled 'The Properties of Language', Yoshimoto, citing several literary texts, both modern Japanese novels and classical poetry, analyses meaning. Again using linguists like Miura and Tokieda, Yoshimoto asserts that to equate meaning simply with subjectivity is inadequate. Linguistic meaning, he writes, is the total sum of relationships embodied in the referential expression of the unconscious (Yoshimoto, 1990: 78). Linguistic meaning links us to the other. He discusses the three properties of value, letters (written scripts) and images as constituents of meaning. Dismissing De Saussure's view of linguistic value as flawed, Yoshimoto defines value as 'the relations arising from the whole of language as seen in the self-expression of consciousness as value' (Yoshimoto, 1990: 89).

The use of written scripts separates expression into both the expression of consciousness and the production of consciousness. Images add an extra dimension to meaning: they provide a link between the referential expression of consciousness (i.e. as sign) and the expression of self. In this discussion, Yoshimoto frequently refers to the French philosopher Jean-Paul Sartre's (1905–80) most famous work *L'être et le néant* (tr. as *Being and Nothingness*, 1956) and to the writings of the Japanese critic Fukuda Tsuneari (1912–94). His stress is on liberty—the free interaction between subjectivity and linguistic expression—as opposed to a vulgar or Soviet Marxist straightjacket imposing a rigid ideology of types on literary expression. Commentators generally read this chapter as the first major exposition of Yoshimoto's poetics (Yoshimoto, 1990: 64–113).

Chapter three (on rhythms, tropes etc) begins with an elaboration of Yoshimoto's dictum in the previous chapter that expression can be divided into the two categories of the expression and production of consciousness. These two categories Yoshimoto now defines as oral and written narrative (although, as he makes clear later, literature can encompass both categories in varying proportions). Yoshimoto stresses how rhythm is important in producing meaning. Following Hegel's opinion in his lectures on aesthetics, Yoshimoto sees rhythm as linked to the subjective realm, rather than an attribute of the formal, objective realm. In his discussion of tropes that follows, Yoshimoto divides troping into two types: semantic and imageraic. The former is conventional, while the latter is surrealistic. The analysis of both rhythm and tropes is confined largely to poetry, with numerous modern poems cited.

Yoshimoto then treats modern poetry written in traditional forms (tanka and haiku) and argues for a unique type of troping in which beauty is constructed on a constant shifting of meaning between the two types of troping defined earlier. This reading of traditional verse, Yoshimoto argues, is entirely new, as previously such poetry was analysed from the perspective of meaning, where the author is the chief focus. Yoshimoto derides this approach as just prose with rhythm. Finally, he treats tropes in modern prose narrative, with several examples from authors like the Nobel prize winner for literature Ōe Kenzaburō. He argues that narrativity—transpositions or shifts in narrative voice—is an important type of trope (Yoshimoto, 1990:114–56).

Language as literary history

Chapter four applies the theoretical model of language developed in the previous three chapters to a history of modern Japanese prose from the late nineteenth century to the late 1950s. Thus this last chapter in volume one of *Beauty* is a rewriting of modern Japanese literary history. Yoshimoto's chief targets appear to be the famous literary critics Nakamura Mitsuo (1911–88) and Hirano Ken (1907–78). Nakamura wrote an influential literary history entitled *Nihon no Kindai Shōsetsu* (Modern Japanese Fiction) in 1954, and Hirano wrote a history of equal importance entitled *Shōwa Bungaku Shi* (A History of Shōwa Literature), published in 1951. Hirano took an explicitly Marxist approach to literary history while Nakamura took a comparative viewpoint (he was originally a specialist in French). Yoshimoto criticises both books numerous times in this chapter, and, therefore, offered a completely new reading of modern Japanese literature that stands in stark opposition to the dominant models represented by Nakamura and Hirano.

Yoshimoto's starting point for his new history of modern Japanese prose is language, so his reading of literature can be seen as essentially rhetorical. In this respect, his standpoint resembles the school of formal or rhetorical criticism called the New Criticism that emerged in the Anglo-American scholarly world at about the same time. Even more interesting is the fact that the New Criticism drew upon many of the same sources as Yoshimoto for its 'scientific' formulation of formal principles of criticism.

For example, in the 1949 volume (often cited as representative of 'New Criticism') *Theory of Literature* written by the scholars René Welleck (b.1903) and Austin Warren, one of the chief sources of authority cited is I.A. Richards (Welleck and Warren, 1973: 16, 140ff). Moreover, the critic Jonathan Culler traces the rise of New Criticism back to the poet T.S. Eliot's (1888–1965) *The Sacred Wood* (1920), through the writings of Richards and his pupil William Empson (1906–84) to Welleck and Warren (Culler, 1988: 9–11). However, despite parallels, Yoshimoto's rhetorical technique of criticism is essentially his own, and, unlike the 'New Criticism', his methodology never achieved a dominant position in Japanese critical discourse, which, though splintered into several traditions, for modern literature at least, has been more influenced by Nakamura and Hirano.

I will not describe chapter four in detail but will focus on several of Yoshimoto's insights into literary history that illustrate his distinctive rhetorical (or linguistic) technique and his originality, often to be found in his close readings of various prose texts. It should also be noted that Yoshimoto's arguments in this section of volume one are articulated almost entirely in the context of Japanese readings of modern Japanese prose, and he rarely mentions any non-Japanese critics (theoretical or otherwise). One of Yoshimoto's principles is his division of style into 'literary style' (bungakutai) and 'oral style' (watai) but by this he does not mean oral or written transmission, rather, these are rhetorical types or categories of expression (as noted earlier) which often overlap. Linguistic type is his principle of recognition, not 'influence' in the conventional literary historical sense (focusing on theme) or the Marxist literary sense (Yoshimoto, 1990: 175–7).

Yoshimoto praises the works of Kōda Rohan (1867–1947) for an innovative move from the literary to the colloquial, both categories deriving from Yoshimoto's own unique schema. He argues that Kōda's novels have an affinity with Futabatei Shimei's (1864–1909) famous novel—often called the first Japanese modern novel—*Ukigumo* (Floating Clouds, 1888). This viewpoint runs contrary to received opinion which holds that Kōda's work is not modern (Yoshimoto, 1990: 190–201). Yoshimoto also asserts that Kunikida Doppo's (1871–1908) novel *Musashino* (Musashino Plain, 1901) portrays landscape as a state of mind or perception, as well as place. This argument is remarkably close to the contemporary literary critic Karatani Kōjin's (b.1941) much-praised thesis in his 1980 study *Nihon Kindai Bungaku no Kigen* (Origins of Japanese Literature) that *Musashino* is among the first modern novels to 'overturn values' in respect of landscape (Yoshimoto, 1990: 207–8; Karatani, 1988: 25).

Yoshimoto also takes up relatively obscure writers such as Suzuki Miekichi (1882–1936) who he praises for the extravagant metaphors in his writing and for his sophisticated use of narrative perspective. Yoshimoto compares Suzuki to the much more famous Izumi Kyōka (1873–1939) who, he argues, did much the same. Again, Yoshimoto's thesis bears some similarity to the much-acclaimed 1980 study *Shōsetsu no Nihongo* (The Language of the Novel) by the contemporary critic Noguchi Takehiko (b.1937) (Yoshimoto, 1990: 211–22; Noguchi, 1980: 211–34). These arguments are put in the context of opposition to the theses of Nakamura and Hirano that 1906 was the year the naturalist novel was born in Japan.

Yoshimoto's reading of postwar literary history is also innovative, with his emphasis on the different dimensions of time represented within postwar novels. This argument leads him to characterise postwar writing as divided into two separate categories: novels of continuity and novels of rupture. In his discussion of immediate postwar fiction, Yoshimoto also proposes a sophisticated re-reading of the relationship between narrative and author which seems to anticipate the American literary critic Wayne Booth's notion of the 'implied author' as expounded in Booth's influential 1988 study *The Company We Keep: An Ethics of Reading* (Yoshimoto, 1990: 318–32; Booth, 1988: 128, 438–57).

Chapter five commences volume two of *Beauty* and in this long chapter (approximately half the book) Yoshimoto rewrites the history of classical Japanese poetry and prose along the same lines as the final chapter of volume one. Again, he stresses the importance of the aesthetic evaluation of texts, in other words, text criticism is the linguistic or formal basis of his methodology. Discussing poetry, he emphasises the aesthetic notion of 'composition' rather than the stress on genre categorisation by traditional schools of Japanese criticism. By 'composition' (kōsei) Yoshimoto means the internal structure of classical poems or songs (Yoshimoto, 1990a: 9–35).

Yoshimoto's view of Orikuchi Shinobu and Yanagita Kunio, the two pioneers of the school of reading literature as ethnology or sociological history, is complex. He praises both writers for their grand visions linking the history of Japanese religiosity with the birth of poetry (or song) but at the same time he often criticises them (Yoshimoto, 1990a: 35–46). He is even more critical of scholars like Saigō Nobutsuna (b.1916) who, especially in his celebrated study *Nihon Kodai Bungakushi* (The History of Classical Japanese Literature, 1951, rev. ed. 1963), took an historical approach to ancient Japanese song, attempting to contextualise the historical evolution of Japanese poetry against a reading of social history. Yoshimoto's analysis of numerous classical poems essentially sees them in figural or tropical terms (Yoshimoto, 1990a: 49–74).

His readings of classical prose are similar, stressing the internal shifts from poetry to prose in such structural features as fictionality. Yoshimoto's concern with fictional elements in prose composition is partially indebted to Orikuchi's research, as he acknowledges (Yoshimoto, 1990a:

96–103). Yoshimoto here, as in chapter four of volume one, focuses on narrativity, arguing that narrative technique is fundamental to the development of advanced prose narratives like the eleventh-century masterpiece *Genji Monogatari* (The Tale of Genji). As Yoshimoto writes: 'The composition of literary works indicates shifts in modes resulting from the expansion of language as seen in semantic production' (Yoshimoto, 1990a: 118).

Yoshimoto's treatment of drama is equally innovative. He criticises theorists like the German dramatist Bertolt Brecht (1898–1956) and Fukuda Tsuneari and emphasises how dramatic literature borrows linguistically from other genres of prose narrative. This shift from drama as tale to drama as expression is primarily a linguistic shift, although it also reflects a change in the audience, and thus in audience expectation (Yoshimoto, 1990a: 134–62). Yoshimoto's analysis becomes more directly historical as he moves on from medieval drama to the Kabuki and Bunraku theatres of the eighteenth and nineteenth centuries. He focuses on the theme of suicide in the classic plays of Chikamatsu Monzaemon to argue that the reason fidelity is the greatest virtue of Chikamatsu's lovers (hence leading to suicide when the lovers' desires cannot be realised) is because of the historical oppression of women. Consequently, Chikamatsu's dramas are ideal fantasies, an idea he borrowed from the poet and theorist Kitamura Tōkoku (1868–94) but which he develops into a larger thesis that modern drama has inherited this as a universal paradox (Yoshimoto, 1990a: 177–214).

Chapter six is a series of reflections on the perennial aesthetic problem of form versus content. Yoshimoto cites a large array of theorists ranging from such Western critics as Hegel, V.G. Belinski (1811–48), Georgi Plekhanov (1857–1918) and Lukács to such Japanese critics as Kurahara Korehito (b.1902), Akutagawa Ryūnosuke (1892–1927), Kobayashi Hideo (1902–83) and Tanikawa Tetsuzō (1895–1989). Apart from Hegel, who Yoshimoto admires, most of the Western critics are vulgar Marxists or vulgar Hegelians who understand neither Marx nor Hegel. On the other hand, for the most part the Japanese critics do understand Hegel correctly so they receive a more appreciative treatment. Yoshimoto's view is: 'Form is [defined as] seeing literary works as an expansion of linguistic self-expression while content is [defined as] viewing literary works as referential expression' (Yoshimoto, 1990a: 223).

The next and last chapter of *Beauty* is one of the most theoretical, in which Yoshimoto attempts to both summarise his earlier views and also to synthesise a view of language and its relationship to meaning in the modern world, and to signs and images in general. He dismisses most contemporary philosophers of language as failing to recognise a fundamental split in modern consciousness: the rupture between language as communication and language as expression. This rupture or alienation is inherent in modern linguistic structures and extends to sign systems as well. The examples Yoshimoto cites to illustrate this rupture are mostly drawn from contemporary Japanese poetry. Language has become displaced from meaning: the poetry of authors like Minoru Yoshioka (1919–90) demonstrates this unequivocally, argues Yoshimoto (Yoshimoto, 1990a: 260). Thus 'collective imaginaries' (gensō no kyōdo-sei), which here means socio-linguistic structures, contain within themselves many layers of meaning, including such complex concepts as alienation, both as an emotional and conceptual dimension, which leads to a double perspective (Yoshimoto, 1990a: 254–77).

Discussing the notion of value, Yoshimoto observes that while experience is individual, desires are shared and are therefore common concepts. Thus he reads Richard's famous *Principles of Literary Criticism* (1924) as establishing that the value of literary work is to create order out of disordered desire, or disordered individual psychologies. But Richards ignores the fundamental importance of language, as Yoshimoto notes: 'The value of literature which is inherent in the artistic expression of language cannot be reduced to consciousness. It thrusts forward outside consciousness, towards the internal structure of expression' (Yoshimoto, 1990a: 282). Yoshimoto's views here strongly resemble modern hermeneutic philosophers like Hans-Georg Gadamer. Finally, Yoshimoto discusses theoretical spaces and sign systems. This discussion deals mainly with Sartre's notion of sign, which Yoshimoto eventually dismisses as inadequate as a theorisation of linguistic construct (Yoshimoto, 1990a: 289–305).

This summary of the two volumes merely notes Yoshimoto's most important points; it cannot convey the sense of newness and freshness that strikes readers even today when they encounter this work. Yoshimoto's unique schema virtually rewrites the whole history of Japanese literature, from the earliest times to the modern era. His judgments originate in his novel and complex distinction between language used for self-expression and for reference. Despite his borrowings from elsewhere, in essence Yoshimoto's conceptualisation of this distinction is entirely his own. This simple binary contrast itself understates the complexity and power of Yoshimoto's approach to literary history and criticism alike—so different from methodologies adopted hitherto that his new paradigm reveals entirely new readings of works long consigned to fixed categories of judgment.

How much of the freshness and interpretative power of his readings of Japanese literature are due to his methodology, and how much to his own intuitive judgment is an open question—the balance between his language-based methodology and his own superb hermeneutic skills is finely maintained, and makes it difficult to distinguish between the two. His discussion of theoretical semantics and philology is exceedingly sophisticated and, as noted earlier, his novel theory anticipates much of the new structuralist language-based criticism that was soon to arrive in Japan from abroad. Let us now examine in detail how *Beauty* was received in Japan in order to fully comprehend its impact upon readers and the underlying intellectual context of this landmark of cultural criticism.

Contemporary reactions to Beauty

Kawakami Haruo wrote in the postscript to the 1990 edition of *Beauty* that the definitive critique of the work had yet to be produced (Kawakami, 1990: 308). However, by the time he wrote this, a large number of critiques and commentaries had been published on the work in Japan. Kawakami also noted that Yoshimoto discussed more than 500 major literary works in the study and this explains why so many critiques of the work generally concentrate only on one or two aspects, rather than attempting to criticise the two volumes as a whole.

Linguists and scholars of language generally view Yoshimoto's arguments as part of a dialogue with Tokieda Motoki (the pre-eminent theorist of language at the time) and assess him accordingly. Nomura Seiichi notes that, unlike the study of Japanese literature in Japan, which is fragmented and open to influences from abroad, Japanese language study in Japan has remained aloof from foreign influences throughout the twentieth century. Nomura here is discussing 'kokugo' or studies of the Japanese language from within the traditional mainstream of teaching Japanese in schools and universities, not studies of language in general or studies of foreign languages. Thus Nomura locates Yoshimoto within the traditional system of discourse, or as it is characterised in this book, insider discourse. Tokieda is the major figure in insider discourse on language and so it was only natural that Yoshimoto took issue with him (Nomura, 1985: 103–7).

Nomura has documented several articles by Yoshimoto prior to the publication of *Beauty* in which Yoshimoto engages in a dialogue with Tokieda. But Tokieda himself wrote in 1966 that he could not understand Yoshimoto's arguments in *Beauty* (Quoted Nomura, 1985: 106). Other linguistic critics like Okubo Tadayoshi and the poet and scholar Fujii Sadakazu argue that Yoshimoto's emphasis is quite different from Tokieda, and so should not be linked to him. On the other hand, Nomura asserts that Yoshimoto understood Tokieda's theory better than most and was ahead of his time in pointing out the problems in Tokieda (Nomura, 1985: 108–9). Nomura summarises his argument that both writers were quite similar by emphasising that both men worked from the same 'nationalistic' (i.e. insider) base, they both opposed Stalinism, and both were critical of Saussurian linguistics (Nomura, 1985: 110–13).

Another scholar of linguistics, Isotani Takashi, working from a background of cultural semiotics or Tartu semiotics, praises Yoshimoto highly for anticipating much of the theory which was introduced into Japan from the West a little later. He argues that Yoshimoto differs from linguists such as himself because he 'intends a theory of expression as thought' but contemporary linguists' 'intention is science' (Isotani, 1985: 123). Isotani finds Yoshimoto to be a kind of cultural semiotician since Yoshimoto puts such stress on consciousness whereas linguists have abandoned the notion of consciousness in their analyses. In this respect, Yoshimoto is closer to older linguists such as I. A. Richards and Roman Jakobson (1896–1982), the influential Russian/American thinker (Isotani, 1985: 124–6). However, much in *Beauty* is useful and well ahead of its time since at the time of its publication nothing resembling the sophistication of Yoshimoto's approach was available in Japanese (Isotani, 1985: 138–9).

In the Marxian feminist Kōno Nobuko's (b. 1927) study of Yoshimoto's thought published in 1986, Kōno emphasises Hegelian influences, arguing that Yoshimoto's logical base is the Hegelian dialectic (Kōno, 1986: 13). Kōno praises Yoshimoto's conceptualisation of literary expression and his sophisticated notion of subjectivity in which the self is constructed through language (Kōno, 1986: 37, 64). We see here how Kōno construes (partially, at least) Yoshimoto's arguments as a reaction to the debate on subjectivity (shutaisei) which had been in full cry in 'progressive' literary circles since the end of World War II (Koschmann, 1996: 45, 41–87). But, as we have seen, Yoshimoto wrote *Beauty* specifically in order to oppose what he described as simplistic Marxist notions of history and subjectivity. Kōno finally declares that Yoshimoto tried to go beyond Hegel's aesthetic theory but failed (Kōno, 1986: 73).

The philosopher Takeda Seiji in his study of Yoshimoto also concluded that Hegel was the dominant influence on *Beauty*. He argues that Yoshimoto's dual concepts of self-expression and referential expression owed much to Hegel's distinction between 'an sich' and 'für sich' or intrinsic and extrinsic consciousness (Takeda, 1996: 198). Takeda's view is that Yoshimoto's notion of self-expression is a subjective expression of the self conceived in relation to a self-consciously realised notion of the other, whereas referential expression is the other seen in terms of the relationship between self and the other. Thus the latter notion conceives of the other as a provisional fact. Then it follows that if the referentiality of language is provisionally conceived of as fact, a notion of self being a production of relation is possible. This view is, in Takeda's eyes, essentially the same as the conceptual categories Hegel creates to imagine or characterise the world (Takeda, 1996: 198–9).

Takeda also likens Yoshimoto's notion of referent to De Saussure's famous concept of 'langue', and Yoshimoto's notion of self to De Saussure's concept of 'parole' (Takeda, 1996: 201). Comparing Yoshimoto's views on the origins and evolution of language to De Saussure's, Takeda notes that Yoshimoto's arguments may seem a little belated but they are actually more advanced when considered as analytic linguistic theory. The reason that some critics see *Beauty* as inferior to structuralist linguistics introduced from the West not long after the publication of the book is because of the vagueness and ambiguity of Yoshimoto's terminology (Takeda, 1996: 190). Takeda especially singles out for praise Yoshimoto's theory of meaning. He finds Yoshimoto's hypotheses superior to contemporary Japanese critics like Karatani Kōjin, and to contemporary Western critics like Gilles Deleuze (b.1925) (Takeda, 1996: 197, 211-12).

Insider semiotics: Karatani on Yoshimoto

Karatani Kōjin in a much-quoted essay first published in 1982 squarely locates Yoshimoto's intellectual endeavours, and most notably *Beauty*, into a context of insider discourse. He argues that Yoshimoto is trying to build a system that can withstand the winds of foreign influence that have determined Japan's culture hitherto (Karatani, 1996: 246). He compares *Beauty* to the great writer Natsume Sōseki's (1867–1916) *Bungakuron* (Theory of Literature, 1906), claiming both men had great ambitions 'to speak like a master' but Yoshimoto chose to attack Marxism (Karatani, 1996: 242–3). Karatani defends Yoshimoto from the attacks on *Beauty* by young Japanese scholars enamoured of French structural and semiotic thought. Their views are superficial, they do not understand *Beauty* at all, he writes (Karatani, 1996: 247).

Karatani makes the point that by attempting to escape from Marxist categories of thought, Yoshimoto became inextricably entwined in them: his system of linguistic analysis is based on a dialectical methodology. He also claims that Yoshimoto's discourse—which he criticises several times for its convoluted neologisms—clearly attacks bourgeois notions of subjectivity, as Yoshimoto's concept of self in *Beauty* has a reflective, relational aspect (Karatani, 1996: 248–50). Karatani also argues that Yoshimoto's categories of self and referential expression are based entirely on Marx's distinction between 'value' and 'use-value' in his famous study *Capital*. Therefore the relationship between the two poles that Yoshimoto posits is a relational, dialectical connection. This discovery, Karatani writes, he only made many years after reading *Beauty* (Karatani, 1996: 251–5).

In a series of brilliant analogies, Karatani explains why he believes Yoshimoto stopped short in his analysis of language. Just as Karl Marx saw the importance of money in the economic superstructure, but the economist John Maynard Keynes only saw a probability analysis, so the young Yoshimoto stopped short at elaborating the fundamentals. Hence *Beauty* is overwhelmingly a study of methodology, a merely structural analysis, not the truly revolutionary study it had the potential to be (Karatani, 1996: 256–7).

Karatani castigates the dominant theoretical discourse in currency at present: semiotics, structuralism etc. use the vocabulary of science but are in no sense scientific, and such vocabulary is barely understood by its practitioners. He argues that De Saussure's ideas, in particular, have not been understood in Japan, as the history of the reception of these ideas is a history of mistranslation and misunderstanding. To a lesser degree, the same is true of De Saussure's reception in France. But, despite Yoshimoto's immense debt to Marx, the notions of language he advocates are closest to De Saussure (Karatani, 1996: 258–61). Earlier, however, Karatani had argued that *Beauty* has no connection to De Saussure or Tokieda, despite several indirect borrowings from both (Karatani, 1996: 258). Finally, Karatani reiterates his belief that *Beauty* is an isolated work, isolated from other studies by Yoshimoto, and isolated from its times. This, however, does not detract from its immense importance (Karatani, 1996: 240–61).

It is fascinating how Karatani has anticipated several revisions, or at least, rethinkings by Yoshimoto himself about *Beauty* and its significance. In his preface to the edition of *An Introduction to Mental Imaginaries* published in his *Collected Works* in 1973, Yoshimoto notes that his views on language have often been criticised on the grounds that foreign philosophers of language had superseded them. But he does not accept this even now (Yoshimoto, 1973: 6). Nevertheless, the fact that soon after *Beauty* was published, a wave of (mainly) French semiotic, structuralist, and poststructuralist linguistic writings washed up on the shores of the Japanese intellectual world and did much to erase his own contribution, and to lessen his impact, must have deeply disappointed him. The insider thinker once again had been thwarted by outsider philosophers.

Moreover, in *On High Images II* (1990), Yoshimoto admits his analysis of De Saussure's ideas in *Beauty* was based on a misunderstanding of De Saussure's major theoretical treatise *Cours de linguistique générale* (Course in General Linguistics, 1916), a reconstruction of lecture notes and other materials by two students. This misunderstanding arises, notes Yoshimoto, out of the fact that this seminal text is itself a reconstruction, and also because the Japanese version Yoshimoto consulted contained numerous errors in translation. Now having access to a new Japanese translation, Yoshimoto revised his views, although he still differs in several respects from De Saussure. In the same essay, he also acknowledges his reliance on Marx's analysis of currency for his basic model of language (Yoshimoto, 1990: 44–59).

The connection between Marx's discussion of value and Yoshimoto's views on value have been commented on in a recent essay by the scholar

Takahashi Jun'ichi who cites two definitions of first, meaning, and then, value, from *An Introduction to Mental Imaginaries* to argue that these views go far beyond contemporary linguistics. These definitions are for meaning: 'The meaning of language is the sum total of all the relations inherent in the linguistic structures which are seen as referents to consciousness'; and for value: 'We can describe the sum total of relations inherent in linguistic structures seen from the self-expression of consciousness as value' (Quoted Takahashi, 1996: 99). This is not poststructuralist or semiotic analysis, argues Takahashi, but something superior: a rewriting (inspired by Marx's theory of value) of linguistic theory based on language itself (Takahashi, 1996: 99). In other words, Takahashi is making a similar claim for Yoshimoto as was made for the 'New Critics'.

There can be no doubt that Yoshimoto borrowed from Marx. Essentially Yoshimoto applies Marx's notion of value, especially his insight in *Capital* that 'value can only manifest itself in the social relation of commodity to commodity', to language (Marx, 1952: 19). This conception of value becomes for Yoshimoto a paradigm or model which he follows as he develops his thesis of linguistic contradiction between expression and referent. But Hegel's theory of aesthetics may be of even more importance. In Hegel's lectures on aesthetics we find the following passage:

'In this sense we may say that the content is at first subjective, something purely inward, with the subjective standing over against it, so that now this gives rise to a demand that the subjective be objectified. Such an opposition between the subjective and the objective contrasted with it, as well as the fact that it ought to be transcended, is simply a universal characteristic running through everything.... Now since the content of our interests and aims is present at first only in the one-sided form of subjectivity, and the one-sidedness is a restriction, this deficiency shows itself at the same time as an unrest, a grief, as something negative. This, as negative, has to cancel itself...'

Hegel, 1975: 96

In this classic statement of Hegelian dialectic, we can find the heart of Yoshimoto's theory of aesthetics or linguistic oppositions. The power that this methodology has in interpreting literature determines its usefulness. In Yoshimoto's literary history, it becomes a powerful tool indeed, leading to insights only taken up by later critics. So, in this respect, the positive re-evaluation in Japan of Yoshimoto's system that we can detect over the past two decades from our survey of the reaction to *Beauty* is justified. Perhaps the most interesting characteristic of *Beauty* is that as a late-twentieth-century product of insider discourse, it speaks as much to, and borrows as much from outsider discourse as internal 'nativist' intellectual currents.

Collective Imaginaries (1968)

Collective Imaginaries is probably the most widely read of Yoshimoto's three major theoretical treatises. The scholar Miura Sukeyuki has written that it was the 'bible' of its era for young people (Miura, 1988: 108). It is also cited frequently by scholars working in the humanities. Furuhashi Nobuyoshi, perhaps the pre-eminent scholar of ancient Japanese poetry today, uses the argument in this book as his basic working model, and he is not alone (Furuhashi, 1995; 1998). The eminent feminist scholar Ueno Chizuko cites the book as a basic starting point for historical discussions of gender (Ueno, 1998: 117). The reason why this study is the most popular of the three probably stems from first, the volume's readability: it is easily the most accessible of the three treatises, with an absence of convoluted neologisms and, second, the content is, in a way, less theoretical than Yoshimoto's other two studies, as it treats Japanese society and the state, topics which are commonly of more interest to the general reader.

The first six chapters (they are called 'studies' [ron] not chapters but this amounts to the same thing) were published between November 1966 and April 1967 in the *Bungei* (Literature) journal. Five newly written chapters, and a new introduction, were added to make up a single volume, first published under the title of *Kyōdō Gensō Ron* (Collective Imaginaries) in December 1968. Typographical errors were corrected for the volume's appearance in the *Collected Works* (1972) but no other changes were made. This is the edition used here.

In the introduction, Yoshimoto justified the need for the book by citing the desire for people to create their own independent conceptual world apart from a shared, collective conceptual world, a desire frustrated by the two worlds intermingling. He also discusses the sociologist Karl Wittfogel's (1896–1941) thesis expressed in his *Oriental Despotism* (1955) that Japan does not fall into Marx's category of the 'Asiatic mode of production' because of its politics and economy. Yoshimoto disputes this, arguing that Japanese internal conceptual systems are borrowed from Asia. His justification for this common Asian imaginary seems remarkably close to the arguments that Yanagita Kunio put forward in *The Ocean Road* (Yoshimoto, 1972a: 5–11).

Yoshimoto defines 'collective imaginary' (kyōdō gensō) thus: 'Here collective imaginary means…the entire conceptual world outside of the psychological worlds of individual humans and their products…. It indicates not humans as individuals, but the proper shapes of concepts that connect to this world as a kind of collectivity' (Yoshimoto, 1972a: 11). This notion is needed, argues Yoshimoto, to fill two conceptual gaps left by *Beauty*: What kind of psychological structure does subjectivity have? And, how is the individual placed in the world? Yoshimoto discusses the Marxist answer to these questions.

The collective imaginary which includes politics, the state, religion and law precedes production and science, it precedes the Marxist notion of the mode of production as a fundamental conceptualisation of society. The collective imaginary, and its corollary, the individual imaginary, is a universal, a conceptual frame that encompasses the world. Totems, customs, myths, religion, law, and the state are all expressions of the collective imaginary which has as its chief material objects cultural anthropology and ancient history, although the notion of a collective imaginary transcends these spheres (Yoshimoto, 1972a: 18–35).

The term 'collective imaginary' appears to derive from the concept of 'représentations collectives' (group ideas) found in the writings of Lucien Lévy-Bruhl, who Yoshimoto frequently cites in this book. Lévy-Bruhl borrowed this idea from the French sociologist Emile Durkheim (1858–1917) in his attempt to account for the differences between primitive and modern people. Lévy-Bruhl stressed the social origin of collective representations governing the mentality of primitive people.

Another notion borrowed from Durkheim which Lévy-Bruhl utilised is 'conscience collective' (collective consciousness), which also seems to have influenced Yoshimoto's notion. In his 1926 study *Les Functions mentales dans les sociétés primitives* (translated as *How Natives Think*), Lévy-Bruhl argues: 'Should not the representations and the connections between the representations be of the same nature? Are they not necessarily a "collective representation"?…both theory and postulate deal with the mental process of the *individual human* mind only.

Collective representations are social phenomena like the institutions for which they account…' (Lévy-Bruhl, 1979: 23). As we shall see, these views clearly resemble Yoshimoto's.

Yoshimoto's use of the term 'gensō' (imaginary) bears some similarity to the French psychoanalyst Jacques Laçan's (1901–81) use of the word 'l'imaginaire' (imaginary) in which the imaginary is the world, the dimension of images, conscious and unconscious; specifically, the subject's relation to an image exterior to him (Grosz, 1989: xviii ff.). But it is unlikely that either had read the other as early as the late 1960s and therefore the possibility of influence on Yoshimoto is negligible.

The first three chapters deal with tabus, (spirit) possession, and seers respectively. The chapter on tabus (kinseiron) focuses on tabus relating to sexuality (incest etc.) and power. Yoshimoto cites Freud's study *Totem and Taboo* (1912–13) where Freud links the tabus inherent in neuroses to those of primitive society. This linkage originates in Freud's belief that there is a congruence between the primitive and neurotic modes of thinking (Gay, 1988: 327). Yoshimoto disagrees with this thesis and argues that one cannot generalise directly from abnormality to normality. Nevertheless, he applies some of Freud's insights to Yanagita Kunio's 1910 work *The Legends of Tōno*, and argues that tabus revealed in these tales fall into two categories: the collective imaginary and the binary imaginary (taigensō), a concept Yoshimoto develops later to refer to individual imaginaries. The tales dealing with fear in *Tōno Legends* can read as relating to individual or collective experience (Yoshimoto, 1972a: 36–54).

Commenting on a passage from Ōoka Shōhei's (1909–88) acclaimed novel *Nobi* (Fires on the Plain, 1952), Yoshimoto argues Ōoka's depiction of a déjà-vu state is an individual imaginary arising from an abnormal fear. This Yoshimoto contrasts with 'dead daughter' and 'disappearance' tales or dreams in various works by Yanagita to argue that such tales concerning the fear of strangers or the punishment meted out to those who break tabus arise from the collective imaginary of the Japanese village. Fears of this type in modern Japan arise, therefore, from a mixture of the two imaginaries (Yoshimoto, 1972a: 54–62).

The second chapter, concerning spirit possession (hyōjinron), again focuses on *Tōno Legends* to create a link between the modern déjà-vu state captured by Ōoka and the desire to escape, to dream that is found in Yanagita's writings. These desires arise from the collective imaginary created by the Tōno tales. Such desires are 'neither abnormal nor pathological', states Yoshimoto (Yoshimoto, 1972a: 65). They symbolise the change from a collective to an individual imaginary and in psycho-analytical terms create a state close to narcolepsy (falling into deep sleep unexpectedly) or epilepsy. Yoshimoto argues that the American thinker William James (1842–1910) described similar states in his famous 1902 study *The Varieties of Religious Experience* when he discussed the loss of the individual to religious experience (i.e. an individual being possessed).

Yoshimoto examines tales of prophecy or omens in *Tōno Legends* and finds that such experiences indicate a hidden desire to be 'other', the same impulse behind spirit possession. Normally, he observes, the collective imaginary is opposed to individual imaginaries but this is not the case in the Tōno tales. There, the two imaginaries work together. Hence, tales of fox possession reflect the actual social reality of rural poverty (Yoshimoto, 1972a: 65–8).

The chapter on seers begins with a quotation from the novelist Ryūnosuke Akutagawa's (1892–1927) story *Haguruma* (Cogwheels, 1927) where the narrator is musing on death, his self-reflections being triggered by seeing himself in a mirror. The crisis of the doppelgänger is, argues Yoshimoto, a crisis of the self—a confusion between self as other and other as self. This crisis creates a somnabulistic state which echoes similar states described by Sasaki Kizen (1886–1933)—a Tōno informant and collaborator with Yanagita—in the *Tōno Monogatari Shūi* (Tōno Tale Collection, 1935), a collection of tales added to the original 1910 volume. In these tales, the collective imaginary creates similar lethargic states as projections of death. But the anomie of modern life, as revealed in Akutagawa's story, cannot be resolved without escaping from the collective imaginary of traditional village society. On the other hand, notes Yoshimoto, 'The desire to return to the collective imaginary of urban working class society is frustrated by suicide, but this frustration represents a search for a kind of liberation from all imaginaries' (Yoshimoto, 1972a: 89).

We see here how the individual imaginary is confused by, caught up with the collective imaginary. Yoshimoto then discusses women who are mediums or seers in these tales. He disagrees with Yanagita's interpretations of these women, arguing that women who are possessed are symbolic of the collective imaginary in that they represent contemporary gender issues and marital problems arising from conflicts between the two imaginaries (Yoshimoto, 1972a: 89–100).

Collective Imaginaries (1968): The Sexual Imaginary

In the preceding three chapters, Yoshimoto has traced the socio-religious base of the modern Japanese state, and argued that the clash between the individual and the collectivity embodied in the village has created a sense of rupture or alienation that continues to the present day. Thus, to this point, we can see how he has been elaborating a thesis first proposed in *Beauty*. But the next four chapters move in a different direction: to investigate issues of gender and sexuality. Chapter four is concerned with female mediums or shamans (mikoron) and introduces a thread occurring at the end of the previous chapter that eventually leads to Yoshimoto's concept of 'binary imaginaries' in chapter eight.

Yoshimoto considers the question of why mediums are generally female. He argues that in oral tradition, and therefore, in the collective imaginary of the village, mediums are sexual objects. He cites Freud on object cathexis, how the self develops in resistance to the opposite sex, and, using Freud's insight, turns again to the Tōno tales. At this point, Yoshimoto proposes the notion of a binary imaginary as a contrary or opposing force to the collective imaginary. However, unlike individual imaginaries, binary imaginaries are predicated on gender oppositions. From the Tōno tales he cites instances of mediums as objects of desire (usually of the gods) who therefore violate tabus and threaten the order of the collective imaginary. He stresses the ritualistic or symbolic aspects or functions of female shamans who represent an uncanny force, a presence alienated from the 'home' of the collective imaginary (Yoshimoto, 1972a: 101–19).

In the next chapter on the other world (takairon), Yoshimoto begins with a quotation from Martin Heidegger's *Sein und Zeit* (Being and Time, 1927) on death as an imagined experience. For Heidegger death is, writes Yoshimoto, 'a mentally "constructed" imaginary, not a mentally "experienced" imaginary' (Yoshimoto, 1972a: 120). This 'intentional' (in the philosophical sense) or constructed notion is contained within the collective imaginary. Primitive people see death as part of the collective imaginary but modern people see it simply as destruction. For evidence of the former assertion, Yoshimoto cites various Tōno tales, and also Lévy-Bruhl's *How Natives Think*.

Next Yoshimoto considers the idea of the 'other world' where old people go to die. In the Tōno tales (both the 1910 and 1935 collections) there are numerous stories of old people being driven out of their communities. This happens because the existence of these elderly people is in opposition to the collective interest of the village. Consequently, as Heidegger notes, 'the other world' does not merely transcend individual biological death but is constructed intentionally on the borders of the village (Yoshimoto, 1972a: 132). Citing various Japanese writers on ceremonial burial, Yoshimoto links Yanagita's division of burials into ceremonial and non-ceremonial categories to notions of the other world and concludes: 'The purging of the collective imaginary [in the modern world] into the categories of individual and binary imaginaries means the death of the collective imaginary as symbolised by the notion of "other world"' (Yoshimoto, 1972a: 138).

Chapter six is concerned with rituals (saigiron), initially as a source of information on the origins of the individual imaginary. Citing Hegel's *Phenomenology of the Mind* (1807), Yoshimoto investigates the development of self-consciousness in the child, the development of ego in the womb. The rituals relating to birth among primitive peoples portray birth (and death) as part of a continuous process, thus life is part of death, and vice versa. Yoshimoto uses the ancient Japanese mythohistorical chronicle the *Kojiki* as his source for narratives which support this hypothesis. Female fecundity and sexuality thus become a metaphor for agriculture: myths relating to goddesses birthing numerous beings reflect the shift in ancient Japan from a hunter–gatherer to a cultivating society. Even more than the Tōno tales, the myths and rituals collected in the *Kojiki* demonstrate the process of transformation, of birth to life; such mythology makes up the basic iconography of the collective imaginary (Yoshimoto, 1972a: 139–49).

Using Japanese scholarship on ritual, Yoshimoto investigates ceremonies relating to rice planting, harvests etc. He demonstrates how in ceremonies to placate the gods no symbolic sacrifice occurs but conjugal sex is celebrated ceremonially. Thus Yoshimoto describes the symbolic collective imaginary of a rice-cultivating society like Japan. He also examines ceremonies associated with the Imperial family and concludes, contrary to the assertions of scholars like Orikuchi Shinobu and Saigō Nobutsuna, that in these rituals the Emperor is conceived of as a god, and simultaneously as mortal. Hence the Emperor is a sublimation, an hallucination. Yoshimoto argues that these ceremonies are fundamentally shamanistic, not nomadic, as proposed by the historian Mori

Masayo (b.1921). However, clear differences exist between Japanese and Asian shamanism (Yoshimoto, 1972a: 149–60).

Next, chapter seven considers matriarchy and motherhood (bose-iron). Yoshimoto refutes the thesis that communal marriage arose in primitive societies to liberate people from jealousy as proposed by Friedrich Engels (1820–95) in his celebrated 1884 study *The Origin of the Family*, which in turn was based on the ethnologist Lewis H. Morgan's (1818–81) classic *Ancient Society*, published in 1877. Yoshimoto proposes the thesis that the binary imaginary of sexual relations is the basis of the collective imaginary and further, that the binary imaginary is founded on the relationship between brother and sister. He cites the *Kojiki* where this sibling relationship becomes legalised in a rite and thus forms the basis of legal authority in the village. This is the Japanese meaning of 'matriarchy' (Yoshimoto, 1972a: 160–70).

Yoshimoto then looks at ancient Okinawa where women combined both religious and practical authority. This is the most developed form of matriarchy found in Japan. Citing Engel's *Origin of the Family*, Yoshimoto argues that for tabus to exist, both the collective and binary imaginaries are necessary. The more common split in Japan with women invested with religious authority and men with political authority can be traced through an investigation of incest tabus which are linked to fictitious kin relations (created to avoid incest) in the collective imaginary. In the *Kojiki*, we can see the symbolic shift from a society based on matriarchy to one based on the clan (Yoshimoto, 1972a: 170–9).

Chapter eight on binary imaginaries draws together some of the threads concerning women and ritual described in the previous four chapters. Yoshimoto defines the family thus: 'The family is born when people who join together both the binary and collective imaginary are alienated from their relatives' (Yoshimoto, 1972a: 181). Thus the basis for the family is the binary imaginary, which is independent from the collective imaginary. Freud argues that relationships between individuals constitute the essence of what Yoshimoto terms the binary imaginary but for Yoshimoto the individual imaginary is possible only when people are separated from their family.

Using examples drawn from fictional works by modern novelists like Natsume Sōseki (1867–1916) and Mori Ōgai (1862–1922), Yoshimoto argues that the question of how to define the family is one of the major issues of modern Japan. In modern fiction, husbands and wives discover binary imaginaries as a kind of self-identity in a different way from a relationship built on their individual identities. The sexual relationship is the basis of the binary imaginary but, in addition, there is the metaphysical recognition of oneself through others—this describes the relationships between parents and children, brothers and sisters etc. This binary imaginary is different from the collective or individual imaginaries: it is a realm of imaginary constructed upon the consciousness of sex (Yoshimoto, 1972a: 179–88).

Thus interpretations of primitive societies which posit sexual utopias established on the principle of free love are false: human beings are not free agents in respect of their sexual identities. Yoshimoto then considers various hypotheses concerning the relationship between sexuality and ritual, and political systems like matriarchy which emerge as a result. He argues that conceptual frames like his invention of the imaginary are capable of analysis and discussion, and moreover, as empirical evidence is lacking for ancient society, in effect, discussion at the level of imaginary is the only means available for us to 'know' the reality of early Japanese society. He then links female sexuality as a biological phenomenon to the diurnal seasonal cycle: ritual celebrates sexuality by creating a binary imaginary (different from the collective imaginary) in which a particular notion of time is produced (Yoshimoto, 1972a: 188–205).

Collective Imaginaries (1968): The Birth of the State

Chapters nine to eleven propose a psycho-social reading of the *Kojiki* as part of a history of the early Japanese state, and in doing so, advance a theory about the origins of the state. In chapter nine, concerning guilt (zaisekiron), Yoshimoto argues that a study of myth enables us to draw a picture of primitive society by means of his conception of the collective imaginary. He cites the famous expulsion of the god Susanoo from the Land of Reeds by his father, which occurs in the *Kojiki*, as not a description of original sin, as proposed by Orikuchi Shinobu, but, rather, the birth of logic. Susanoo is rejecting patriarchy for matriarchy (he wishes to go to the land of his mother). Thus we see here a symbolic conflict between agricultural society and the monarchic Yamato proto-state—this contradiction is celebrated in ritual form in festivals. Later a reconciliation occurs, and Yoshimoto reads this as a symbolic reconciliation of the religious institution (the elder sister in the *Kojiki*) with the agricultural polity (Susanoo, the younger brother) (Yoshimoto, 1972a: 204–14).

Yoshimoto analyses other sibling conflicts in *Kojiki*, seeing them as clashes within a polity built on blood relations. Hero narratives are thus interpreted as symbolic representations of differing clan traditions, creating versions of history or myth different to the dominant religio-mystical matriarchy, that is, the Imperial lineage (Yoshimoto, 1972a: 214–27).

Chapter ten is concerned with models (kihenron) but the models discussed in this chapter relate solely to the law. Yoshimoto is seeking to trace the process by which law evolves out of religious sanctions, or, more broadly, how law comes into being as a result of people becoming alienated from nature. Yoshimoto's various hypotheses are based on close readings of various passages from the *Kojiki*. This also allows him to propose a historical reading of the *Kojiki* (following the scholar Misumi Hiroshi) which sees Yamato rule as a union between a native population and a ruling group from elsewhere. Yoshimoto also explores the differences between religion and civil sanctions. He examines the typology of expiatory ceremonies that indicate a shift in the collective imaginary from a religious to a civil or legal process (Yoshimoto, 1972a: 227–50).

The final chapter, chapter eleven, on origins (kigenron), arises out of the recent boom in Japan of books exploring the origins of the Japanese state. We see here how Yanagita's famous 1960 study *The Ocean Road* provides a direct stimulus for Yoshimoto's discussion. He asks the question: What does the collective imaginary of village society signify when it becomes independent from a clan- or family-based state polity (Yoshimoto, 1972a: 250)? Yoshimoto compares the descriptions of ancient Japanese society in the Chinese records to that provided in the *Kojiki*. He stresses how fundamental shamanistic religio-magical beliefs were for kingship in early Japan. He argues that the Chinese chronicles reveal a much more sophisticated state than we see in the *Kojiki*. In other words, by the time of the chronicles (the first four centuries A.D.), the Yamato state has separated political from religious authority. Yoshimoto then links his analysis of the early Japanese state with the development of law. He also considers the ethnic origins of the Imperial line (Yoshimoto, 1972a: 250–75).

In his postscript to the version of *Collective Imaginaries* published in his *Collected Works*, Yoshimoto notes that his intention in this book was to analyse two classic texts: *The Legends of Tōno* and the *Kojiki*. He wanted to examine the collective imaginary of primitive Japanese society and trace the formation of the collective imaginary of the state. But, he emphasises, this is not a historical study, rather, a study of the time before history began (Yoshimoto, 1972a: 276–8). In the postscript, the editor of this volume, Kawakami Haruo, argues that this book is an attempt to grasp the fundamental structure of the entire domain of the human imaginary using the three axes of collective, binary, and individual imaginary. Moreover, Yoshimoto's methodology—his invention of the notion of 'imaginary'—is entirely original (Quoted Yoshimoto, 1972a: 278–83).

Shortly, we will investigate the impact of this book on Yoshimoto's contemporaries, but first we need to assess the work as a whole. Yoshimoto clearly saw the state as a concept encompassing both society and culture, and so his analysis utilises his notion of collective imaginary to conceptualise the early Japanese state in the process of the formation of its most crucial elements. He also uses this quite original notion to construct a psycho-social reading of traditional agrarian culture and social beliefs (including religion), and also the institutions that arise from them. The sources from which he draws his picture of the culture and society of early, prehistoric Japan are those utilised by Yanagita—collections of folk tales, legends, myths, modern anthropological and ethnographic Japanese scholarship, and literature. The key texts are the two versions of the Tōno tales and the *Kojiki*.

Thus, in his use of sources, Yoshimoto borrows heavily from the approach pioneered by insider writers like Yanagita and Orikuchi. Naturally, his readings of these sources are entirely his own. But the most remarkable aspect of this study is the conceptual vocabulary or methodology that Yoshimoto invented to analyse and categorise his source texts. The idea of the imaginary, and also the three varieties of imaginary that Yoshimoto theorises, while influenced by Lévy-Bruhl's concept of 'représentations collectives', is clearly an original, and quite daring formulation. By utilising this methodology, Yoshimoto drew links between a congeries of disparate phenomenon and data to produce an exciting and coherent rewriting of the social, political, and cultural origins of the Japanese state, and an alternative reading of its historical evolution. Yoshimoto reconstructs the Japanese state as the product of an Asian mode of kingship that is essentially shamanistic in its origins, and, moreover, privileges female kinship over male.

This rewriting of the basis of Japanese culture and identity must be seen in the context of the political debates, referred to earlier, that raged throughout the 1960s. Yoshimoto, while using a number of important

Western theorists like Freud and Engels, is proposing a thesis relating to Japanese identity that radically separates the idea of Japan from Western notions of culture, statehood and society. Thus, in a very real sense, Yanagita's book (first serialised during the 1950s) was the fuse that sparked these debates. This re-imagining of Japan as a typically Asian politico-religious construct affirms an identity that is more Asian than Western. Such a conceptualisation is a clear assertion of independence—intellectual, cultural, and religious—quite contrary to the Westernised conceptualisation of Japan advocated by thinkers like Maruyama Masao. The notion of a binary imaginary predicated upon gender, and one that stresses the importance of the female, is also a radical rewriting of a Western masculine script that sees patriarchy rather than matriarchy as the dominant mode of early statehood.

Finally, Yoshimoto's methodology in this book is a radical departure from conventional Western modes of social-scientific, cultural, or intellectual analysis. Yet, it is, in essence, a universal paradigm that can, in theory, be used to analyse the West as well as Japan. Not merely is Yoshimoto's radical conceptualisation of the 'imaginary' a powerful affirmation of insider discourse and theory but it purports to transcend its insider origins and become an outsider discourse.

The impact of Collective Imaginaries (1968) on contemporary Japan

Nakata Hitoshi, the translator of *Collective Imaginaries* into French, has argued in his 1999 study of Foucault and *Collective Imaginaries* that Yoshimoto's volume is the first Japanese philosophy of history that can be utilised by international intellectual discourse (Nakata, 1999: 10). He further asserts that *Collective Imaginaries* is an attempt to combine two different conceptions of the state, that of the West and Japan. He singles out Yoshimoto's notion of 'binary imaginaries' as an entirely original reading of the relationship between humans and society. The similarity of Yoshimoto's analysis here and Hamaguchi Eshun's notion of 'man-in-nexus' (discussed in chapter one) hardly needs to be elaborated, and perhaps confirms Nakata's point about the originality of this idea (Nakata, 1999: 60–9).

Comparing Foucault's *Les mots et les choses* to *Collective Imaginaries*, Nakata argues that both books, were, in part, inspired by similar sources.

Just as Foucault's volume is, he writes, a response to the French philosopher Maurice Merlau-Ponty's late anti-Marxist essays, so Yoshimoto's study is preceded by Jean-Paul Sartre's 1957 essay 'Search for a Method' (Nakata, 1999: 8). Despite finding terms which resemble Yoshimoto's notion of 'gensō' (imaginary) in the writings of Marx, Nakata believes Yoshimoto's idea is entirely unique and a major contribution to intellectual debate (Nakata, 1999: 191). Furthermore, the realisation of this concept in *Collective Imaginaries* fulfils a dream that Foucault discusses in chapter ten of his book: '…psychoanalysis and ethnology are not so much two human sciences among others, but they span the entire domain of those sciences, they animate its whole surface, spread their concepts throughout it, and are able to propound their methods of decipherment and their interpretations everywhere' (Foucault, 1973: 380). Nakata argues that in the quotation above Foucault dreams of a certain formal structure to consciousness, and that *Collective Imaginaries* is the fulfilment of this dream.

One or two objections to this would include the fact that Foucault's words do not necessarily mean that he has ruled out his own conceptualisation as a formal structure of the unconscious, most notably his idea of 'episteme' (Foucault, 1973: xxii). Further, Foucault himself notes in his foreword to the English edition that in his book he is attempting to 'reveal a positive unconscious of knowledge' (Foucault, 1973: xi). Also, interestingly, after reading *Les mots et les choses*, Yoshimoto wrote that he had never imagined any connection between Foucault's work and his own (Quoted Nakata, 1999: 69).

Nevertheless, a number of Japanese commentators besides Nakata have likened *Collective Imaginaries* to Foucault's book, and, in terms of their impact on their respective societies (Japan and France), this may be a fair comparison. Naturally, only time will tell which book has more significance for readers generally. In a 1980 survey of the many critical reactions to Yoshimoto's study, the anthropologist Yamaguchi Masao's 1969 article on the book received much attention. Yamaguchi was astonished at Yoshimoto's scholarship which he compares in its scope and power to the work of authors such as De Saussure and Lévi-Strauss but he criticised Yoshimoto for not focusing more on indigenous symbolic systems (Cited Haniya, 1985: 141–2). A legal historian, Ishio Yoshihisa, nominates the German sociologist Max Weber's (1864–1920) notion of 'legitimacy' as comparable to certain aspects of the collective imaginary. He also compares Yoshimoto's arguments on tabu to those of the German/American psychologist Erich Fromm (1900–80) and has no doubt that *Collective Imaginaries* is a major study (Ishio, 1985: 143–61).

Kasai Kiyoshi in a 1985 essay on the book reads it as very much influenced by Japan's defeat during World War II. He argues that in a series of publications from the 1950s onwards, Yoshimoto tried to develop a new theory of the state and the Emperor as a reaction to the humiliation of defeat. He cites several statements by Yoshimoto in which he confessed his despair at the defeat. Unlike the orthodox left who saw the defeat as a liberation, Yoshimoto, he writes, saw it as a humiliation. Yoshimoto's attempts to construct a new conceptualisation of the Japanese state rest on an acceptance of the famous historian Tōyama Shigeki's (b.1914) view that Imperial absolutism was the source of weakness in the Japanese state. Thus Yoshimoto's search for a new notion of the state and history that would replace the traditional, prewar Emperor-centred perspective was a reaction to his sense of betrayal by the 'Emperor system'.

Kasai cites a famous sentence from Yoshimoto's introduction to the Kadokawa paperback edition of the text: 'The state is a collective imaginary. Customs and religion and law are all collective imaginaries' (Quoted Kasai, 1985: 150). The notion of the collective imaginary is Yoshimoto's reconceptualisation of the state—a view which Kasai reads as a fundamental critique of the Emperor, the first such since the defeat. The collective imaginary combines two different conceptions of the state: the Japanese view that the state is the sum total of all the people or all families and the Western view that the state is an invisible structure built upon society. The notion of collective imaginary explains how the ancient agricultural society of Japan was absorbed into the Imperial Yamato state through the process of religion developing into law, which creates the state structure. Yoshimoto's emphasis on Okinawa as a source for Japanese religiosity, writes Kasai, also undermines Marxist theses about Imperial absolutism (Kasai, 1985: 146–57).

With Kasai's essay, we have a partial explanation of the personal context in which Yoshimoto developed his notion of the 'collective imaginary'. But, as noted earlier, the book also develops ideas touched upon in *Beauty*, and thus can be seen as a continuing exploration of certain fundamental threads in Yoshimoto's writings. One of the most important of these threads is the formulation of fundamental paradigms, applicable as Yoshimoto sees it, to a general discourse on culture and intellectual history, an outsider discourse, not merely a contribution to the postwar Japanese debate, the fundamental rethinking about the state that occurred at the time.

Certainly, in Japan, Yoshimoto's terminology has been very influential, with numerous publications on the ancient culture and society of Japan using the terms 'kyōdō gensō' (collective imaginary) in their discussion. The notion of the imaginary seems to have enabled many investigators of Japanese culture to discuss particular cultural phenomenon outside a strict Marxian framework which posits an economic base to cultural phenomena, although this is not to say that Yoshimoto does not take account of economic circumstances.

One other point worth making is that Yoshimoto's analysis openly borrows much from his insider predecessors on culture, especially Yanagita Kunio and Orikuchi Shinobu. Again, only time will tell whether Yoshimoto's paradigm will replace the conceptual frames developed by his precursors. Finally, as we have seen with *Beauty*, Yoshimoto draws openly and without reservation on outsider theorists like Hegel, Engels and Lévy-Bruhl in constructing his notion of the imaginary.

On Mass Images (1984)

We have seen how Yoshimoto first expressed interest in images and sign systems at the conclusion of *Beauty*. *Collective Imaginaries* uses a different vocabulary to analyse society and culture. But by the mid 1980s, Yoshimoto began to focus more attention on cultural phenomena which drew from non-literary sources like comics and movies. *Masu Imēji Ron* (On Mass Images) is the first detailed study by Yoshimoto which covers popular culture as well as serious literature. The book was first serialised in the journal *Kaion* between March 1982 and February 1983. It was revised over the course of the following year and was first published as a single volume in July 1984. The volume was later reissued as a paperback (without any additions or corrections) in May 1988, and subsequently reprinted in 1994. This latter edition is used here. It is a precursor to the later trilogy of 'High Images' volumes published between 1989 and 1994, which engage a large range of cultural phenomena but still maintain a keen interest in serious literature.

On Mass Images is divided into twelve essays, which will be treated here as equivalent to chapters, as the underlying links and concerns enable the study to be read as a thematic whole. The first chapter is on metamorphosis (henseiron) and begins with an extended study of the Czech writer Franz Kafka's (1883–1924) famous novella *Metamorphosis* (1916). Through a close reading of the text, Yoshimoto asserts that Kafka, through the metamorphosis of Gregor into an insect, embodies for his readers the experience of a loss of autonomy. Further, he notes, 'this image of metamorphosis turns the world into one of schizophrenia' (Yoshimoto, 1994: 17). Yoshimoto argues that such a metamorphosis has been added to the human condition in the present.

After examining the monologue of a schizophrenic patient to confirm his hypothesis, Yoshimoto considers stories by the contemporary novelists Tsutsui Yasutaka (b.1934) and Murakami Haruki (b.1949), the latter's text co-written with the copywriter and essayist Itoi Shigesato (b.1948). These stories describe delusional worlds constructed of camera images or transient TV realities. Yoshimoto notes that such young, contemporary authors attempt to create language to match the present reality of images alone but eventually their words are defeated by the power of images. He praises the novelist Takahashi Gen'ichirō's (b.1951) award-winning 1981 story 'Sayonara, Gyangutachi' (Goodbye to the Gang) for capturing the reality of TV images, and praises the air of cynicism and nihilism that pervades the work.

Yoshimoto notes that the work reads like a 'dramatic cartoon', a genre of Japanese manga called 'gekiga' which emerged in the 1970s and treated adult themes; one translation of the term is 'graphic novel'. Yoshimoto's conclusion is that the delusional, schizophrenic world of the present disappears in the work of the contemporary novelists that he discusses. But the cynicism championed in these fictions leads to an acceptance of the world of images created by the governors. Thus metamorphosis 'celebrates the sad love of those who govern the sick' (Yoshimoto, 1994: 34). There is no doubt the target of Yoshimoto's criticism is the imagery of commodity capitalism (Yoshimoto, 1994: 6–34). In some respects, his criticisms here resemble those contained in the celebrated 1964 study *One Dimensional Man* by the German/American philosopher Herbert Marcuse whose ideas are often seen as contributing to the rise of the New Left in Europe and the USA.

Chapter two concerns stagnation (teitairon) and led to much criticism of Yoshimoto after its first publication as an essay. The reason for this is that it targets an appeal orchestrated by the novelist Nakano Kōji (b.1925) for writers to sign an anti-nuclear, pro-disarmament document. Yoshimoto sees this document as a 'soft Stalinist' attack on the USA (Yoshimoto, 1994: 37). As he writes: 'Is the major intellectual current in modern "Europe" lamenting the danger of nuclear war? Or is it lamenting the danger of the forcible ascendancy over Europe of the Soviet military–bureaucratic complex through its control of Poland? To my mind, the latter is a far more believable, and more universally significant portent of modern Europe' (Yoshimoto, 1994: 39).

Castigating this document as a fake designed to fool people into supporting Stalinism, Yoshimoto argues that Nakano's language in this declaration is exactly the same as avant-garde science fiction (SF) *animé* (movie-length animated SF cartoons). So he asks 'why does Nakano Kōji—famous for writing realist fiction—now unconsciously slip into the old clichéd intellectual milieu of anime and cartoon writers' (Yoshimoto, 1994: 41). Yoshimoto's answer to his own question is that this kind of utopian SF derives from a view of humanity or human nature as unchanging and that this viewpoint has led people into stagnation. By stagnation, Yoshimoto means first, the consciousness of the collective imaginary of agricultural solidarity; and second, the contemporary form of mass production. Thus Nakano's stagnation stems from an attempt to insert the collective consciousness of a rural utopia into modern society (Yoshimoto, 1994: 41–2).

Yoshimoto deconstructs stagnation in two famous works: the TV personality Kuroyanagi Tetsuko's (b.1933) celebrated 1981 book *Madogiwa no Totto Chan* (Totto-chan: The Little Girl at the Window) and the Catholic novelist Ōhara Tomie's (b.1912) award-winning novel *Aburahamu no Makuya* (Abraham's Tent, 1981). The former book, which has become an international best-seller, and is taught in schools around the world, Yoshimoto criticises for its idealisation of a nonexistent past, its nostalgia for a world in which children can be free, where children unawares can possess a special kind of narcissism. But this is impossible in the present. So the stagnation of today lies in the evocation of the nostalgic ideal in the readers of Kuroyanagi's book.

The reason why this is impossible is because of state control, and a structure of regulation to which civil society is continually exposed.

Yoshimoto argues that Kuroyanagi's fantasy 'bears no resemblance whatever to the mass images of capitalism equalling free competition; on the contrary, civil society in its role as a means of economic and social production is subject to invisible, artificial control and manipulation by the state' (Yoshimoto, 1994: 49). Again, we see sentiments that could have come straight from Marcuse's *One Dimensional Man*.

Nevertheless, Yoshimoto is not entirely negative about Kuroyanagi's work for he allows that the longing in the book for an absolute liberal idea can counter contemporary stagnation. Ōhara's novel is based on real-life testimony by clients of a charitable organisation called 'Christ's Arc', which accepts and helps victims of domestic violence etc. Yoshimoto is inspired by this real-life attempt to console victims of the present and writes: 'We will not permit the present stagnation to contract into the spectacle of the past, we will look to the future' (Yoshimoto, 1994: 55).

The next chapter is concerned with reasoning (suiriron) but also with mysteries, as the Japanese word 'suiri' also means mystery when applied to novels. Examining Edgar Allan Poe's (1809–49) short story 'The Murders in the Rue Morgue' (1841), Yoshimoto argues that the substance of the process of reasoning of Dupin, Poe's detective hero, is coincidence, images derived from a sense of déjà-vu, as well as the construction within the reader (or projected reader) of assent to Dupin's analytical power. The narrator's consciousness intersects with the author's at the point where the knowledge of the assailant, despite the narrator's ignorance of his 'identity', seems to be a recollection of something forgotten.

This characteristic Yoshimoto also finds in writers like Dostoevsky and Miyazawa Kenji (1896–1933). His conclusion is that: 'conceptualised worldviews are not déjà-vu or unfixed reality, rather, they only exist as déjà-vu experiences' (Yoshimoto, 1994: 65–6). This follows from his assertion that: 'We are brought back to the fact that transcendental concepts [in Kantian terms, Yoshimoto refers to a priori cognition] are born from the discrepancies with empirical fact that language has in terms of its significance as language' (Yoshimoto, 1994: 65).

Yoshimoto's rather startling, yet illuminating contention is used to analyse reasoning as a quality in a number of contemporary Japanese SF novels which he finds inferior to Poe's fiction since these novels fail to encounter mystery at the heart of their reasoning. Finally, Yoshimoto discusses two stories by Ryūnosuke Akutagawa. These stories concern delusion; as Yoshimoto notes, for Akutagawa 'connections between phenomena are vital and this concern with connections grows in intensity and scope until it becomes a delusional connection' (Yoshimoto, 1994: 77). This rather difficult chapter is probing further the delusional world of the present, a world where metamorphosis (the constant condition of change underlying the present) leads to stagnation, where images conceal a contradictory longing to break free from the delusion of commodity capitalism, where, as he writes of Akutagawa's fiction: 'We readers are able to describe the desire to instantly connect [ourselves to] a faraway place, and also the desire to fuse past and future together into a mystery [but Yoshimoto also means here a process of ratiocination]' (Yoshimoto, 1994: 78).

Chapter four discusses the world (sekairon). Yoshimoto criticises Nakano Kōji once again for his artificial divisions of the world of literature into categories like atomic bomb literature, Vietnam war literature, resistance literature, and so on. Yoshimoto argues that this conflates literature with ethics but 'if we had that [ethical] wall, all the myths and ideology and superstitions and lies about human nature will be destroyed' (Yoshimoto, 1994: 81). The book of the world consists of different orders, lineages, and structures, and we read these structures via the medium of ethics. Yoshimoto rejects the fake ethics of Nakano— there is no universal principle behind his discussions. He rejects as a lie the notion that such sentiments equal the ethical world. Authors create their own ethical worlds, argues Yoshimoto (Yoshimoto, 1994: 79–88).

This view follows logically from Yoshimoto's insistence on the idea that the world contains all things and categories, including literature and ethics. To theorise the world, as Yoshimoto does in books like *Beauty* and *Collective Imaginaries*, means in a sense to create the world. Thus Nakano's ideological version of what we now call 'identity politics' trivialises this process of world-making as it applies to literature. To demonstrate his point, Yoshimoto analyses two novels in depth: Nakagami Kenji's (1946–92) long novel *Sennen no Yūraku* (A Thousand Years of Pleasure, 1982) and Ōe Kenzaburō's novel *Oyogu Otoko–Mizu no Naka no Rein Tsurii* (The Swimming Man–Rain Trees in Water, 1982), which was later published as part of a quintet of novels called *Rein Tsurii o Kiku Onna Tachi* (The Women Who Listen to the Rain Trees, 1982).

Both novels create worlds, and both, therefore, are 'unethical'. They transcend ethics (as ethics exist only as part of their created worlds) and attempt to shatter our worlds or worldview. This reading of fiction is close to various attempts by aesthetic philosophers like Theodor Adorno and Nelson Goodman to theorise art as symbolic world-making. The activity of world-making in art or literature also hints at a solution to the crisis of the present, of stagnation, that we have encountered hitherto.

On Mass Images (1984): Making Fictional Worlds

In chapter five Yoshimoto selects artistic works which do, in his view, construct worlds, and therefore challenge the existing order. But in this chapter on difference (sairon), Yoshimoto analyses fiction by three writers—Inoue Yasushi (1907–91), Yasuoka Shōtarō (b.1920) and Kaga Otohiko (b.1929)—to demonstrate how unsuccessful all but one are in creating new worlds. In chapter five, Yoshimoto swaps the word 'world' with 'difference' (sai), contending that great art establishes difference but inferior art seeks to erase it. Yoshimoto asks the questions: How do we construct the artefact (sakuhin) that is the world? Why do we attempt to construct the world as an artefact? Because it is the only world we can know but 'we cannot transcend perfectly our limited world of the present' (Yoshimoto, 1994: 107). Yet this is how we enter the present: 'our artefacts all exist within a universal artificiality' (Yoshimoto, 1994: 108).

Yoshimoto discusses Inoue's attempt in his 1981 novel *Honkakubō Ibun* (The Priest Honkaku's Testament) to eliminate difference. The author's motive is to negate or deny personal death, speculates Yoshimoto. But death is not eliminated by denial. The same error of logic or judgment is the motive behind all Inoue's historical fictions. Yasuoka, on the other hand, succeeds in the story 'Ga' (Moth) where the narrative voice introduces a sense of difference. But Yasuoka's long historical narrative *Ryūritan* (Tales of Wanderings, 1981) fails in that the differences between the sensibility of the author's world and the world itself are erased. The strongest criticism Yoshimoto reserves for Kaga's 1982 novel *Ikari no Nai Fune* (Ship Without an Anchor), which erases real differences in the world by being constructed on an ideological model. Yoshimoto castigates such novelists who are now being overtaken by popular literature, saying that writings such as theirs represent the ideals of a literature in stagnation (Yoshimoto, 1994: 103–30).

In chapter six, on compression (shukuyōron), Yoshimoto expands on world-making: 'We all sense obstacles, hardnesses, and in an unbiased way select from various angles, and according to the particular layering, compress everything into a flat plane where we wish to construct as an artefact an image of another, identical world. This may be illusory since compression only exists as an unconscious defence, thus an artificially constructed compression is impossible. But, other than experiencing doubts about the pre-existing world of the present, we can do nothing else' (Yoshimoto, 1994: 131). The desire to abstract or compress incomprehensible reality into comprehensible art through world-making ultimately fails, as Yoshimoto implies here, but, as he also notes, it is the only means we have to comprehend the world.

This chapter deals explicitly with what Yoshimoto later described as subcultures: specifically the subculture of cartoons, skits, and advertising copy-style scripts. He argues that high and low art are now in the process of being reversed. We are faced with a flat world where both are identical. Yoshimoto praises three examples of Japanese manga or cartoons for portraying powerfully the breakdown of the modern family. A new world of expression is created in flat-plane cartoons, a monologic, compressed world. Yoshimoto singles out especially skits and scripts written by the famous advertising copywriter Itoi Shigesato in combination with the writer Hashimoto Osamu (b.1948) and Kamasaki Tetsuo.

He argues that this kind of pop culture is a far stronger literature of resistance than traditional leftist fiction. He stresses that for writers such as Itoi, the spoken language has superseded traditional genres of written style. He observes that the unconscious reality of the present—something no longer disclosed by serious highbrow literature—is revealed in popular mass culture, contrary to its image of revealing only surface reality. In a similar vein, he applauds the writing of the so-called 'hippy' author, American novelist and poet Richard Brautigan (1935–84), another iconic 'pop' writer (Yoshimoto, 1994: 131–53).

Chapter seven concerns anatomy (kaitairon), namely, the anatomy of the present. Mass culture, according to Yoshimoto, is a response to the invisible system of control, which here we may read as 'culture', not a response to the visible system of politics and economics. He argues that we are enmeshed in this invisible system: even the pop art of resistance evokes in us a sense of déjà-vu. These views, once more, strongly resemble those of Marcuse. He examines a number of novels that attempt to reveal the anatomy of the system. He praises Shiina Makoto's (b.1944) 1981–2 novel *Aishū no Machi ni Kiri ga Furu no da* (Mist Rises in the Grief Stricken Town), noting that it dramatises the meaningless minutia of daily life for the young. Shiina's works symbolise the violence brought about by the desire to break the rules.

He showers similar praise on Ōe Kenzaburō's 'rain tree' novel mentioned earlier, and on Murakami Haruki's novel *Hitsuji o Meguru Bōken* (The Wild Sheep Chase, 1982), where the 'sheepman' in Murakami's story represents the unease of the present. Finally, Yoshimoto compares Ōe's 'rain tree' novel to the American SF fantasy writer Ray Bradbury's (b.1920) story 'Halloween is Here!'. Ōe is the superior writer as his anatomy of the present, a nihilistic, pessimistic version, is the more convincing (Yoshimoto, 1994: 153–73).

Chapter eight is concerned with tropes in modern poetry (impōron), and resembles somewhat Yoshimoto's arguments in his *Study of Postwar Poetry*, which had been published in an expanded form in 1983. He argues that tropes or metaphors express something that cannot be expressed in words, but which can only be expressed through troping. He examines the poetry of a number of contemporary women poets—Mochizuki Noriko, Itō Hiromi (b.1955) and Isaka Yōko (b.1949). He declares that their poetry is brilliant, especially in their representation of female subjectivity which clearly reveals how they are treated by men, and thus their work is an attack upon male chauvinism. However, the language they use is closed, not open. He cites others with similar drawbacks, like the singer–songwriter Nakajima Miyuki (b.1952) and the musician Matsutōya Yumi (b.1954).

Citing work by other contemporary poets, Yoshimoto repeats the point he had made in his *Study of Postwar Poetry*, that such poetry is a solipsistic exercise using metaphorical language for purely private (not public) matters, thus it is closed, not open to readers. He praises the poet and novelist Nejiime Shōichi (b.1948) for his clever erotic satires on modern society but there is no sense of collectivity (kyōdōtai) in his work, thus it too suffers from the same flaw. The only poet he champions for being open to readers is Arakawa Yōji (b.1949) (Yoshimoto, 1994: 174–203).

Chapter nine on poetic vocabulary (shigoron) further explores the dilemma of contemporary poetry. Yoshimoto argues that there should be a relationship between words, and here he means the language of poetry, and the present. The closed worlds that contemporary poets create are therefore problematic. Yoshimoto states that poets are wrestling with fundamental problems of meaning and representation: Given that our world is created by words, how can poets seek other-world realities? He cites the work of the poet Inagawa Masato (b.1949) to illustrate how, by using difficult and obstructive language, poets like Inagawa create new, self-conscious reflexive worlds.

Another difficult poet, Hiraide Takashi (b.1950), creates linguistic barriers between the image of the real world and the poem so that the poem deconstructs the real world. Thus Yoshimoto's viewpoint is complex—while understanding both the difficulties and real achievements of contemporary poets, he is nevertheless critical of their overall approach. He cites older poets of the 'postwar generation', the generation of writers with whom Yoshimoto himself is usually associated, as exemplars, as they base their poetry on images of the real world, they confront the real world (Yoshimoto, 1994: 204–22).

Chapter ten on 'the times' (jiseiron) shifts from a consideration of contemporary poetry to an examination of models of the world drawn from both classical and modern prose. But the main discussion in this chapter is on the contemporary novelist Kojima Nobuo (b.1915). Yoshimoto compares the positioning of classical prose narratives (monogatari) in time and space to Kojima's award-winning multi-volume novel *Wakareru Riyū* (Reasons for Separation, 1968–89). The classical narratives all establish a sense of time and place through a shared consciousness or imaginary but Kojima's novel does not—indeed, the tragedy of the novel's protagonist, the English professor Maeda Eizō, is 'the great demonic system of the present' (Yoshimoto, 1994: 232).

In a long, detailed comparison of the novels of Sōseki to Kojima, Yoshimoto argues that, in contrast to the love triangles in Sōseki's fiction, Kojima's love relationships always culminate in a sexual resolution. *Reasons for Separation* ends with a revelation of the present, an uncertain present, which confirms that the world created by contemporary fiction is changing and discontinuous in contrast to the unchanging, continuous world of classical prose narrative (Yoshimoto, 1994: 223–47).

Chapter eleven on images (gazōron) deals with television, specifically with TV advertising. The TV camera has radically changed our perception of the world, argues Yoshimoto. As the gaze of television is close to real sight, so TV images are more real than the real thing. As the purpose of TV advertising is to increase the exchange value of the commodities advertised, *images* alone are sold. Consequently, image and reality becomes confused, and images come to exist to produce images. Analysing a large number of TV commercials, Yoshimoto attempts an anatomy of image, creating a rhetoric or grammar of advertising. When story or drama is used as the narrative instrument in certain advertisements, as we as viewers enter the story, then we forget the product being advertised and thus the advertisement contains its own contradiction. This is because of the copywriters' creative ability to override the frame of the advertisement with their own subjectivity.

Advertisements compete directly against each other, the product becomes secondary to this process. Yoshimoto evaluates advertisements against certain criteria: how close to or apart from reality the image is; how disruptive of order the advertisement is. Finally, he nominates an advertisement for a toilet that includes a bidet as the most appropriate form of radicalism for the present. People are reduced to bodies, to mere objects, as sexual narcissism becomes the keynote. Yoshimoto writes that the advertisement suggests infantile satisfaction with motherly toilet training: such is the present, he writes (Yoshimoto, 1994: 248–71).

The last chapter on verbal surface or appearance (gosōron) analyses cartoons or comics. Yoshimoto praises the manga genre as a new cultural form which combines word and image. He analyses various well-known cartoon artists including Yamagishi Ryōko (b.1947), Tsuge Yoshiharu (b.1937), Ōtomo Katsuhiro (b.1954), Okada Fumiko, Hagio Moto (b.1949) and Takano Fumiko (b.1957). He demonstrates how Yamagishi uses narrative devices effectively in her comics. Yoshimoto cites Tsuge's work for its radical mixture of pornographic image and word. Okada's work interests him because of the depiction of the characters as an aspect of the narrative's consciousness. Yoshimoto is also fascinated by graphic techniques such as reversed perspectives and differential construction which he discusses in the comics of Hagio and Takano. Yoshimoto takes this subculture seriously as a mode of artistic production (Yoshimoto, 1994: 272–97).

This summary of *On Mass Images* is long and laboured but given the diverse nature of topics that Yoshimoto treats in this book, and given the original method of publication where each chapter is serialised as a separate essay, this is inevitable if readers are to gain some idea of the contents. It is unlikely that this book will be translated into English in the foreseeable future and thus it is important to have as complete a description as possible. Much of the book is an attempt to weld the various readings Yoshimoto makes of several literary works published in the 1970s and the 1980s into a coherent argument and so the detail of each work discussed must be taken into account in any critical evaluation of the book as a whole.

Yoshimoto's superb skills as a literary critic are much in evidence in the individual readings he gives of the many Japanese novels discussed in the text. Does the conceptual frame of world-making, arising out of a situation of cultural stagnation in traditional modes of fiction, and the notion of 'difference' manage to provide an adequate linkage between the themes of these several works? The answer is, for the most part, yes. The evidence for this conclusion lies in the way Yoshimoto's readings became the starting point for much of the subsequent critical reception of these works in Japan. But, as with *Beauty*, Yoshimoto has negative appraisals of works (fiction and poetry) that he identifies as embodying the themes he dislikes.

He identifies his opponent early as a crude 'Old Left' reading of literature and history epitomised in Nakano Kōji's appeal. This is the stagnation that he writes of—a Cold War reading of culture. In a sense then, his opponent is ideology itself. At the same time, though, at various places in the text, he evokes the New Left reading of ideology most famously expressed in Marcuse's *One Dimensional Man*. Perhaps this is why his conceptual vocabulary slides about, avoiding precise definition, and generally baffled many of his contemporaries. Yoshimoto's critique of Cold War cultural polemic is tethered to an embrace of the glitzy consumerist culture of the 1970s that he finds in TV advertising, some examples of fiction, and in manga. He argues that the dystopian or subversive (visually as well as intellectually) themes these subgenres—traditionally seen as 'low' culture—champion are a more effective rejoinder to the stagnation of the present: they make a difference.

There is a contradiction here: an ambiguity about ideology (although he rarely mentions this term) that allows for it to be condemned yet utilised as an unacknowledged source of his notion of the 'present'. This contradiction weakens Yoshimoto's argument as a whole. Nevertheless, his attempt to conceptualise Japanese culture during a period of rapid change, where it splintered into numerous subgenres such as manga under the impact of commodified consumerism, is a heroic and ambitious attempt to bring the diverse phenomena he surveys into a single frame, which thus permits him to evaluate these works using the same aesthetic criteria. Added to the ambition of the study as a whole is Yoshimoto's determined effort to construct his conceptual frame as an insider mode of discourse, avoiding the overuse of outsider theorists like the Frankfurt School, and also avoiding their vocabulary, especially the key term of ideology.

Culture as commodity: reactions to On Mass Images (1984)

In his postscript to *On Mass Images*, Yoshimoto locates his study on the border between high culture and subculture. He writes that this work is an attempt to grasp culture and subculture as a whole, despite the great difficulties involved. He also records how he lost friends over his criticism of the anti-nuclear declaration (Yoshimoto, 1994: 298–301). In the commentary attached to the paperback edition of the book by the TV critic Ura Tatsuya, we find a sense of indignation that the high priest of cultural criticism has descended from the clouds to analyse 'subcultural' phenomena like advertising copy and comics. This criticism is echoed by other commentators writing at the time, as we shall see.

However, Ura argues that Yoshimoto is a true leftist as he has fulfilled his own definition in *On High Images*: 'Only those continually searching are the true Left' (Yoshimoto, 1994: 307–8). Ura also quotes Yoshimoto's own words from a dialogue between the two to further elaborate on his motives: 'Unless I discuss all these phenomena—contemporary "pure literature" and the products of the intelligentsia which are clearly not in that category—on a level surface using the same language then I will not be able to grasp contemporary issues' (Yoshimoto, 1994: 308).

Ura also notes that Yoshimoto's approach, mixing the genres of high and low culture together, and analysing them 'on a level surface' is fundamentally different from treatments of mass culture in the past. Yoshimoto characterised his book as difficult and dark but urged that it be read lightly. It is fair to say that the reception to the volume was mixed, not only as a result of Yoshimoto's daring decision to treat high and low culture on an equal plane but also because of the difficulty of his language. It is interesting to note, however, that some of Yoshimoto's key terms, like 'sai' (difference), were immediately taken up and used widely in intellectual discourse, in the same way as earlier phrases from Yoshimoto's work had been.

The contemporary cultural critic Watanabe Naomi in a long, difficult critique of both *On Mass Images* and *On High Images*, argues that Yoshimoto's central concept of the 'world' is ill-defined, and that the closer one approaches it, the further it recedes into the horizon. He also notes how death plays an important role in Yoshimoto's analysis, with near-death experiences and other narratives dealing with death recurring frequently. Is Yoshimoto's conceptualisation of the world, his world-making, a kind of response to an emptiness (kokū), a death he perceives at the heart of the world, he asks (Watanabe, 1988: 91). Later in his essay, Watanabe appears to link this emptiness to the boundless nature of the present, and also to the diverse cultural phenomena that Yoshimoto champions in *On Mass Images*. Watanabe seems to doubt Yoshimoto's high evaluation of 'low' cultural phenomena, which could just as easily be seen as ephemeral in nature (Watanabe, 1988: 95).

Karatani Kōjin also questions Yoshimoto's new methodology, or as some critics have suggested (on the basis that the methodology is unchanged), his new terminology. Karatani wonders why Yoshimoto does not persist with the vocabulary qua conceptualisations he developed during the 1960s. Karatani believes that Yoshimoto's real target in *On Mass Images* is the critical doctrine known as 'postmodernism' (Karatani, 1985: 63–7). As Karatani does not have much time for postmodernism, it follows logically that he is not especially taken with the 'subcultures' Yoshimoto chooses to highlight, and, in some cases, to praise. As Karatani puts it: 'I have little faith in the "pop" writers taken up by Yoshimoto' (Karatani, 1985: 68).

A number of critics found *On Mass Images* incomprehensible. The playwright Kitamura Sō (b.1952) likens the volume to a puzzle by Lewis Carroll (Kitamura, 1985: 267–8). A commentator on subculture, Fukutomi Tadayori, also notes that some readers will find the work incomprehensible, especially in regard to the notion of 'mass images'. Yoshimoto's critical vocabulary, especially neologisms he invents to describe new conceptualisations, has always proved a barrier to readers, as Yoshimoto himself has appeared to recognise recently with rewritings of some works like *Beauty* to make them easier to read.

Fukutomi remarks on the usefulness of notions like 'the present' to deal with cultural phenomena as diverse as contemporary poetry, cinema, and comics (Fukutomi, 1985: 269–73). He observes that if Yoshimoto had retained the critical vocabulary of *Beauty*, he would not have been able to treat popular culture. Fukutomi traces a prehistory of 'imēji' (images) in the use of similar terms like 'shizō' or 'zō' in *An Introduction to Mental Imaginaries* and *Beauty*. He argues that this notion is a ground-breaking discovery, as culture itself is made conscious through this domain. Thus Yoshimoto's book is 'the revelation of "the present" in images' (Fukutomi, 1985: 278).

Yamamoto Tetsuji has argued that *On Mass Images* signals a new direction in Yoshimoto's oeuvre, a shift in emphasis from industrial to consumer societies. This explains the move away from language (Yamamoto, 1996: 110). But Yoshimoto's focus on consumer commodities has dismayed some critics. Kuroko Kazuo characterises books like *On Mass Images* as poems of praise for consumer capitalism, and criticises Yoshimoto for ignoring harsher realities (Kuroko, 1990: '107).

Conclusion

As we noted earlier, Yoshimoto is still very much a work in progress. It is exceedingly difficult, therefore, to attempt to characterise the contribution he has made to discourse on culture in Japan. It goes without saying that he is one of a handful of figures of whom it can be said that they have shaped, and, in some cases, created modern Japanese culture. His readings of 'high' culture such as literature and Japanese history, thought, and linguistics have had an enormous impact on his contemporaries, and, in certain fields of thought, still constitute important landmarks that all investigators take account of as a matter of course.

His research into 'low' culture such as cinema, television, comics and fashion helped to make this a respectable field of intellectual enquiry in Japan. Although his first impact in Japan was in the area of politics, he is now considered far more significant as a commentator on culture and society generally. In short, he has followed in the tradition of Yanagita Kunio in that he has been, and continues to be, one of the figures most responsible for the insider perspective on Japan, and the world.

He is always seen as propounding an insider viewpoint, as arguing from the distinctive Japanese experience in his attempts to make sense of history and culture. Yoshimoto himself often writes that his critical perspective is 'Asian', both in the sense of Marx's notion of an Asian mode of production, and in the sense that in a world dominated by the Western worldview (which, then, becomes outsider discourse) there exists a different way of seeing and interpreting reality. Long ago he abandoned a Marxist perspective but, as numerous critics point out, his critical vocabulary, and indeed his worldview, still borrows very much from Marxian ideas. Whether this allows him to be classified as a leader of the Japanese 'New Left' depends upon the definition one uses, but some critics persist in classifying him thus. Therefore, although we have characterised his achievements as belonging to insider discourse, para-doxically, he draws almost as much from non-Japanese as indigenous sources for his ideas.

Yoshimoto has often declared in his writings that his intention is to open a dialogue with Western or outsider discourse. But, given the lack of translations of his work—a dilemma shared with most significant Japanese thinkers of the twentieth century—we can state fairly unequivocally that at this point in time the dialogue has yet to be joined, despite the various interviews held between Yoshimoto and his Western equivalents, like Foucault. Too often these dialogues record two separate conversations, two separate discourses, going in parallel direc-tions but rarely joining to make a real exchange of views. His intellec-tual successors, for example Karatani Kōjin, who have had some of their work made available in translation have, perhaps, been more successful in opening dialogues with Western thinkers, although the suspicion remains that they are read mainly by Western specialists on Japan.

Yoshimoto, like all contemporary insider critics, at times takes out-sider perspectives. And his writings always conduct an internal dialogue between his preferred Western thinkers and writers, and their Japanese equivalents. He is still active in this pursuit, and his views are always chal-lenging, as few Japanese thinkers of his generation have anything like his intellectual breadth or depth. His massive body of work stands as a monument to a half-century of unrelenting analysis of Japanese culture and society, an achievement almost unmatched in contemporary Japan.

4

The Literature of Contemporary Japan

All poetry is rhetoric
Writing this
I still continue to write

Tanikawa Shuntarō, from 'Toba 7' (Tanikawa, 1990: 239)

One of the most important and enduring expressions of culture is literature. This is especially so for Japan, which boasts one of the oldest and most distinguished literary cultures in the world. Poetry and literary prose have always played a vital role in the formation of Japanese culture, as we have seen in the writings of critics like Yanagita Kunio and Yoshimoto Takaaki.

This chapter will attempt to provide a snapshot of modern Japanese literature by examining some of the most important creations of a few of the most significant authors of postwar and contemporary Japan. For reasons of space, my discussion will be restricted to a handful of representative novelists, and poets of free-style verse. Fortunately for readers of English, there now exist excellent surveys of modern Japanese writing, including Donald Keene's acclaimed 1984 study *Dawn to the West* that provides a description of Japanese literature from the late nineteenth century to the 1970s. This chapter covers some of the same writers but will also treat contemporary authors not discussed by Keene. In addition, numerous translations now exist of much of the most significant literature produced in Japan in modern times (including most of the works discussed here).

The writers investigated in this chapter will be read primarily through the filter of insider discourse. Most critics of literature in Japan, by definition, are insider authors as the literature they discuss is written in Japanese and, usually, it is aimed primarily at a Japanese readership. There are a few exceptions to this rule—writers who deliberately seek out an international audience—but even these authors write in Japanese, with Japanese readers as their initial market. The vast majority of literary critics, and virtually all the commentators cited herein, are insiders, writing for a Japanese audience first and foremost. Naturally, this is true of most literary critics the world over. But the insights gained by using an insider lens in the case of Japanese literature are especially valuable as, traditionally, Japanese literature is much more context-dependent than many other literatures.

The Japanese language, unlike such European languages as English, French, or Spanish, is restricted to Japan, thus its immediate literary context is limited to this one society. The only exception to this is the literature produced in the prewar and wartime Japanese colonial territories—too specialised a topic to be dealt with in a study of this kind. Hence, it is only natural to use as guides to interpret the literature produced by this society those readers who are most familiar with it: namely, insider commentators. Nevertheless, from time to time, the hybrid and international nature of some contemporary Japanese writing will come under scrutiny by explicit comparison with its Western counterpart.

Postwar heretic: Mishima Yukio

The scholar Tsuge Teruhiko has identified six major categories of writing in postwar Japan; by 'writing', basically he means fiction. The first category is fiction in which the individual explores social and political realities; writers listed in this group include Noma Hiroshi (1915–91) and Shiina Rinzō. The second category is writing which seeks to portray a totally realistic world in the novel and includes the same group of novelists as the first category. The third category consists of novelists who emphasise play and parody, and includes Dazai Osamu (1909–48) and Sakaguchi Ango (1906–55). The fourth category includes such novelists as Mishima Yukio (1925–70) and Ōoka Shōhei who construct fictional tales in which little trace can be found of the author. The fifth category deals with intellectual or ideological fiction (at the time often influenced by existentialism) written by authors such as Haniya Yutaka. The final category is concerned with novels that focus on the relationship between the self and other and includes writers such as Dazai and Takeda Taijun (1912–76) (Tsuge, 1989: 4–5).

This description implies an orderly historical narrative of various schools of postwar fiction covering the several categories enumerated above. Nevertheless, as these different categories were dominant at different times in the first two decades after 1945, and as several categories overlapped, the reality was neither as neat nor as orderly as the above description states. For example, the appearance of existentialist fiction like Haniya Yutaka's famous postwar novel *Shirei* (Ghosts, 1946–76) led to a debate between Haniya and Yoshimoto Takaaki on such fiction where Yoshimoto declared that these were 'readerless' novels (Quoted: Kuritsubo, 1997: 6–14). The category in which Mishima Yukio was placed, therefore, implicitly champions a novel for readers, a more traditional style of novel with a strong story line. Moreover, as postwar literature is a commercial product sold as a commodity by professional authors whose income depends upon sales, all the above types of fiction were in competition for much the same market.

The critic Oketani Hideaki has argued that Mishima was a 'heretic' (itansha) or outlaw because he went against prevailing trends in postwar literature. Oketani's view is that the immediate postwar generation of authors wrote principally about the war, or, as a reaction to the war, focused on the depression—spiritual as well as material—which resulted from the defeat. He writes that Mishima instead mourned the ending of the war on the grounds that something valuable had been lost. What was lost for Mishima, argues Oketani, is the day-to-day prospect of death (Oketani, 1972: 154–5). The critic Nakamura Mitsuo argued a similar case, claiming Mishima's emphasis on sexuality clearly opposed the dominant humanistic and progressive trend of postwar writing (Nakamura, 1968: 161).

Oketani's viewpoint arises, in the main, from a reading of Mishima's first major novel *Kamen no Kokuhaku* (Confessions of a Mask, 1949). It is fascinating how many well-known generalisations made about Mishima's writing by Japanese critics can also be applied to *Confessions of a Mask*. It is as if the novel is so typical of Mishima's oeuvre that it can stand as a litmus test on views about his literature as a whole. Nibuya Takashi argues that Mishima's plot structures are simplicity itself: an expression of a fundamental alienation from life, and then the story of the protagonist's attempts to escape that alienation (Nibuya, 1991: 50–1).

The distinguished critic Sasaki Kiichi, writing in 1951, forty years before Nibuya, argues that Mishima's writing is rooted in paradox and parody, and thus, ironically, disappoints readers' more prosaic expectations (Sasaki, 1972: 1). As Takeda Katsuhiko's 1989 survey of forty years of critical responses to *Confessions of a Mask* reveals, such views are not at all uncommon among the myriad reactions that the novel has stimulated (Takeda, 1989: 145–9).

From almost the day it was published, *Confessions of a Mask* has been recognised as one of Mishima's major works: the first truly important novel he had published since his decision to become a full-time author in September 1948, a decision taken only ten months before the publication of *Confessions* (hereafter, this abbreviated title will be used) in July 1949. As Mishima's biographer John Nathan records, the novel became an instant best-seller, and provoked as many negative as positive reviews (Nathan, 1974: 100).

The story of *Confessions* is quite straightforward. Told in the first person, it is an autobiography of a sensitive youth who from his first memories of childhood is attracted to men. The autobiography or confession quite explicitly links memories to the protagonist's sexuality—the narrator's first ejaculation occurred as a result of the impact upon his senses of Guido Reni's medieval painting of St Sebastian pierced through his bare chest by arrows. At the onset of adolescence, the narrator determines to wear a mask: to conceal his true nature from the world, and pose as heterosexual. But his pose is complex: he decides that he can love a woman without any sexual desire. He manages to achieve this unlikely aim by falling in love with a girl called Sonoko (by this time in the narrative we are in the midst of World War II). But realising his love for Sonoko is incomplete and hollow, he even contemplates suicide as a form of escape. In the end, she marries someone else and the protagonist, while grateful for his escape, is still torn by desires he feels are illicit.

This plot summary shows that the 'plot' or the action of the novel is not all that important. The chief merit of the work is the fine, sensitive, at times, brilliant portrait of the narrator—related in Mishima's glittering tragicomic style. One interesting point is that, as far as I can tell, the narrator's name is given at only one place in the narrative. The English translator Meredith Weatherby romanises this name as 'Kōchan' (little Kō) but the Chinese character may better be read as 'Kimi-chan' (little Kimi) (Mishima, 1949: 52; Mishima, 1958: 113). Kimitake is Mishima's real name, whereas Yukio (like Mishima) is a pen-name, and Mishima was probably called 'Kimi-chan' as a child.

The question of whether the novel is truly autobiographical, and whether the 'confessions' of latent homosexuality by the protagonist are actually those of Mishima himself, has been debated endlessly. Nathan's interviews with Mishima's mother confirm that the love affair in the second half of the novel, where the protagonist tries to convince himself he loves the seventeen-year-old Sonoko, is based on reality (Nathan, 1974: 79–80). But Mishima also wrote more than once that it was not autobiographical, stating famously that the novel was 'a pure fabrication', and that he had 'attempted to create a perfectly fictional confession' (Quoted Mushiaki, 1973: 8; Miyoshi, 1974: 149).

Although this debate will continue for many years yet, it is worth noting that a novel-memoir about Mishima written by Fukushima Jirō, in which he claims to have been Mishima's lover around the time *Confessions* was written, was pulped by court order on publication in 1998 after the author was charged with slander by Mishima's relatives (Fukushima, 1998: 61–137; Okamura, 1998: 44–50). However, as numerous critics have noted, in an important sense, it is irrelevant whether *Confessions* is an accurate representation of Mishima's life at the time. As the scholar Miyoshi Masao writes (in the best critique of the novel to appear in English to date), memoirs, when recorded as literature, are always the product of selection and arrangement, and are thus ultimately fictional (Miyoshi, 1974: 147).

The novel has an uneven tempo, as if Mishima could not make up his mind as to what is meant to be a parody of the traditional genre of autobiographical fiction or *watakushi shōsetsu* (I-novel), as it is known, and what is meant to be an authentic portrait of a young man struggling to come to terms with his homosexual tendencies. Both elements feature in the novel: the parody evident in the stylised descriptions of sadistic fantasy and over-ratiocinated self-analysis indulged in by the protagonist–narrator, and the authentic note of realism in the description of the protagonist's love (a purely emotional and asexual love) for Sonoko.

The narratorial voice, especially in the second half of the novel, where the narrator comes to realise the impossibility of his love for Sonoko, is quite convincing. The histrionic absurdities of the narration in the first half also add to the verisimilitude of narratorial presence while providing a doubled sense of readerly pleasure, as the presence of Mishima as playful author is superimposed subtly onto the narrative. Thus Mishima creates a doubled text—narrator as character, narrator as author—in this stylistic tour de force.

If the dislocations of the war, and the effect that the constant fear of death has on the individual psyche, create an important element of the structure of *Confessions*, then a more overt response to the spiritual crisis of postwar Japan can be easily discerned in *Kinkakuji* (The Temple of the Golden Pavilion, 1956), perhaps Mishima's greatest novel.

The novel is based upon a real event, an arson attempt by a young monk on the famous Kinkakuji (Temple of the Golden Pavilion) in Kyoto in July 1950. Compared to *Confessions*, it is a much more complex and dense work. The density derives not merely from the intricate stylistic variations in language—the novel contains several quotations from Buddhist sutras, frequent lyrical descriptive tableau and a large number of characters speaking in the distinctly captivating Kyoto dialect—but also from its complex construction. Numerous dualities structure the narrative: the relationship of the acolyte monk Mizoguchi to his evil undergraduate classmate Kashiwagi explicitly contrasted to his relationship with his saintlike classmate Tsurukawa; Mizoguchi's relationships with his good and evil superiors; and, most significantly, his relationships with the females in his life beginning with his adolescent infatuation with Uiko, his love–hate antagonism towards his mother, and ending in the unsatisfactory erotic connections with the warwidow, and the prostitute Mariko. Mizoguchi oscillates between good and evil, swayed first by an attraction to one, then the other.

The story is, like *Confessions of A Mask*, told in the first person by Mizoguchi, who relates the difficulties of his childhood, which he links to his stuttering. This created a residue of bitterness in the young man that festers and turns to malevolent evil. The son of a priest, he follows in his father's footsteps and becomes an acolyte at the Temple of the Golden Pavilion, one of the most beautiful and celebrated temples in Japan. His fellow-acolyte Tsurukawa is the embodiment of good, while Kashiwagi, a classmate at Ōtani Buddhist University, where Mizoguchi studies after the war, is the embodiment of evil. After Tsurukawa dies suddenly, Kashiwagi takes his place—good is replaced by evil, further corrupting Mizoguchi. The struggle against good is symbolised in Mizoguchi's twisted mind by the Golden Temple; to destroy good, he resolves to burn it down. When the temple is burning, he flees into the mountains, and there the story ends.

Mizoguchi himself is depicted as struggling within the aura cast by the evil, the alienation inherent in his own self, symbolised by his stammering. Paradoxically, to banish the evil, to live as a normal human being, he has to burn down the temple, which in his eyes represents a beauty so far beyond his normal state that it is a threat. Mishima linked the theme of beauty and the arson attack on Kinkakuji as early as two months after the attack, according to the critic Muramatsu Takeshi, who in his 1990 book on Mishima, cites as evidence Mishima's published response (issued in September 1950) to an article by the distinguished critic Kobayashi Hideo on the arson (Muramatsu, 1990: 250–1). Oddly enough, both Mishima and Kobayashi returned to a discussion of beauty but linked it to the novel in a well-known dialogue published in January 1957, only three months after the novel's publication in a single volume (it had been serialised over the preceding eleven months).

In this dialogue, Mishima noted that the arsonist had no real motive for the attack. According to his research, the arsonist committed the crime out of petty envy. Kobayashi argued that the novel was not really a novel, being unconcerned with social issues and not dealing with arson at all. According to Kobayashi, the novel was really 'a lyric poem' (Mishima, 1957: 286). Presumably Kobayashi meant by this the powerful aesthetic effect created by Mishima's stylistic legerdemain, which focuses upon the brooding beauty of the Golden Temple. However, strong views to the contrary were soon in evidence. Nakamura Mitsuo wrote a much-cited critique in December 1957 where he argued that the character of Mizoguchi represents the youth of Mishima's generation, an 'objectification' of the dilemmas of that generation (Quoted: Mushiaki, 1973: 10–11).

Looking back from the perspective of nearly half a century later, this viewpoint seems most prescient. If we place the novel in its historical context, then we can see how the rejection of the beauty of the Golden Temple by Mizoguchi can be interpreted as a rejection of the traditions of the past, and by extension, of the past itself, by Mishima's generation.

Japanese tradition (used in various ways as an all-encompassing propaganda tool by the wartime authorities) had led the nation to defeat, had left the postwar generation with nothing but ashes. What more appropriate way to destroy that past than by exorcising the darkness of the generation who came of age after the war, but who experienced the war's full horror, by a symbolic conflagration as proposed in Mishima's novel?

More than any other example of Mishima's fiction, *The Temple of the Golden Pavilion* has served as a touchstone to debate over the meaning of Mishima's suicide in 1970. As a result of the suicide, the well-known critic Miyoshi Yukio reversed his famous view that the last line of the novel: 'I wanted to live' (Ikiyō to watashi wa omotta)—in the translation by Ivan Morris—meant that Mishima had 'banished.... Mizoguchi into the real world', to argue, that on the contrary it was Mizoguchi who had 'banished Mishima Yukio into the world of art' (Quoted Kitani, 1998: 83–4).

Here Miyoshi, taking up the debate in the novel about knowledge and action, is arguing that action is superior, that Mizoguchi's act of arson prefigures Mishima's suicide, thus reversing his earlier view that the discourse of the novel, the aesthetics of the text, so to speak, triumphed over Mizoguchi's action. Much in the novel defies clear explanation, and this deliberate obscuring of event and psychology by the author perhaps mimics real life, and adds a strong note of authenticity, if only in the verisimilitude of perception, to the otherwise artfully constructed novel. It may also explain the novel's initial success with readers and its continuing significance today for a generation of readers for whom the war is not even a memory.

The body politic: Ōe Kenzaburō

Ōe Kenzaburō was born in 1935, ten years later than Mishima, and this may be the reason that, despite the parallel course of their careers (until Mishima's suicide), Ōe seems clearly to represent a different generation from Mishima. However, his early fiction can be read equally as a strong, if not dissimilar, reaction to the war, and the impact it had on the generations who came to maturity afterwards.

Ōe achieved fame very early in life: while still a student at Tokyo University he was awarded the Akutagawa Prize for his novella 'Shiiku' (The Catch, 1958). (This distinguished prize is given annually for the best work of fiction written that year by a new writer.) This story, written when Ōe was only 23, is typical of the outpouring of fiction that exploded from his pen in his early twenties. Ōe castigated postwar Japan for its narrow-minded, almost xenophobic ethnocentrism, which he perceived as the dark side of the new democratic postwar state. Far from Japan embracing democratic principles, in work after work Ōe took his fellow countrymen to task for barely understanding those principles in their narrow-minded pursuit of material wealth. Ōe wrote numerous essays that established him as a spokesman for the democratic left fighting against a hegemonic conservative state structure centred on the Emperor.

Thus it came as a surprise that after writing at helter-skelter pace a body of explicitly political work, at the age of twenty-nine Ōe turned to something resembling autobiography. After the birth the previous year of his first son Hikari, with significant brain damage, Ōe wrote a novel called *Kojinteki na Taiken* (A Personal Matter, 1964) that seemingly dramatised this most traumatic event. In fact, to what degree the novel is autobiographical is an issue still raging among critics even today. Kuroko Kazuo in his 1989 study of Ōe, criticises his fellow critic Hasumi Shigehiko's view that the novel is 'a universalisation of a personal matter' (Kuroko, 1989: 147). Kuroko's opinion is that the novel has many themes other than the obvious one of the dilemma that the protagonist 'Bird' falls into when confronted by the birth of his deformed son.

In the novel, Bird loses his job as a teacher at a college prep school after an alcoholic binge, and stays for a night or two of non-stop sex with an old girlfriend called Himiko. The cause of Bird's dissipation is the dilemma of whether he should authorise an operation on his infant son, which may well kill the child or leave him a vegetable, or simply let him die. In the end, he approves the operation that saves the infant's life and decides to return to his wife to make a new life with their son.

There is no doubt the events described parallel the real events in Ōe's life, at least in the dilemma of what to do about the infant born with a brain hernia. The critic Ichijō Takao reads the novel as the exploration of a new life, a new beginning—an explicitly autobiographical reading (Ichijō, 1985: 35). Ōe himself in his 1987 novel *Natsukashii Toshi e no Tegami* (Letters to Wistful Years), which reads very much like an ironic self-reflexive attempt at autobiography, discusses *A Personal Matter* almost entirely as an exercise in autobiography. In the guise of his narrator 'K',

Ōe notes the criticism directed at the novel by his contemporaries, led by Mishima Yukio, that the 'happy ending' was contrived and out of character with the dark, pessimistic tone of the rest of the work. In a letter from another character Gii to K, Gii argues that the happy ending is absolutely necessary and appropriate, given the probable reactions of K's family, especially his wife (in the novel, K's wife is Yū, in reality Kenzaburō's wife is Yukari) to him writing anything other than the truth (Ōe, 1992: 460–1).

Karatani Kōjin seems to agree with Hasumi when he states that Gii's discussion of the novel confirms the universal nature of the character 'I' (meaning, in a sense, the 'I'—the first-person narrator—of both novels) (Karatani, 1996a: 153). Whether because the novel was so different from the political fiction that preceded it, *A Personal Matter* received great critical acclaim. Ichijō writes that the novel's success overturned the generally negative critical views of Ōe's writing that had been on the increase immediately prior to its publication (Ichijō, 1985: 28). But this is not to say that the novel is universally praised.

Karatani, while discussing Mishima's critique of the ending as neither here nor there, argues that the implied connections between the deformed infant and the H-bomb testing mentioned in the novel is, despite Ōe's intention to make the link, simple self-deception. Ōe's elaborations of the infant into a universal victim (here Karatani is pointing to other representations of Hikari-like figures in later novels) are false to the individual realities of the victims, as the image of the grotesque child is merely a version of Ōe's own alienated self (Karatani, 1990: 301–2).

Karatani is correct in pointing out the plot defect of the deformed infant taking on symbolic dimensions not justified by the text itself. Other flaws are obvious: not the decision to 'save' the infant, but the absurdity of Himiko fulfilling Bird's fantasy to travel to Zanzibar. Indeed, despite the praise showered on the creation of Himiko by the American scholar Susan Napier, she appears as yet another version of the deeply unhappy yet madly promiscuous sexpot with a heart of gold—a literary cliché if ever there was one (Napier, 1991: 91). Even with these flaws, the novel is a success, as contemporary critics recognised.

The power of the youthful Ōe's language, which approaches poetry with its deliberately extravagant imagery, invests Bird with immense force—his anguish described in rhetoric so strained it approaches Gerard

Manley Hopkins' famous 'no worst, there is none' sonnet. One odd piece of synchronicity is the fact that Bird's much-discussed anal intercourse with Himiko—which restores his virility—parallels a similar scene in Norman Mailer's famous novel *An American Dream*, written and serialised at much the same time as *A Personal Matter*. Both scenes became notorious among contemporary readers for their breaking of the taboo of anal sex; whether Ōe was influenced by Mailer is an open question.

In 1967 Ōe published *Man'en Gannen no Futtobōru* (translated as *The Silent Cry*) in serial form from January to July in the *Gunzō* magazine. Two months after its publication in September 1967 as a single volume, it was awarded the Tanizaki Jun'ichichirō prize. The novel has received almost unqualified praise since its appearance. If length is any index of serious content, it is interesting to note that the novel was the longest work Ōe had written to date. The novel returned once again to the political themes that had largely concerned him before *A Personal Matter*. In addition, the novel is largely set in a remote village in a valley in what seems clear is Shikoku, Ōe's birthplace: this is a return to the settings of his early short stories.

The plot revolves around the relationship of two brothers, the elder Mitsusaburō (shortened to 'Mitsu' in the story) and the younger Takashi (shortened to 'Taka'). Takashi returns to Tokyo from the USA whence he had fled in order to avoid complications arising from his involvement in the anti-US riots and demonstrations of the 1960s over the re-signing of the US–Japan Security Treaty. He proposes to Mitsu that they return to their native village to help the villagers in a scheme to organise trade with the Korean owner of a supermarket chain, called the 'Emperor' locally, and so bring about a revitalisation of the village. The family has traditionally been the 'lords' of the manor, and lives in a majestic mansion overlooking the village. Mitsu agrees and returns to the village with his wife Natsumi. But Mitsu has been deceived by Taka who has sold the mansion to the 'Emperor', pretending it was his brother's decision.

Taka increasingly sees his destiny as repeating the experience of his great-grandfather's younger brother who led a village rebellion against the authorities in the 1860s and was killed (so Taka believes) by his older brother, Mitsu's great-grandfather. Taka enlists the support of the local youths in an attack on the village supermarket, a re-enactment of the earlier rebellion. Mitsu knows the 'rebellion' is something of a lie, and refuses to play the role of his great-grandfather in Taka's violent fantasy.

Natsumi, who is an alcoholic due to the birth of her deformed son left in care in Tokyo, leaves her husband for the charismatic Taka. Mitsu is left alone translating English literature in the attic, refusing to take part in his brother's shenanigans. In a climactic scene, Taka tells Mitsu that he has raped and murdered a young woman, and when his brother refuses to believe him (saying he was sure it was an accident), confesses to incest with their retarded younger sister, which led to her suicide. Mitsu castigates Taka for his 'heroic fantasies', and refuses to answer his question of: 'Why have you always disliked me?' Soon after, Taka shoots himself, leaving behind the message, 'I told the truth' (Ōe, 1974: 243–4).

The novel is full of complex ironies: the parallel plots of the contemporary brothers repeating the drama of their ancestors are full of ironic reversals, with revelation after revelation of yet another layer of deception in both sets of relationships. The actual family history, with their older brother being killed by Koreans after World War II attempting a similar attack to that a hundred years previously, adds yet another layer of ironic repetition. Even the Japanese title—Football in the First Year of the Man'en Era (1860)—is ironic as the era only lasted the one year. Taka's quixotic and meaningless death seems to presage Mishima Yukio's own meaningless suicide three years later. Indeed, in Taka's political rhetoric, which Mitsu continually undermines, pointing out the numerous contradictions and absurdities, we almost see a Mishima-like caricature.

The novel itself is, for most Japanese readers then and now, a most political work. Most readers have read the story as an attack on authoritarianism, both the authoritarianism of the Japanese government in the 1960s, and especially during the anti-American riots that occurred in 1960 (thus, again, the irony of the title), and the authoritarianism of the anti-government protesters. Kuroko Kazuo argues this way, extending his interpretation to contend that the novel questions the whole notion of modernity, constructing a dystopian fantasy (while seemingly realistic) questioning Japanese government policies of the sixties. Kuroko sees the influence of Yanagita Kunio and Orikuchi Shinobu in Ōe's creation of the village as a site of an alternative history to the official one (Kuroko, 1989: 27–34).

Karatani Kōjin holds similar views but reads the novel as an allegory, arguing that it is not directly about 1960 but rather is an attempt to save the self (both Mitsu's and Taka's lives seem fixed on an inexorable downwards slope) as well as save the state, and modern Japanese history, by foregrounding the violence inherent in the state as revealed in the savagery associated in the novel with Japanese involvement with Asia (S's complicity in war crimes on the Asian continent, the attack on Koreans etc). Thus the village is a unique cosmos unto itself, an individual space that cannot, except by allegory, be related to the transcendent structures of history. However, Karatani's conclusion is that the novel foretells the end of 'modern literature' (Karatani, 1996a: 52–88).

This reading of the novel as allegorical is inspired, in part, by the increasing use by Ōe of similar allegorised sites in the dystopian fictions that followed. Susan Napier takes this line of reasoning to an extreme by reading the novel almost entirely as a mythos, an exploration of sacrifice in the wasteland romance (Napier, 1991: 181–96). The same kind of structural analysis can be found in Michiko N. Wilson's 1986 book on Ōe, the first monograph-length study of Ōe in English, which focuses on the ironic transpositions of 1860 to 1960 in its analysis of the novel (Wilson, 1986: 48–60).

One of the major reasons for the novel's success is the powerful balance between the political and the personal that Ōe achieves. The tension between the two brothers—a complex mixture of love and guilt—is beautifully conveyed in Mitsu's jazz-like poetic first-person narrative. This balance is doubled in the contrasting political perspectives that the two brothers hold. In a sense, we listen to both voices: to the extreme anti-capitalist left (which approaches the authoritarian right—demonstrated in the history of Mitsu's family) in Taka's wild, narcissistic but violent and conspiracy-ridden fantasies; and the liberal or progressive left in Mitsu's cynical but sympathetic revulsion for consumer capitalism.

The novel ends when Mitsu goes to Africa to work (a little more realistic than Ōe's previous utopian evocations of Africa) and Natsumi bears Taka's child, which henceforth the couple will raise as their own. Both viewpoints are thus reconciled in the birth of new life, a constant theme in Ōe's writing, though it is often expressed as rebirth or resurrection. Ōe being awarded the Nobel Prize for Literature in 1994 represents, perhaps, a recognition that these themes are not uniquely Japanese but are common to many of the significant authors of the twentieth century.

Postwar poetry

The scholar Kokai Eiji has divided postwar verse into six different categories: 'democratic poetry', which established workers' circles to encourage working-class and rural poets, and which therefore had a leftist (i.e. anti-American) political colouration; the 'Arechi' (Wasteland) group of poets led by Ayukawa Nobuo (1920–86), which dominated the poetry scene until the mid-1950s; an explicitly leftist group of poets associated with the *Rettō* (Archipelago) journal which, in the poet Sekine Hiroshi's (b.1920) words, spoke of 'resisting the current situation of Japan as a colony [of the US]' (Quoted Kokai, 1977: 14); such poets as Ōoka Makoto (b.1931) and Tanikawa Shuntarō (b.1931) who had no wartime service experience (unlike the 'Wasteland' poets); poets who emerged in the affluent 1960s not aligned with any particular poetic faction; and, finally, a new generation of poets who began writing from the 1960s onwards (Kokai, 1977: 3, 3–23; Kokai, 1973).

By 'postwar', Kokai means the first twenty or so years after the war, but this periodisation is contested by many poets as Kokai himself is the first to admit (Kokai, 1973: 3–25). Where do we draw the dividing line between postwar and 'modern' (gendai)? If we label verse that is clearly influenced by the war, in that it is documentary poetry recording the horrors of the war, as 'postwar' then we can classify much of the poetry written until 1960 as falling into this category. Kokai identifies a large part of the verse of poets like Ayukawa, Andō Tsuguo (b.1919), Akiya Yutaka (b.1922), and Ryūichi Tamura (b.1923) as explicitly documentary in nature (Kokai, 1973: 26–60).

Even women poets like Ibaragi Noriko (b.1926), Ishigaki Rin (b.1920), and Yoshihara Sachiko (b.1932), who write from a feminist perspective on a variety of themes, composed much poetry bearing on the war, if only indirectly. Ibaragi's famous poem 'Watashi ga Ichiban Kirei Datta Toki' (When I was My Most Beautiful), published in her second verse collection issued in 1958, lamented how the war had robbed her of her youth, although it ends on an optimistic note describing how she will spend her mature years like Rouault who 'painted the most beautiful paintings' (Quoted Kokai, 1977: 231–2).

Before discussing the Wasteland poets in more detail, we will take a brief look at some of the other notable collections of poetry produced during these years outside the Wasteland aesthetic. The poet Tanigawa

Gan (1923–95) took up the issue of peasant or rural poetry in a number of well-known essays published between 1945 and 1957. In 1958, he was associated with a magazine entitled *Minzoku Shijin* (Ethnic Poets) that raised these issues, and published such poetry. One of the most important collections produced by this movement was the Osaka poet Inoue Toshio's (b.1922) award-winning 1956 collection *No ni Kakaru Niji* (Rainbow in the Fields). Not only did this collection paint the harsh lives lived by the peasantry in Japan (little changed in some respects from a century ago) in realistic colours but it did so with a poignant lyricism.

The poem 'Chibusa' (Breasts) from this collection describes the lowly position of a farm wife who has to wait until her neighbours finish to use the bath, which is now filled with dirty water. Her ample breasts, a symbol of her womanhood, are thus wasted as her position is equivalent to that of a slave (Kokai, 1973: 232–49). This poem can be contrasted with Ishigaki Rin's poem 'Sentō De' (At the Bathhouse), written twenty years later, which describes working-class women at an urban bathhouse, so poor that they cannot afford to lose even one-yen coins in the soapy water, but who also have a certain unstated pride in their nakedness (Morton, 1997: 85–6).

Another collection that revealed the difficult conditions of postwar Japan was Kuroda Saburō's (1912–80) 1960 collection *Chiisana Yuri to* (With Tiny Yuri), which consists of twelve poems, described by the poet in his postscript as 'a record of my heart', about the six months the poet spent raising his small daughter Yuri while his wife was hospitalised. Kuroda had to continue to work during this time, and this moving collection records his sadness at not being able to fulfil the roles of husband, father, and breadwinner adequately (Kokai, 1973: 146–7).

The impact that the war had on Japan was not confined to the years immediately after the war. The poet Soh Sakon's famous 1968 book-length poem *Moeru Haha* (Mother Burning), about the death of his mother on 25 May 1945 while attempting to evacuate her from Tokyo during a massive US air force incendiary raid, and the subsequent burden of guilt on the poet, demonstrates perfectly how the war remained a major theme for poets long after the event had receded into historical memory (Morton, 1991: 88–96; Morton, 1992: 161–7).

The scholar Sawa Masahiro argues that the Wasteland group was simply unable to escape from the impact of the war. (Sawa, 1996: 105–11) One of the poets associated with this group, Nakagiri Masao (1919–83), wrote in the second *Wasteland* journal published in 1947 that his was the 'lost generation', thus taking up the theme that Ibaragi later immortalised in her poem (Quoted Sawa, 1996: 108). According to one of the founding members, the poet Kuroda Saburō, the group had lost its intensity by 1954, although it still commanded a powerful presence in contemporary poetry circles (Kokai, 1982: 432).

Tanikawa Shuntarō commented on the postwar poetry environment in an interview in 1997, noting that 'that there was a time when poetry, especially the poets known as the "Wasteland" group, occupied a very powerful position... The distinguished poet and critic Ōoka Makoto later used the phrase "a festival of sensibility" to sum up the poetry of my [younger] generation. We were opposed to the notion that poetry should be constructed as a critique of society or follow a particular ideology' (Morton, 1988: 8). Hence Tanikawa clearly implies that the Wasteland poets were pursuing a distinctly critical social ideology. Ōoka Makoto has described the verse of the Wasteland poets as a 'poetry of themes', making the point that their poetry was opposed to tradition, whether that be the millennia-old tradition of lyric poetry or the prewar tradition of modernist poetry, and thus came to be focused on social and political themes (Ōoka, 1978: 207–8, 234).

The polemical essay 'Dedication to X' (usually assumed to be written by Ayukawa) included in the first Wasteland anthology published in July 1951 is generally considered to be the manifesto of the group, and explains their position in transparent terms. The manifesto declares that the present is a wasteland and goes on to say: 'If you and we have a future, it will emerge from us not despairing of life today... Ignoring peace, asking questions, using the most sensitive organ—the ear—judiciously; and deepening our understanding of our lives, continuing our intellectual quest most patiently—using all the painful endeavours of the spirit, we must face this wasteland of the present... If you can grasp our meaning in this nameless, mass society, in which we are linked so closely, then you will understand all the more' (Quoted Kokai, 1973: 48–9). However, by being critical of the present, poets were free of the burden of the past, as Ayukawa wrote in a 1950 essay entitled 'Sokoku Naki Seishin' (Poetry without a Fatherland): 'It is still too easy for us to possess a fatherland. We are the world's beggars. We've got nothing in our pockets. But we can walk anywhere we want to go' (Quoted Kurihara, 1988: 199).

This statement recalls the difficult circumstances of postwar Japan with its poverty and lack of material resources. But the freedom that

Ayukawa mentioned in his essay was not matched by a corresponding valorisation of freedom in his verse, as Sawa has pointed out. The freedom in thought and action that postwar Japan gave to its citizens was celebrated in poetry by a younger generation who, by and large, were too young to fight in the war.

The clarion call of this generation was first heard in the essay 'Sekai e' (To the World) by Tanikawa Shuntarō, published in the first issue of the *Yuriika* magazine in October 1956: 'What we need to give to people is inspiration. It's not necessary for us to have a profound philosophy or definite worldview or sharp social analysis. Such things render poetry of no use, and thus poetic inspiration is lost. Through inspiration poets give birth to poetry and this links us to people... We don't live in order to write poetry. We write poetry in order to go on living or because we are alive. I am not in love with poetry, I am in love with the world. In reality, no poet in the Japan of 1956 can eat because of his poetry. But that is not a reason to isolate poetry. We have to strive to sell poetry. Because the fact that poetry sells means people are enjoying it...we can slip poetry into songs, thriller movies, even strip shows' (Quoted Takahashi, 1997: 330–3).

Tanikawa fulfilled his own prescription and has since become the best-known and most widely read poet in contemporary Japan. He burst onto the literary scene in 1952 at the age of twenty-one with his collection *Nijū Oku Kōnen no Kodoku* (Twenty Billion Light Years of Loneliness). His verse was fresh and new, his focus on the quotidian issues of daily life appeared in sharp contrast to older, postwar poets who still focused on the war and unresolved issues arising from it. Tanikawa's poetry rarely grappled directly with politics, in stark contrast to the postwar school. And this disengagement from ideology and a turn to a new sensibility proved immensely popular among readers. It is instructive to compare the last stanza of Tanikawa's three-stanza poem 'Haru' (Spring) from *Twenty Billion Light Years of Loneliness* to the famous poem 'Tenki' (Weather) from Nishiwaki Junzaburō's (1894–1982) 1933 collection *Ambarvalia*. Tanikawa's stanza reads:

> A moment in spring
> With god
> I had a quiet chat

Tanikawa, 1986: 99

While Nishiwaki's poem reads:

> Morning like an (upturn'd gem)
> Someone whispers at the doorway to someone else
> Today is the birthday of a god

Nishiwaki, 1991: 14

Nishiwaki's prewar modernist gem of formalist displacement stands in stark contrast to Tanikawa's down-to-earth, even childish (although this is more obvious in Japanese than English) diction, which grounds and demythologises the notion of divinity. The rest of the poem speaks of a journey to the clouds, and the narrator is 'always climbing'. But he does not meet Nishiwaki's god. Tanikawa's god is, perhaps, nature, or simply aspiration, quite a mundane divinity. Tanikawa's work at this moment is a classic demonstration of Ōoka Makoto's phrase 'a festival of sensibility'. Ōoka's expression is often read as indicating the turn to language that occurred in the 1960s, which can be paraphrased as a 'festival of language', as opposed to the 1950s emphasis on themes.

The turn to language poetry

Kokai Eiji has identified several poetry collections published at this time which focus on language as the subject of poetry: Naka Tarō's (b.1922) 1965 collection *Ongaku* (Music), especially the poem 'Mayu' (Cocoon); Nakae Toshio's (b.1919) 1969 collection *Goishū* (Words); Fujitomi Yasuo's (b.1928) various collections including *Koruku no Sara* (Cork Plates, 1953), *Hachigatsu no Nanika* (August Something, 1954), and *Seikaku na Aimai* (Precise Vagueness, 1961); and especially Suzuki Shiroyasu's (b.1935) 1967 collection *Kansei Dōsei Mata wa Kansei e no Tōsō* (Tin Cohabitation or an Escape from the Trap), which featured an extraordinary ten-poem sequence entitled 'Shishōsetsu teki Puapua' (An Autobiographical Puapua), a tour de force of erotic language that had quite an effect on contemporary poetry (Kokai, 1973: 299–306).

However, the dominant poet of the 1950s and 1960s was Yoshioka Minoru (1919–90) whose two major collections of the time, *Seibutsu* (Still Life, 1955) and *Sōryo* (Monks, 1958), continued the older, prewar modernist tradition of the avant-garde actively discouraged by the wartime authorities, and trenchantly criticised by such postwar poet-critics as

Yoshimoto Takaaki who preferred the metaphysical existentialist verse of the Wasteland poets. Indeed, in some respects, we can argue that Yoshioka was a language poet maudit.

The American scholar Marjorie Perloff in her study of the legacy of French symbolism, *The Poetics of Indeterminacy* (1981), identifies two distinct linguistic traditions inherited by poets in the West: the symbolist and anti-symbolist. The symbolist mode of writing is inherited from Charles Baudelaire, and in it, the whole coheres despite a complex layering of symbolic threads; in Perloff's words, 'the relationship of the word to its referents, of signifier to signified, remains essentially intact'. The anti-symbolist mode is characterised by an 'indeterminacy or "indecidability", of literalness and free play' that was inherited from Arthur Rimbaud (Perloff, 1981: 17).

We can apply Perloff's conceptual framework to modern Japanese verse as well which, as many commentators have noted, was more influenced by French poetry than any other comparable body of verse. Using Perloff's conceptual frame, we can see that Yoshioka was undoubtedly the major poet of indeterminacy in postwar Japanese verse. As Ōoka Makoto has written, 'Only after World War Two was Japanese poetry ready to absorb concretely the real meaning of European movements such as dada, surrealism, expressionism, Neue Sachlichkeit, and existentialism... it was only after the Japanese experienced nuclear war, rubble and hunger that the real force of these movements came home to them' (Quoted Yoshioka, 1985: 19).

Hence, Yoshioka was the spiritual heir to 1920s poets, being more determinately indeterminate than older poets such as Nishiwaki. Yoshioka himself wrote about his method of composition, 'I become calmly saturated with a certain consciousness and a certain composition, and reality is established. Then come moments of white heat. I'm visited with ennui, and then by despair. I see a certain painting. A female body is imagined. I touch a substance hard as a tortoise-shell...' (Quoted Yoshioka, 1985: 26). As the translator of this passage Tsuruoka Yoshihisa remarks, this reminds us of automatic writing, the staple technique of twenties 'undecidable verse'.

Yoshioka's poetry of this time, while indeterminate, nevertheless retains some of Nishiwaki's characteristic associative thrust, with the logic of the verse seemingly explicable on some conceptual level. Part seven of *Monks* in Onuma Tadayoshi's translation reads:

four monks
one of them writes the origin of the temple and
the histories of the four
another writes the lives of the world's flower queens
a third writes the histories of the axe and the
chariot and the monkey
a fourth because he is dead
hides himself from the others and burns one
after another
the histories that the other three write

Yoshioka, 1985: 56

In Yoshioka's later poetry the sense of conceptual displacement grows stronger, as does the use of the collage technique. Thus the later poems are less amenable to translation, although their impact in contemporary poetry circles was considerable. One such conceptual poem is 'Dōbutsu' (Animal) from the 1976 collection *Safuran Tsumi* (Saffron Gathering):

I hear that
In the rain
It seemed to be an animal, a live animal in fact
Gathering many 'lines'
It raced towards the base of the cliff
The shadow of the red swollen heart of an animal
Pricking its ears
Not showing its back
Like a rhino grazing on the grass
Standing in the corner of a white wall
It seemed, beyond doubt, to be a moistened leather chair
Bending its body in the middle
Placing its hair and bones underneath the table
Towards its lonely den
It walks slowly
What on earth could
This 'animal' be?
Already incorporating many 'facets'
Together with phantasmagorical children
Now it's about to cross a long rope

> Beneath it may be a desert
> Exceeding the jarring of our recognition
> The night trails a string
> The dead animal lets out a cry
> At the springboard it turns one somersault
> And is finally buried beneath the froth
> Display its feet
> Hiding its eyes
> It ends a single 'poem'

Yoshioka, 1983: 104–5

Yoshioka was the heir to poets of the jazz era of the twenties, such as Nishiwaki Junzaburō (although Nishiwaki and others like him continued to write poetry). Yoshioka's poetry is, at times, difficult and obscure but a focus on the complexity of meaning can easily be seen as another kind of response to the debased language of ideology born of the totalitarian politics of war. Yoshioka's poetry is also controversial, with a variety of critical viewpoints contending for dominance. Ōoka Makoto argues that, despite the clearly undecidable or ambiguous nature—Ōoka's preferred description is 'rich and polysemous'—of most of Yoshioka's collections, ambiguity as a technique is not characteristic of his early writing (Ōoka, 1978: 207). The poet–critic Shimaoka Shin, in his 1998 one-volume history of modern Japanese poetry, argues that Yoshioka was undeniably a surrealist poet who sublimated his own wartime experiences in his verse. He cites the poet Kiyooka Takuyuki's phrase 'internal documentary' as characteristic of Yoshioka's technique. Shimaoka, like most other critics, also notes how influential Yoshioka was for the poets of his and later generations (Shimaoka, 1998: 248–51).

The scholar Tsuboi Hideto takes up both issues of surrealist influence and Yoshioka's technique to argue that the poet was much influenced in his characteristic diction by his early studies in classical Japanese verse, and also declares that the impact of prewar modernist poets on Yoshioka was decisive, citing evidence of Yoshioka's stylistic borrowing from Katue Kitasono (1902–78), the leading avant-garde poet of the 1920s and 1930s (Tsuboi, 1989: 264). However, Yoshimoto Takaaki finds that *Monks* is neither surrealist nor an example of 'automatic writing'; rather, he argues that it is 'pre-realistic', and has a clear connection with phenomenal reality (Yoshimoto, 1983: 64–6).

Here Yoshimoto is attempting to link Yoshioka's technique in this collection with later sixties poets like Irisawa Yasuo (1931–99) who created long epic poems that used language in an ironic yet visionary way. The critic Shinoda Hajime makes the point that Yoshioka's technique in *Monks* is satirical and sarcastic (Shinoda, 1985: 70). The Yoshioka specialist Shiroto Shuri grasps the gauntlet to argue that, despite the poet himself declaring that he was indeed a modernist and surrealist poet, he was not. He also notes how the poet himself described *Saffron Gathering* as 'quotation poetry' (i.e. collage), and also notes how well received the collection was (Shiroto, 1995: 28–31).

Much of this debate hinges on whether the modernism or surrealism under discussion is the much-criticised prewar Japanese version or the French original. No doubt Yoshioka differed much from his postwar confreres, and no doubt he was sincere in his generous acknowledgments of the various influences (both domestic and foreign) on his writing. But he was a truly, even startlingly original poet, whose originality was recognised by all his contemporaries, and was paid the ultimate compliment of being widely imitated for years after.

Politics as a theme for poetry was briefly revived once again in the early 1960s when the problem of the renewal of the US–Japan Security Treaty became the focus for mass action and large-scale riots. A new generation of politically committed poets like Amazawa Taijirō (b. 1936) and Yoshimoto Takaaki literally donned demonstrators' helmets once again to take to the streets in protest, and in the process produced much charged verse. The scholar Satō Ken'ichi argues that this was the point where 'postwar poetry' came to an end, and 'modern poetry' began.

However, the political poetry produced by Amazawa in the magazine *Batten*, which in Amazawa's own words 'tried to capture…the essence of the students' political radicalism', heralded something of a false dawn, as many commentators have pointed out (Satō, 1998: 255–7). For the sixties was also the time when Japan entered the consumer age, and affluence led to massive changes in Japanese society. Poetry had become commercialised. This change in publishing from coterie presses to commercial presses was symbolised by the founding of the magazine *Gendai Shi Techō* (Modern Poetry Notebook) in 1959 by the large publishing house Shichōsha, and it was no coincidence that many of the poets published in the journal soon had individual volumes issued by Shichōsha.

By the end of the decade, poets with the theme of 'words words words', to quote Kokai, had become dominant (Kokai, 1973: 277).

Yoshimoto Takaaki launched his famous attack on such poetry in 1968 with his book *Sengoshiron* (A Study of Postwar Poetry) where he castigated poets for the solipsism of their verse that he branded mere 'rhetoric' (Yoshimoto, 1983: 172–3, 216–33). However, Yoshimoto's critique did little to stem the tide.

A number of outstanding collections appeared at this time, including Irisawa Yasuo's award-winning 1968 collection (actually one long poem) *Waga Izumo Waga Chinkon* (My Izumo My Requiem), which built a vast alternative myth of Japanese history, ironic and serious at the same time (Morton, 1993: 163–76). Soh Sakon's collection *Kappa* was published in 1964 featuring fifty-four poems all written about the mythical creature called a 'kappa' but which is actually an embodiment of the poet's guilt at abandoning his mother transformed into the image of the poet as a foetus in his mother's womb. That the kappa is Soh himself as a foetus is revealed in *Mother Burning*.

Yamamoto Tarō (1925–88) published his book-length poem *Yurishiizu* (Ulysses) in 1975, which re-created the story of Ulysses but in a distinctly Japanese context (Morton, 1993: 101–17). Shiraishi Kazuko (b.1931), who is the leading woman poet of her generation, published her book-length poem *Sei naru Inja no Kisetsu* (Seasons of the Sacred Lecher) in 1970. This book is an autobiographical narrative based on Shiraishi's experiences in the USA travelling with various jazz musicians.

But the 1970s took a different turn from the previous decade, in some respects resembling the 1920s jazz age. The craze for consumer culture commented upon by Yoshimoto in his 1984 book *On Mass Images* led to the revival of the famous catchcry of the twenties: 'ero, guro, nansensu' (eroticism, grotesquery, nonsense). We will investigate the poetry produced in this decade and afterwards a little later. First, we need to examine the fiction of this era by beginning with the most famous novelist of the 1970s: Murakami Haruki.

The world of Murakami Haruki

Murakami Haruki is the most popular author of serious fiction in contemporary Japan. He was born in Kyoto in 1949 but, soon after, the family moved to Kobe where Haruki was brought up. Haruki left home at the age of nineteen to attend Waseda University in Tokyo where he majored in film and theatre studies. He was married in 1971 while still a student and subsequently opened a jazz coffee shop. Graduating from Waseda in 1975 with a thesis on the journey motif in American cinema, Haruki began his career as a novelist by winning in 1979 the Gunzō new author's prize with his story *Kaze no uta o kike!* (Hear the Wind Sing).

Soon, Haruki was translating F. Scott Fitzgerald and writing articles on American film and literature. The ironic, 'cool', first-person male protagonists (or protagonist—the same character frequently appears as the narrator in several stories) he usually employs in his fiction sound almost trans-Atlantic in their admiration of American popular culture, although it is simultaneously Japanese popular culture that is being described.

In 1981 Murakami decided to become a full-time writer. Between 1981 and 2001 he has published eight full-length novels (which have won many literary prizes and have all been translated into English), several volumes of short stories, various volumes of essays, and works of non-fiction, including *Andāguraundo* (Underground) in 1997, a study of the human impact of the gas attacks on the Tokyo subways. He has also produced numerous translations of twentieth-century and contemporary American fiction by such authors as John Irving, Raymond Carver and Truman Capote.

Murakami was raised in the relentlessly bourgeois environment of the upper-class Kobe suburb of Shukugawa, and graduated from a junior high school in Ashiya (another upper-class Kobe suburb). Of his background, he wrote: 'I was born and raised in Kansai (western Japan). My father is the son of a Kyoto Buddhist priest and my mother is the daughter of a Senba [a wealthy suburb of Ōsaka] merchant so I guess you can describe me as 100% made in Kansai. Therefore, as a matter of course, I grew up using the Kansai dialect. Other varieties of Japanese are foreign to me, so to speak; I received a fairly parochial education where people using standard [Tokyo] Japanese were hardly respectable…' (Quoted Imai, 1997: 303).

This statement reflects the pride of the native of Kansai, the region which is regarded as the birthplace of Japanese culture, and which for most of Japan's history housed the capital. Kansai culture is also quite different in its speech and cuisine, and in other respects, from Tokyo, its great rival. Ashiya, where Murakami went to school, is filled with the homes of the rich and successful. However, Kobe was originally a treaty port open to the West, and has enthusiastically adopted Western culture, boasting several famous foreign restaurants and academies.

This comfortable, middle-class and quite cosmopolitan environment has left its mark on Murakami's fiction.

Hear the Wind Sing is mostly set in that environment, although the seaside town where the action (what little there is) takes place is left unnamed. Murakami's dislike yet comfortable embrace of the bourgeois prosperity of his hometown is evident from early in the novel. The plot is slight. Most of the action concerns the narrator driving around the town, going swimming at fashionable hotels, and chatting in J's bar. The protagonist called 'Boku' or 'I' is relating the tale (or writing the novel) in the first person in 1978 but the events he is recalling occur between 8 and 26 August 8 1970.

He tells us of his relationship with a girl who had only four fingers on her hand, and of his friendship with the 'Rat', with whom he habitually drinks at J's bar. We hear the Rat's tale as well as the four-fingered girl's tale, and other tales. 'I' tells us he had three girlfriends with whom he had sex. The third unnamed girlfriend (as all the characters are unnamed) committed suicide. The four-fingered girl appears to have had an abortion, which she confesses to the narrator at the end of the novel. She also confesses how miserable her life has been, and there is a very subtle implication that she may be contemplating suicide. Rat's story, which parallels the other stories, is about his decision to leave the town to become a novelist.

Yet, despite the novel being a cavalcade of tales narrated by conversations with very little action, a number of other elements make the work much more complex than appears on a first reading. In addition to being studded with references to iconic subcultural (to use Yoshimoto Takaaki's formulation in *On Mass Images*) moments of the late sixties like Western pop music and movies, the novel is full of references to the high literary culture of the West. 'I' cites Nietzsche, Henry James, Flaubert and Molière, among others, at various points in the narrative. Another subtext is the self-conscious references to writing that discusses philosophy, writing itself, and various other weighty matters. Finally there are the few, fleeting references to the student riots of the late 1960s, which have closed the university in Tokyo where the narrator and 'Rat' are enrolled, thus making their summer break in their hometown (presumably Ashiya) a little more intriguing.

This last element has been discussed in excruciating detail by several Japanese critics (although they usually combine discussion of this novel with the novel that follows a year later with all the same characters). Fukami Haruka in his 1990 book on Murakami, cites a long discussion between Murakami and Itoi Shigesato, a collaborator of Murakami (their collaboration is discussed in Yoshimoto's *On Mass Images*), about the dislike Murakami feels towards the sixties radicals, and especially the Zenkyōtō student union leaders who he thinks were hypocrites. Fukami also cites an interview Murakami gave in 1985 where he emphasised how he was a child of the seventies and noted how there was some 'unfinished business' remaining from the late-sixties and early-seventies student riots (Fukami, 1990:20, 22–4).

The critic Kasai Kiyoshi argues that the suicide of the narrator's girl-friend is a marker of the uncertainty of the seventies—symbolised by Zenkyōtō and the Red Army. By this he means the idealism of the sixties becoming the terrorism of the seventies (Kasai, 1991: 20). We will take up the political thread in Murakami's writing a little later but the more important and more obvious theme is death, and the loss it occasions.

The death of the narrator's girlfriend is mentioned several times in the narrative, and the sense of loss that all the characters feel appears related to death. Yet despite this overarching sadness, the novel is nar-rated in a witty, light tone with numerous amusing anecdotes and apho-risms, which give the story its strong appeal. The powerful sense of historicity provided by the author's frequent citations of Western, that is, Japanese pop culture is driven by an inventive chatty narrative consist-ing either of the narrator's monologues or conversation. Thus 'I', the only real character (as several critics have pointed out, the 'Rat' is a kind of alter ego of 'Boku'), is sympathetically and powerfully portrayed as a kind of new-age seventies man, kind and responsible, especially in his relationships with women.

Exactly the same two characters appear in *1973 no Pinbōru* (Pinball, 1973) published a year later. In fact, these two novels make up the first half of a tetralogy, but there is a clear division between the first two novels, and the later two: *Hitsuji o Meguru Bōken* (A Wild Sheep Chase, 1982) and *Dansu Dansu Dansu* (Dance Dance Dance, 1988). *Pinball, 1973* features two parallel tales, one about 'Boku', the other the Rat's tale. The political thread is stronger in this novel with several references to the campus violence of the late sixties and early seventies, although the novel is set in 1973. The narrator, the same 'Boku' or 'I', is living in Tokyo with a pair of twin girls with whom he has, it appears, a most satisfactory sex life. The Rat is back in Ashiya (although it is unnamed), chatting with the Chinese bar owner 'J' and attempting to disentangle himself from a sexual relationship with an unnamed woman. 'I' has graduated from university and runs a translation agency with a friend, and spends his spare time having sex or reading Kant's *Critique of Pure Reason*. He embarks on a quest to find a mysterious 'Spaceship' pinball machine that he finally discovers in a chicken farm's refrigerated warehouse.

The style of *Pinball, 1973* is identical with its predecessor, being constructed of I's monologue and conversations, with numerous subtexts, although the Rat's tale (narrated in the third person) has a larger share of the story. The iconic pop and high culture references recur, as does the wistful melancholy of the earlier novel. The girlfriend who committed suicide, though, is given a name: Naoko and her death seems to haunt 'Boku'.

The appeal of the novel is much the same as *Hear the Wind Sing* in that it lies in the character of 'I': gentle, witty, and sensitive. The fantasy wish-fulfilment element (the sexual utopia of twin bed partners) is stronger in *Pinball, 1973* and thus makes it a less successful novel than the earlier story. In 1989 Karatani Kōjin wrote a much-cited powerful critique of these first two novels, mainly focusing on *Pinball, 1973*. Karatani emphasises the various subtexts to the point where the main text—the story of I's monologues about himself and relationships, and the Rat's search for identity—becomes almost irrelevant. Karatani argues, firstly, that the 'I' experiences reality and time entirely from a Kantian perspective. Namely, that 'Boku' is a true Kantian—his judgments derive solely from taste and inclination, thus he is an example of Kant's transcendental subjectivity, both as expounded in the *Critique of Pure Reason* and *Critique of Judgement*. Secondly, Karatani argues that Murakami's style owes little to American literature, contrary to the viewpoint of just about every other critic writing on Murakami; rather, his novels are pastiches.

Murakami's fiction has no historicity; the use of dates, pop culture, and lists, ubiquitous in his writing, is a pastiche and thus meaningless. Murakami, claims Karatani, constructs the past—here he is referring to the political references—from the bricolage of pop culture and negates historicity by the use of irony. Values collapse in Murakami's fiction; irony renders everything as a subjective fantasy of the transcendental ego. Thus, he states, *Pinball, 1973* is a pastiche of Ōe's *The Silent Cry* but it is constructed on premises that contradict Ōe's work: for Murakami, history does not exist (Karatani, 1996a: 89–113 *passim*). Karatani is contrasting Ōe's vision of the 1960s with Murakami's: his conclusion is that Murakami opposes the values that Ōe champions. We shall return to this critique shortly but, despite the weakness of Karatani concentrating his attention on the subtext rather than the main text, it is nevertheless a powerful and important criticism of Murakami's fiction.

A Wild Sheep Chase represents a change in Murakami's style, which Murakami himself noted, observing that his first two novels (written at night after work) did not escape the limits of trial runs but that *A Wild Sheep Chase* as his first work as a full-time author was very different, with a much stronger storyline (Murakami, 1990: vii; 1990a: 111). The changed emphasis on the plot, as opposed to the rather plotless first two novels, and also the strong introduction of fantasy or science fiction (SF) elements strikes the reader immediately. *A Wild Sheep Chase* is, fundamentally, a thriller, a mystery novel about a right-wing conspiracy to gain control of the supernatural powers of a sheep, powers that are represented in the term 'Will', which clearly is meant to remind us of fascism and Nazism.

'Boku' is now co-partner in a thriving copywriting business, just divorced from his former secretary. He is sent on a wild sheep chase to Hokkaido to find a mysterious sheep who is a supernatural entity. He is accompanied by a woman with perfect ears, a call-girl who is his lover. 'I' also discovers he is retracing the footsteps of the 'Rat'. The action takes place mostly in 1978–9. In the end, the Rat, who has committed suicide, shows 'I' how to kill the evil right-wing figure who is blackmailing him to undertake the quest. We finally discover that the right-wing leader is the Rat's father (he also dies).

A Wild Sheep Chase became a bestseller in Japan, and started a spectacular run by Murakami in which he broke all previous records for publication. The culmination of his commercial success was his two-volume novel *Noruwei no Mori* (Norwegian Wood, 1987), telling the tragic tale of Naoko (Boku's girlfriend who committed suicide in the earlier novels), which sold more than four million copies in Japan. The massive commercial success of *A Wild Sheep Chase* seems to have given Murakami's critics pause. It is noticeable that Karatani does not criticise this novel in as much detail as the earlier works. But criticise it he does. *A Wild Sheep Chase* is not a psychological mystery, argues

Karatani; rather the real theme of the novel is the triumph of the will. The myth of the transcendental ego replaces a mythical god in this work. Murakami's vision of the world, as revealed in this book, is actually an escape from the real world, a romantic denial of the real world and history (Karatani, 1996a: 113–35). Hence Karatani reads the conspiracy as mere irony that evades the political realities of 1980s Japan.

However, a more positive reading of Murakami's work, which subsequently became quite well known, also emerged in 1989. This was Yoshimoto Takaaki's essay on the appeal of *Dance Dance Dance*, the last novel of the tetralogy (excluding *Norwegian Wood*, though this is an arguable move). *Dance Dance Dance* is set in 1983 and converts the supernatural elements in *A Wild Sheep Chase* mostly to psychology. The novel is again modelled on a quest or a 'treasure hunt', as the critic Hasumi Shigehiko describes the essential plot structure of *A Wild Sheep Chase* (Hasumi, 1994: 19).

'I' is searching for 'Kiki', the girl with perfect ears who disappeared at the end of *A Wild Sheep Chase*. I's search leads him into the seamy world of prostitution as he investigates the secret call-girl ring where Kiki was employed. The 'sheepman' of the previous novel now only emerges in his imagination, in a dark room of the now-demolished Dolphin Hotel in Sapporo. This vision he shares with a hotel receptionist called Yumiyoshi, who eventually becomes the real object of his quest, which, we learn, is a search for love. Another character is I's old high-school acquaintance, Gotanda, who we suspect from almost their first meeting may well be a serial killer who has murdered Kiki (but 'Boku'/'I' never catches on until the last). 'Boku' also has to act as a surrogate father for Yuki, a precocious thirteen-year-old girl with psychic gifts who is shamefully neglected by her rich, divorced parents.

This novel thus can be read cynically as the culmination of the author's ten-year search for a plot. The tetralogy could almost be subtitled as 'four characters in search of a plot', but to conclude that a conventional, realistic, psychological thriller is the end-result of Murakami's fictional endeavours is to trivialise his achievement, as Yoshimoto points out. Yoshimoto's conclusion to his essay is that a trite mixture of love story and adventure tale becomes something immeasurably more significant by means of the blending of several structural and plot elements in the novel. The mystery, fantasy, metaphysical discussions, and strong psychological metaphors—

mainly focusing on darkness and light—which characterise the novel create a fairy-tale atmosphere (otogibanashi). Thus we find strong fantasy elements in the work (Yoshimoto, 1997: 220).

'Boku' could not possibly exist in real life, argues Yoshimoto, as he is too much an idealisation of an 'ordinary' (read extraordinary) new-age seventies male. Yuki similarly is a fairy-tale princess (in the novel she absolutely forbids 'I' from using this word to refer to herself) with magic powers that enable 'I' to see that his buddy Gotanda is a murderer. But, as Yoshimoto notes, this is a fairy-tale for the eighties, with detailed sex scenes and harsh, realistic depictions of the emptiness of the consumer paradise that Japan and Hawaii (where part of the second half of the novel is set) have become (Yoshimoto, 1997: 215–29). Murakami's eponymous hero has moved closer to Ōe's heroes: he is seeking his salvation through love. The last chapters of the novel capture the overwhelming urgency, the divine madness, of love in an extremely convincing and powerful manner, with the contrast between love and sexual desire made transparent by the narrator's ruminations on his love-making with Yumiyoshi, his true love, and sex with the call-girls.

Unfortunately, the numerous cuts and abridgements in the English translation make the above argument much easier to follow in the original Japanese. In contrast to the other novels in Murakami's tetralogy, the English translation of *Dance Dance Dance* is, in several respects, different from the Japanese original, especially concerning Murakami's portrayal of Yumiyoshi who is a much harder individual in the translated version, with the deletion of several phrases that soften her character.

Fiction at the end of the twentieth century

As Murakami has increased his audience by writing longer and longer novels—his last major novel *Nejimaki-dori Kuronikuru* (The Wind-up Bird Chronicle, 1994–95) was originally published in three volumes in Japanese—so his plot construction has become much more conventional and less experimental. Hasumi Shigehiko wrote a book-length study entitled *Shōsetsu kara Tōku Hanarete* (A Long Way from the Novel, 1994) on the explosion of massive multi-volume novels in Japan in the 1970s, 1980s, and 1990s and concluded that the tale is 'telling' the author, rather than the author telling the tale (Hasumi, 1994: 62).

In other words, the structures of these massive, long novels have become increasingly similar to the point where one can speak of a single structure incorporating common elements like a 'treasure-hunt'-style quest, the common appearance of twins, the absence of women as significant players in these fictional quests, the theme of a 'lost child', constant repetition, the use of mythic motifs and so on (Hasumi, 1994). Hasumi took as his specific case studies Murakami's *A Wild Sheep Chase*, Inoue Hisashi's (b.1934) *Kirikirijin* (The Kirikiri Tribe, 1981), Maruya Saiichi's (b.1925) *Uragoe de Utae Kimigayo* (Sing the National Anthem in Falsetto, 1982), and Murakami Ryū's (b.1952) *Koin Rokkā Beibiizu* (Coin Locker Babies, 1980). Indeed, claims Hasumi, it is the very sameness of the structures of these novels that attracts readers (Hasumi, 1994: 52).

Hasumi's attitude towards this structure or model is, as one would expect, quite negative. He states that he wrote his book to expose the flatness of the landscape that he finds described in these works, although, he states, in many cases this is not the intention of the authors (Hasumi, 1994: 61). However, Hasumi mentions two novels that seem to escape this structure, which he calls variously a 'story' (setsuwaron) or 'tale' (monogatari) as opposed to a 'novel' (shōsetsu). These are Nakagami Kenji's *Karekinada* (Withered Tree Straits, 1977) and Ōe Kenzaburō's *Dōjidai Gēmu* (The Game of Contemporaneity, 1979) (Hasumi, 1994: 139–207). Nakagami and Ōe write novels through the medium of language or style, which is the key determinant of fiction. But the tales or stories told by Murakami Ryū, Murakami Haruki and Maruya Saiichi do not depend upon language in the sense of style. They are simply plot structures with fixed narrative elements that can be told by anybody (Hasumi, 1994: 281–7).

Thus, Hasumi stresses linguistic expression in a way strikingly similar to Yoshimoto Takaaki who declared: 'The value of literature which is inherent in the artistic expression of language cannot be reduced to consciousness' (Yoshimoto, 1990a: 282). If we read 'consciousness' here as referring to a collective consciousness of tale or story, then we see Hasumi's assertion for modern fiction restated in a broader context.

Nakagami, who died prematurely of cancer at the age of 46, was a brilliant story-teller. He began with autobiographical novels of his youth in Shingū as a member of the 'untouchable' class of burakumin. His story 'Misaki' (The Cape, 1976), which was awarded the Akutagawa

Prize, is the first in a sequence of works written on this theme. These works form an interlocking whole in which the same characters reappear in a family saga format. The next work in this sequence is the novel *Withered Tree Straits*, followed by *Hōsenka* (Touch-Me-Not, 1979) and concluding with *Chi no Hate Shijō no Toki* (The Sublime Time at the Ends of the Earth, 1983). Other works also connect to this theme. Alan Tansman argues that with these novels Nakagami attempted to create a metanarrative or narrative of narratives, a circular never-ending tale (Tansman, 1998). This adds another dimension of meaning to the texts but does not necessarily subvert their fundamental thematic coherence.

In addition, Nakagami wrote works using Japanese mythology or set in ancient times, many of which focus on the same region as his tetralogy, such as his collection of tales about Kumano, *Kumano Shū* (1984). As Kuritsubo Yoshiki points out in his summary of Nakagami criticism until 1991, most Japanese readers of Nakagami emphasise his skills as a story-teller (monogatari). Furuhashi Nobuyoshi puts it thus: 'the characters, the narrator and the audience are woven into the same space' (Quoted Kuritsubo, 1991: 126). Next, the connection with the 'alleys' (roji) or ghetto of his childhood, the 'other world' revealed in his writings of the undercaste, has commanded most attention among Japanese readers (Kuritsubo, 1991: 128–9).

Maria Flutsch has written that if Nakagami's standpoint was writing from the ghetto, then Murakami Ryū 'writes from the "kichi", the Sasebo American military base beside which he spent his childhood' (Flutsch, 1994: 94). With the award of the Akutagawa Prize for his novel *Kagirinaku Tōmei ni Chikai Burū* (Almost Transparent Blue, 1976), Murakami Ryū became known as the *enfant terrible* of contemporary Japanese fiction. This novel about the sex and drugs culture of the youth close to the US bases in Japan shocked readers but established the author as the chronicler of life on the margins. His novel *Koin Rokkā Beibiizu* (Coin Locker Babies, 1980) is an SF dystopia set in a parallel Japan that represents his efforts to 'demolish [my] relationship with the novel form' (Quoted Snyder, 1999: 209).

Story-telling may not be as much at the heart of Murakami's fiction as Nakagami's—*Almost Transparent Blue* has little sense of a plot—but it is important nonetheless. Murakami Ryū's novel *69* (1987) is an autobiographical memoir about the author's time as a high school student, laced with his characteristic irony, but with a strong emphasis on character and story. Recently, Murakami has become known more for his harsh and probing exploration in novels and films (he is also a filmmaker) of sex and violence. Ueshima Keiji questions whether a recent novel *Kokkusakkā Burūsu* (Cocksucker Blues, 1991) is pornography (Quoted Snyder, 1991: 205). But this thematic combination of sex and violence has become equally a dilemma for contemporary authors writing in other languages, as we can see in the American novelist Bret Easton Ellis' controversial *American Psycho* (1991).

The renewed stress on story-telling in contemporary ·fiction, the emphasis on conventional genres of novel—whether mystery, fantasy, SF, romance, or whatever—stands in stark contrast to a parallel mode of fiction that works primarily as parody and pastiche. And, if Karatani is correct, then we have already encountered this mode in Murakami Haruki's writing. However, there are many more explicit parodists or satirists who have serious claims to be important writers (cf Aoyama, 1994).

Ogino Anna (b.1956) famously declared when she had not yet written any fiction that she would be awarded the Akutagawa Prize for her writing before she turned thirty. However, she could not match her boast and was only awarded the prize in 1991, when she was thirty-four (Kodaira, 1997: 43), for her story 'Seoi Mizu' (Burden of Water, 1991). Subsequently, Ogino published a collection of short pieces in a single volume entitled *Watashi no Aidokusho* (My Favourite Poisonous Books, 1991), which were all parodies of modern Japanese literary classics. The most well-known story in the collection is 'Yukiguni no Odoriko' (The Snow Country Dancer), which is a parody of the famous two novels *Izu no Odoriko* (The Izu Dancer, 1926) and *Yukiguni* (Snow Country, 1937) by Kawabata Yasunari (1899–1972), who was awarded the Nobel Prize for Literature in 1968, the first Japanese writer so honoured.

Ogino's parody is also a commentary on the story as the protagonist, a Filipino dancer called 'Kaoru', quotes and 'explains' sections of Kawabata's *Snow Country* to the young man she meets on a train journey. The tragicomic, yet zestful monologue of Kaoru conveys with great comic wit her effervescent personality as well as delightfully dissecting Kawabata's story (unconsciously) from a feminist perspective. Naturally, the story also describes the reality of female foreign entertainers in contemporary Japan (Ogino, 1994: 84–118).

According to Hiraoka Masaaki, Ogino so admires Marilyn Monroe that she dresses in the same clothing made famous by the actress and plays out some of her favourite scenes around Tokyo (this was later the subject of a photo exhibition) (Hiraoka, 1998: 240–1). That admiration, if not obsession, is evident in the collection of short stories collectively titled *Meitantei Maririn* (Famous Detective Marilyn), first published in 1995. The stories are written from various perspectives but all revolve around Marilyn Monroe. Here, rather than parody, Ogino writes humorous yet affectionate pastiches of Monroe's life and films.

Ogino's parodies tend to be short stories or episodes but the novelist Shimada Masahiko's (b.1961) parodies tend to be more linguistic parodies, or, more precisely, satires. Shimada made his literary debut while still a student with his novella *Yasashii Sayoku no tame no Kiyūkyoku* (A Divertimento for Gentle Leftists, 1983), a gentle satire on leftist student politics. He produced a large number of novels over the next decade, of which probably the most well-known are *Boku wa Mozō Ningen* (I am an Artificial Man, 1986), *Yumetsukai* (Dream Messenger, 1989) and *Higan Sensei* (Professor Other Side, 1992).

I am an Artificial Man is a satire both of didactic novels and autobiographies. The immediate target is Mishima's *Confessions of a Mask*. There are numerous references to Mishima's last work, the tetralogy *Hōjō no Umi* (The Sea of Fertility, 1971) in the text. The protagonist is called 'Akuma Kazuto' (Evil One) and eventually meets Mishima as a woman called 'Yukiko' in a dream. But the novel as a whole is an autobiography deliberately mimicking, or more accurately, parodying *Confessions of a Mask*. The work culminates in the rebirth of the protagonist as an artificial man.

Dream Messenger is the story of Mika Amino, a wealthy second-generation Japanese–American, middle-aged widow who is searching for her lost son Masao who was kidnapped by his father when he was three. We soon discover he is now Matthew. As Matthew, he was raised at the Rental Child agency in New York where he was rented out to 'Orpharents', adults who rent children. The narrative is a complex patchwork of a myriad voices, as is often the case in Shimada's fiction. Matthew has numerous internal dialogues with Mikinaito, who Matthew calls his guardian spirit (originally it was the name the child Masao gave to his pillow). Using Mikinaito's powers, Matthew is a Dream Messenger, and can break into the dreams of his clients. He has become a kind of universal prostitute–nurse who seeks to help both body and soul. At the end he is reunited with his mother but the real story is a series of frenzied observations on contemporary Tokyo and New York, seen through the eyes of several characters. These stories are interwoven through Matthew into a complex tapestry of tales and lives lived at the margin.

The end of the novel has a quasi-religious epiphany where Matthew dreams the creation of the universe—this directly follows the revelation that Maiko Rokuyo, who is the detective hired by Mrs. Amino, has fallen pregnant with Matthew's child (the two have fallen in love). This shift from dystopia to utopia (at least in dream), or a religious epiphany is mirrored at the end of *Professor Other Side*, which ends with a letter espousing Buddhism.

Professor Other Side is a deliberate parody of the distinguished novelist Natsume Sōseki's most acclaimed novel *Kokoro* (The Heart, 1914), although there are also some connections with another, less popular, novel by Sōseki called *Higan Sugi Made* (To the Spring Equinox and Beyond, 1912). *The Heart* tells the story of the relationship between a youth and his mentor whom he calls 'sensei' (Professor). The novel is divided into three sections: 'Sensei and I', 'My parents and I', and 'Sensei and his Testament'. The story is told in the first person by the youth, apart from section three which is a long letter to the youth. The testament makes the youth suspect 'sensei' will commit suicide because of his betrayal of a friend by marrying his friend's true love, and thus the youth is torn between his affection for sensei and his filial duty to his dying father. The novel is a modern classic, commonly regarded as a brilliant study of individual morality.

Shimada's novel is similarly structured, with the first four chapters being told in the first person from the perspective of a youth called 'Kikuhito' who has become captivated by a married novelist he calls 'sensei'. The next four chapters are sensei's diary, and various other autobiographical writings that reveal his dissolute life in the USA, his numerous sexual liaisons and his descent into madness and possible suicide. The last chapter (with the same title as another Sōseki novel) summarises the fates of the main protagonists. Thus, the novel can be read as an 'anti-Kokoro'. Shimada revealed his intentions in a book he later wrote called *Sōseki o Kaku* (Writing Sōseki, 1993) where he stated: 'What I planned with *Professor Other Side* is extremely straightforward. I wanted to rewrite Sōseki at a completely different level from destroying or deconstructing

Sōseki's image, which has been constructed critically by the discourse of Sōseki scholarship. As a matter of course, I meant to translate Sōseki into a dubious, immoral text using the form of the novel. More simply, I planned to write pornography, in the consciousness of Sōseki' (Quoted Komori, 1994: 184).

The scholar Komori Yōichi, in a brilliant article on the novel published in 1994, has demonstrated just how ambitious, radical, and complex Shimada's destruction of Sōseki has been. Shimada's tour de force goes beyond mere parody to launch a powerful attack on various foundations of Japanese culture: race, sexuality and the family being the main targets. Komori shows how Sōseki's novel has been read historically as an exemplum of moral virtue; he further shows how this is an official reading but an incorrect one, as it leaves out entirely the issue of sexuality which is an integral (but hidden) part of the original novel. Shimada not only restores sexuality to centre stage in his novel and makes 'sensei' to be a Don Juan of extraordinary proportions but also problematises the whole notion of truth (Komori, 1994: 182–90).

Contemporary women's fiction

This brief survey of contemporary fiction will conclude with a look at some women writers, only a small sampling of the many new women writers who have captured a large audience, both in Japan and internationally.

With *Trash* (1996)—an amalgam of two Japanese stories—Yamada Amy (b.1959) recently had her first major English translation published. *Trash* is a typical Yamada tale of a streetwise Japanese girl in love with two African–American males. Yamada's first important novel *Beddo Taimu Aizu* (Bedtime Eyes, 1985) was also the story of a love affair between 'Spoon', a black GI runaway from the US base at Yokosuka and a Japanese girl called Kim. The novel, like most of Yamada's stories, is written in the first person with Kim telling events solely from her perspective. Kim's language is composed of the sensual metaphors of sex. One striking aspect of Yamada's heroine–narrators is their innocence—despite their sexual hunger and prowess—and their goodness. Through their love for their African-American men, they sanctify sexuality, which only enhances their pleasure in sex. This innocence, often associated with immaturity, is conveyed through Yamada's first-person perspective.

Yet if we compare the two works, it is the number of dissimilarities that leave the strongest impression. In *Trash*, Yamada and her translator Sonya Johnson have fashioned an entertaining English-language novel based on the New York scene. The independent but caring heroine Koko is caught between her love for a drunken, dissolute man called Rick who has a young son, and a much younger man called Randy. Although both men are African–Americans, race is a background issue, and is not foregrounded as in *Bedtime Eyes*. *Trash* focuses, as does the earlier novel, on the feelings of the female narrator but in *Trash* a number of other characters interact with Koko, and numerous references to New York ground the novel in its particular milieu (Yamada, 1994).

Bedtime Eyes, as noted above, is almost a prose poem, the narrative driven by Kim's love for Joseph Johnson or 'Spoon', as he is called. Kim's feelings express themselves in numerous internal monologues triggered by thoughts of Spoon's body, and their many sexual encounters. However, the language of love is not pornographic (despite its frankness—Yamada uses English four-letter words to refer to their genitals) but, rather, beautiful. The beauty is expressed through smells—the various scents of Spoon's body—frequently likened to exotic spices and 'soul food'. By using poetic language as the currency of Kim's monologues, Yamada creates a moving and powerful portrait of a young woman's love, which manages to overcome Spoon's often degrading and brutal behaviour towards her. His unfortunate character, Yamada implies, is the result of years of racial discrimination. The plot device of the loving woman attempting to 'save' an unworthy male through the strength of her love is not new, of course.

Apart from descriptions of drinking and lovemaking, the only significant plot development in the novel is Maria's—Kim's closest friend who works as a strip dancer at the club where Kim sings—seduction of Spoon out of her jealousy (she confides to Kim that she loves her) (Yamada, 1987: 87–8). This stimulates in Kim her awareness that she truly loves Spoon, the first time she has ever loved anyone. At the end of the novel, Spoon is taken away by the authorities on charges of selling classified US documents to a foreign power (Yamada, 1987: 121–38). This twist recalls the famous novel *Aru Onna* (A Certain Woman, 1919) by Arishima Takeo (1878–1923) where the heroine Yōko's lover Kurachi commits a similar crime. The passionate, sensuous and frank eroticism of Yōko and Kurachi's lovemaking parallels Yamada's descriptions of Spoon and Kim's amorous liaisons. Whether Yamada was influenced by Arishima is unknown; although she did major in Japanese literature at university (she did not complete a degree), she is reputed to have preferred foreign authors like Françoise Sagan (b.1935) and Boris Vian (1920–59) to homegrown writers (Takakuwa, 1997: 196).

Yamada is an extremely productive writer, with numerous publications including essays and non-fiction. But her fiction, according to Takakuwa Noriko, can be divided into two types: stories of interracial love, and coming-of-age stories of young women (Takakuwa, 1997: 196). The innocent sensibility of the strong female narrators, however, is common to both. Yoshimoto Takaaki argues that Yamada's novels are often built around an equation of eating and sex, and that the sexual sensibility expressed by her female narrators is powerful and aggressive. This overt female dominance dissolves other social and conceptual categories to construct 'a new order of power' (Yoshimoto, 1989: 266). Two other notable characteristics of Yamada's fiction stand out: her concern with race (her metaphors are often explicitly racial) and the American setting of many of her novels. However, the international nature of her writing has not been appreciated by all, such as Nina Cornyetz's criticism of her fiction as 'reproducing a discourse of colonisation' due to her stereotypical presentation of black men and Japanese women in some of her novels (Cornyetz, 1996: 453).

When she was young, Yamada dabbled in creating cartoons. A much more successful and famous writer of comics is Uchida Shungicu (b.1948) who in the 1990s made a successful debut as a novelist. As a comic book artist, Uchida became famous for her cartoons depicting sex, and feminist topics like childbirth. In 1993 her novel *Fāzā Fakkā* (Father Fucker) became something of a sensation because of the strong autobiographical implications inherent in the work. The novel is narrated in the first person by Shizuko who tells of how in her teenage years she was a rebel, falling pregnant to a schoolmate called Hiroki. Her baby is taken away from her at birth, and she is continually subjected to verbal attacks by her mother and stepfather. At this point, when she is only fifteen, her stepfather who until then had been quite strict towards her begins to rape her (Uchida, 1996: 161). Her mother closes her eyes to the rape. After repeated rapes, and growing violence towards her, at the end of the novel Shizuko runs away from home. This plot summary paints a grim picture but the tone of Uchida's narrator captures the same quality of innocence that some of Yamada's female narrators possess. Moreover, the projection of self in the narrator's monologue is powerful and convincing.

Yoshimoto Banana (b.1964) is the last of this group of female novelists we will discuss but she is certainly the most popular, and the most famous. Indeed, Yoshimoto approaches Murakami Haruki in her sales, and like Murakami, has had several of her novels published in English translation. Yoshimoto's real name is Mahoko and she is the second daughter of Yoshimoto Takaaki. This was one of the reasons why the eminent scholar of classical Japanese literature, Furuhashi Nobuyoshi, decided to study her fiction, which resulted in his 1990 book on Yoshimoto and the popular contemporary tanka poet Tawara Machi (b.1962). Furuhashi argues that Yoshimoto may represent the birth of a fundamentally different kind of literature in the 1970s and 1980s (Furuhashi, 1990: 193). We shall return to Furuhashi's study later but this sense of the birth of something new is pervasive among the many critiques and studies of Yoshimoto that have emerged over the past decade or so.

In 1994, the literary historian Suzuki Sadami wrote that the division between highbrow or elite literature and popular literature had finally broken down (Suzuki, 1994: 274). Suzuki specifically noted the period from 1984 to 1994 as the time when this change occurred. Suzuki links this change to the rise of television and movies—visual media—as rivals to traditional print media. The challenge of the visual (and we could include comics here) has fundamentally changed literature, argues Suzuki (Suzuki, 1994: 276). By this he means the massive diversification of the Japanese market and the growth of high-quality fiction in what had previously been considered popular or genre writing: areas like SF and thrillers. Furuhashi, referring specifically to Yoshimoto, notes how her sales have approached three million in Japan and argues that her approach is fundamentally different from her peers, especially older paragons of Japanese literature like Ōe Kenzaburō and Nakagami Kenji, who, he notes consider 'much more deeply [than Yoshimoto] the issues of the self, society and literature' (Furuhashi, 1990: 45, 188).

There is no doubt Yoshimoto is a 'popular' writer in the old, pre-1980s pejorative sense. Her style is much easier to read than someone like Ōe, with very few words using Chinese characters, as Furuhashi remarks (Furuhashi, 1990: 187). He also observes that her approach to fiction is not plot-driven but is concerned, overwhelmingly, with the sensibility of the young, female narrators of her novels. Yoshimoto is writing monogatari, not novels—here we see similarities to Hasumi's reading of contemporary fiction—and though the themes of death, the past and the family are ubiquitous in her writing, nevertheless the tales are recounted through the medium of the female protagonist as a series of scenes (rather than as a plot line) which linger in the memory, constructed along the same lines as classical narratives (Furuhashi, 1990: 43–5; 185–8). Yoshimoto herself, as several commentators have noted, has talked of how she was influenced by comics, the fiction of Stephen King and the postmodern punk novelist Kathy Acker (b.1948) (Yoshimoto, 1992: 107–12, 68–72; Yoshimoto, 1995: 45).

Yoshimoto's success came with her first published novel *Kitchin* (Kitchen, 1988), which was awarded the Izumi Kyōka Prize. The novel was based upon two stories published the previous year. The 'plot' of *Kitchen* is almost incidental to its substance, which is how the healing power of love can overcome the sadness and depression brought about by death. The narrator is a young woman called Sakurai Mikage who is orphaned at an early age and raised by her grandmother. When her grandmother dies, she moves in with Tanabe Yūichi, a student at the same university attended by Mikage, and who worked part-time at her grandmother's shop. In the apartment shared by Yūichi and his mother Eriko, Mikage comes to know peace and happiness, and eventually, love.

The fact that Eriko was originally a man, while responsible for much of the notoriety of the novel, is hardly highlighted at all in the work. But when Eriko is murdered by a patron, Yūichi's subsequent depression (which frightens Mikage, presumably because of the possibility of his suicide) awakens in Mikage her love for Yūichi which is symbolised in her delivery to him by taxi late at night of a dish of delicious deep-fried crumbed pork cutlets on rice ('katsudon'). Yūichi has gone to a country inn, and Mikage, sensing his desperation, leaves her own inn (where she is working on a job) to bring him her gift, risking life and limb by climbing up the ledge of the locked inn to his room.

Food, and the site of its preparation, is one of the key motifs of the work, which often dwells on the everyday reality of cooking and its pleasures. The monologue style is a tone-poem to the struggle between light and darkness, day and night, optimism and depression. Yoshimoto's imagery is focused on these commonplace contrasts, which occur in nearly all of her stories, as Ueno Yūko has demonstrated (Ueno, 1995).

The kitchen is marked by the absence of adult males (Yūichi is a feminised youth, like most of Yoshimoto's young male characters), and this absence, which has been conflated into the phenomenon of 'the absent father' (fathers are almost always dead or divorced in Yoshimoto's fiction), has been taken up by numerous critics. Apart from noting the obvious connection to the contemporary social problem of Japanese fathers working long hours and thus returning home late at night to leave early in the morning, we can also speculate that constructing fictions with no father-figure is a useful strategy for dealing with the endless speculation about Yoshimoto's real father.

Kitchen was followed by other novels—*Kanashii Yokan* (A Sad Premonition, 1988), the award-winning *Tugumi* (1989), and the recently translated *Shirakawa Yofune* (Night and Night's Travellers, 1989). In 1990, Yoshimoto wrote *N.P.*, a longer and more substantial novel than some of her previous works. It is a darker novel than *Kitchen* but shares similar concerns. The novel is narrated by a female protagonist who is called Kanō Kazami. Kazami's old boyfriend Shōji was translating a book of ninety-seven stories by a writer called Takase Sarao who, while resident in the USA, after penning these successful stories in English had committed suicide. Shōji, too, committed suicide. And Kazami comes to believe that there is a curse on the volume. Kazami's parents were divorced when she was young and now she lives with her mother, a freelance translator into English. Kazami meets Takase's children, the twenty-four-year-old Otohiko and his twin sister Saki. Kazami quickly learns that Otohiko's strange girlfriend Sui is the twins' stepsister. Sui tells Kazami that she committed incest with her father but maintains her incestual sexual relationship with Otohiko is completely moral because they do not have the same mother. The ninety-eighth story for which Sui is searching is the tale of Sui's incest with her father.

Kazami is strangely attracted to Sui who virtually kidnaps her and later assaults her in her attempt to steal Kazami's copy of the ninety-eighth story. She also learns that Sui is Shōji's old girlfriend. The relationship between Sui and Kazami comes to dominate Kazami's monologic narrative and the exchange of feelings between the two approaches love. But the occult enters into the narrative when Sui tells Kazami she is cursed, as was her father. The source of the evil spirit possessing them both is the book, says Sui, but there is an implication that the real source is their incest. Kazami increasingly comes to feel Sui is suicidal after learning Sui is pregnant with Otohiko's child. At this point, Sui poisons Kazami with the intent of a double suicide but Kazami survives. In a long letter, Sui apologises and says she is making a new life for herself and her child with another man. At the end of the novel, Kazami and Otohiko discover their love for each other.

In the afterword, Yoshimoto tells the readers that Sui may be read as a fallen woman or as a bodhisattva. But Kazami's compassion and love for both Sui and Otohiko tend to persuade us that she, Kazami, is more likely to be a bodhisattva than the troubled Sui. Ann Sherif, the English translator of this novel, has argued that *N.P.* 'promotes an essentialist view of Japanese national identity' by proposing that the curse actually represents the world outside Japan which 'brings with it…corruption and contamination' (Sherif, 1999: 290). Thus for Sherif, the concern with translation is the major theme. This proposition is arguable. As Yoshimoto herself hints in the afterword, the issue of incest, its tragic effects on Sui, and the healing compassion that Kazami displays are foregrounded far more than any specific references to Japanese identity. The occult or mystery element shapes the narrative into a more conventional 'treasure-hunt' (to borrow Hasumi's term). Nevertheless, Yoshimoto's focus is firmly on healing, which Sherif also notes is one of Yoshimoto's major themes (Sherif, 1999: 279).

Undoubtedly, Yoshimoto's most ambitious novel to date is also her longest—*Amurita* (Amrita, 1994). This work represents, perhaps, her first attempt to construct a mega fiction along the lines of the massive novels of her contemporaries. Yoshimoto herself wrote that with this novel, she 'wanted to describe the leisurely daily life of another world…the way the occult and New Age is overcome by reality…how sheltered families can begin to recover their functions' (Yoshimoto, 1995: 35–6). Yoshimoto also mentioned how the novel took two years to write and that she adopted a new narrative technique of real-time diary-style recounting of events on a month-to-month basis (Yoshimoto, 1995: 17–18).

Unfortunately, despite Yoshimoto's narrative experiments, at times the novel is tedious and laboured. The author in chapter twenty-two (with the English title 'This Used to Be My Playground' in the Japanese edition, however in the English translation all chapter titles are omitted) even provides us with a plot summary of the novel in the form of a list in case we have forgotten what happened previously. As this is the last chapter, followed by a final prologue, this is a somewhat curious strategy (does

Yoshimoto expect readers to absorb the novel slowly, not in one reading?). In the context of the novel, the protagonist-narrator Watanabe Sakumi writes a list of all that has happened to her over the past few years.

As the list makes clear, this is a novel where the 'plot' is of little importance. We learn that Sakumi's beautiful actress sister has committed suicide, that Sakumi has suffered a concussion that leaves her with severe amnesia—thus creating two versions of Sakumi in the same person (before and after regaining her memory, later the two are reunited)—and that Sakumi has fallen in love with her sister's old flame, the novelist Ryūichirō. But the main narrative thread is really Sakumi's kid brother Yoshio who is clairvoyant but, as a result, refuses to attend primary school and is thus put into an institution for troubled children. Yoshio is never far from his older sister–narrator's thoughts.

Two trips, one to Kōchi with her brother, and more importantly, another trip to Saipan with Ryūichirō and, later, Yoshio are important catalysts for action. The latter trip especially, where Sakumi meets Ryūichirō's friends, the psychic Saseko and her partly psychic husband Kozumi, creates in Sakumi the seed of a vision of happiness that sustains her as she attempts to heal the wounds of her sister's suicide, the dissolution of her almost all-female household (consisting of her mother, her mother's female friend Junko and her college student cousin Makiko) with its sole male Yoshio, and the final complication of Yoshio's adult friend, the beautiful psychic Kaname, and her one-time lover 'Mr. Mesmer'.

More than most novels by Yoshimoto, this work concentrates on the sublimity inherent in the everyday, quotidian facts of normal life. This is the theme that Yoshimoto herself stresses in the 'Afterword to the American Edition', and her emphasis on the unending yet magical cycle of life is relentless, with inconsequential detail after inconsequential detail piled on top of one another. The same technique is applied to Sakumi's 'quotable' philosophical or poetic musings about life, another familiar characteristic of Yoshimoto's female protagonists and remarkably similar to the musings of Murakami's 'Boku'.

The 'other world' reality is powerfully conveyed; the Saipan trip is idealised, as the near-past is often idealised in Yoshimoto's fiction, as Furuhashi notes in a general observation (Furuhashi, 1990: 59). This, conversely, emphasises the present: complex, sad, and mysterious, fulfilled in the self-consciousness of the protagonist, which encompasses the varied and complex realities of the many other characters in a clear, transparent way. Others' thoughts are not available to the protagonist except by direct report through conversation (which, nevertheless, reports dreams and other psychic occurrences). Rather than historicising nostalgia for the past, as John Treat argues, such a narrative technique puts the reader into the midst of a polyphonic tale of the ungraspable present, as we too are privy to those many conversations on an equal footing with the narrator (Treat, 1993: 384). This novel, perhaps, realises this particular gift of Yoshimoto in a more powerful way than any other of her works, and, this achievement may well compensate for the longueur of this most ambitious experiment.

The era of nonsense

The poet and literary historian Shimaoka Shin in his history of modern poetry characterises the 1970s as the era of nonsense. He cites as evidence the critic Tanemura Suehiro's article, 'Nansensu Shijin no Shōzō' (A Portrait of Nonsense Poets), serialised in the journal *Modern Poetry Notebook* between 1968 and 1969. In 1977, Tanemura published an expanded version of this essay where he wrote that young poets were trying to shatter 'the control society (or planned society) cut off from dreams and madness and impossible expressions, the existence of which it attempts to deny...it is only natural for students in the 1970s to sing a different tune from this control society, to make as their catchcries slogans like "we have no trust in language" and "nonsense"' (Quoted Shimaoka, 1998: 284). The student riots in Paris in 1968 and the storming of Tokyo University the following year by Japanese student radicals represented the last gasp of 1960s radicalism. What followed, writes Shimaoka, was the slow turning away from radicalism: from the Age of Aquarius, LSD, and hippies (Shimaoka, 1998: 286).

In this environment, the two leaders of nonsense poetry were Tanikawa Shuntarō and Terayama Shūji (1935–83). Terayama wrote verse dramas for underground theatre, produced videos and wrote radio poetry. In 1960, when he was only twenty-four, Terayama wrote a famous essay entitled 'Kōi to Sono Hokori—Chimata no Gendaishi to Action Poem no Mondai' (Action and Its Boasts—The Issue of the Fork in Modern Verse and Action Poems) in which he criticised poets' obsession with print media. He characterised jazz poetry and graffiti in public toilets as 'action poems', which were 'revelations of life overflowing in forks in the road' (Quoted Shimaoka, 1998: 275). In the late sixties and early seventies, poetry recitals and performances became extremely popular. Shimaoka cites Terayama's 1973 action poem 'Jikanwari' (Timetable)—a sketch of how to experience poetry by drawing in chalk a square on a concrete footpath and dividing it into various zones—as typical of the kind of verse (or performance) activity that Terayama championed (Shimaoka, 1998: 276–7). The poetry publishing house Shichōsha fanned the trend for performance poetry, which resulted in overflow audiences for verse readings. This spurt of activity gave rise to a 'mini-boom' in poetry publishing, with numerous sets of poets being issued at this time.

Thus, the mid-seventies represented a peak in popularity for poetry that has never been regained since. Shimaoka writes that single volumes of the thirty-four-volume set *Nihon Shijin Zenshū* (A Collection of Japanese Poetry), produced by Shinchōsha at the time, sold over 100,000 copies (Shimaoka, 1998: 279). The scholar Takahashi Seori argues that the seventies saw a fundamental split between performance poets like Terayama and elite print-oriented poets who rejected this trend, writing ever more obscure and difficult 'language' poetry (Takahashi, 1997: 337–9). While Terayama explored the motifs of 'clowning', 'laughter', and 'deconstruction' in his poetry, poets of an opposing persuasion developed poetry in a direction similar to abstract art—this kind of poetry Takahashi calls 'conceptual art' (Takahashi, 1997: 337–9). Before we examine such poetry in more detail, we need to investigate the other major 'performance poet' of the 1970s: Tanikawa Shuntarō.

Tanikawa's activities during the decade include in 1970 translating the 'Peanuts' comic strip into Japanese, going on a poetry-reading tour of the USA the following year, writing scenarios for the famous movie director Ichikawa Kon during 1972–3 and translating the Mother Goose nursery rhymes into Japanese in 1975. In the midst of this activity, in 1973 Tanikawa wrote his volume *Kotoba Asobi Uta* (Word-Play Songs). In a way, as the poet himself confessed in a 1997 interview, this volume was written as a counter-strategy to poetry as conceptual art. Tanikawa remarked, 'modern poetry has become too intellectual, too sterile and, as a result, readers have gradually been lost. So I thought I'd try to revive poetry.... I decided to do something different, to try rhyme. In the end, I thought that if I didn't make rhymes that sounded like bad puns it would not interest my Japanese audience. That's how I came to compose *Word-Play Songs*' (Morton, 1998: 28).

We can see the result in the following poem 'Tane' (Seed) from that collection:

> had see
> a nap
> dreamt see
> fire's
> extinguished see
> damn
> see ya
> tomorrow see
> moon's out tonight see
> sowed
> rapeseed see
> bud's out see

Morton, 1993: 243

According to the scholar Tsuboi Hideto, the leading poet of the conceptual art school in the 1970s was Arakawa Yōji (b.1949). Arakawa wrote four volumes of poetry during this time: the two most famous collections are *Shōfuron* (A Study of Prostitutes, 1971) and *Suieki* (Water-Station, 1975). The latter volume was awarded the Mr. H Poetry Prize in 1975, by far the most prestigious of the many poetry prizes awarded annually in Japan. Of *Water-Station*, Yoshimoto Takaaki wrote in *On Mass Images* that Arakawa was: 'The first and greatest poet who changed the meaning of the metaphor for young, modern verse', but the poet Iijima Kōichi (b.1930) wrote of the same volume: 'poetry for the era of air-conditioning with the most comfortable temperature adjustment' (Quoted Tsuboi, 1998: 272).

Shimaoka explains that the characters 'suieki' can also be read 'mizu-umaya', an old term found in classical literature that means a post-station or portside inn beside a watercourse, and this association with classical literature invests Arakawa's complex poem with a certain austere elegance (Shimaoka, 1998: 297–8). Nevertheless, the poem 'Water-Station', like many of the poems in the collection, constitutes 'an exchange between meaning and non-meaning', as Shimaoka puts it, and so creates a newness of technique that was immediately noticed by Arakawa's contemporaries (Shimaoka, 1998: 298).

Indeed, Arakawa's emphasis on technique brought about a swift counter-attack from up-and-coming poets like Inagawa Masato (b.1949) and Hiraide Takashi (b.1950). Ironically, the latter poet was himself attacked by Yoshimoto Takaaki in his 1968 book on postwar poetry for the obscurity of his 'rhetorical verse'. Arakawa's article 'Gijutsu no Ikaku' (The Menace of Technique) was published in the October 1977 issue of *Modern Poetry Notebook* where he stated that poets need to work alone with technique, not sensibility or feeling, thus repudiating the poetic ethos of the sixties, and this provoked the reaction of the two younger poets. Their reply appeared in the next issue of the same journal in an article entitled 'Kifū no Jizoku o ou: Arakawa Yōji Hihan' (We Need to Maintain the Ethos: A Criticism of Arakawa Yōji) where they argued the need to inherit the critical ethos of the sixties (Tsuboi, 1998: 273–4).

In 1997, two leading poets of the 1990s, Nomura Kiwao and Shiroto Shuri, wrote an influential study entitled *Tōgi Sengoshi—Shi no Runnesansu e* (Discussions of Postwar Poetry—Towards a Renaissance in Verse), in which they argued that Arakawa's theoretical stance on poetry was not matched in his actual verse practice. Tsuboi observes that Arakawa's poetry style changed considerably in the 1980s in collections such as *Heroin* (Heroine, 1986) where he grew closer to performance poets, composing verse described by the poet–critic Kitagawa Tōru (b.1935) as 'pop poetry' (Tsuboi, 1998: 274–5). It is also interesting to note that the contemporary poet Yoshida Fuminori (b.1947) describes *Water-Station* as a mere copy of Irisawa Yasuo's 1968 collection *My Izumo My Requiem*, which emphasises again how epoch-making Irisawa's volume was for later poets. Yoshida goes on to argue that this book was an ironic manifesto declaring the loss of meaning or originality in poetry as words simply became playful symbols. Thus, he declares, the volume was a turning point for Japanese poetry (Yoshida, 1996: 119–20).

Naturally, other poets belonging to the school of conceptual art produced volumes of interest during this decade. The stress on myth and magic that we see in Irisawa's volume was imitated by poets like Yoshimasu Gōzō (b.1939) with his 1970 collection *Ōgon Shihen* (Golden Poems), his 1973 collection *Ōkoku* (Kingdom) and especially his long poem *Neppū, A Thousand Steps* (Devil's Wind, A Thousand Steps, 1979). In 1984, Yoshimasu published another long book–poem

Oshirisu, Ishi no Kami (Osiris, the God of Stone) which, like *Neppū*, was awarded a major poetry prize. Hiroaki Satō's 1989 complete translation of *Osiris* has given English-language readers a chance to appreciate this major poet's achievements (Yoshimasu, 1989).

The revival of prose–poetry continued in this era, with a number of poets already mentioned writing books using this genre of verse. Probably the most influential poet writing prose–poetry at this point in time was Iijima Kōichi who published several collections, which were acclaimed critically by his peers, notably *Goya no Fāsuto Nēmu* (Goya's First Name, 1974) and *Baruserona* (Barcelona, 1976). One unusual feature of Iijima's work is how his prose–poetry began to slip into his prose during this period, with several of his novels (he was awarded the Akutagawa Prize for fiction in 1970) sharing the same text-fragments as his prose–poetry (Tsuboi, 1989: 268–9). In 1979, Iijima wrote a volume of poetry called *Miyako* about Miyako island in Okinawa, which confirmed the interest in Okinawa of several mainland poets during this decade.

After the reversion of Okinawa to Japan from US occupation in 1972, as Ōshiro Sadatoshi has noted, there was a revival of poetry produced in Okinawa itself. The search for a new Okinawan identity led in the 1970s to an interest in language, as Okinawan writers sought new modes of expression to accommodate the new political and social reality. The necessity of maintaining their ethnicity, for want of a better term, produced much experimentation among Okinawan poets (both Okinawan-born, and poets who were born on the mainland but migrated to Okinawa) at this time (Ōshiro, 1989: 114). Ōshiro reported that the number of literary and cultural journals increased threefold in the 1970s and this explosion of publishing outlets led to an outpouring of poetry (Ōshiro, 1989: 117).

Poets like Mizuna Akira (b.1942) and Yamaguchi Kōji (b.1940) produced important collections with a focus on language and identity throughout this period. One of the best-known poets who came to prominence at this time was Iraha Morio (b.1942). In 1972 he published the collection *Taiken* (Experience), followed by *Memai* (Vertigo, 1975), *Ōto* (Vomit, 1978), *Maboroshi no Mikojima* (Phantom Shamaness Island, 1979), and *Kanashi Den* (The Tale of Kanashi, 1980). *Phantom Shamaness Island* was awarded the Yamanoguchi Baku Prize, the most prestigious poetry prize awarded in Okinawa. The collection concerns Iraha's birthplace Ikema island, which he calls the phantom island of female mediums or shamans, and mixes legend and myth into a complex genealogy of origins, though not as ironically as Irisawa's similar evocation of his birthplace Izumo in his 1968 collection (Iraha, 1979).

The explosion of poetry produced in Okinawa at this time was later paralleled by an explosion of prose, although for the most part, this did not receive comparable recognition until the 1990s, with the award of the Akutagawa Prize to Matayoshi Eiki's (b.1947) novel *Buta no Mukui* (The Pig's Revenge) in 1996 signalling the beginning of a trend. The only significant Okinawan prose writer to receive recognition before then was the novelist Ōshiro Tatsuhiro (b.1925).

The revolution in women's poetry

Several commentators have pointed to the 1980s as being the decade of women's poetry. A number of events brought about this explosion in women's writing and publishing. Kunimine Teruko in her review of women's poetry serialised in *Modern Poetry Notebook* from March 1993 to January 1994 points to 1983 as a key year. The poetry journal *Gendaishi Ra Mēru* (Modern Poetry Journal: La Mer), edited by the two veteran women poets Shinkawa Kazue (b.1929) and Yoshihara Sachiko, and which originally printed poetry solely by women (and mostly adhered to that policy), started publication that year.

The first award of a new poetry prize from Shichōsha (which was the original publisher of *La Mer*) went to the Osaka woman poet Hirata Toshiko (b.1955) which caused the *Mainichi* newspaper to exclaim 'Not another woman!' (Kunimine, 1993: 152). The reason for the *Mainichi's* indignation was that four out of the five previous recipients of the *Modern Poetry Notebook* poetry prize had been women. Similarly, the prestigious Mr. H Poetry prize-winners for 1982 and 1983 were both women. But, as Kunimine points out, no woman had been awarded the Mr. H prize for the ten years prior to 1992 (Kunimine, 1993: 152).

Consequently, the women's poetry 'boom' progressed at a rapid pace. In 1984, Suzuki Yuriika (b.1941) was awarded the inaugural La Mer poetry prize and also the Mr. H Poetry prize for her first volume of verse *MOBILE Ai* (Mobile Love, 1984). Her second volume of poetry *Umi no Baiorin ga Kikoeru* (I can Hear the Violin of the Sea, 1985) was awarded another poetry prize. Hirata Toshiko's successor in

1984 for the Shichōsha poetry prize was another new woman poet, Nakamoto Michiyo (b.1949). *La Mer* quickly became a success: 7000 copies were printed of the first issue alone (Kunimine, 1993: 152). Moreover, the birth of *La Mer* was accompanied by a hugely successful new series of selected woman poets, which had commenced publication the year before in 1982. This library of women poets was called the *Joseishi no Genzai Shiriizu* (Series of Contemporary Woman Poets) and was published by Shichōsha, which did much to initiate the 'boom'. A number of young poets like Shiraishi Kōko (b.1960) and Matsui Keiko (b.1948) were published in this series, which rode on a wave of journalistic acclaim leaving a deep impression on the reading public (Isaka, 1986: 68).

Shiraishi Kazuko, the doyen of Japanese women's poetry, wrote that the eighties generation brought about a revolution in female verse (Shiraishi, 1991: 68–9). But, Itō Hiromi, one of the most radical and most notorious of this new generation of women poets, was much less impressed with the entire phenomenon. In 1983, she wrote a much-quoted article in *La Mer* in which she stated that 'for male readers, Kōko, Yōko, Hiromi, Michiko and Junko are all just the generic woman poet', thus expressing her irritation and deep mistrust of this sudden rage for women's poetry (Quoted Tsuboi, 1989a: 24).

Before exploring the impact Itō made, and continues to make, upon the poetry scene, we will pause briefly to reconstruct a short history of women's poetry over the previous two decades. Ishigaki Rin established a firm position among the ranks of significant poets through the sixties and seventies. During this period, she published her second and third volumes of poetry: *Hyōsatsu Nado* (Nameplates etc, 1968) and *Yasashii Kotoba* (Soft Words, 1984). These books further enhanced her reputation as a poet concerned with the ordinary day-to-day lives of working women. The subjects of her poetry are mundane: such topics as toilets, cooking, plucking wildflowers, and the public bath. Yet the complex irony inherent in her verse does not lend itself to a simple, uncomplicated reading. Her poetry reveals a clear concern with social and political issues (Morton, 1997: 80–6).

Tomioka Taeko (b.1935) is another feminist poet whose work, despite its complexity and difficulty, left a huge impact on her contemporaries. Tomioka published throughout the 1950s and 1960s, eventually abandoning poetry for prose in 1973. In her several collections, she introduced a type of poem that was to become her trademark: the 'monogatari shi' or tale poem. Tomioka's tale poetry seems to tell a story but the story goes on and on. Her poems often take the form of dialogues addressing you (kimi), and these dialogues—which actually resemble endless monologues after the style of the poet Gertrude Stein (1874–1946) whose work she translated—often focus on relationships. Thus, Tomioka created a new, distinctly female speaking voice: a voice for women alone, a voice ambiguous and indefinite, speaking in dialect rather than standard Japanese, standing in stark contrast to an authoritative, univocal narrative whether that be cast in a traditional masculine mode or in a feminine mode (Morton, 1997: 86–91).

Both Ishigaki and Tomioka have distinctive linguistic styles. The same can be said of Shiraishi Kazuko who in the 1970s and 1980s moved on from the 'performance' or 'beat' poetry that had established her reputation in the 1960s. In this respect, her famous 1970 collection *Seasons of the Sacred Lecher*, notorious for its breaking of several taboos relating to the depiction of sex in verse, can be seen as the end of one stage of her evolution as a poet. Her 1982 prize-winning collection *Sunazoku* (Sun Clan) explored religious motifs across deserts in the USA, the Middle East, and the Pacific. Her 1988 collection *Furenama, Furemon, Furumon* (The Touched, Loonies, Full Moon) continued this exploration of religion and identity. Shiraishi's long, multi-sequence poems explore spirituality in a way not dissimilar to Yoshimasu Gōzō, continually searching out new and unexplored territory (Morton, 1993: 195–230).

However, the most famous of the younger woman poets who emerged in the 1980s is Itō Hiromi. In this decade, Itō published two landmark volumes: *Teritorii Ron 2* (On Territory 2, 1985) and *Teritorii Ron* (On Territory 1, 1987). The first of the volumes established Itō's reputation as the 'shussan shijin' or 'child-birth' poet. Perhaps the most celebrated poem from this book is 'Kanoko Goroshi' (Killing Kanoko) where two texts are juxtaposed, one at the top of the page, the other at the bottom. The polyphonous nature of the text is made even more transparent when Itō performs the poem at public readings. She plays a tape-recording of her voice declaiming the lower text or poem while simultaneously reading live the upper text (Morton, 1993: 383–9; Tsuboi, 1989a: 34). The upper text plays with notions of abortion and infanticide, thus, postnatal depression is a major theme of the upper text. The lower text relates the story of the suicide of a friend called Hiromi.

Ayukawa Nobuo, in his review of the book, was much impressed by this work but was also shocked by the fact that Itō's daughter is actually called Kanoko (Quoted Tsuboi, 1989a: 33). In the poem, the unborn foetus Kanoko and the newborn Kanoko are murdered several times over by the mother.

The first six or seven poems in *On Territory I*, published two years later, are photographic/poetic collages composed with the photographer Araki Nobuyoshi (b.1940). The poet herself said in an interview about the volume, 'I want to give a sadistic kick to the words born from within me.... I see language as just one element in art. I want to make my art purely visual. I want to eliminate the meaning contained in the words, the flow, the story; I am possessed by this masochistic desire' (Quoted Tsuboi, 1990: 49).

Among the first group of poems in the book, we find 'Triptych', a collage based mainly on quotations from the British painter Francis Bacon (1909–92), and photography that may be dog vomit or a squashed cat. 'Otōsan wa Burū' (Dad is Blue) is a retelling of Freud's famous Little Hans case, except that the author substitutes a 'woman/self' for Little Hans and 'father' for Freud's mother, thus totally reversing Freud's discourse (Itō, 1987). And where in Freud's account the father's 'phallus' appears, the author substitutes 'poo'. Itō also substitutes 'I' for 'Little Hans', thus combining two of her favourite motifs, 'evacuation' and 'desire'. Grammatical subject and semantic subject are completely disengaged.

Takeda Nobuaki, commenting on the late seventies verse of Itō and Yōko Isaka, argues that their poetry problematised the issue of gender, and especially the notion of a gendered self. The self created in their verse is not a subjectivised but an objectivised self (Takeda, 1989: 132–3). This fracturing of gender in Itō's verse—she creates a simulacrum of herself and then destroys it—is her most notable achievement.

The poet Matsuura Hisaki argues that 1980s poetry displayed the symptoms of a kind of exhaustion. He observes that the popularity of poetry diminished as consumer values flourished, and there was a burst of new subcultural (or mass-culture) activity in areas like cinema and comics as a result of the growth of info-capitalism. The expansion of the 1980s 'bubble economy' also played a role in fostering fashions, television, the Internet, and also forms of popular culture, which eventually pushed poetry to the cultural margins; naturally, he is writing of poetry as conceptual art. The bursting of the bubble further accelerated this trend (Matsuura, 1996: 126).

According to such a reading of cultural history, the increased emphasis on issues like sexuality and gender, inherent in the women's poetry boom, is but a symptom of a splintering of social and political concerns in literature and a shift towards the personal as poets like Itō focus on notions of selfhood.

Therefore, we might expect that male poets also displayed similar concerns in their work. Shimaoka Shin argues that the attention paid to issues of transgressive sexuality and sexual taboos in Itō's poetry is matched, if not directly influenced by similar concerns in the poetry of Nejime Shōichi (b.1948) (Shimaoka, 1998: 291). Nejime studied poetry under Suzuki Shiroyasu, the poet who with his 1967 'Puapua' poems had first combined 'language' poetry with sexual themes. His first book *Fu*, published in 1979, was awarded the Mr. H Poetry prize. But the volumes he published in the early eighties, like *Getabaki Sungeki* (An Unpretentious Sideshow, 1980) and *Nōmaku Menma* (Brain Meninges Pickles, 1983), display a virtuoso skill in word-plays centred on transgressive sex. To a degree, Nejime continued in the 'showman' tradition of Terayama Shūji, working extensively on radio, and in the late eighties began to establish a solid reputation as a novelist concentrating on stories about the inner-city life of small shopkeepers (the environment in which he was raised).

The 'conceptual art' tradition of word-plays was continued in the same decade, predominantly by male poets like Hiraide Takashi, especially with his 1987 volume *Ie no Ryokusenkō* (Green Flash in the House), which is a complex play of parallel short prose-poems using a 'green ray' motif taken from Jules Verne (Morton, 1993: 309–18). With Inagawa Masato, who also wrote one of the landmark collections of this decade in *Fūin* (Seal, 1985), these two 'rhetorical' (to use Yoshimoto Takaaki's pejorative term) poets constituted one of the main centres of poetic activity (Shimaoka, 1998: 219).

It is difficult to evaluate the 1990s, as this decade has witnessed the arrival of a whole new group of exciting young poets like Nomura Kiwao, Shiroto Shuri and Seo Ikuo (b.1948). But the nineties have also seen the publication of what is possibly Tanikawa Shuntarō's best collection ever: his 1993 book *Seken Shirazu* (The Naïf). The most celebrated work in this collection is the poem 'Chichi no Shi' (My Father's Death), which mourns the death of the poet's father Tanikawa Tetsuzō, a famous philosopher and literary critic. This long, complex poem has been hailed by several critics as one of the best poems published in decades, combining self-ridicule, irony, sadness and a sense of stillness which gives the work great power. The fact that a few years after the publication of this volume, Tanikawa declared that he would write no more poetry has also added to the significance of this collection (Morton, 1998: 29).

Two stanzas at the heart of this poem sum up its strength:

> While you are asleep, Death,
> With its silent, swift hand
> Sweeps away all the details of life but
> For us who talk away the small time
> Until the flowers placed as offerings on the altar fade
> There is no end to foolish chatter
> Death is the unknown
>
> In the unknown there is no detail
> This resembles poetry
> Both Death and poetry tend to abridge life but
> Those who are left alive rejoice in puzzling detail
> Rather than abridgement

Tanikawa, 1993: 12–13

5

Mass Culture:
TV, Cinema, and Manga

I saw the mob
Shoot itself
Unbearably sad
On the TV screen
Light snow is falling

Takizawa Wataru, 1925–96 (Okai, 1997: 132)

This chapter will sketch an outline of three areas of mass culture: television, cinema and manga (comics). The stress will be on the recent
development of some of the more vital areas of interest as perceived by
contemporary Japanese commentators, rather than a detailed history of
the evolution of these cultural media over the past seventy or eighty
years. Naturally, television is the newest of these three cultural forms,
and is still in a state of rapid change. The sheer magnitude of television
product demands a highly selective approach, and here the focus will be
on a few areas of contention identified by influential commentators. In
discussing Japanese cinema, I will concentrate on postwar cinema and
the films of a few celebrated directors rather than attempt a detailed
overview, as such an overview is already available in English through the
writings of such commentators as Donald Richie and Joseph Anderson
(Anderson and Richie, 1982) and David Desser (Desser, 1988). Finally,
manga, because of its ephemerality, and sheer volume, will be subjected

to the same kind of analysis with attention paid only to a small group of influential practitioners in the modern era.

The same kinds of generalisation relating to insider discourse as apply to literature also apply to mass culture, although this might seem a paradoxical statement. Although neither TV, cinema nor comics originated in Japan, and indeed in the early history of these cultural genres much of the technology and content was imported from abroad, as modes of communication they are intricately and ineluctably linked to contemporary Japanese society. So comprehension and criticism of Japanese popular culture invariably forms part of an insider dialogue. Few critics working on these three cultural modes would call themselves outsider commentators and most would avoid any explicit comparison with examples drawn from outside Japan.

However, it should be noted that quite early pioneers of the study of mass culture (generally excluding cinema), especially those working in universities, saw such investigations as explicitly rooted in outsider theory imported from the West. The focus of this group, unlike the indigenous discourse referred to above, centred not on aesthetic or thematic concerns but, rather, on the role popular culture plays in society as a whole. This small group pioneered academic study of popular culture in the 1950s, exactly at the same time that TV was introduced to Japan, and that manga was beginning to assume its current significance. As these media themselves boomed in the 1960s and after, such pioneering writers were largely overtaken by a broad coalition of insider authors on mass culture, and this trend has continued to the present day, although several academics have inherited the mantle of those pioneers, and work in their tradition.

As with the study of mass culture elsewhere, in general, non-journalistic criticism and research has only begun to emerge in quantity over recent decades. Japanese film theory and criticism has the longest history of the three genres of mass culture under investigation here but even this body of work is relatively small, especially when compared to what is available on older expressions of culture such as literature and art. Serious and substantial critiques of Japanese TV and comics have emerged only of late and, as yet, no single theoretical conceptualisation is accepted in Japan—debates about the history, provenance, and aesthetic significance of these modes of cultural expression have commenced only recently. Yomota Inuhiko (b.1953) is typical of the group of younger scholars who are now engaged in building the framework for indigenous Japanese theories of popular culture, so it is no accident that this chapter draws frequently upon his research. In the main, current criticism in these fields is still based in the broad structure of discourse established by insider predecessors like Yoshimoto Takaaki.

From the above account, it is clear that it is no easy task to describe the intellectual and cultural context in which TV, cinema, and manga operated throughout the period under investigation. The combination of masses of raw data, and the lack of a concrete analytic framework dictate that this must be so. Therefore, the few commentators and practitioners chosen for discussion here play crucial roles in constructing that context; this is particularly noticeable in the case of contemporary cinema, which explains why this chapter pays such attention to contemporary critics of Japanese film.

Television the powerful

Television broadcasting began in Japan in 1953. The spread of television into Japanese households was very rapid, with the total production of television sets rising 9.3 times in the four years from 1955 to 1959. After the unprecedented success of the broadcast of the royal wedding between Crown Prince Akihito and Shōda Michiko on 10 April 1959, when fifteen million Japanese tuned in to watch the event—the biggest TV audience yet in Japanese history—the popularity of TV increased even more. By 1960, the audience for television encompassed 29.1% of households, nearly double the 1959 figure. In 1964, TV Tokyo—the youngest of the major networks—was founded. From this time, Japanese television has consisted of the government network NHK (Japan Broadcasting Corporation) and four commercial networks: Asahi National Broadcasting Co. Ltd (TV Asahi), Fuji Television Network (Fuji TV), Nippon Television Network (NTV), and Tokyo Broadcasting Corporation Inc. (TBS) (Schilling, 1997: 15, 33–6).

Over the past decade and a half, a number of technological developments have further spread the influence of TV. The introduction of cable television to Japan will increase that trend even though, to date, it has only been taken up in a small way. By 1996, only three million out of forty-two million TV households subscribed to multi-channel cable. Clearly, the potential exists for expansion. Satellite TV has only a few channels thus far—two extra NHK channels and a few entertainment channels like Wowow. Yet by 1997, some eight million reception contracts had been signed for NHK satellite TV (Kawai, 1997: 268).

'High Vision' TV was introduced to Japan at the time of the Seoul Olympics but the battle between the differing technologies employed by NHK and overseas competitors has hindered large-scale expansion (Schilling, 1997: 15, 33–6; Yoshimoto, 1995a: 71–7). Nevertheless, Japan's success as an exporter of colour televisions to the USA from 1975 onwards (commercial production of colour TVs in Japan began in 1959) demonstrates how Japan had soon become a world leader, not a follower, in TV technology (Schilling, 1997: 36). Moreover, despite Japan lagging behind the USA in Internet technologies, by the late 1990s a number of the commercial Japanese TV channels were available over the Internet.

The dominance of television over other media as a provider of news, information and entertainment is well documented. In a 1999 survey conducted by NHK, television scored first as the source of information preferred by all age cohorts except the fifty to sixty age group for males, where it was second to newspapers. However, for all other age cohorts (from sixteen to seventy and above), television was the chief source of information; and, for women, nothing surpassed TV (Cited Kusano, 2000: 23). Andrew Painter raises some doubts about NHK surveys but he admits how powerful TV is as a medium shaping perceptions on a large variety of topics. He even cites 1992 statistics indicating that the average household in Japan has the TV set turned on for an average of between seven and a half and eight hours per day (Painter, 1993: 296). Given that forty-two million households possessed TVs in 1996, we can see just how pervasive television is for the vast majority of Japanese.

Mark Schilling notes that after the start of TV broadcasts, many programs were modified versions of overseas originals. NHK repackaged American quiz shows to adapt them for Japanese audiences. Further, with the growth in commercial networks in the late 1950s and early 1960s, lack of product became a crucial issue. This gap in programming was filled by imports, mainly from the USA, with programs like *Laramie*, *Ben Casey*, *Combat*, and *Bewitched* gaining large Japanese audiences. But by the 1970s, imported programs, other than movies, had been largely replaced by Japanese programs created by the large networks (Schilling, 1997: 10).

Yoshimoto Takaaki's critique of television

Next, we will outline a critical overview of Japanese television. Such a critique has been provided by Yoshimoto Takaaki in his 1991 study *Jōkyō to Shite no Gazō—Kōdo Shihonshugika no 'Terebi'* (A Portrait of the State of Affairs—'Television' under High Capitalism), reprinted in 1995 as a paperback. Yoshimoto originally published the twenty-five chapters of the book in serial form in the monthly *TBS Chōsa Hōhō* (TBS Data Survey) between September 1987 and September 1989.

Yoshimoto viewed numerous programs and channels over this period, apparently keeping detailed notes. In his introductory chapter, 'Terebi wa Doko e Yuku ka' (Whither Television), he made clear his overall disappointment with Japanese TV. According to Yoshimoto, television is a 'frightened medium' that survives on the repetition of the familiar (Yoshimoto, 1995a: 15). He notes how complete is the construction of a simulacrum reality on television: the whole day is divided into one-hour packages, and there are only two seasons, spring and autumn, since ratings are only taken seriously at these times. Another characteristic of Japanese TV pointed out by Yoshimoto is how the faces of the on-screen personalities essentially create amateur personas. Japanese television deliberately shies away from announcers or hosts who might cultivate an air of elitism or professionalism; rather, they appear to be amateurs, just like us. Thus, his initial conclusion is that television is an 'empty imaginary', a view he had already hinted at in his 1994 book *On Mass Images* (Yoshimoto, 1995a: 15–32).

Based on his intensive viewing, Yoshimoto wrote two chapters on news and current affairs programs. He argues that 'infotainment' has become predominant on the 'wide-shows' that dramatise news for viewers. This has been accomplished with technology that enables news to be packaged from anywhere in the world and instantly translated onto the small screen. When issues such as international terrorism are presented on news and current affairs shows, because no point of view or position is held by the producers or commentators of these programs, viewers are given no insight into the causes and context behind these events. Whether viewers are meant to see these events as tragic or comic or whatever is impossible to know. A partial exception to this analysis is allowed by Yoshimoto for NHK news, but commercial news shows such as TV Asahi's popular *News Station*, hosted by the former comedian

Kume Hiroshi (b.1944), are disappointing because of a lack of editorial focus (Yoshimoto, 1995a: 34–46).

Kume Hiroshi's success has stimulated a flood of Japanese publications about this newscaster who during 1992 ran what some considered a vendetta on his show against the government kingmaker, the veteran politician Kanemaru Shin, who was accused of accepting massive illegal campaign contributions. When Kanemaru resigned in October 1992, many attributed his fall to Kume's attacks. Kume's brash style—where the on-screen presenter becomes a personality—was imitated by most other commercial channels but in the late 1990s he became enmeshed in sexual scandal (Schilling, 1997: 160–3).

Yoshimoto conducted a detailed analysis of the popularity of various programs: in 1988, these were a mixture of NHK historical dramas, quizzes and samurai dramas. Yoshimoto lists several reasons for their popularity. Firstly, the top five programs were serials. NHK's historical drama *Takeda Shingen*, dramatising the life of the famous medieval warlord Takeda Shingen (1521–73), for instance, held down the number-one spot and consisted of serialised episodes from Takeda's life. As Yoshimoto noted, the fact of serialisation creates suspense and raises expectations, a clear use of narrative to enhance viewer interest. Secondly, the broadcast time slots were those that traditionally captured the most viewers. Thirdly, the content of the various programs sustained viewer interest throughout the season. And, finally, the celebrities and actors appearing on these programs were at the peak of their popularity. In analysing content, Yoshimoto highlighted the clever pacing and innovative story lines used in the dramas. The first two top-rating shows in 1988 were dramas; the number-two spot was occupied by *Hassei Sensei*, a wartime drama. The famous emcee Kyosen Ōhashi (b.1934) occupied the number-three place with *Quiz Derby*, one of the many quizzes this personality has been associated with over a long career in TV (Yoshimoto, 1995a: 63–77).

Yoshimoto also embarked upon an analysis of the top personalities or 'tarento' (talents), as they are sometimes called. His list included Hagimoto Kin'ichi (b.1941), Beat Takeshi (b.1947), Tamori (Morita Kazuyoshi, b.1945), and Akashiya Samma (b.1955). What these (all male) personalities, or better, comedians, had in common, apart from their longevity as TV stars, was an ability to make themselves the object of their humour, which let the audience laugh with them as much as at them. Yoshimoto noted that Tamori, the star of the long-running Fuji TV program *Waratte ii Tomo* (Go Ahead and Laugh!)—described by Painter as a 'hodgepodge of skits, quizzes, monologues, dialogues and performances'—was able to give the appearance of continually ad-libbing (despite the carefully orchestrated nature of the ad-libs) but in a steady tone of voice that reassured audiences of the predictable nature of the humour (Painter, 1993: 301; Yoshimoto, 1995a: 108). Tamori spent much time abasing himself, as did Akashiya, his erstwhile foil on some seasons of *Waratte ii Tomo*. Akashiya, a younger Osaka comedian, made a good partner for the Tokyo-educated but Kyushu-raised Tamori, with elements of their humour arising from the two distinctly different dialects employed by them.

Discussing how major news events were treated by the networks, Yoshimoto praised the coverage by Japanese television of the death and funeral of Emperor Hirohito. Yoshimoto argued that Japanese TV had opened to scrutiny much that had been hitherto hidden from the public gaze. But he strongly criticised coverage of the 'Recruit' company scandal by Japanese TV—where again bribes were allegedly given to politicians to curry influence—since, he observed, newscasters had forgotten the notion of the presumption of innocence (Yoshimoto, 1995a: 152–9).

In conclusion, Yoshimoto notes that television has the unique quality of eliminating the distance between the self and other, and hence, allows viewers to be virtually written over by the scripts of the various programs. However, Yoshimoto's own observations and critiques—and, generally speaking, he is very critical of TV—tend to contradict this viewpoint (Yoshimoto, 1995a: 189–97). Nevertheless, Yoshimoto's views are echoed by many commentators on Japanese TV, whether Japanese or not.

Other perspectives

The scholar Kusano Atsushi (b.1947) in his study of news reporting on Japanese TV, *Terebi Hōdō no Tadashii Mikata* (The Correct Way to View Television News), published in 2000, agrees with many of Yoshimoto's criticisms. Kusano focuses on the coverage of a few important issues, mainly confining his analysis to NHK. One broadcast that he subjected to a minute analysis was a special program on the fifth anniversary of the Kobe-Hanshin earthquake, broadcast on NHK TV on 7 January 2000, called *Fukkō e no Teigen: Toruko, Taiwan Soshite Kobe* (Proposal for

Reconstruction: Turkey, Taiwan and Kobe). Kusano takes NHK to task for several shortcomings he identified in the program. He argues that the program was deliberately biased against the government, with a clear antigovernment cast revealed both in the structure of the program and the commentators who appeared on it (Kusano, 2000: 32–7).

Kusano's contention is supported by his critical analysis of the program, which goes into much detail to probe the facts behind Japan's assistance to the survivors of the massive earthquake in Turkey, portrayed as inadequate on the program, and which finds similarities with the government's response to the Kobe-Hanshin earthquake. Kusano's main interest is in the assistance provided to Turkey, and the general question of overseas aid. However, he tempers his criticism somewhat by acknowledging that the inherent limitations (in time, and depth of analysis) imposed upon documentaries by the medium of TV may well have caused some of the problems he sees in the presentation (Kusano, 2000: 26–59).

One intriguing aspect of Kusano's critique is the section where he describes the various official responses to his criticisms. Although he slates these responses from NHK as entirely inadequate, nevertheless his account reveals how carefully vetted by community groups such programs are, and how skilfully NHK has constructed a network of interlocking committees to provide community feedback on its programming. The relative openness of NHK to criticism is itself quite noteworthy, especially when compared to government TV networks run by some of Japan's Asian neighbours (Kusano, 2000: 76–86).

As any reading of the Japanese press over the last decade will demonstrate, TV viewers in Japan are not shy about criticising TV programming. Several TV 'scandals' have been exposed in the press in recent years relating to incidents such as the coverage of the sarin gas attack by the Aum sect on the Tokyo underground, and of Aum itself, and most recently of an NHK documentary aired in January 2001 covering the unofficial war crimes tribunal held in Tokyo on the so-called 'comfort women'—women who were pressed into prostitution as sex slaves during World War II. These incidents concern the censorship of programs by the networks concerned.

A number of debates among the intelligentsia have accompanied the growth of TV over the decades since its introduction to Japan. The sociologist Sakurai Tetsuo's (b.1949) 1994 book *TV Mahō no Media* (TV:

The Magic Media) traces many of these debates. The initial impulse behind the book was to counter the writer Tsutsui Yasutaka's famous dystopian vision of TV as expressed in a 1965 collection of science fiction (SF) stories called *48 Oku no Mōsō* (48 Billion Hallucinations), which sparked a debate over the possibilities and dangers of TV. Sakurai's perspective is not as pessimistic as Tsutsui's but, nonetheless, he praises the novelist for his grasp of the myriad future possibilities of this medium (Sakurai, 1994: 18–29).

Another interesting debate examined by Sakurai relates to the 1980s controversy about the large number of faked programs and episodes on Japanese TV. These fakes (yarase) Sakurai identifies as occurring across a broad band of broadcasters including NHK, Television Osaka, and TBS (Sakurai, 1994: 138–41). Fakery, of course, is not confined to Japanese TV, and nor did it end on Japanese TV in the 1980s, with several similar episodes having come to light in the 1990s. Sakurai often compares and contrasts issues relating to TV in Japan with similar problems abroad. In this, he inherits the tradition of outsider discourse on the mass media created by the pioneer scholars of the 1950s.

Andrew Painter conducted nineteen months of fieldwork during 1988–89 within a production department of a major Osaka TV station. His analysis of this experience is built upon a conceptual frame which posits that 'much of Japanese television produces representations of quasi-intimate communication…between TV performers and viewers…patterned…on informal interaction of the sort found in *uchi* (in-group) contexts' (Painter, 1993: 321–2). Thus TV is both public and private at the same time, but as it is a one-way communication from TV to viewer, the viewing audience is represented by 'talents', panels etc. This conclusion agrees with Yoshimoto's remarks on amateurism. Painter argues that 'the goal of TV producers is not to homogenise society or to mislead viewers to serve some hidden, political purpose or class interest' but, he also notes that producers do not question 'cultural and ideological presumptions that underlie everyday practices of television production and consumption' (Painter, 1993: 323–4).

Painter observes that TV 'in Japan, as elsewhere, does not merely reflect society—it transforms it' (Painter, 1993: 324). But, while acknowledging that the representation of society does marginalise certain groups who never appear on the screen, Painter stresses that 'there is something unusual and human about the Japanese experience of television' (Painter: 1993: 325). Earlier, he wrote that 'Japanese viewers no doubt recognise that the unity offered by television is illusory, but they enjoy vicarious participation in TV's electronic *uchi* all the same' (Painter, 1993: 324). Painter's analysis uses as evidence for his contentions 'waidoshō', wide-shows of the sort treated by Yoshimoto, and also *Waratte ii Tomo* and a morning news program called *Zūmu-in Asa* (Zoom In Morning).

Paul Harvey, on the other hand, concentrates his analysis on 'asadora' or morning dramas. These programs are serialised soap operas broadcast in the morning on NHK and aimed at predominantly female audiences, but which have an impressively large viewing audience, and thus, claims Harvey, exercise a significant influence over society (Harvey, 1998: 133–4).

The first asadora were screened in 1961 as a direct response to the popularity of postwar radio soap opera. The programs are screened daily for about fifteen minutes and usually last for six months, normally about 160 episodes with approximately thirty-six hours of air time. Harvey argues that these programs are not soap operas, although they are very close to Western series like the British soaps *Coronation Street* and *EastEnders* or the Australian soap *Neighbours*. Harvey also argues that asadora are based on the home as opposed to Western soaps, which are based on the community (Harvey, 1998: 134–5). The stories, however, are all formulaic in that they are based on their heroines succeeding in their chosen path against all odds. The use of the word 'heroine' is justified on the grounds that forty-three out of fifty leading characters in NHK asadora between 1961 and 1991 were females.

The 1983 asadora *Oshin* telling the life story of Oshin, which neatly encapsulated all the major events of twentieth-century Japanese history into this one woman's lifetime, was easily the most successful internationally, being sold to TV networks all over the world. The ratings for these programs are exceedingly high by any standards; *Nonchan no Yume* (Nonchan's Dream, 1988), a drama about a young woman in the immediate postwar era struggling to balance the demands of her work as a publisher against her love for a man called Takeno, peaked at 50% of all viewers in the Tokyo region. In February 1984 *Oshin* captured 62.5% of the viewing audience, nearly double the ratings of any other program. The effects of these programs on the region in which they are set are often profound. In the case of *Oshin*, a tourist industry sprang up in the town of Sakata within two months of the start of broadcasting (Harvey, 1998: 141, 139).

Harvey notes how NHK has a deliberate policy of shifting from region to region with its asadora, and the didactic morality behind the documenting of women's self-achievement in the dramas is easy to discern. Here, perhaps, we find a direct link between the rationale of a taxpayer-funded channel and program content (Harvey, 1998: 139). Harvey also points out how the key to the popularity of these dramas is the idealised families portrayed in them. Naturally, similar conclusions can be drawn about families and communities portrayed in Western soaps, for example, the Australian publicly funded ABC drama *Seachange* (1998–2000).

We can see in the accounts given here how commentators attempt to link program content with ideology or at least to link content with social issues. The logic of viewer choice dictates the latter approach; and the logic of advertising-driven programming dictates the former. However, it is noticeable how many innovative programs try to subvert conventions which may be said to embody ideologies. This is especially true of comedy programs, at least when they begin broadcasting.

The most successful comedy duo of the 1990s has been the team called 'Downtown', made up of Matsumoto Hitoshi (b.1963) and Hamada Masatoshi (b.1963) who began on TV in 1987 but achieved fame with their program *Gaki no Tsukai* (No Job for Kids), which was aired throughout the 1990s on the NTV network. Often described as subversive, their comedy is similar to the US show *Saturday Night Live* but with no political jokes. Perhaps their form of ribald, irreverent, loony humour is closer to British Goon-style comedy, seen in programs such as *Monty Python's Flying Circus*. The paradox of this kind of stand-up Osaka comedy, called 'manzai', is that the vast bulk of such comedians are employed by the Osaka company Yoshimoto Kōgyō, which has frequently been criticised for its dictatorial control of TV comedy (Schilling, 1997: 45–52).

Beat Takeshi, often described as the 'king' of Japanese TV for the large number of popular programs he has hosted over the last quarter of a century, is also seen in Japan as an anarchic, comic genius who does not care how many sacred cows he offends. Yet, in a famous incident in 1986, his 'army' of supporters invaded and ransacked the Tokyo editorial office of *Friday* magazine, which had run pictures of a college student with whom he reportedly was having an affair (Schilling, 1997: 256). We will examine Takeshi's career as a movie director (under his real name of Kitano Takeshi) later but this mixture of rebellion and arrogance, simultaneously celebrating and undermining capitalist consumer values, is a common characteristic of Japanese TV.

Postwar Japanese cinema

Before embarking upon a discussion of two important postwar directors, namely, Kurosawa Akira (1910–98) and Kitano Takeshi, I will provide a brief outline of postwar Japanese cinema. This account is based primarily, but not exclusively, upon the recent study *Nihon Eiga Shi Hyakunen* (A Hundred Years of Japanese Cinema History, 2000) by Yomota Inuhiko.

Yomota argues that most studies of Japanese cinema focus upon the masterpieces and ignore the majority of films produced for the mass market. As he notes, 'the history of cinema is never the history of masterpieces' (Yomota, 2000: 11). He observes that there are two generally acknowledged 'golden eras' in Japanese cinema: from 1920 to 1930 and from 1950 to 1960. Before the war, Japan was one of the world's most powerful centres of film production. For example, in 1941 Japan ranked second behind the USA, producing approximately 500 movies per year. With the onset of World War II, and the subsequent devastation suffered by the major population centres, production fell dramatically but due to the 1950s boom, by 1960 the industry had surpassed prewar production levels, with 547 films made that year; this peak has not been overtaken since (Yomota, 2000: 34–5).

Movies made in the immediate postwar era were subject to censorship by American occupation authorities and thus period dramas or samurai dramas, which according to Tsutsui Kiyotada made up almost half of all prewar Japanese films, were more or less banned on the grounds that they smacked of prewar military ideology. Tsutsui in his study *Jidaigeki Eiga no Shisō: Nosutarujii no Yukue* (The Ideology of Period Drama Cinema: The Home of Nostalgia), published in 2000, describes the ordinance issued on 19 November 1945 as 'the law banning chambara'—'chambara' being the slang term used to describe sword-fighting, samurai dramas (Tsutsui, 2000: 50). Thus, Yomota argues, the Americans encouraged 'ideas cinema' as a substitute; that is, movies that promoted

American democratic values and ideas. An example of such a movie is Kurosawa Akira's *Waga Seishun ni Kui Nashi* (No Regrets for My Youth, 1946) which centred around the anti-war movement in prewar Japan (Yomota, 2000: 130).

As Yomota notes, it is difficult to evaluate the effect of the American occupation on subsequent Japanese cinema. But, it is striking that once censorship and American controls were lifted in 1952, a massive revival in period dramas began (Yomota, 2000: 136–8). Tsutsui links this revival with the beginning of the second 'golden age' of Japanese cinema and describes the revival as a 'reaction' to the occupation, in other words, a reassertion of Japanese values (Tsutsui, 2000: 55). During this period, when cinema dominated the entertainment industry, the six major studios—Tōhō, Daiei, Shōchiku, Tōei, Nikkatsu, and Shintōhō—concentrated on what Yomota calls 'program pictures', or formula or genre films for a mass audience (Yomota, 2000: 160).

This was also the era when the West discovered Japanese cinema with a number of Japanese films, including Kurosawa's *Rashōmon* (The Rashō Gate, 1951), *Sanshō Dayū* (Sanshō the Bailiff, 1954) directed by Mizoguchi Kenji (1898–1956) and *Jigokumon* (Hell Gate, 1954) directed by Kinugasa Teinosuke (1896–1982), winning major film awards in Europe. Yomota singles out three reasons for the West's sudden embrace of Japanese cinema: first, the exotic nature of 'Oriental' film; second, the emphasis on the auteur or director as primarily responsible for a film; and third, the strong overseas promotion of Japanese cinema led by the then president of Daiei, Nagata Masaichi (1906–85) (Yomota, 2000: 142).

Independent cinema also thrived in the fifties, mainly producing left-wing dramas, but such efforts faded as consolidation appeared in the 1960s. The major studios produced formula films for a mass audience; nevertheless each studio had its preferred audience and made product to suit. A large number of series appeared in the 1950s: the director Ōba Hideo's (b.1910) female-oriented sequence of melodramas under the title *Kimi no Na Wa?* (What is Your Name?) produced by Shōchiku; the monster movie series initiated by the director Honda Inoshirō (1911–93) featuring monsters like Gojira, Matadon, Radon, Mosura, and Kingugidora; the chambara series *Zenigata Heiji Torimono Chō* (Case-Files of Heiji Zenigata) from 1951 to 1961 featuring a samurai detective played by the famous actor Hasegawa Kazuo (1908–84); and the boom in youth movies started by Nikkatsu after its rebirth in 1954 with young staff and directors. Yomota argues that films produced by Nikkatsu in this period, for example the 1956 hit *Taiyō no Kisetsu* (Season of the Sun) directed by Furukawa Takumi from the novel by Ishihara Shintarō (b.1932), who was later to become a politician (elected as governor of Tokyo), created a new image of the Japanese (Yomota, 2000: 145–60).

During the 1960s, however, the cinema boom collapsed. Ticket sales declined from a peak of 1.1 billion in 1961 to roughly half that in 1963. Most commentators attribute the loss of audience to television, which came to dominate the world of entertainment by the mid-sixties. By 1971 both Daiei and Nikkatsu had ceased production. Nikkatsu resumed production after three months but it took three years for Daiei to recover. The film industry fought back with cinemascope and colour (during most of the 1960s, black-and-white movies predominated) but to no avail. However, the sixties also saw outstanding achievements by the postwar generation of directors. Yomota argues that unlike the fifties-era independents (many of the 'new wave' sixties directors operated as independents), these directors had no interest in socialist realism. Rather, their movies are often dark and cynical portrayals of the desolation of postwar Japan. Yomota nominates as outstanding among this group such directors as Imamura Shōhei (b.1926), Ōshima Nagisa (b.1932), Nakahira Kō (1926–78), Suzuki Seijun (b.1923), Shinoda Masahiro (b.1931), Fukasaku Kinji (b.1930), and Teshigahara Hiroshi (b.1927) (Yomota, 2000: 160–4).

David Desser has written a well-known study of the 1960s directors, *Eros Plus Massacre: An Introduction to the Japanese New Wave Cinema* (1988), in which he finds affinities between these directors and such Western equivalents as Jean-Luc Godard (b.1930). However, Desser notes that during this era of great creativity, audiences still declined, with the number of movie theatres falling from 7457 in 1960 to 3246 in 1970. Moreover, Desser argues that by 1978 most movies were 'pink [i.e. erotic] movies, *roman poruno* (soft-core porn), and other marginal sex exploitation pictures' (Desser, 1988: 9). Many of the movies produced by the 1960s directors became well known in the West as Japanese art cinema and, like their 1950s predecessors, won several awards. Teshigahara's *Suna no Onna* (Woman of the Dunes, 1963) was especially popular abroad, winning a prize at the Cannes film festival. Yomota notes that Teshigahara's trilogy of films based on the novels and screenplays of the avant-garde writer and playwright Abe Kōbō (1924–93)—including *Woman of the Dunes*—preaches a philosophy close to the Spanish filmmaker Luis Buñuel (1900–83), and also shares his black humour (Yomota, 2000: 179).

But formula or genre films continued to be produced during this period. Okamoto Kihachi (b.1924), a journeyman director who directed numerous movies during the 1960s and 1970s, always had an eye to entertaining the audience, with musicals, SF and movie spectaculars among the films with which he is usually associated. Yomota described Okamoto's 1959 movie *Dokuritsu Gurentai* (Desperado Outpost), set at the end of World War II, as a most intriguing 'macaroni Western' (Yomota, 2000: 164; Tayama 1991: 47–9). Another formula series beloved by audiences was the Zatōichi movies starring Katsu Shintarō (1931–97) about a blind masseur who is a famed swordsman. This series ran from 1962 to 1971, with two or three films released annually, and its popularity was such that in the 1970s it was turned into a TV series, which achieved fame outside Japan (Yomota, 2000: 165).

Yomota observes that, in terms of aesthetic excellence, Japanese cinema hit rock bottom in the 1970s. The sixties directors who specialised in erotic movies often had a leftist, utopian tinge to their films but, in the seventies, the student movement (the main audience for such films) collapsed as Japan became wealthy due to high economic growth. The cynicism of the younger generation—more specifically, the collapse of the utopian values espoused by youth a decade earlier—is symbolised in Yomota's mind by the suicide of Mishima Yukio in 1970 and the violence wrought by the Red Army—a point of view we have encountered earlier in critical reactions to the literature of this period (Yomota, 2000: 180–2). In 1971, porn movies made up a quarter of all films produced, and by 1978 this had risen to three-quarters (Yomota, 2000: 184; Anderson and Richie, 1982: 456).

The arrival of roman poruno (romantic or soft-core porn) as a major genre of film was signalled by the decision by police in 1972 not to prosecute one such movie for obscenity. This series produced by Nikkatsu continued to 1988, with approximately two movies made a week. The 'king' of the pink-movie genre was Wakamatsu Kōji (b.1936) but numerous other directors such as Kumashiro Tatsumi (b.1927), Konuma Masaru (b.1937), Tanaka Noboru (b.1937), Obara Kōyū, Katō Akira, and Sone Chūsei (b.1937) were associated with the famous

Nikkatsu conveyor belt. The latter director also made Nikkatsu youth movies like the popular *Aa Hana no Ōendan* (Ah, Super Cheer Squad, 1976–77) based on the manga of the same name. Yomota also notes how 1970s erotic movies had been aimed solely at male audiences, but that by the 1980s such films had also started to target a female audience (Yomota, 2000: 180–2, 186–8).

Whether because of the impact of Kurosawa's realistic period dramas, as Tsutsui argues, or for other reasons, chambara and yakuza (gangster) movies in the seventies lost their innocence and sentimentality (Tsutsui, 2000: 94). Instead, they depicted the brutal violence of postwar Japan by analogy in period dramas, or directly through depicting contemporary society in harsh, realistic terms with no nostalgia. The five-part series *Jingi Naki Tatakai* (Battles Without Honour or Humanity) produced during 1973–74, directed by Fukasaku Kinji, stripped the Japanese gangster film of its sentimentality and revealed the poverty and greed behind crime. Fukasaku had a huge box-office hit with these five movies and so it was no surprise that he went on to make several other movies over the next few years that further explored this theme.

But perhaps the most successful film series in world movie history also emerged during the 1970s. The first movie in this series was *Otoko wa Tsurai yo* (It's Tough Being a Man, 1969) and starred Atsumi Kiyoshi (1928–97), who continued in the lead role until his death. The series was directed by Yamada Yōji (b.1931), the most commercially successful filmmaker of his time; and a decade before the forty-eighth and last movie in the sequence, which continued unbroken from 1969 to 1997, he commenced writing a new series from 1989, directed first by Kuriyama Tomio (b.1941) and later by Morisaki Azuma (b.1927), called *Tsuribaka Nisshi* (The Chronicles of Fishing Fanatics) and starring Nishida Toshiyuki (b.1947). This was, in some ways, a clone of the earlier series modernised for the 1990s generation. By 1999, some ten movies had been made in the new series.

'Tora-san', the character played by Atsumi in *Otoko wa Tsurai yo*, was a lovable pedlar who was forever trying to help people out of difficulties, and was always thwarted in love. Tora-san's Japan was a fantasy drawn from an idealised, rose-tinted portrait of the close-knit, impoverished community of the inner-city tenements, as much based on premodern Japan as on postwar Tokyo. The series kept Shōchiku afloat when many of its competitors were going broke, and the sentimentality and humour of the movies spawned many imitators (Yomota, 2000: 171, 191–2).

Contemporary Japanese cinema

Yomota argues that by the end of the 1970s the age of formula films was over. The major studios gradually fell into decline, and individual film-makers were forced to step out on their own through cooperatives, verifying a trend that had been evident a decade or more earlier. The demise of the majors and the studio system associated with them was confirmed by 1986 when just three major studios were still in business. Only twenty-four movies were made that year (Yomota, 2000: 193, 195–202). The majors had lost control of how and by whom movies were made. Nikkatsu's roman poruno was killed off by a massive explosion in 'adult videos', which featured hard-core pornography ostensibly obscured by an out-of-focus lens but which could be easily restored to clarity by use of a simple device available from the local electronics store. Nikkatsu abandoned the production of erotic movies in 1988 but by then Nikkatsu itself could not be saved (Yomota, 2000: 195–203).

From the late seventies, individual filmmakers established reputations in low-budget genre films. Ōbayashi Nobuhiko (b.1938) made his name at this time by directing pastiches of horror movies, for example his 1977 production *House*. In the 1980s, he continued this trend with movies such as *Toki o Kakeru Shōjo* (The Girl Who Ran Through Time, 1983). Many of the experimental, avant-garde filmmakers of the eighties were influenced by the multitalented Terayama Shūji whose performance poetry was investigated in chapter four. Such conceptual, experimental movies as *Den'en ni Shisu* (Dying in the Country, 1974) had a great influence on the succeeding generation. However, the collapse of Nikkatsu, in particular, dealt a severe blow to the industry, as this studio was responsible for fostering most of the new eighties generation of directors, including names now acclaimed in Japan—Morita Yoshimitsu (b.1951), Negishi Kichitarō (b.1950), Ikeda Toshiharu, Nakahara Shun (b.1951), and Nasu Hiroyuki (b.1952) (Yomota, 2000: 202–3).

Despite the catastrophic downturn in movie production, the collapse of the studio system and the rise of independent film-making companies meant the eighties was a time of great experimentation. New filmmakers entered the market in droves, and many made movies that fell outside hitherto dominant genres: documentaries and animated films flourished, especially towards the end of the decade. Hara Kazuo and Takamine Gō both achieved prominence as documentary filmmakers at this time. Hara invented the 'action documentary', examples of which are *Yukiyukite, Shingun* (Go, Go Divine Army, 1987), and *Zenshin Shōsetsuka* (The Complete Novelist, 1994). Takamine made films about Okinawa, his birthplace, usually using the Okinawan dialect with Japanese subtitles as in *Untamagirū* (1989), parallelling a similar eighties trend in the West with movies made in Welsh and Breton (Yomota, 2000: 204–6).

The 1980s also saw major directors of the sixties, who had lapsed into silence during the intervening decade, make come-backs. Kurosawa Akira made two period epics in the 1980s: *Kagemusha* (1980) and *Ran* (1985). Suzuki Seijun (b.1923), who was fired by Nikkatsu in 1968 for making incomprehensible movies (but praised by many critics like Satō Tadao), returned to prominence with three films that Yomota describes as being imbued with the erotic, poetic spirit of the novelist Izumi Kyōka: *Tsuigoineruwaizen* (Zigeunerweisen, 1980), *Kagerōza* (Gossamer Theatre, 1981), and *Yumeji* (1991). New directors making mixed-genre feature films like Sōmai Shinji (b.1948), with his massive hit *Sērāfuku to Kikanjū* (High School Girl and Machine Gun, 1981) and *Shonben Raidā* (Piss Rider, 1983), also made their debuts during this most complex decade. This was also when Kadokawa Haruki (b.1942) made his biggest impact as a film producer, with his top box-office star, the actress Yakushimaru Hiroko (b.1964), earning large profits for Kadokawa films, starring in *The Girl Who Ran Through Time* and *High School Girl and Machine Gun* (Yomota, 2000: 206–10; Satō, 1987: 221–62; Schilling, 1997: 81–5).

Other new, exciting talents included the actor and essayist Itami Jūzō (1933–97) with his international hits *O Sōshiki* (The Funeral, 1984), *Tampopo* (Dandelion, 1987), the two-part *Marusa no Onna* (A Taxing Woman, 1987, 1988) and *Ageman* (Lucky Charm, 1990). The director Morita Yoshimitsu's witty satire on middle-class Japan *Kazoku Gēmu* (The Family Game, 1983) had similar international success. Another new talent, Yanagimachi Mitsuo (b.1945), adapted two of Nakagami Kenji's novels for the screen, notably *Hi Matsuri* (Fire Festival, 1985), and received high praise. But perhaps the most significant director to achieve international success during the eighties was Miyazaki Hayao (b.1941) whose animated films became increasingly noticed abroad. *Kaze no Tani no Naushika* (Nausicaä of the Valley of the Wind, 1983), an SF eco-drama, brought him to international attention, as did his *Tonari no Totoro* (My Neighbour Totoro, 1988). Miyazaki's poetic fables contrasted with the harder, technopia (that is, technological utopia) style of other animated movies like Ōtomo Katsuhiro's (b.1954) film version of his own manga *Akira* (1988) (Yomota, 2000: 209–29; Schilling, 1997: 173–6).

The fact that, for the first time in a decade, Japanese films were beginning to find an overseas audience indicated the beginning of a revival in the Japanese film industry. This has been borne out by the experience of the 1990s. After thirty years of declining production, a reverse has occurred with a steady increase in output, especially after the middle of the decade. In 1996, the average attendance hovered around 119 million, the lowest on record, but just two years later, average audiences had increased to 150 million. The average yearly movie production during the nineties was 200 films, a significant increase over the previous decade. In fact, in 1996, some 289 movies were released (Yomota, 2000: 217–18).

By this time, the three major studios—Shōchiku, Tōhō and Tōei—were competing with a large number of independent filmmakers backed by a variety of firms with no experience in movie-making. The extra returns generated by free-to-air TV, satellite TV, and videos enticed a number of media and other companies into financing film production. However, the bursting of the bubble economy by the mid-1990s, and the economic downturn triggered by the Kobe-Hanshin earthquake, curbed some of the more extravagant ventures, like the theatre chains owned by independent filmmakers, and the producer Okuyama Kazuyoshi's 'Cinema Japanesque' venture at Shōchiku to accommodate new filmmakers (Yomota, 2000: 216–17).

Yomota noted a new trend towards ethnicity in films made in this decade, although often this was only skin-deep. Yanagimachi Mitsuo's *Ai ni Tsuite, Tokyo* (About Love, Tokyo, 1992) focused on the situation of Chinese residents of Tokyo. Kōhei Oguri's (b.1945) *Nemureru Otoko* (Sleeping Men, 1996) used Indonesian and Korean actors but not terribly successfully. Sai Yōichi (b.1949), the son of a Korean resident in Japan, made a comic but radical film about Korean residents called *Tsuki wa Dotchi ni Dete Iru* (Where Does the Moon Rise, 1994). Other filmmakers touching on this theme include Yamamoto Seiji and Tsukamoto Shinji—the latter's 'iron man' series *Tetsu Otoko* (Iron Man, 1989) transcends ethnicity, argues Yomota (Yomota, 2000: 220–2).

Formula movies continued to be produced during this period; Yomota points to Ōmori Kazuki's (b.1952) remakes of the Gojira (Godzilla) series as one example. Like-minded mainstream directors also created a pastiche style, which Yomota finds in the films of Itami Jūzō and Morita Yoshimitsu, especially the latter's remake of the Natsume Sōseki novel *Sorekara* (And Then) in 1985. Another example of a post-modern, pastiche-style film that appeals to nostalgia, argues Yomota, is Suō Masayuki's *Shall We Dance* (1998), which achieved much acclaim abroad (Yomota, 2000: 212, 223–4).

Animated movies also became increasingly profitable. Miyazaki Hayao's immensely popular 1997 movie *Mononoke Hime* (Princess Mononoke) appeared to many Japanese film-goers to issue a challenge to the Disney dominance of animated film. But art films continued to win prizes abroad, demonstrating how successfully the Japanese film industry had revived during this decade. The famous Kabuki actor Bandō Tamasaburō (b.1950) made two films based on Izumi Kyōka and Nagai Kafū's novels—*Gekashitsu* (The Operating Theatre, 1991) and *Yume no Onna* (Dream Woman, 1993)—that brought him much critical praise. Kitano Takeshi's films, which we will examine shortly, also won many prizes at international film festivals. The latest Japanese filmmaker to achieve success abroad is Kawase Naomi (b.1969) who won the Cannes d'Or award for new directors at Cannes in 1997 for *Moe no Suzaku* (Suzaku, 1996), at the same time as the veteran director Imamura Shōhei won a Cannes prize for *Unagi* (Eel, 1996). Kawase's latest feature *Hotaru* (Fireflies, 2000) also achieved much critical success in Japan and she is perhaps typical of the new breed of filmmakers who will lead Japan onto a larger stage in the twenty-first century, as Japanese films become a regular part of the international movie scene (Yomota, 2000: 225–9).

The later films of Kurosawa Akira

Although Yomota Inuhiko has argued that lists of the 'best-10 films' in any given year should be treated with caution, nevertheless some polls are, perhaps, more significant than others. In the November 1995 edition of Japan's leading film journal *Kinema Junpō* (Cinema Journal), a list of the best ten Japanese movies of all time or, more precisely, of the 100 years from 1887 (when the Japanese film industry started) to 1995, had Kurosawa Akira capturing nearly a third of the films with three movies being selected: *Shichinin no Samurai* (Seven Samurai, 1954) at number two, *Rashōmon* (1950) at number seven and *Ikiru* (Living, 1952) at number eight. Kurosawa had three times as many films as any other director in the list, which was selected by 104 professionals involved in the Japanese film industry (*Kinema Junpō*, 1995: 8–22). Such praise for Kurosawa in Japan has been echoed in the West on a number of occasions.

Kurosawa directed thirty-one films in his lifetime but, given the vast library of books on Kurosawa in Japanese and English (far more than any other Japanese director), here we will examine a mere handful of his creations, mainly focusing on some of the movies he made after *Akahige* (Red Beard) in 1965. Many Japanese commentators see this period as a turning point in the director's career. In a volume published in 1994 entitled *Isetsu Kurosawa Akira* (Contrary Views of Kurosawa Akira), which was devoted to examining the movies he made after *Red Beard*, the editors describe this period as a 'dislocation' (dansō) dividing his films into two separate groups. Before 1965, Kurosawa averaged a film a year, but afterwards the average was a new movie every five years. Moreover, after *Red Beard* Kurosawa stopped using Mifune Toshirō (1920–97) as his leading actor, preferring Nakadai Tatsuya (b.1932) in later samurai epics like *Kagemusha* (1980) and *Ran* (1985). He also switched from black-and-white to colour movies at this time (Bungei Shunjū, 1994: 2–3).

The two main factors related to this dislocation in Kurosawa's career are generally seen to be his failed involvement in the movie *Tora Tora Tora* about Japan's sneak attack on Pearl Harbour during World War II, jointly produced by Twentieth Century Fox and Tōei in 1969, where it was announced that Kurosawa had withdrawn from the project due to 'mental stress' (noirōze), and his attempted suicide on 22 December 1971. Without attempting any analysis of these two complex events, we may surmise that they are symptomatic of a change in direction or viewpoint, or simply represent a watershed where the director needed to draw a line between one phase in his career and another (Bungei Shunjū, 1994: 77).

The three commentators who discuss these issues in the 1994 volume which serves as the basis of our account are Shirai Yoshio (b.1922), a distinguished movie critic and one-time editor of *Kinema Junpō*; Okata Toshio (b.1955), a film critic who wrote an important study of Kurosawa in 1991; and Hayakawa Hikaru (b.1961), a director and essayist. In contrast to the *Kinema Junpō* 1995 poll, all three commentators evaluate Kurosawa's later films more highly than the earlier, more famous movies. Shirai does not include any of the earlier films in his top-ten Kurosawa movies but evaluates *Dodesukaden* (1970) quite positively. Okata places *Derusu Uzāra* (Dersu Uzala, 1975) at the top of his list, followed next by *Dodesukaden*; Hayakawa evaluates both films very highly. It is noticeable that from the *Kinema Junpō* list, only *Living* and *Seven Samurai* receive qualified praise from the three commentators (Bungei Shunjū, 1994: 17–21).

The contrast between movies like *Living* and *Seven Samurai*, and the post-1969 films could not be greater. *Living* is the story of Watanabe Kanji, a civil servant working in a city office who discovers he only has six months to live. Watanabe, played brilliantly by Shimura Takashi (1905–82), tries dissipation and romance as a means to satisfy the emptiness in his heart left after twenty-five years of bureaucratic service. In the end, he is still unsatisfied so in an attempt to do something meaningful in his last days he takes up a petition to turn a section of waste land into a park. Initially opposed by the city officials, he succeeds in this. In a series of flashbacks, we see how his death has forced his colleagues and family into re-evaluating both his and their own lives.

Seven Samurai has Shimura again in the lead role as the chief samurai Kanbei who is recruited by a group of peasants from a remote village to hire other samurai to protect them against the attacks of bandits. After a brilliant, and poetic battle, the samurai succeed. The heroism of the samurai and their noble sacrifices are contrasted with the timeless nobility of the peasants' labour, and the film ends with Kanbei noting that 'the farmers are the winners. Not us' (Kurosawa, 1992: 225).

Seven Samurai and *Living* were both written by Kurosawa and his usual script collaborators. *Red Beard* was adapted from a novel by Yamamoto Shūgorō (1903–67). This movie about a nineteenth-century doctor, played by Mifune Toshirō, who helps the poor and attempts to practice humane and scientific medicine, celebrates some of the same noble ideals dramatised in the earlier two films. However, *Dodesukaden*—the title refers to the noise a train makes passing over tracks—is a much more theatrical, almost bizarre experience which, by portraying the slum-dwellers living in a rubbish-tip, seeks to satirise the situation of contemporary Japan, and is a much more difficult and complex film than the previous period dramas.

The movie tells the several stories of the fringe-dwellers but *Dersu Uzala* tells the story of one man—the Siberian hunter who acts as a guide for a Russian army expedition in the last years of the nineteenth century. This film is a masterpiece of image and colour, the camera brooding on the bleak but beautiful forests of Siberia with a poetic intensity. It foreshadows the later *Dreams*, where Kurosawa tells a group of stories as dreams, a nostalgic exploration of the director's childhood where an early twentieth-century rural Japan is depicted from a child's perspective as magical and cruel, beautiful and yet lost.

When we consider the style of Kurosawa's post-1969 movies, it is fascinating how many commentators liken the visual style of these films to painting or art. The actor Tsuchiya Yoshio (b.1927) who appeared in a number of Kurosawa films, indeed in virtually all the period dramas until 1969, when interviewed for a special Kurosawa edition of *Kinema Junpō* in August 1998 noted that '*Red Beard* was the last Kurosawa movie in which I appeared…. From then on Kurosawa went into the world of visual art and so I thought it would be better to view his films than appear in them…. I felt in *Dersu Uzala* he achieved a certain maturity, and *Dreams* was fascinating, pure Kurosawa' (Quoted *Kinema Junpō*, 1998: 121). The formalistic nature of these later films is evident in other respects as well. The critic Nishi Kanenari, in the same issue of *Kinema Junpō*, discussing Kurosawa and Noh drama, states that 'Kurosawa adapted substantially the dramaturgy of Dream Noh (where the dead speak) in the expression of *Kagemusha*…' (Quoted *Kinema Junpō*, 1998: 202).

Shirai Yoshio notes something similar about *Dodesukaden*, comparing the movie to the German expressionist masterpiece of early twentieth-century cinema *The Cabinet of Dr. Caligari* (1919), directed by Robert Wiene. The self-conscious use of colour in this movie, Kurosawa's first colour film, allowed the director to experiment with various cinematic techniques and styles of acting. Matsue Yōichi (b.1930), who produced the movie, remarked that it was one of Kurosawa's most experimental pieces. Okata Toshio pointed to the influence of television on some elements in the framing and narrative of the movie, and it appeared that Kurosawa became interested in television from about this time (Bungei Shunjū, 1993: 84–8, 137, 166).

Harada Masato (b.1949), a director and film journalist who was an associate of Kurosawa, conducted two long interviews with the director in 1991 that were published in book form under the title *Kurosawa Akira*

Kataru (Kurosawa Akira Speaks, 1995). In a long postscript to this book, Harada praises *Dodesukaden* as one of Kurosawa's finest films. He describes it as the 'sequel' to Kurosawa's 1951 movie *Hakuchi* (The Idiot), an adaptation of Dostoevsky's novel of the same name, which featured Mori Masayuki (1911–73) in the lead role in a stunning performance (and ample justification for the November 1995 *Kinema Junpō* poll placing him first as the all-time best Japanese actor). Presumably Harada means that the idea that purity or innocence is, in some sense, incorruptible (Christ's gift to humankind)—one of the major themes of *The Idiot*—is also a strong element in the make-up of various characters inhabiting the surrealistic rubbish-tip that is home to the fringe-dwellers portrayed in *Dodesukaden*, especially the boy often seen as an idealised self-portrait of the director (Harada, 1995: 204–5).

Shirai Yoshio describes the cinematic narrative of *Dersu Uzala* as documentary realism and, like many Japanese critics, showers extravagant praise on the film. The film's producer, Matsue Yōichi, noted that the massive costs involved in the three years of production in bleak, inaccessible locations in Siberia could not have been possible without the full financial backing of the Soviet government, which expended enormous amounts of money on the movie and provided Kurosawa with a huge crew. Kurosawa's oft-quoted remark that making the film was totally exhausting is testimony to the immense physical challenge the director faced (Harada, 1995: 100). Okata Toshio praised the film for its lack of sentimentality, which prevented the air of melancholy that pervaded the movie lapsing into bathos (Bungei Shunjū, 1994: 121). Although the atmosphere of late nineteenth-century Siberia is beautifully evoked in this story, which ends in the hunter pursuing his wild prey, it is fascinating that, as the producer has revealed, the story was originally conceived by Kurosawa in the 1940s, and was set in the northern island of Hokkaidō, with an early script having the central character leave the northern wilderness to come to Tokyo (Bungei Shunjū, 1994: 168).

The critics assembled for Bungei Shunjū's 1994 book generally do not evaluate very highly the movies Kurosawa made after *Dersu Uzala*. Shirai argues that in *Ran* (Kurosawa's version of *King Lear*) and *Kagemusha*, both period dramas focusing on central characters played by Nakadai Tatsuya, Kurosawa was forced into a familiar Japanese aesthetic, which emphasised elements of Japanese thought associated with traditional culture, because of the use of the wide screen and vista colour; and also because of the increasingly painterly vision of the director. This, he implies, led to a loss of vitality compared to earlier films (Bungei Shunjū, 1994: 141).

Okata sees both these movies, and also *Dreams* especially, as being nostalgic evocations of the past: clearly, the creation of a filmmaker more and more preoccupied with the process of ageing, and its inevitable consequence. Yomota Inuhiko argues that *Kagemusha* and *Ran* both express the director's 'lyrical style'. With *Dreams*, as Yomota notes, Kurosawa needed the assistance of Honda Inoshirō, a colleague known for his monster movies. More than any other, this film expressed Kurosawa's long-held attraction to visual art and painting (Yomota, 2000: 207). Finally, Tsutsui Kiyotada argues that Kurosawa's period dramas (presumably including *Ran* and *Kagemusha*) could not be described as typical of the genre, indeed, they were atypical, but in some sense precisely because they were atypical, they were masterpieces (Tsutsui, 2000: 166–7).

Filmmaker Kitano Takeshi

Kitano Takeshi's complete list of TV appearances is staggering, whether as a guest, star, or emcee of quiz programs, variety programs, comedies, the list goes on…. Suffice to say that since his television debut as a comedian, he has appeared regularly since 1975, and has hundreds, more likely, thousands of TV credits to his name. Since the early 1980s Kitano also has a number of credits as an actor in TV dramas. His first appearance as a serious actor in films dates from 1981. He initially came to the attention of Western audiences with his role in the 1983 film *Merry Christmas, Mr. Lawrence* directed by Ōshima Nagisa, and based on a novel by Laurens van der Post. With the participation of the popular singer David Bowie, who played a British officer incarcerated in a World War II POW camp in Java run by the Japanese (he was subsequently executed), Kitano's debut in Western films made him an instant celebrity. He has since acted in another Western movie, Robert Longo's *Johnny Mnemonic* (1995) playing a gang boss. Since directing his first film, *Sono Otoko, Kyōbō ni Tsuki* (Because That Man is Violent) in 1989, Kitano has also regularly starred in his own movies (Kitano, 1988: 394). *Because That Man is Violent* won three awards, and is the only movie of the eight he has made to date that he did not also write.

That Kitano's skills should also include writing does not come as any surprise as he is the author of over fifty books covering such diverse topics as movie criticism, fiction, autobiographical narratives, updated versions of literary classics like Aesop's fables, history, comedy, and political and social criticism (Kitano, 1998: 391, 401–3). What astonished most commentators about Kitano's first film was the level of violence portrayed on the screen, which rose exponentially as the cop played by Kitano sought revenge on his various enemies. Kitano's well-known remark that on-screen violence is nothing compared to the real thing did little to mollify critics like Tayama Rikiya, who, nevertheless saw the movie as marking an auspicious debut (Tayama, 1991: 217–18).

In a 1998 essay, Kitano remarked that he had no intention of criticising Yamada Yōichi and his 'Tora-san' series but criticise him he did, noting that the success of this series 'destroyed Japanese cinema'. He went on to say that it was just the same as a TV series, and the fact that so many Japanese saw the films was a 'sad' reflection on the country. Reacting to a critique which judged his movies as inferior to those of Itami Jūzō, Kitano declared that Itami's films were just the same—mere TV dramas (Biito, 1998: 10). In another essay in the same collection on the character 'Tora-san', Kitano relents a little by stating that at first he liked the movies, too, but the hypocrisy and sentimental falsehoods that Tora-san exemplifies eventually turned him against the series (Biito, 1998: 87–8).

Perhaps it was in reaction to such sentimentality that Kitano took recourse to graphic violence. His second movie, *3-4x10 Gatsu* (3-4x October, 1990), was equally violent, telling the tale of innocents being caught up in the underworld. Tayama Rikiya described this movie as 'mediocre' (Tayama, 1991: 218). Perhaps that is a reaction to the way in which Kitano's vision differed from other filmmakers at the time. The commentator Fukuma Kenji spoke of his shock at how different the movie was from conventional pictures (Fukuma and Zeze, 1994: 52). However, Kitano's next movie *Ano Natsu, Ichiban Shizuka na Umi* (That Summer, The Most Tranquil Sea, 1991) won a number of awards. Sono Shion in a 1994 article on Kitano described how impressed he was by the total disregard for the demands of commerce (and the audience) the director displayed in the former movie: Sono noted its total absence of music and the complete lack of sentimentality. But the latter film he described as being decorated by 'utterly sweet music', implying a complete backflip by Kitano in this movie about a deaf surfer searching for the perfect wave (Sono, 1994: 84). Although garnering some critical acclaim, neither film, nor his earlier movies, achieved box office success. This may be why Kitano has gradually changed his style to create more audience-friendly movies.

His next movie was *Sonachine* (Sonatine, 1993), about gang warfare in Okinawa. The box-office failure of the film led its producer Okuyama Kazuyoshi to lose his job as Shōchiku's head of production, and was presumably the reason why he launched an attack on Kitano as an amateur, ego-tripping at the expense of his audience, as Mark Schilling puts it (Schilling, 1997: 262). However, the film was a hit in overseas art cinemas, and brought Kitano recognition in the West. In Japan, critical reaction was mixed; *Kinema Junpō* rated it fourth on the list of best ten Japanese films for 1993.

In the February 1994 issue (vol.1125) of *Kinema Junpō* where the poll was conducted, the staff writer Ōtaka Hiroo wrote that *Sonatine* elevated Kitano above such famed directors as Ōzu, Mizoguchi and Naruse. The poet, architect, and film critic Watanabe Takanobu (b.1938) noted that the movie forced us to peer into a dark pit, describing the director's vision as nihilistic while arguing that 'he must be called a genius'. Another commentator, the newspaper editor Ishii Makoto, remarked that after seeing *Sonatine*, his dislike of Kitano's films, due to their excessive violence, changed: only by staring violence directly in the face could the theme of the film be realised (*Kinema Junpō*, 1994: 76, 94, 97–8). Yomota described the violence as a 'necrophiliac desire' on the part of the director, which was, however, the source of the film's success (Yomota, 2000: 228).

Kitano's next film was his first comedy *Minna Yatteru ka* (Getting Any, 1994), filmed before his motorscooter crash in August 1994 when he almost died. In March 1995, after seven months of rehabilitation, Kitano returned to work and the movie was released. The film was reminiscent of his TV comedies; the plot centred around the ridiculous attempts of the simple-minded hero to succeed in sex. As one would expect, it attracted little critical attention in Japan but Ōtaka, who had previously praised *Sonatine* extravagantly, in the February 1996 issue of *Kinema Junpō* (vol.1184) wrote that he loved the film, finding the slapstick comedy irresistible (*Kinema Junpō*, 1996: 103; Schilling, 1997: 262).

Kizzu Retān (Kid's Return, 1996) followed a year or so later, and was the first Kitano movie to succeed at the Japanese box office. This movie concerned the adventures of two schoolboy friends who become involved with yakuza (gangsters) before returning to the safer world of everyday life. One of the boys actually embarks upon the life of a gangster but his gang forces him to corrupt his friend—a budding boxer—and both eventually escape back to normality. It was a very personal film about growing up, and it definitely appeared as if the director was mellowing somewhat, as his trademark violence was expressed within a strong moralistic frame.

HANA-BI (1997) won numerous prizes both in Japan and overseas. *Kinema Junpō* judged it the best film of the year, and this was the general view. The film is a powerful mixture of violence and sentimentality wrapped up in a trademark Kitano plot of a cop (played by Kitano) gone bad for a good cause who wreaks havoc on his enemies. The cop eventually kills his wife (after blowing away the bad guys), who is suffering from a terminal disease, and then commits suicide. The film also featured some of the director's own paintings, reminding his audience of Kurosawa doing the same in *Dodesukaden*. The relationship between the cop and his wife is central to the film, as his love for her provides the audience with a sharp contrast to his utter lack of mercy for his enemies, and in exploring the complexities of that relationship we see a shift in theme from anarchic violence to something equally enigmatic but much more capable of comprehension. One other fact worth mentioning is that although the film has a conventional story-telling structure, it was filmed in chronological sequence, which is a quite unusual method of film-making (Kitano, 1998: 102–3).

One of Kitano's most recent films is *Kikujirō no Natsu* (Kikujiro, 1999). This movie is easily his most sentimental. The plot concerns the relationship between a father figure, Kikujirō (played by Kitano), and a young boy as they journey together to seek out the boy's mother. The fact that Kitano's real father was called 'Kikujirō', and that the relationship between him and his son was troubled at the best of times, provides a clue to some of the motivations that lie behind the film. Interestingly, before embarking on production of this movie, Kitano wrote that as the main theme of *HANA-BI* was violence, and that he hated to repeat himself, the theme of his next film was to be love, with the leading character resembling Mother Teresa (Biito, 1998: 14–15). Even allowing for Kitano's characteristic sarcasm, there may be an element of truth in this statement. The father figure lies to the boy to conceal the fact that he has found his mother in order to protect both the boy and his mother, who has made a separate life. Towards the end of the movie, Kikujirō and the boy join a group of oddballs and misfits who entertain the boy. This sequence is almost identical to Kitano's TV comedy, and even the actors are the same, another indication that the populist comedian and the art director are converging in style.

On various occasions Kitano has claimed publicly that movie-making is a mere sideline, an indulgence to be pursued while he goes about the serious business of making a living through comedy. This remark is reminiscent of the statements by some of Japan's most famous poets that while their poetry makes them famous, they earn their living from translations, journalism, or non-fiction. There is a paradox between the two personalities revealed by Kitano's different names: 'Beat Takeshi', the anarchic, vulgar comedian and 'Kitano Takeshi', the refined director of art movies overflowing with nihilistic violence. Some critics see a deliberate disjunction between the early, uncompromising, non-commercial films and the TV work of the crass, utterly commercial comedian. This disjunction is resolved or dissolves in the later movies, which have become increasingly mainstream. But such an analysis ignores the personal elements common to both.

Kitano, by his own admission, grew up in an impoverished, violent, inner-city environment made worse by his drunken, physically abusive father. Yet, according to many who have worked with him, and the testimony of his own daughter, the singer Matsuda Shōko, he is an exceedingly gentle man who in private life abhors violent language. As such, he stands in contrast to the bullying, domineering style of most well-known Japanese directors, especially Kurosawa Akira who was notorious for his perfectionism and haranguing of crew and actors. It would appear that violence and, lately, love, play the major roles in his art, not only in his films but also in his TV comedy, which is often dark and satirical. However, as we know from numerous studies, the expression of private demons in public art is a phenomenon common to many great filmmakers and writers and needs no special explanation (Kitano, 1998: 52–65, 68–116).

Manga: an introduction

As the doyen of Japanese comic authors Tezuka Osamu (1926–89) noted in his introduction to Frederik Schodt's groundbreaking 1983 study

Manga! Manga! The World of Japanese Comics, 'The Japanese comics industry first began to show signs of heating up to this [present] fever pitch
after World War II' (Quoted Schodt, 1983: 11). Schodt reported that
1.16 billion comics or manga had been produced in 1980, making up
27% of the total publications for that year (Schodt, 1983: 12). In 1994,
Toren Smith reported that total sales of manga magazines (excluding
manga storybooks) alone had sold 1.5 billion copies, and that sales had
doubled since 1982. In 1992 manga made up 40% of the total publications of books and magazines (Smith, 1993: 1). Thus, we can see that
since Tezuka Osamu's comments in 1983, in just over a decade the
manga boom had increased to incredible heights. However, this exponentially rising curve in manga readership slowed in 1995, with sales for
that year dropping 0.5% over the previous year (Japanese Book News,
1996: 21). It was noticeable that book sales also fell in 1995, compared
to 1994, the first time this had happened since 1958. By 1998, manga
amounted to 36.7% of all books and magazines sold, a marked decrease
on the 1992 figure (Sōseki, 2000: 2).

Readers of manga in 1996 were about 60% male, and 40% female.
The majority of adult readers were attracted to 'story' manga (or narrative comics) as opposed to gag comic strips or political lampoons.
Indeed, as the manga specialist Takeuchi Osamu points out, the postwar
genre of manga is based on 'story manga'. Japanese scholarship on manga
began in the mid 1960s, and has been steadily increasing since (Takeuchi,
1996: 15). Much of this scholarship is devoted to 'story' manga (and its
later child 'gekiga' or 'graphic novels'), which has often been turned into
movies (animated and live-action), TV series, and novels.

Prewar comics were much closer to their Western counterparts.
Shimizu Isao in his 1991 book *Manga no Rekishi* (A History of Comics)
devotes a chapter to the turn-of-the-century magazines *Punch* and
Japan Punch, the latter an obvious copy of the British original. Shimizu
begins his discussion of Japanese manga in 1834 with the publication
of the *Hokusai Manga,* as is the practice of many manga historians, but
he sources modern manga back to copies of their Western equivalents
in the late nineteenth century (Shimizu, 1991). However, Shimizu, like
Tezuka, draws a line between prewar and postwar manga. Shimizu
argues that in the 1950s the mass production of comics on a huge
scale, which expanded the readership enormously and also created new
markets for teenage and adult readers, came about as a result of

'kashihon'ya'—lending libraries that enabled one manga to be read by a hundred readers (Shimizu, 1991: 189). Later, manga as 'visual novels' expanded rapidly under the influence of TV and animated movies, where numerous tie-ups resulted (Shimizu, 1991: 195).

The manga historian Ishiko Jun (b.1935), in his massive history of Japanese comics *Nihon Manga Shi* (A History of Japanese Comics, 1988), also points to TV and movies as a key factor behind the manga boom, but notes the equal importance of the shift from monthly to weekly manga magazines in the fifties (Ishiko, 1988: 305–17). The influence of the master comic artist Tezuka Osamu is noted by all commentators. In his autobiography, Tezuka explained how he developed his unique, and soon to be copied, style (in Schodt's translation): 'I felt [after the war] that existing comics were limiting.... Most were drawn...as if seated in an audience viewing a stage.... This made it impossible to create dramatic or psychological effects, so I began to use cinematic techniques.... I experimented with close-ups and different angles...' (Quoted Schodt, 1983: 63). We will examine Tezuka's achievements later but what is important here is that Tezuka's career, which began after the war and blossomed in the 1950s when many of his most famous series like *Tetsuwan Atomu* (Mighty Atom—renamed 'Astroboy' in the West when it appeared as a TV cartoon) began, coincided with the birth of the manga boom. The connection is there for all to see.

Tezuka's remarks about his use of cinematic technique illuminates many of the visual characteristics of modern manga. In a sense, they make up the visual architecture of the visual or graphic 'novel', which later became the mainstay of manga. Various explanations have been advanced for the popularity of manga in Japan; most relate the artistic form to the nature of the Japanese language. Frederik Schodt describes the various visual conventions that have become standard in manga, relating the ubiquitousness of onomatopoeia to the frequent use of onomatopoeia in the Japanese language, and also to the various orthographic scripts used to write Japanese, especially 'kanji' (or Chinese characters). He also speculated about why Japanese comics are speed-read by their audience—which allows massive, narrative comics to find a market—and this method of reading also creates a certain visual and verbal style (Schodt, 1983: 18–27). Other commentators focus less on the formal qualities of the art, and stress the story.

Dana Lewis, an American manga translator and journalist, argues that 'American or European readers picking up a manga for the first time today are far less likely to be amazed by that heavy list of "special characteristics"...indeed they might find the artwork...dull and plodding compared with the work of new young artists publishing...in the United States and elsewhere.' Lewis believes it is not the art or cinematic flow that set manga apart from their Western counterparts but their content (Lewis, 2000: 9). What Lewis finds remarkable about manga is the complexity and variety of their stories: 'from period swordplay to far-future SF, scatological gag strips to Fortune 500 corporate strategy, from intimate psychological studies of a young girl's coming of age to the most outrageous erotica' (Lewis, 2000: 11). She could have added manga about games (Japanese chess, mah-jongg, athletics etc.), businesses, history, science, childbirth, and much, much more.

Manga cover every conceivable subject and are often used as educational tools—retelling Japanese literary classics, for example (although this is also popular in the West). Their range is infinitely larger than Western comics. Nevertheless, a number of manga artists 'graduate' to fiction or non-fiction writing or movie-making as a career, and the immense popularity of books in Japan testifies to a complex and variegated literary culture that caters to a variety of readers, from children to adults. Perhaps the sheer range of manga goes some way to explaining why they are read by all ages and occupations but, in many cases, they do not displace other kinds of reading or visual entertainment but accompany them, despite the traditional complaint that people who read comics don't read books (also heard in the West).

Manga master: Tezuka Osamu

Tezuka Osamu grew up in prewar Takarazuka, a relatively affluent area in the Kansai region around Osaka famous for the all-girls Takarazuka review located in the centre of a vast entertainment complex established by the founder of the Hankyū railways line, which opened up that region to housing. Nevertheless, in the cartoonist's youth, the area was still in the process of being developed, as the following remarks by Tezuka reveal: 'I lived in Takarazuka and on my way home from school, I used to pass by a lonely marsh. I often used to daydream about it when I was in primary school and junior high. Beside the marsh a mysterious, trembling creature used to lie in wait for me. I would capture it and bring it home. I'd close the storm shutters so it wouldn't escape, and lock up the doors so it had no way to get out but, facing material reality, usually I'd awaken from my dream' (Quoted Sakurai, 1990: 41).

Tezuka graduated from the medical school of Osaka University in 1951, being licensed as a physician the following year. In 1961 he was awarded a doctorate for a research thesis on snail sperm. But as he later wrote, 'I neglected my medical studies at Osaka University in favour of drawing manga' (Quoted Ishiko, 1991: 17). Tezuka's enthusiasm for manga quickly turned him into a professional with his comic *Shintakarajima* (New Treasure Island, 1947), written when he was only twenty, achieving astonishing sales of between 400,000 and 800,000 copies (Schodt, 1983: 62).

Another reason for Tezuka choosing the way of the cartoonist over the way of the physician may have been that his basic training as a doctor was essentially that of an army medic, a fact that he concealed until his death, claiming to have graduated from the Medical Faculty of Osaka University rather than the specialist college at Osaka University which he actually attended (Sakurai, 1990: 58–9). But his success as a manga artist helped make respectable a career that had never been viewed in that light hitherto, and inspired virtually all the significant postwar cartoonists who saw Tezuka's innovations as creating a template for their craft (Schodt, 1983: 64).

The cinematic techniques Tezuka employed with *New Treasure Island* and the others that followed, especially *Astroboy* and *Janguru Taitei* (renamed *Kimba, the White Lion* in the West) led inevitably to their transformation into animated cartoon series. *Astroboy* began serialisation in the boys' magazine *Shōnen* (Boys) in April 1951, undergoing a few name changes until Tezuka settled on 'Tetsuwan Atomu'. The serialisation of this story comic continued for sixteen years, one of the longest Tezuka ever wrote. Afterwards, a sequel was serialised for two years, from January 1967, in the *Sankei* newspaper under the title of *Atomu Ima Monogatari* (Tales of Astroboy) (Ishiko, 1991: 31–2).

Ishiko Jun in his 1991 study of Tezuka argues that the motive behind *Astroboy* was to alert readers to the changes that the rapid advance of science and technology could bring to society at large (Ishiko, 1991: 32–3). Sakurai Tetsuo in his 1990 study of Tezuka remarks in a similar vein that the early theme of the confrontation between different ethnicities (symbolised by the robot Astroboy) was later replaced by the larger theme of the conflict between humans and robots (or technology). Sakurai summarises the theme as the 'clash with a different culture' (Sakurai, 1990: 88). This reading is a more overtly political reading than that of Ishiko's, and clearly sees the theme of this most famous series as, partly at least, the product of Japan's involvement in World War II, and the clash of cultures this entailed.

Astroboy was made into Japan's first animated TV series in 1963 by Tezuka's production company. Ishiko finds this event epoch-making. He claims Tezuka's marriage of manga and movies changed the course of future TV, manga, and movies (Ishiko, 1991: 30–1). There is no doubt that in Japan, at least, this is the view held by most of Tezuka's successors. One thing is certain: without Tezuka's manga being made into an animated series for TV, it is unlikely that he would have achieved the overseas success that he did and paved the way for future overseas exports of animated cartoons and animated movies (anime) from Japan. Although Tezuka's animated cartoons were successful abroad, being dubbed into several languages, they cost so much to make that (despite several innovative cost-cutting animation techniques) in Japan they failed to turn a profit. This led to the bankruptcy of Tezuka's animation company in 1973 (Schilling, 1997: 266).

Naturally, as Tezuka became more famous, so the occasional critic of his work emerged. Sakurai singles out two or three for comment. Kusamori Shin'ichi in 1966 criticised Tezuka for allowing his own high standards to lapse by creating manga too quickly, and thus the quality of the stories declined. Another critic was Ishiko Junzō (1929–77), a well-known manga commentator, who in 1975 criticised Tezuka for being a bad businessman, arguing that his ineptness as a manager was the chief cause of the collapse of his animation company (Cited Sakurai, 1990: 149–50). However, both critics acknowledge Tezuka's enormous skills as a manga artist.

Tezuka is often praised for being the real inventor of the long story-comic for girls. Tezuka accomplished this with his story-comic *Ribon no Kishi* (Princess Knight), which he commenced in 1953 in the girls' magazine *Shōjo Kurabu* (Girls' Club). As Schodt comments: '[the comic] was a sensation among girls in Japan and had many of the ingredients of today's successful girls' comics: a love story, a foreign setting, and a heroine with large eyes and a somewhat bisexual personality' (Schodt, 1983: 96). Sakurai argues that the pioneering technical innovations incorporated into this manga were of even more significance than the gender-bending story where the heroine Sapphire pretends to be Crown Prince in a mythological European kingdom and vanquishes her foes with her sword (Sakurai, 1990: 116).

In a book entitled *Manga no Kakikata* (How to Write Manga, 1977), Tezuka formulated his various principles or 'rights' that manga artists should respect when creating their works. Ishiko Jun summarises them thus: firstly, never mock victims of war or calamity; secondly, never disparage any specific occupation; and thirdly, never ridicule the people at large (Ishiko, 1991: 57–8). Commentators find evidence of Tezuka's moral perspective in much of his work, and thus the principles he enunciates above are a reasonably faithful statement of his own ethical practices. This accounts, no doubt, for much of the respect in which he was held by his peers, and also must have played some role in helping to establish his popularity among readers.

Tezuka's most ambitious manga and, according to some, his greatest, is the long story-comic *Hi no Tori* (Phoenix). Tezuka began drawing this comic in 1954, and was still drawing it at the time of his death. Ishiko divides the composition of the work into four specific periods: from 1954 to 1957; then after nine years in which he did not work on it at all 1967 to 1972; 1976 to 1981; and finally from 1986 to 1988. Thus the writing of this still incomplete work covered thirty-four years. In the artist's own words: 'It is my life work, and I imagine I'll still be writing it until the day I die' (Quoted Ishiko, 1991: 69). Schodt notes that the work is actually twelve separate stories, 'each one independent yet linked to the rest, with the titles *Dawn, Future, Yamato, Universe, Hō-ō, Resurrection, Robe of Feathers, Nostalgia, Civil War, Life, Strange Beings* and *Sun*' (Schodt, 1996: 262). The comic is over 3000 pages long and is set on the earth, in outer space, in the future, in the past, and has a huge cast of characters. The central unifying symbol is the phoenix, which is immortal and unchanging, unlike humans who are constantly reincarnated as they pursue their individual karmas or fates.

As is obvious from the above, the comic is based upon Buddhist notions of rebirth and karma, and the huge expanses of time that make up the Buddhist cosmos. Ishiko likens the composition of the work to a symphony with various movements, and his view of the theme agrees with Tezuka's as expressed in an essay the author wrote in 1967 where he remarked:

> Humankind for millions of years has lived for today in order to live for tomorrow. Our anxiety about tomorrow is an anxiety about death; our fear of the night is linked to our fear of the next world of perpetual darkness. At every age in the past the fight for existence occurred; all religions, philosophies and civilisations advanced in step with the passion for life.
>
> *Phoenix* is a drama which has as its theme the issues of life and death. The struggle with the phoenix—eternal life—continues from ancient times into the future, and for humankind represents a kind of fate.
>
> *Quoted Ishiko, 1991: 80*

This work treats themes difficult to encapsulate in fiction or film, save for the most speculative and ambitious science fiction or fantasy, which often struggles to find a readership or audience. However, the visual dimension that manga provides may well make it easier to represent such a vast panorama of human experience and such a huge variety of interrelated tales. The rich visual symbolism of Tezuka's artwork creates a common template or fabric upon which the various stories are worked out. But, despite the unalloyed praise of critics like Ishiko and Schodt, the work has its detractors.

Sakurai does not think *Phoenix* is a success, describing it as an 'incoherent' work. He asks why Tezuka did not limit the major theme to exploring Japan from ancient to medieval times? (Japan is the subject of most of Tezuka's later comics, claims Sakurai.) He argues that praise for the comic as expressing the philosophy of rebirth or the eternal return is overblown and exaggerates the quality of the work (Sakurai, 1990: 179). Sakurai quotes the novelist Mishima Yukio as stating the work made Tezuka into the mouthpiece of the left-wing teachers' union, thus implying a clear ideological bias (Sakurai, 1990: 38). This comment appears somewhat mysterious considering that Mishima's last work, the tetralogy *Hōjō no Umi* (The Sea of Fertility), is constructed around the theme of Buddhist rebirth. However, the *Phoenix* stakes a claim to be considered as art, perhaps art of a subculture, as Yoshimoto Takaaki has argued, but art nevertheless. No one makes such a claim about the overwhelming majority of manga produced in Japan. Just as Tezuka had no real progenitors, he has precious few successors.

Uchida Shungicu and women's Manga

Sharon Kinsella in a 1996 article has noted how respectable manga has become of late. This is due to the ageing of readership since 1959 when the first successful weekly magazines were published and the boom began. Manga now occupies an important part of the cultural menu of Japanese adults; as she notes, profit margins are high compared to other media, with the total gross income of the manga industry in 1994 three times that of the domestic film industry (Kinsella, 1996: 104). Once piracy—in the form of sharing magazines and free reading in bookshops—is included, manga readership figures are massive. The leading manga magazine in 1994, *Jump*, was read by twenty million people a week—about one-fifth of the entire population of Japan (Kinsella, 1996: 104).

Tezuka is an example of a manga artist whose work was aimed primarily at children (the major market for manga until the fifties and sixties) but who was taken up by a much larger readership. The largest audience for manga in the 1990s was adolescent and adult males, which in 1994 comprised well over 60% of the total market (Kinsella, 1996: 105). Other adult readers include women who continued reading manga after adolescence. In his 1996 collection of essays on manga, Frederik Schodt discusses the growth in 'ladies comics' since their first appearance in the 1980s. He reports that these magazines targeted adult women—'college students, office workers, and housewives'—who made up a readership of 120 million (based on circulation figures) by 1993 (Schodt, 1996: 124). Many of these magazines focused on erotica for women, mostly written by women. Erotica here covers hard-core pornographic tales of sexual adventure or softer stories of Mills and Boon-type romance or even magazines written by women for women on gay-male-love erotic comic themes. *Comic Amour*, identified by Schodt as the 'top erotic magazine for women in Japan [in 1996]', sold around 430,000 copies per month (Schodt, 1996: 120–4).

Manga artists who achieve success in Japan are, as one would expect, rich beyond the wildest dreams of the average manga reader. A number of women artists belong to this select group of manga millionaires. But certain women artists are equally famous for their treatment of erotic themes. Schodt discusses two in particular: Morizono Milk who is famous for her 'sexually charged S & M flavoured stories' and Uchida Shungicu whose debut as a novelist was examined in chapter four. Morizono is actually an artist of considerable gravity who has penned a two-volume story about AIDS and also a story about Marilyn Monroe, with a subplot about Robert Kennedy and the CIA (Schodt, 1996: 207–12). The similarities between Morizono's work and the fiction of female authors like Yamada Amy are obvious.

Before considering some famous manga by Uchida in detail, I will attempt a brief overview of erotic manga. This genre of manga is the one most noticed, and most criticised by Western commentators on popular culture. Ian Buruma in his 1984 book *A Japanese Mirror: Heroes and Villains of Japanese Culture* uses the universal tendency to characterise woman as either madonna or whore to explain the violent fantasies concerning women that he discovers in erotic comics; in the Japanese context, the image of madonna is replaced by a maternal image more suited to Japan's matriarchal child-raising practices. He points to a 1977 comic by Kamimura Kazuo about a motherly prostitute named Sachiko, whose maternal, loving nature is contrasted to another prostitute who sleeps with her clients out of sexual desire, and not a desire to comfort, and thus is disembowelled quite graphically as punishment (Buruma, 1985: 55, 104–8, 225). Buruma sees erotic manga as pornographic and violent.

A similar picture, though significantly more complex, is painted by Anne Allison in her 1996 book *Permitted and Prohibited Desires: Mothers, Comics and Censorship in Japan* where she examines male and female readership of erotic manga using psychoanalytic theory to argue that male readers situated as viewers and voyeurs are not necessarily empowered by their reading of such manga (Allison, 1996: 49). Allison identifies a pattern of dominance in sexual comics that 'encodes…relations of power in which unremitting submission is demanded', and further, that 'women are the targets for *manga* violence even in comics aimed at women' (Allison, 1996: 78). While acknowledging that the type of pornographic manga examined by Buruma and Allison is still being produced in Japan today, we can also find erotic manga that are considerably less problematic. Such manga may also undermine the common characterisation of the portrayals of females in manga as passive objects subject to male domination. It is important to note here that non-erotic manga can also empower women, as with the 'shōjo manga' or comics about young women who are distinctly heroic, following the tradition of Tezuka's Princess Knight (Napier, 1998).

Uchida Shungicu's manga can be read as both empowering and liberating in their portrayal of female sexuality. Uchida began her career as a professional manga artist in 1984 working for such magazines as the avant-garde *Garo* rather than girls' or women's comics. Uchida has drawn in a variety of genres including humour and thriller pieces. Schodt mentions her 1986 series *Hen na Kudamono* (Strange Fruit) where Uchida constructs a comedy about three women visiting a family restaurant (Schodt, 1996: 174–5). Uchida's concern with the everyday can also be glimpsed in her essays. In an essay collection published in the same year, Uchida wrote a number of illustrated short pieces about food (among other things) with titles like *Naze 'Oryōri' na no* (Why 'Cooking'?) and *Hazukashii kedo Tabemono no Hanashi* (I'm Ashamed of It But Here's a Chat about Food) (Uchida, 1995: 60–5, 72–6). But even these essays reveal an interest in the erotic, with Uchida's many illustrations mostly being of young women in various states of undress.

Uchida's 1987 long story-comic or graphic novel *Maboroshi no Futsū Shōjo* (The Illusory Ordinary Girl) does not, as Schodt claims, depict 'the underbelly of Japanese society…broken families, unwanted pregnancies, juvenile delinquency and drug use' but rather tells a sensitive story of the heroine, a senior high-school student called Yamashita Sayuri living happily with her mother, and her sexual awakening. Sayuri falls in love with a young office worker, Toyama Yōji (Schodt, 1996: 175). She falls pregnant to Yōji but, with his support, has an abortion. Yōji is depicted as just as naïve as Sayuri, and when the story ends, he is portrayed as the innocent being educated as to the realities of love, parenthood, and adult responsibility by Sayuri who, in the course of the 196-page comic, comes to grow in maturity and self-understanding. There are a variety of subplots involving Yōji's 'OL' (office girl) girlfriend Shirai Noriko, Sayuri's best friend Sakata, and Sayuri's former high-school boyfriend Nakamura Shin'ichi, but the main story focuses on Sayuri and her journey to maturity, her struggle to become an 'ordinary girl', a struggle she comes to see as naïve and illusory (Uchida, 1988).

The comic depicts Sayuri's journey to self-knowledge as arising initially from her sexuality. When she is caught in a sexual embrace which approaches rape with Shin'ichi—who she is about to abandon—he whispers to her 'You're my woman!'; her immediate reaction is: 'Ah, at a time like this, his words disgust me' (Uchida, 1988: 55–6). Later, when making love to Yōji, she says to him afterwards, 'Just now I felt strange. I was moved.' She muses: 'I must have come, just now. How wonderful!' She objects to being called a 'high-school girl' by Yōji, and says 'Just "woman" will do' (Uchida, 1988: 90–1). Her first orgasm is depicted by Uchida by focusing on the movements of her hands, in three panels, where her two hands make elegant shapes, as if in a traditional Japanese dance.

In a postscript, Uchida conducts an interview with a psychologist, Kishida Hide, whose writings Uchida credits with changing her life. Discussing how some overseas critics read Uchida's comics as obscene or pornographic, because her frank depictions of sex can be seen by children, Uchida says, on the contrary, her comics 'do children a service' (Uchida, 1988: 200). The fact that Sayuri has almost no consciousness of guilt in her sexual relations, nor is there any subtext criticising her first experiments in sex, clearly demonstrates Uchida's didactic and, from the author's own perspective, highly moral attitude towards the depiction of sexuality.

Uchida's moral values, as revealed in her manga and other writings, argue for a woman's right to control her sexuality, and to enjoy sex for the pleasures it brings. In this sense, she follows in one tradition of women's writing which portrays sexual pleasure as liberating, and empowering for women. Uchida's collection of thirteen comics published in 1993 in paperback under the title of *Ai no Sei Kashira* (Love's Consequences?) explores this theme in an even bolder fashion. *The Sex of It*, the fifth story, begins with a short paragraph directly expressing female lust, and the pleasures of sex (Uchida, 1998: 52). Then the comic begins with a graphic ten-panel sequence of lovemaking.

The same unnamed couple is portrayed in five further lovemaking sequences including such variations on the theme as bondage and the use of sex-aids. The perspective seems primarily from the male point of view but the female clearly enjoys sex as much as the male, although, as the dialogue is so limited, little sense of a story emerges. The second-last sequence involves the male forcing the female to go on a public walk with him with a vibrator secretly lodged in her vagina. This sequence seems to stress the pleasure of a female submitting to male domination, and also the pleasures of display (Uchida, 1998: 52–70).

The theme of older woman and younger man is explored in *Kare no Kureta Powasson* (The Poison He Gave Me), the story of a love affair between Horide Hideko, the editor of a magazine, and Chino Shinji, a 25-year-old man 10 years her junior who works as a writer on the magazine. The older woman's fascination with the young man's youth and innocence is emphasised. After Hideko performs fellatio on Shinji, he is so overcome with emotion that he hugs her tightly, and she thinks to herself, 'How sweet he is!' Then, she muses: 'He expresses his emotions so directly.... I'll give him everything he wants' (Uchida, 1998: 198). Later, the sexual pleasure the older woman derives from the younger man is expressed even more forcefully, when with his consent, she gently sodomises him and, in a reverse of the scene in *The Sex of It*, brings him to an ecstatic orgasm with a vibrator. This reversal is quite deliberate as Uchida here explores the eroticism of domination but with the female as the dominant partner introducing the male to female pleasure, again, quite explicitly in the context of a consensual, loving relationship (Uchida, 1998: 169–208).

All the erotic comics collected in the volume are quite explicitly illustrated, and would be banned on the grounds of pornography in many other countries. Yet, there is a complete absence of pain in the sexuality depicted therein, with the sexual variations enjoyed by the couples clearly a matter of mutual consent. The only exception to this are the comics jointly written by Uchida and Asakura Sekaiichi which enact a series of reverse disembowelments (the knife closes the wound in the male character's stomach) (Uchida, 1998: 237–62). In other words, Uchida's portrayal of sexual pleasure in these stories stands in stark contrast to the sado-masochistic comics condemned by Allison and others. The illustrator Minami Shinbō makes this point in his commentary on the volume in his postscript, when he argues that Uchida creates a female eroticism from a unique feminine perspective, unlike conventional comics (Uchida, 1998: 320–1).

The most remarkable expression of this kind of eroticism is Uchida's short comic *Aru Henka* (A Metamorphosis) in the same volume, where the female protagonist grows a penis on a third limb extending out of her stomach. She also grows a fourth hand on the opposite side of her belly. This may be a dream, as it takes place as she awakens from sleep in the morning. But whether she is dreaming or not, at the end, the protagonist, at first appalled by the prospect of these growths on her otherwise normal female body, decides that the male organ will surprise and delight her boyfriend as she fantasises sodomising him. The hermaphroditic sexuality described here makes explicit what is already implicit in many girls' manga, as numerous observers have noted (Uchida, 1998: 269–88).

Uchida's most famous manga to date is her 1994 book *Watashitachi wa Hanshoku Shite Iru* (We Are Reproducing) which Schodt observed won a prestigious literary award (Schodt, 1996: 177). The book begins with a comic showing clearly the pregnant protagonist's journey from early pregnancy to birth. At the end of the book is another story depicting the postnatal experience of a couple coping with a newborn baby at home. In between Uchida explores in a series of explanatory-style graphic sequences (eight panels to a page) all the possible permutations of the process of pregnancy and childbirth including breast-feeding, postnatal sex, the mechanics of the delivery, and so on. Uchida's motive would clearly appear to be educational, as the book contains a wealth of information relating to childbirth and associated issues. Uchida also divides the graphic strips by four short essays in which she explains that, although some of what is written in the book arises from her personal experience of childbirth and motherhood, nevertheless most of it is fiction derived from other sources. By 'fiction', presumably Uchida means non-fictional accounts of childbirths and pregnancy. In the short essays, Uchida also refers from time to time to her own personal experiences (Uchida, 1996a).

Yet, despite the obvious practicality and usefulness of the book as an illustrated guide for parents-to-be, Uchida states at the very beginning of her first essay that 'You might have bought this book expecting a useful comic on childbirth? You've made a mistake. Didn't you see the author's name?…. Nowhere is it written that this book is useful. Just as the title indicates, it describes in an entirely irresponsible way what I thought was interesting about how living human beings make babies' (Uchida, 1996a: 48). This statement presumably emphasises the author's artistic intent, and also acts as a kind of disclaimer for people whose experience of childbirth might differ from that depicted in the book. Also, Uchida's concern with the erotic and sensuous nature of childbirth is evident, with comparisons of breast-feeding to sex, and suggestions that the best way not to traumatise the baby while making love in bed together is to tie up the man so that mother appears to the baby to be clearly in charge and enjoying herself; she also mentions breast-feeding as an aid to seduction (Uchida, 1996a: 74, 100, 111).

It is interesting to note that this has been done before. The poet Itō Hiromi, discussed in the previous chapter, has written a number of books and poems about childbirth. Her two books *Ii Oppai Warui Oppai* (Good Breast Bad Breast, 1992) and *Onaka Hoppe Oshiri* (Belly Cheek Bottom, 1993) are both liberally illustrated by her own manga and graphics, which cover much of the same ground as Uchida. Moreover, in 1985 and 1987 respectively, Itō wrote the two verse collections *On Territory 2* and *On Territory 1* which established her reputation as the 'childbirth' poet. In *On Territory 2*, Itō uses the phrase 'hanshoku suru' (reproducing) in one famous poem called 'Mikaijin no Seiseikatsu' (The Sex-Life of a Barbarian) and in the later volume penned her well-known poem 'Warui Oppai' (Bad Breasts) where she repeats the line 'plants/insects are reproducing' as a refrain (Itō, 1988: 110; Itō, 1987). As Itō has been taken up widely by the media as a feminist poet, it is not too difficult to speculate upon possible influences on Uchida.

Nevertheless, Uchida's influence is undoubtedly much greater than Itō's, irrespective of any shared perspective since readers of manga far outnumber those of non-fiction or poetry. And as Uchida has a strong following, no doubt partially encouraged by the success of her autobiographical fiction and her other artistic achievements as an actor and musician, her ideas wield much influence over the thinking of young people. The proposition that her open embrace of female sexuality as an empowering force has done much to mould the views of Japanese women in the 1990s is therefore relatively uncontroversial.

Epilogue

Night deepens
The rain stops
Reading aloud, my voice
Reverberates thickly
Against the walls

Yoshida Issui, 1898–1973 (Yoshida, 1982: 453)

One question that arises from this study is to what degree does insider discourse on culture in Japan differ from its equivalent in other societies? Looking from the perspective of Australia, it is clear that the differences are marked, both in the sheer quantity of such discourse produced in Japan, and also by the quality and depth of the thinkers who create this discourse. At first glance, such a comparison may not seem all that useful since Japan is a much older society than Australia, nor is Japan a society settled by immigrants from abroad. Yet one resemblance, however imprecise, can be discerned between the two. Australia is a post-colonial society, and thus the various conceptualisations and expressions of culture created by its people over the past two centuries have often been characterised as either direct borrowings from overseas—chiefly from its colonial overlord Britain, and also, in the twentieth and twenty-first centuries, from the USA—or reactions to them in the form of adaptations of such borrowings.

Japan was not colonised by a European power, and yet the impact of first the Meiji Restoration of 1868, and then the post-World War II American occupation, have occasionally been interpreted by Japanese thinkers as a kind of cultural colonisation. We have seen in chapter four that the poet Sekine Hiroshi explicitly stated that Japan had become a US colony. He was certainly not alone in that view, and the comparison of Japan's experience of Western imperialism in the nineteenth century and the US occupation in the twentieth century to the process of colonisation, is not uncommon. Therefore, a comparison of insider discourses on culture in Australia and Japan may not seem as odd as first appears.

As a post-colonial society, Australia has struggled to create a culture that reflects the massive historical, social, political, geographic, and physical differences between itself and Britain. Even the process of naming, which fixes landscape and geography in historical memory, is subject to the post-colonial experience, as we know from the writer Paul Carter's acclaimed 1987 study *The Road to Botany Bay: An Essay in Spatial History* where Carter attempts to unravel this process as a means to constructing a history closer to indigenous concerns. Carter is one of the many Australian practitioners of insider discourse. However, no Australian insider theorists on culture have had the impact on their own culture equivalent to modern writers such as Yanagita Kunio and Yoshimoto Takaaki on Japan. Moreover, the sheer quantity of insider writers in contemporary Japan far exceeds in percentage terms their counterparts in Australia. Even Australian literature and cinema—two of the most robust and praised areas of modern Australian culture— pale beside the quantity and quality of what has been produced in Japan over the last century.

We can conclude from this that in Japan the insider discourse on culture, and expressions of this culture, occupy a much greater share of the intellectual and social space than the equivalent in Australia. Obviously, Japan's long history, well in excess of a thousand years, has something to do with this (and especially the weight accorded to culture over the course of that history), as does the much larger population and its much richer cultural heritage. Nevertheless, the differences are striking, and if we are to extend comparisons of insider discourse to other societies, say Indonesia or Korea, which have had similar disruptive experiences (colonial and otherwise) of the West, then again the clear magnitude and importance of what is produced in Japan becomes all too evident.

One reason for the great importance Japanese place upon culture, and the insider discourse that accompanies it, is the context-dependent nature of Japanese society or, to put it another way, the contextual basis of Japanese social relations. This is a feature of Japanese society noted by numerous observers and has led to the use of phrases such as the 'Japanese tribe' or 'Japan Inc.' to describe Japan. Often, this feature of Japanese society is linked to the Japanese language and the way it is used in modern Japan.

Without wishing to enter into this debate, and face the need to question exactly how accurate these descriptions are, the point is that ethnocentric or indigenous discourse, or as I have characterised it in this book, insider discourse is the logical outcome of a context-rich cultural and intellectual environment where, to a larger degree than elsewhere, conceptualisations of culture look inwards to indigenous formulations, and share a common set of assumptions about the nature of the society that produced this culture. This tendency has been exacerbated as part of a Japanese version of post-colonialism, where Japanese see themselves as struggling against the dominance of Western conceptualisations of culture and discourse. Naturally, insider discourse is part of a process of contestation and debate where different views of culture are challenged, and new views proposed—but rarely do these proposals originate wholly from, or point to paradigms of culture that are explicitly comparative or universal in nature.

We have seen how many of the insider theorists investigated in this study borrow or draw from outsider theories and views on culture but, nonetheless, they tend to limit their conclusions and applications to Japan alone. And, the views that these writers on culture put, as I have demonstrated, are immensely influential within Japan. In a real sense, they define the body and genre of insider discourse in contemporary Japan. Nevertheless, it is worth repeating that only a tiny number out of a much larger group of these writers have been able to be touched upon in what is essentially an introductory study.

The fact that discourse on culture in Japan arises from shared assumptions concerning the nature of this culture is evident in the frequency with which commentators on Japanese culture, whether writing from inside or outside that society, borrow from the same conceptual vocabulary. This illustrates the immense difficulty of actually creating an entirely new vocabulary to deal with these issues. We have seen how many

Japanese thinkers have lamented the fact that in post-Meiji Japan, indigenous conceptualisations of cultural issues were largely displaced by imported ones. Yanagita Kunio has been cited several times as one such thinker. But when Yanagita invented new terms to describe particular cultural phenomena his vocabulary almost immediately became itself a matter of contestation. Many critics of Yanagita explicitly based their critiques in an imported schema arising from Marxist discourse.

Similarly, when Yoshimoto Takaaki developed entirely new conceptual systems to describe Japanese culture, the immense difficulty in comprehending his neologisms and their precise meanings led to much confusion and, eventually, to another set of neologisms. This is not merely a problem of vocabulary, or even of concepts, but of how much Japanese society and culture is the product of its own unique history; therefore, to what degree can conceptual vocabulary derived from other societies and histories be adequate to describe it?

Yet all who consider this issue in our study recognise that the same dilemma applies to all human cultures; in other words, we recognise the ancient debate over particular versus general. Generalised concepts that are inherently comparative (indeed all concepts, by definition, must be at least implicitly comparative insofar as referentiality is concerned) are the basic building blocks of any intellectual discourse and, in practice, their use cannot be avoided. This study attempts, as far as humanly possible, to consciously problematise this dilemma during its interrogation of the various insider and outsider guides who constitute the object of analysis. The basic axis of insider and outsider discourse that this study is built upon is the ultimate recognition of this dilemma.

Another thread that is taken up more than once by the thinkers examined in this book is the degree to which cultural expression serves as a guide to social reality or sensibility. Religious belief of whatever stripe plays a major role in the social life of all human societies. This truth has been brought home to us in a powerful and disturbing way with the revival, for instance, of fundamentalist Christian and Islamic faiths in the politics of many nations; and, in the case of modern Japan, with the shocking attack of the Aum sect on the government and people of Japan, most notably in the sarin gas assault on the Tokyo subway system in 1995 which left many dead and severely injured.

Literally thousands of books and articles have been written about Aum and its implications for the fate of contemporary Japan. Two of the figures discussed in this study—Yoshimoto Takaaki and Murakami Haruki—have devoted much effort to unravelling the various issues surrounding this terrible crime, in their attempts to open a dialogue with its perpetrators and its victims. One difficulty in understanding Aum is the complex religious background to the sect, which draws upon far more than just Japanese Buddhist sources for its doctrines. We have touched upon Japanese religiosity in a number of places in this book, and have often used culture as an aid to understanding the manifest complications of religious belief for contemporary Japanese.

In a sense, then, what is at issue here is the complex and fluid permeability of cultural phenomena. That is to say, culture does not merely express or reflect social reality, it actively shapes and creates it. Similarly, the interpreters or guides, whether insider or outsider, that we have used as a means to grapple with modern Japanese culture have had an influence far beyond mere conceptualisation. The views of thinkers like Yanagita, Yoshimoto, Maruyama Masao, and others, as well as the cultural expressions of artists like Mishima Yukio, Yoshimoto Banana, Kurosawa Akira, Kitano Takeshi, and Uchida Shungicu play a far more important role than merely acting as a mirror to reflect social reality. In a sense, they shape and create it by focusing attention on this or that social issue, and thus problematise matters that otherwise would not come to public attention.

This raises the question of how we 'read' the culture of modern Japan. As explained in the introduction, the perspective here is to see the phenomena described as dynamic, in a state of constant change, rather than as fixed and unchanging. But this is not to deny the force of tradition on people's lives, while recognising that the tradition itself is fluid, subject to changing interpretation. Consequently, this book has sought to tread a fine line between describing and presenting data, and problematising and contextualising its interpretation. It has consciously sought to devote as much energy to the latter, as to the former, for the reasons outlined above.

The context-dependent nature of modern Japanese culture, indeed of the society at large, has dictated the course of this study, with much attention paid to the body of discourse that both creates the environment in which culture is produced, and also shapes the reception and interpretation of the various expressions of culture that emerge from it. Perhaps the most significant of those trends occurring over the last three or four decades is the move towards a hybridisation of culture. This is not merely a hybrid of different cultural genres but also of specifically Japanese and international influences.

Examples of the former tendency would include the cross-over trend of writers of manga becoming film directors working on animated and live action features, and also becoming novelists. Another example of the hybridity of cultural genres is contemporary Japanese poets becoming multimedia artists, producing their work in digital form with image and music, thus enabling it to be accessed through CDs and over the Internet. The resulting performance is as much theatre (in some cases, musical theatre) as written text—this trend is evident in the work of such contemporary poets as Itō Hiromi and Yoshimasu Gōzō.

Examples of the latter trend of a blend of indigenous and international influences include much contemporary manga, which has moved away from the template established by Tezuka Osamu (which, arguably, was also influenced by Walt Disney) to a more avant-garde style of manga art influenced by contemporary American and French cartoonists, although the American cartoonist Stan Lee has always been acknowledged as a source by modern Japanese manga artists. This works two ways, with many contemporary Western cartoonists and directors seeking a 'Japanese' look, and attempting to imitate Japanese manga styles and trends. The same cross-over of influence has long been true of literature where contemporary novelists like Murakami Haruki or Yoshimoto Banana openly admit their debt to contemporary Western authors. And recently, a number of contemporary Western novelists have repaid the favour by imitating Murakami in particular.

The hybridisation of cinema and television has been accepted as a fact since their early history. The links between literature and cinema and TV in Japan are well established—even contemporary novelists like Yamada Amy have had several stories made into films and TV films or series. When George Lucas can state several times that his 'Star Wars' series of movies are explicitly based on Kurosawa period movies (and several of these are based on well-known Japanese historical novels), and when movies like *The Seven Samurai* have been remade into Hollywood series ('The Magnificent Seven' cowboy movie series), then hybridity becomes the norm rather than the exception.

It may be possible to argue along similar lines for some of the cultural theorists considered here—except that, in the absence of more definitive evidence, the paradigm changes to one of synchronicity or convergence rather than direct imitation. The similarities between the writings on culture of Yoshimoto Takaaki and Michel Foucault have been noted several times by commentators, even to the extent of a book having been written exploring these similarities. However, it would appear that this is a case of convergence or synchronicity rather than direct imitation. Perhaps the same case can be made for Japanese thinkers advocating an ecological theory of culture such as Umehara Takeshi, for, as we know, a similar case has been made by numerous Western writers over the past two decades.

However, it is important for us to know what these writers and thinkers are saying, and what context produces the type of discourse on culture that has exploded out of Japan over the course of the twentieth century. This book attempts to answer those questions by a preliminary examination of the issues; here this has meant an introduction to the writings of some of the giants of insider discourse, and a summary of some selected but highly significant areas of Japanese culture as they have developed over the past four or five decades.

References

Akasaka, Norio *Yanagita Kunio no Yomikata: Mō Hitotsu no Minzokugaku wa Kanō ka?* (Tokyo: Chikuma Shinsho, 1994).

Akimoto, Yoshio (ed.) *Fudoki* (Tokyo: Iwanami Shoten, 1958).

Allison, Anne *Permitted and Prohibited Desires: Mothers, Comics and Censorship in Japan* (Boulder, Colorado: Westview Press, 1996).

Alston, William P. 'Quine on Meaning' in Hahn, Lewis Edwin and Schilpp, Paul (eds) *The Philosophy of W.V. Quine* [The Library of Living Philosophers V.18] (La Salle, Illinois: Open Court Publishing Company, 1987) pp. 49–73.

Anderson, Benedict *Imagined Communities: Reflections on the Origins and Spread of Nationalism* (London: Verso, 1983, 6th repr. 1990).

Anderson, Joseph L. and Richie, Donald *The Japanese Film: Art and Industry* [Expanded Edition] (Princeton, New Jersey: Princeton University Press, 1982).

Anzai, Hitoshi *Chēhofu no Ryōjū* (Tokyo: Kashinsha, 1988).

Aoki, Tamotsu *'Nihon Bunka Ron' no Hen'yō—Sengo Nihon no Bunka to Aidentitii* (Tokyo: Chūō Kōronsha, 1991).

Aoyama, Tomoko 'The Love that Poisons: Japanese Parody and the New Literacy' in *Japan Forum* Vol. 6, No. 1. (Apr. 1994) pp. 35–46.

Arisaka, Yōko 'The Nishida Enigma: "The Principle of the New World Order"' in *Monumenta Nipponica* 51: 1 (Spring 1996) pp. 81–105.

Asabuki, Ryōji *Opus* (Tokyo: Shichōsha, 1988).

Barnes, Gina 'The "idea of prehistory" in Japan' in *Antiquity* 64 (1990) pp. 929–40.

Benedict, Ruth *The Chrysanthemum and the Sword: Patterns of Japanese Culture* (Boston: Houghton Mifflin Co., 1946).

'The Best Pictures in 1993' in *Kinema Junpō*, Kessan Tokubetsugō (Feb. 1994) No. 1125, pp. 72–166.

Biito, Takeshi *Watashi wa Sekai de Kirawareru* (Tokyo: Shinchō Bunko, 1998).

Booth, Wayne *The Company We Keep: An Ethics of Reading* (Berkeley: University of California Press, 1988).

Bungei Shunjū (ed.) *Isetsu Kurosawa Akira* (Tokyo: Bunshun Bunko, 1994).

Buruma, Ian *A Japanese Mirror: Heroes and Villains of Japanese Culture* (Harmondsworth, Middlesex: Penguin Books, 1985).

Carter, Paul *The Road to Botany Bay: An Essay in Spatial History* (London, Boston: Faber and Faber, 1987).

Cassirer, Ernst *The Philosophy of Symbolic Forms* Vol. 1 (New Haven and London: Yale University Press, 1955).

Clarke, Hugh 'Japonesia, the Black Current and the Origins of the Japanese' in *The Journal of the Oriental Society of Australia* Vol. 17 (1985) pp. 7–21.

Clarke, Hugh 'The Great Dialect Debate: The State and Language Policy in Okinawa' in Elise K. Tipton (ed.) *Society and the State in Interwar Japan* (London and New York: Routledge, 1997) pp. 193–218.

Clifford, James *The Predicament of Culture: Twentieth-Century Ethnography, Literature and Art* (Cambridge and London: Harvard University Press, 1988).

Cornyetz, Nina 'Power and Gender in the Narratives of Yamada Eimi' in Paul Schallow and James Walker (eds) *The Women's Hand: Gender and Theory in Japanese Women's Writing* (Stanford, California: Stanford University Press, 1996).

Culler, Jonathon *Framing The Sign: Criticism and its Institutions* (Oxford: Basil Blackwell Ltd, 1988).

Dale, Peter N. *The Myth of Japanese Uniqueness* (New York: St. Martin's Press, 1986).

Desser, David *Eros Plus Massacre: An Introduction to the Japanese New Wave Cinema* (Bloomington and Indianapolis: Indiana University Press, 1988).

Doak, Kevin M. *Dreams of Difference: The Japan Romantic School and the Crisis of Modernity* (Berkeley, California: University of California Press, 1994).

Doak, Kevin M. 'Ethnic Nationalism and Romanticism in Early Twentieth-Century Japan' in *The Journal of Japanese Studies* 22:1 (Winter 1996) pp. 77–103.

Feleppa, Robert *Convention, Translation and Understanding: Philosophical Problems in the Comparative Study of Culture* (Albany, New York: State University of New York Press, 1988).

Flutsch, Maria 'Myth and the Dispossessed: Recent Stories by Four Contemporary Writers' in *Japanese Studies Bulletin* Vol. 14, No. 3 (Dec. 1994) pp. 78–88.

Foucault, Michel *The Order of Things: An Archeology of the Human Sciences* (New York: Vintage Books, 1973).

Fukami, Haruka *Murakami Haruki no Uta* (Tokyo: Seikyūsha, 1990).

Fukuda, Ajio 'Kaisetsu (Kainan Shōki, Kaijō no Michi)' in *Yanagita Kunio Zenshū* Vol. 1 [Chikuma Bunko] (Tokyo: Chikuma Shobō, 1994) pp. 689–703.

Fukuda, Ajio 'Kaisetsu (Kyōdo Seikatsu no Kenkyū hō, Minkan Denshō Ron)' in *Yanagita Kunio Zenshū* Vol. 28 [Chikuma Bunko] (Tokyo: Chikuma Shobō, 1996) pp. 631–44.

Fukuma, Kenji & Zeze, Takahira 'Nihon Eiga no Chihei wa Ugoite Kite iru' in *Gendai Shi Techō* 37:7 (July 1994) pp. 50–9.

Fukushima, Jirō *Mishima Yukio: Tsurugi to Kanbeni* (Tokyo: Bungei Shunjū, 1998).

Fukutomi, Tadayori '*Masu Imēji Ron*: Masu Imēji To Iu Hōhō' in *Yoshimoto Takaaki Variant* (Kyoto: Hokusōsha, 1985) pp. 264–81.

Fukuzawa, Yukichi (trans. by David A. Dilworth and Umeko Hirano) *An Encouragement of Learning* (Tokyo: Sophia University, 1968).

Furuhashi, Nobuyoshi *Kodai Waka no Hassei* (Tokyo: Tokyo Daigaku Shuppankai, 1988).

Furuhashi, Nobuyoshi *Yoshimoto Banana to Tawara Machi* (Tokyo: Chikuma Shobō, 1990).

Furuhashi, Nobuyoshi *Kodai no Ren'ai Seikatsu* (Tokyo: NHK Bukkusu, 1995).

Gabriel, Philip 'Rethinking the margins: Shimao Toshio and *Yaponesia*' in *Japan Forum* 8:2 (1996), pp. 205–20.

Gadamer, Hans-Georg *Truth and Method* trans. revised by Joel Weisheimer and Donald G. Marshall [Second Revised Edition] (New York: Continuum, 1994).

Gay, Peter *Freud: A Life For Our Time* (London: Papermac, 1988)

Gō, Kajiki 'Yanagitagaku to Orikuchigaku' in Keiō Gijuku Daigaku Kokubungaku Kenkyūkai (ed.) *Orikuchigaku to Kodaigaku* (Tokyo: Ōfusha, 1989) pp. 37–86.

Goodman, Nelson *Languages of Art: An Approach to the Theory of Symbols* (Indianapolis: Bobbs-Merrill, 1968).

Grosz, Elizabeth *Sexual Subversions: Three French Feminists* (Sydney: Allen and Unwin, 1989).

Hagiwara, Sakutarō *Hagiwara Sakutarō Zenshū* (eds) Itō Shinkichi et al. (Tokyo: Chikuma Shobō, 1984) Vol. 10.

Hakeda, Yoshito S. *Kūkai: Major Works* (New York and London: Columbia University Press, 1972).

Hamaguchi, Eshun 'A Contextual Model of the Japanese: Towards a Methodological Innovation in Japan Studies' in *The Journal of Japanese Studies* 11:21 (1985) pp. 289–321.

Hamaguchi, Eshun '*Nihon Rashisa*' no Sai Hakken (Tokyo: Kōdansha Gakujutsu Bunko, 1998).

Hanihara, Kazurō (ed.) *Nihonjin to Nihon Bunka no Keisei* (Tokyo: Kokusai Nihon Bunka Kenkyū Sentā, 1993).

Haniya, Yutaka et al. (ed.) *Yoshimoto Takaaki o Yomu* (Tokyo: Gendai Kikakushitsu, 1985).

Harada, Masato *Kurosawa Akira Kataru* (Tokyo: Fukutake Bunko, 1995).

Harootunian, H.D. 'Disciplinizing Native Knowledge and Producing Place: Yanagita Kunio, Origuchi Shinobu, Takata Yasuma' in Thomas Rimer (ed.) *Culture and Identity: Japanese Intellectuals During the Interwar Years* (Princeton, New Jersey: Princeton University Press, 1990) pp. 99–127.

Harootunian, H.D. 'Figuring the Folk: History, Poetics and Representation' in Stephen Vlastos (ed.) *Mirror of Modernity: Inverted Traditions of Modern Japan* (Berkeley, California: University of California Press, 1998) pp. 144–59.

Harvey, Paul A.S. 'Nonchan's Dream: NHK Morning Serialized Television Novels' in D. P. Martinez (ed.) *The World of Japanese Popular Culture* (Cambridge: Cambridge University Press, 1998) pp. 133–51.

Hashimoto, Mitsuru 'Chihō: Yanagita Kunio's Japan' in Stephen Vlastos (ed.) *Mirror of Modernity* (Berkeley, California: University of California Press, 1998) pp. 133–43.

Hasumi, Shigehiko *Shōsetsu kara Tōku Hanarete* (Tokyo: Kawade Shobō Shinsha, 1994).

Hegel, G.W.F. *Aesthetics: Lectures on Fine Art* trans. T. M. Knox Vol. 1 (Oxford: Clarendon Press, 1975).

Hiraoka, Masaaki 'Ogino Anna, Joyū to Shite' in Ogino, Anna *Meitantei Maririn* (Tokyo: Asahi Bunko, 1998).

Hiromatsu, Wataru *Kindai no Chōkoku Ron: Shōwa Shisōshi e no Shikaku* (Tokyo: Kōdansha Gakujutsu Bunko, 1989, repr. 1993).

Ichihara, Chikako *Umi no Tonneru* (Tokyo: Shinbisha, 1985).

Ichijō, Takao *Ōe Kenzaburō no Sekai* (Osaka: Izumi Shoin, 1985).

Imafuku, Ryūta 'Masao Yamaguchi: A Hermes-Harlequin in the Field of Semiotics' in Thomas A. Sebeok & Jean Uniker-Sebeok (eds) *The Semiotic Web 1987* (Berlin, New York, Amsterdam: Mouton de Gruyter, 1988) pp. 94–108.

Imai, Kiyoto 'Murakami Haruki Nenpyō' in *[Gunzō Nihon no Sakka] Murakami Haruki* (Tokyo: Shōgakukan, 1997) pp. 303–12.

Inaga, Shigemi 'Negative Capability of Tolerance—the Assassination of Hitoshi Igarashi' in James W. Fernandes & Milton B. Singer (eds) *The Conditions of Reciprocal Understanding* (Chicago: The Center for International Studies, The University of Chicago, 1995) pp. 304–36.

Inaga, Shigemi *Kaiga no Tasogare: Edouaru Mane Botsugo no Tōsō* (Nagoya: Nagoya Daigaku Shuppankai, 1997).

Inaga, Shigemi 'Mediators, Sacrifice, and Forgiveness: Laurens van der Post's Vision of Japan in the P.O.W. camp in reference to Takeyama Michio and Ghost Plays of the Noh theatre' in *Nichibunken Japan Review* No. 13 (2001) pp. 129–43.

Iraha, Morio *Maboroshi no Mikojima* (Tokyo: Yatate Shuppan, 1979).

Isaka Yōko 'Josei to iu Shizen' *La Mer* Vol. 14 (Autumn 1986) pp. 64–71.

Ishiko, Jun *Manga Shijin: Tezuka Osamu* (Tokyo: Shin Nihonshinsho, 1991).

Ishiko, Jun *Nihon Manga Shi* (Tokyo: Gendai Kyōyō Bunko, 1988).

Ishio, Yoshihisa 'Shihai no Seitōsei to Kyōdō Gensō' in *Yoshimoto Takaaki o Yomu* (Tokyo: Gendai Kikakushitsu, 1985) pp. 143–66.

Isoda, Kōichi 'Nihon Kaiki to Sensōshi no Ichi' in *Gendaishi Tokuhon: Hagiwara Sakutarō* (Tokyo: Shichōsha, 1983) pp. 204–9.

Isotani, Takashi 'Yoshimoto Shigaku no Meta Gengo ni Tsuite' in *Yoshimoto Takaaki o Yomu* (Tokyo: Gendai Kikakushitsu, 1985) pp. 118–39.

Itō, Hiromi *Teritorii Ron 1* (Tokyo: Shichōsha, 1987).

Itō, Hiromi *Teritorii Ron 2* (Tokyo: Shichōsha, 1985, 2nd edn. 1988).

Ivy, Marilyn *Discourses of The Vanishing: Modernity, Phantasm, Japan* (Chicago and London: University of Chicago Press, 1995).

Izumo, Osamu (annot.) *Nihon Ryōiki* (Tokyo: Iwanami Shoten, 1996 [Shin Nihon Koten Bungaku Taikei 30]).

Karatani, Kōjin *Hihyō to Posuto Modan* (Tokyo: Fukutake Shoten, 1985).

Karatani, Kōjin *Nihon Kindai Bungaku no Kigen* (Tokyo: Kōdansha [Bungei Bunko], 1988).

Karatani, Kōjin 'One Spirit, Two Nineteenth Centuries' in Masao Miyoshi and H. D. Harootunian (eds) *Post modernism and Japan* (Durham and London: Duke University Press, 1989) pp. 259–72.

Karatani, Kōjin *Ifusuru Ningen* (Tokyo: Kōdansha Bungei Bunko, 1990).

Karatani, Kōjin *Sai to Shite no Basho* (Tokyo: Kōdansha Gakujutsu Bunko, 1996).

Karatani, Kōjin *Shūen o Megutte* (Tokyo: Kōdansha Gakujutsu Bunko, 1996a).

Kasai, Kiyoshi 'Haisen Taiken to *Kyōdō Gensō' Ron'* in *Yoshimoto Takaaki Variant Genzai no Chijiku* (Tokyo: Hokusōsha, 1985) pp. 146–56.

Kasai, Kiyoshi et al. *Murakami Haruki o Meguru Bōken* (Tokyo: Kawade Shobō Shinsha, 1991).

Kashimoto, Mitsuru '*Chihō*: Yanagita Kunio's Japan' in Stephen Vlastos (ed.) *Mirror of Modernity* (Berkeley, California: University of California Press, 1998) pp. 133–43.

Kawada, Minoru *The Origin of Ethnography in Japan: Yanagita Kunio and His Times* trans. Toshiko Kishida-Ellis (London and New York: Kegan Paul International, 1993).

Kawai, Hayao *Kage no Genshōgaku* (Tokyo: Kōdansha Bunko, 1987).

Kawai, Hayao *Dreams, Myths and Fairy Tales in Japan* (Einsiedeln, Switzerland: Daimon, 1995).

Kawai, Nobukazu (ed.) *Asahi Shinbun Japan Almanac 1998* (Tokyo: Asahi Shinbun Sha, 1997).

Kawakami, Haruo 'Kaidai' in Yoshimoto, Takaaki *[Teihon] Gengo no Bi to wa Nanika I* (Tokyo: Kadokawa Shoten [Kadokawa Sensho 200], 1990) pp. 306–10.

Kawakami, Haruo 'Kaidai' in Yoshimoto, Takaaki *[Teihon]Gengo no Bi to wa Nanika II* (Tokyo: Kadokawa Shoten [Kadokawa Sensho 200], 1990a) pp. 356–8.

Kawamura, Nozomu *Sociology and Society in Early Modern Japan* (Melbourne: La Trobe University, 1980).

Kawamura, Nozomu 'Sociology and Socialism in the Interwar Period' in J. Thomas Rimer (ed.) *Culture and Identity* (Princeton: Princeton University Press, 1990) pp. 61–82.

Kawamura, Nozomu *Nihon Shihonshugi to Minkan Shintō* (Tokyo: Taga Shuppan, 1992).

Kawamura, Nozomu *Sociology and Society of Japan* (London: Kegan Paul International, 1994).

Keiō Gijuku Daigaku Kokubungaku Kenkyūkai (ed.) *Orikuchigaku to Kodaigaku* (Tokyo: Ōfūsha, 1989).

Kinsella, Sharon 'Change in the social status, form and content of adult manga, 1896–1996' in *Japan Forum* 8:1 (1996) pp. 103–12.

Kitamura, Sō 'Masu Imēji Ron: Mirai wa Sukunasugiru' in *Yoshimoto Takaaki Variant* (Tokyo: Hokusōsha, 1985) pp. 267–8.

Kitani, Nobufumi 'Mishima Yukio "Kinkakuji" Kenkyū no Genzai' in *Geijutsu Shijō Shugi Bungei* Vol. 24 (1998) pp. 83–93.

Kitano, Takeshi *Komanechi—Biito Takeshi Zen Kiroku* (Tokyo: Shinchō Bunko, 1998).

Kodaira, Maiko 'Ogino Anna' in *Kokubungaku: Kaishaku to Kyōzai no Kenkyū* Vol. 44, No. 3 (1997) pp. 42–3.

Kokai, Eiji *Nihon Sengo Shi no Tenbō* (Tokyo: Kenkyūsha Sōshō, 1973).

Kokai, Eiji *Gendai Shi no Kozu: Sengo Nihon no Shi to Shijin* (Tokyo: Yūseidō, 1977).

Kokai, Eiji 'Sengo Nihon no Shi Undō – "Arechi" no Baai' in Kokai, Eiji (ed.) *Kanshō Nihon Gendai Bungaku: Gendaishi* (Tokyo: Kadokawa Shoten, 1982) Vol. 31, pp. 431–43.

Kolakowski, Leszek *Main Currents of Marxism [Vol. 1, The Founders]* trans. P. Falla (Oxford: Oxford University Press, 1981a).

Kolakowski, Leszek *Main Currents of Marxism [Vol. 2, The Golden Age]* trans. P. Falla (Oxford: Oxford University Press, 1981).

Komori Yōichi 'Sei e no Akui, Shi e no Akui' in *Yuriika*, Vol. 26, No. 6 (1994) pp. 182–93.

Kōno, Nobuko *Yoshimoto Takaaki Ron* (Tokyo: Chūsekisha, 1986).

Koschmann, J. Victor, Ōiwa, Keibō, Yamashita, Shinji (eds) *International Perspectives on Yanagita Kunio and Japanese Folklore Studies* (Ithaca, New York: East Asia Program, Cornell University [Cornell East Asia Papers No. 37], 1988).

Koschmann, J. Victor *Revolution and Subjectivity in Postwar Japan* (Chicago and London: The University of Chicago Press, 1996).

Kubota, Jun et al. (eds) *Iwanami Kōza Nihon Bungakushi* 18 Vols.(Tokyo: Iwanami Shoten, 1977).

Kuki, Shūzō *'Iki' no Kōzō* (Tokyo: Iwanami Bunko, 1979).

Kuki, Shūzō *Reflections in Japanese Taste: The Structure of 'Iki'* trans. John Clark (Sydney: Power Publications, 1997).

Kunimine, Teruko 'Joseishi no Kōmyaku: Josei Shi 3' in *Gendai Shi Techō* Vol. 36, No. 7 (May 1993) pp. 152–3.

Kurano, Kenji (ed.) *Kojiki* (Tokyo: Iwanami Shoten, 1963).

Kurihara, Atsushi ' "Arechi" kara no Shuppatsu' in Katsumi Tōgō et al. (eds) *Shōwa Bungakushi: Yokuatsu to Kaihō* Vol. 3 (Tokyo: Yūseidō, 1988) pp. 195–204.

Kuritsubo, Yoshiki 'Gendai Nihon Bungakuron' in Kubota, Jun et al. (eds) *Iwanami Kōza Nihon Bungakushi* Vol. 14 (Tokyo: Iwanami Shoten, 1997) pp. 1–54.

Kuritsubo, Yoshiki 'Nakagami Kenji no Genzai' in *Kokubungaku: Kaishaku to Kyōzai to Kenkyū* Vol. 36, No. 14 (March 1991) pp. 126–9.

Kuroko, Kazuo *Ōe Kenzaburō Ron: Mori no Shisō to Ikikata no Genri* (Tokyo: Saiyūsha, 1989).

Kuroko, Kazuo *Murakami Haruki to Dōjidai no Bungaku* (Tokyo: Kawaii Shuppan, 1990).

Kurosawa, Akira *Seven Samurai and Other Screenplays* (London: Faber and Faber Ltd, 1992).

Kusano, Atsushi *Terebi Hōdō no Tadashii Mikata* (Tokyo: PHP Shinsho, 2000).

Lavelle, Pierre 'The Political Thought of Nishida Kitarō' in *Monumenta Nipponica* 49:2 (Summer 1993) pp. 139–65.

Lévy-Bruhl, Lucien *How Natives Think* trans. Lilian A. Clare (New York: Arno Press Reprint, 1979).

Lewis, Dana 'Unlikely Ambassadors: The Surprising Appeal of *Manga* Overseas' in *The Japan Foundation Newsletter* 27:3-4 (March 2000) pp. 7–11.

Marshall, Robert C. Review of *The Myth of Japanese Uniqueness* in *The Journal of Japanese Studies* 19:1 (Winter 1989) pp. 260–72.

Martinez, D.P. (ed.) *The Worlds of Japanese Popular Culture: Gender, Shifting Boundaries and Global Cultures* (Cambridge: Cambridge University Press, 1998).

Maruyama, Masao *Gendai Seiji no Shisō to Kōdō* 2 Vols (Tokyo: Miraisha, 1956).

Maruyama, Masao *Nihon no Shisō* (Tokyo: Iwanami Shinsho [434], 1961, 1981).

Marx, Karl *Capital* (ed.) Friedrich Engels (trans. S. Moore and E. Aveling) (Chicago: Encyclopedia Britannia, 1952).

Matsuura, Hisaki 'Akarui Haibō no Kanata e: 80 Nendai no Shi' in *Kokubungaku* Vol. 41, No. 13 (Nov. 1996) pp. 126–31.

Matsuzawa, Masahiro *Haruki Banana Gen'ichirō* (Tokyo: Seikyūsha, 1989).

Minami, Hiroshi *Nihonjinron no Keifu* (Tokyo: Kōdansha Gendai Shinsho, 1980).

Minami, Hiroshi *Nihonjinron—Meiji kara Konnichi made* (Tokyo: Iwanami Shoten, 1994).

Mishima, Yukio *Confessions of a Mask* trans. Meredith Weatherby (New York: New Directions, 1958).

Mishima, Yukio *The Temple of the Golden Pavilion* trans. Ivan Morris (New York: Alfred A. Knopf, 1959).

Mishima, Yukio *Kamen no Kokuhaku* (1949) in *Mishima Yukio* [Gendai no Bungaku 11] (Tokyo: Kōdansha, 1972).

Mishima, Yukio *Mishima Yukio Zenshū* 36 Vols. (eds) Saeki, Shōichi et al. (Tokyo: Shinchōsha, 1973).

Mishima, Yukio 'Bi no Katachi' (1957) in *Mishima Yukio Zenshū* (Tokyo: Shinchōsha, 1976). Supplementary Vol. 1 (eds) Saeki, Shōichi et al., pp. 285–304.

Mishima, Yukio 'Yanagita Kunio "Tōno Monogatari"' in *[Bungei Tokuhon] Yanagita Kunio* (Tokyo: Kawade Shobō Shinsha, 1992) pp. 44–6.

Miura Sukeyuki 'Yanagita Kunio Ron no Kansei' in *Kokubungaku: Kaishaku to Kyōzai no Kenkyū* 33:3 (March 1988) pp. 83–8.

Miyoshi, Masao *Accomplices of Silence: The Modern Japanese Novel* (Berkeley California: University of California Press, 1974).

Miyoshi, Yukio (ed.) *Mishima Yukio Hikkei* (Tokyo: Gakutōsha, 1989).

Morris-Suzuki, Tessa 'Rewriting History: Civilization Theory in Contemporary Japan' in *positions: east asia cultures critique* 1: 2 (Fall, 1993) pp. 526–49.

Morris-Suzuki, Tessa 'The Invention and Reinvention of "Japanese Culture" ' in *The Journal of Asian Studies* 54: 3 (Aug. 1995) pp. 759–80.

Morse, Ronald A. 'Yanagita Kunio, and the Modern Japanese Consciousness' in *International Perspectives on Yanagita Kunio and Japanese Folklore Studies* (Ithaca, New York: East Asian Program Cornell University [Cornell East Asian Papers] 1988) pp. 11–28.

Morton, Leith 'Feminist Strategies in Contemporary Japanese Women's Poetry' in *Journal of the Association of Teachers of Japanese* 31:2 (Oct. 1997) pp. 73–108.

Morton, Leith 'An Interview with Tanikawa Shuntarō' in *Southerly* 68:1 (Autumn 1998) pp. 6–30.

Morton, Leith 'The Paradox of Pain: The Poetry of Paul Celan and Sō Sakon' in *Literature and Aesthetics: The Journal of the Sydney Society of Literature and Aesthetics* 1:1 (Spring 1991) pp. 82–96.

Morton, Leith 'Translating Japanese Poetry: Reading As Practice' in *Journal of the Association of Teachers of Japanese* 26:2 (1992) pp. 141–79.

Morton, Leith *An Anthology of Contemporary Japanese Poetry* (New York and London: Garland Publishing Inc., 1993).

Moto, Yuriko 'Multiculturalism and Feminism for Women Belonging to Minorities' in *East Asian Review* Vol. 6 (2002) pp. 45–66.

Mouer, Ross and Sugimoto Yoshio, *Images of Japanese Society* (London: Kegan Paul International, 1986).

Murai, Osamu *Nantō Ideorogii no Hassei—Yanagita Kunio to Shokuminchishugi* (Tokyo: Ōta Shuppan, 1995).

Murakami, Haruki *Hear The Wind Sing* trans. Alfred Birnbaum (Tokyo: Kodansha International, 1979).

Murakami, Haruki *Pinball, 1973* trans. Alfred Birnbaum (Tokyo: Kodansha International, 1985).

Murakami, Haruki *Dansu Dansu Dansu* 2 Vols (Tokyo: Kōdansha, 1988).

Murakami, Haruki *A Wild Sheep Chase* trans. Alfred Birnbaum (Tokyo: Kodansha International, 1989).

Murakami, Haruki *Norwegian Wood* 2 Vols trans. Alfred Birnbaum (Tokyo: Kodansha International, 1989).

Murakami, Haruki *Murakami Haruki Zensakuhin 1979–1982* 5 Vols (Tokyo: Kōdansha, 1990).

Murakami, Haruki *Murakami Haruki Zensakuhin 1979–1982* 'Jisaku o Kataru (1)' Vol. 1. (Tokyo: Kōdansha, 1990).

Murakami, Haruki *Murakami Haruki Zensakuhin 1979–1982* 'Jisaku o Kataru (2)' Vol. 2. (Tokyo: Kōdansha, 1990a).

Murakami, Haruki *Dance Dance Dance* trans. Alfred Birnbaum (Tokyo: Kodansha International, 1994).

Muramatsu, Takeshi *Mishima Yukio no Sekai* (Tokyo: Shinchōsha, 1990).

Mushiaki, Aromu 'Kokumen no Kokuhaku o Megutte' in *Mishima Yukio Zenshū* (Tokyo: Shinchōsha, 1973) Vol. 3 'Furoku' pp. 8–15.

Mushiaki, Aromu 'Shu to shite "Kinkakuji" o Megutte' in *Mishima Yukio Zenshū* (Tokyo: Shinchōsha, 1973) Vol. 10 'Furoku' pp. 8–15.

Nagaike, Kenji 'Kaisetsu' in *Yanagita Kunio Zenshū* Vol. 4 [Chikuma Bunko] (Tokyo: Chikuma Shobō, 1994) pp. 507–35.

Nakagami, Kenji *The Cape and Other Stories from the Japanese Ghetto* trans. Eve Zimmerman (Berkeley, California: Stone Bridge Press, 1999).

Nakamura, Mitsuo *Nihon no Gendai Shōsetsu* (Tokyo: Iwanami Bunko, 1968).

Nakamura, Mitsuo *Fūzoku Shōsetsu Ron* (Tokyo: Shinchō Bunko, 1958, repr. 1971).

Nakamura, Mitsuo *Nihon no Kindai Shōsetsu* (Tokyo: Iwanami Shinsho, 1954, repr. 1975).

Nakane, Chie *Japanese Society* (London: Weidenfeld and Nicolson, 1970).

Nakata, Hitoshi & Yoshimoto, Takaaki *Misheru Fūkō to Kyōdō Gensō Ron* (Tokyo: Kōbōsha, 1999).

Napier, Susan J. 'Vampires, Psychic Girls, Flying Women and Sailor Scouts: Four Faces of the Young Female in Japanese Popular Culture' in D.P. Martinez (ed.) *The Worlds of Japanese Popular Culture* (Cambridge: Cambridge University Press, 1998) pp. 91–109.

Napier, Susan J. *Escape from the Wasteland: Romanticism and Realism in the Fiction of Mishima Yukio and Ōe Kenzaburō* (Cambridge, Massachusetts and London: Council on East Asian Studies, Harvard University, 1991).

Nathan, John *Mishima: A Biography* (Tokyo: Charles E. Tuttle Co., 1974)

Natsume, Fusanosuke 'Japan's Manga Culture' in *The Japan Foundation Newsletter* 27:3-4 (March 2000) pp. 1–6.

Natsume, Sōseki *Sōseki Zenshū* Vol. 12 (Tokyo: Iwanami Shoten, 1979).

Nibuya, Takashi 'Tsuki to Suisen' in Satō, Hideaki (ed.) *Mishima Yukio: Bi no Erosu to Ronri* (Tokyo: Yūseidō, 1991) pp. 50–75.

Nihon Bungaku Kenkyū Shiryō Sōsho (ed.) *Yanagita Kunio* (Tokyo: Yūseidō, 1976).

'Nihon Eiga Ōru Taimu Besuto Ten' in *Kinema Junpō*, Rinji Zōkan (Nov. 1995) No. 1176, pp. 8–22.

Nishi, Kanenari 'Kurosawa Jidai to Nō no Doramaturugii' in *Kinema Junpō*, Rinji Zōkan (Aug. 1998) No. 1262, pp. 198–205.

Nishida, Kitarō *Nihon no Meicho: Nishida Kitarō* Vol. 47 (ed.) Ueyama Shinpei (Tokyo: Chūō Kōronsha, 1970).

Nishiwaki, Junzaburō *Nishiwaki Junzaburō Shishū* (ed.) Naka, Tarō (Tokyo: Iwanami Bunko, 1991).

Noguchi, Takehiko *Nihongo no Shōsetsu* (Tokyo: Chūō Kōron, 1980).

Nomura, Seiichi 'Hyōgen to shite no Gengo: Yoshimoto Takaaki to Tokieda Motoki no Sōgu to Kōsho' in *Yoshimoto Takaaki o Yomu* pp. 103–17.

Ōe, Kenzaburō *Man'en Gannen no Futtobōru* in *Ōe Kenzaburō Zensakuhin (Dainikki)* Vol. 1 (Tokyo: Shinchōsha, 1977).

Ōe, Kenzaburō *The Silent Cry* trans. John Bester (Tokyo: Kodansha International, 1974).

Ōe, Kenzaburō *Ōe Kenzaburō Zensakuhin (Dainikki)* 6 Vols (Tokyo: Shinchōsha, 1977).

Ōe, Kenzaburō *A Personal Matter* trans. John Nathan (Tokyo: Charles E. Tuttle Co., 1988).

Ōe, Kenzaburō *Natsukashii Toshi e no Tegami* (Tokyo: Kōdansha Bunko, 1992).

Ogino, Anna *Watashi no Aidokusho* (Tokyo: Fukutake Bunko, 1994).

Ohnuki-Tierney, Emiko *Illness and Culture in Contemporary Japan: An Anthropological View* (Cambridge, New York: Cambridge University Press, 1984).

Ohnuki-Tierney, Emiko *The Monkey as Mirror: Symbolic Transformations in Japanese History and Ritual* (Princeton, New Jersey: Princeton University Press, 1987).

Okai, Takashi (ed.) *Gendai Hyakunin Isshu* (Tokyo: Asahi Bungei Bunko, 1997).

Okamura, Keita 'Mishima Yukio Bungaku ni okeru "Kamen" ni tsuite: Fukushima Jirō no chosaku ni furete' in *Geijutsu Shijō Shugi Bungei* Vol. 24 (1998) pp. 44–51.

Oketani, Hideaki 'Mishima Yukio to Sengo Bungaku' in *Nihon Bungaku Kenkyū Shiryō Soshō: Mishima Yukio* (Tokyo: Yūseidō, 1972) pp. 154–8.

Oketani, Hideaki *Shōwa Seishin Shi* (Tokyo: Bunshun Bunko, 1996).

Olson, Lawrence *Ambivalent Moderns: Portraits of Japanese Cultural Identity* (Maryland: Rowman and Littlefield Publishers Inc, 1992).

Omoto, Kiichi *Bunshijinruigaku to Nihonjin no Kigen* (Tokyo: Shokadō, 1996).

Ōoka, Makoto *Tōji no Keifu: Nihon Gendaishi no Ayumi* (Tokyo: Shichōsha, 1978).

Ophüls-Kashima, Reinhold *Yoshimoto Takaaki—Ein Kritiker Zwischen Dialektik und Differenz* (Wiesbaden: Harrassowitz Verlag, 1998).

Ōshiro, Sadatoshi *Okinawa Sengo Shishi* (Naha: Henshū Kōbō Baku, 1989).

Painter, Andrew A. 'Japanese Daytime Television, Popular Culture, and Ideology' in *The Journal of Japanese Studies* 19:3 (Summer 1993) pp. 295–325.

Perloff, Marjorie *The Poetics of Indeterminancy: Rimbaud to Cage* (Princeton, New Jersey: Princeton University Press, 1981).

Pike, Kenneth *Language in Relation to a Unified Theory of the Structure of Human Behaviour: Part One* (Glendale, California: Summer Institute of Linguistics, 1954).

Pollack, David *The Fracture of Meaning: Japan's Synthesis of China from the Eighth through the Eighteenth Centuries* (Princeton, New Jersey: Princeton University Press, 1986).

Quine, Willard Van Orman *Word and Object* (Cambridge, Massachusetts: The M. I. T. Press, 1960).

Rorty, Richard *Objectivity, Relativism and Truth: Philosophical Papers Volume 1* (Cambridge and New York: Cambridge University Press, 1991).

Sakurai, Tetsuo *Tezuka Osamu: Jidai to Kirimusubu Hyōgensha* (Tokyo: Kōdansha Gendai Shinsho, 1990).

Sakurai, Tetsuo *TV Mahō no Media* (Tokyo: Chikuma Shinsho, 1994).

Sasaki, Kenichi *Serifu no Kōzō* (Tokyo: Kōdansha Gakujutsu Bunko, rev. ed. 1994).

Sasaki, Kiichi 'Mishima Yukio Ron: Gyakusetsu to Parodiei no Engi' in *Nihon Bungaku Kenkyū Shiryō Soshō: Mishima Yukio* (Tokyo: Yūseidō, 1972) pp. 1–2.

Satō, Hideaki (ed.) *Mishima Yukio: Bi no Erosu to Ronri* (Tokyo: Yūseidō, 1991).

Satō, Ken'ichi 'Radeikaru na Shi no Kūkan' in Hirofumi Wada (ed.) *Kingendai Shi o Manabu Hito no Tame ni* (Kyoto: Sekai Shisōsha, 1998) pp. 248–62.

Satō, Tadao *Currents in Japanese Cinema* trans. Barrett, Gregory (Tokyo: Kodansha International, 1987).

Sawa, Masahiro 'Rinen to shite no "sengo": "Sengoshi"' in *Kokubungaku: Kaishaku to Kyōzai no Kenkyū* 41:13 (Nov. 1996) pp. 105–11.

Schama, Simon *Landscape and Memory* (London: Fontana Press, 1995).

Schilling, Mark *The Encyclopedia of Japanese Pop Culture* (New York: Weatherhill Inc., 1997).

Schodt, Frederik L. *Manga! Manga! The World of Japanese Comics* (New York: Kodansha International, 1983).

Schodt, Frederik L. *Dreamland Japan: Writings on Modern Manga* (Berkeley, California: Stone Bridge Press, 1996).

Shanks, Hershel *The Mystery and Meaning of the Dead Sea Scrolls* (New York: Random House, 1998).

Sherif, Ann 'Japanese Without Apology: Yoshimoto Banana and Healing' in *Ōe and Beyond: Fiction in Contemporary Japan* (Honolulu: University of Hawaii Press, 1999) pp. 278–301.

Shimada, Masahiko *Dream Messenger* trans. Philip Gabriel (Tokyo: Kodansha International, 1992).

Shimada, Masahiko *Higan Sensei* (Tokyo: Fukutake Shoten, 1992).

Shimao, Toshio 'Yaponeshia to Ryūkyū Ko' in *Okinawa Bungaku Zenshū* (Tokyo: Kokusho Kankōkai, 1992) Vol. 18, pp. 264–79.

Shimaoka, Shin *Shi to wa Nanika* (Tokyo: Shinchō Senso, 1998).

Shimazaki, Tōson *Hatsukoi: Shimazaki Tōson Shishū* (Tokyo: Shūeisha Bunko, 1991).

Shimizu, Isao *Manga no Rekishi* (Tokyo: Iwanami Bunko, 1991).

Shinoda, Hajime *Gendai Shijin Chō* (Tokyo: Shinchōsha, 1985).

Shiraishi, Kazuko 'Hachijū Nendai to Joseishi: Fueminizumu Undō to Heikō Shite' in *Gendai Shi Techō* Vol. 34, No. 9 (Sept. 1991) pp. 64–9.

Shiroto, Shuri '"Yoshioka Minoru" o Genzai to shite' in *Gendai Shi Techō* 38:2 (Feb. 1995) pp. 27–32.

Smith, Toren 'The World of Manga' in *Japanese Book News* No. 2 (Spring 1993) pp. 1–3.

Snyder, Stephen 'Extreme Imagination: The Fiction of Murakami Ryū' in Stephen Snyder & Philip Gabriel (eds) *Ōe and Beyond: Fiction in Contemporary Japan* (Honolulu: University of Hawaii Press, 1999) pp. 199–218.

Soh, Sakon *Jōmon Rentō* (Tokyo: Shichōsha, 1992).

Sono, Shion 'Kitano Takeshi wa Gyangu Eiga Sakka de Aru' in *Gendai Shi Techō* 37:7 (July 1994) pp. 84–7.

Steiner, George *After Babel: Aspects of Language and Translation* (New York and London: Oxford University Press, 1975)

Sugimoto, Yoshio & Mouer, Ross E. (eds) *Constructs for Understanding Japan* (London and New York: Kegan Paul International 1989).

Suzuki, Sadami *Nihon no 'Bungaku' o Kangaeru* (Tokyo: Kadokawa Sensho, 1994).

Suzuki, Sadami 'Nishida Kitarō as Vitalist, Part I: The Ideology of the Imperial Way in Nishida's *The Problem of Japanese Culture* and the Symposia on "The World Historical Standpoint and Japan"' in *Nichibunken Japan Review* No. 9, 1997.

Tada, Michitarō 'Japanese Sensibility: An "Imitation of Yanagita"' in J. Victor Koschmann, Ōiwa Keibō and Yamashita Shinji (eds) *International Perspectives on Yanagita Kunio and Japanese Folklore Studies* (Ithaca, New York: East Asian Program Cornall University [Cornell East Asian Papers] 1988) pp. 97–120.

Taira, Kōji 'Troubled National identity: The Ryūkyūans/Okinawans' in Michael Weiner (ed.) *Japan's Minorities: The Illusion of Homogeneity* (London and New York: Routledge, 1997) pp. 140–77.

Takahashi, Jun'ichi 'Kachi no Shigan to Higan—Gengo ni Totte Bi to wa Nanika Kara' in Yamamoto Tetsuji et al. (eds) *On the Pre-Asian Practique: Yoshimoto Takaaki no Bunkagaku* (Tokyo: Bunka Kagaku Kōtō Kenkyūin Shuppan Kyoku, 1996) pp. 87–102.

Takahashi, Seori 'Shiteki Gengo no Genzai' in Kubota Jun et al. (eds) *Iwanami Kōza Nihon Bungakushi* Vol. 14 (Tokyo: Iwanami Shoten, 1997) pp. 329–43.

Takakuwa, Noriko 'Yamada Eimi' in *Kokubungaku: Kaishaku to Kyōzai to Kenkyū* Vol. 44, No. 3 (1997) pp. 196–7.

Takeda, Katsuhiko 'Sakuhinbetsu: Mishima Yukio Kenkyūshi (Kamen no Kokuhaku)' in Miyoshi Yukio (ed.) *Mishima Yukio Hikkei* (Tokyo: Gakutōsha, 1989) pp. 145–9.

Takeda, Kiyoko *Seitō to Itan no 'Aida'—Nihon Shisōshi Kenkyū Shiron* (Tokyo: Tokyo Daigaku Shuppankai, 1976).

Takeda, Nobuaki 'Onna no Nishijō/Onna no Hinichijō' in Katsumi Sōgō et al. (eds) *Kōza Shōwa Bungakushi* Vol. 5 (Tokyo: Yūseidō, 1989) pp. 130–40.

Takeda, Seiji *Sekai to iu Hairi: Kobayashi Hideo to Yoshimoto Takaaki* (Tokyo: Kōdansha Gakujutsu Bunko, 1996).

Takeuchi, Osamu 'Japanese Manga: Research and Criticism' in *Japanese Book News* No. 15 (Fall 1996) pp. 1–3.

Tamanoi, Mariko Asano 'Gender, Nationalism and Japanese Native Ethnology' in *positions: east asia studies critique* 4:1 (Spring 1996) pp. 59–86.

Tanaka, Stefan *Japan's Orient: Rendering Pasts into History* (Berkeley and Los Angeles, California: University of California Press, 1993).

Tanigawa, Ken'ichi *Yanagita Kunio no Minzokugaku* (Tokyo: Iwanami Shinsho, 2001).

Tanikawa, Shuntarō *Tanikawa Shuntarō Shishū* (Tokyo: Shichōsha, 1986).

Tanikawa Shuntarō *Sora no Aosa o Mitsumeteiru To: Tanikawa Shuntarō Shishū* (Tokyo: Kakodawa Bunko, 1990).

Tanikawa, Shuntarō *Seken Shirazu* (Tokyo: Shichōsha, 1993).

Tansman, Alan 'History, Repetition, and Freedom in the Narratives of Nakagami Kenji' in *Journal of Japanese Studies* Vol. 24, No. 2 (1998), pp. 257–89.

Tayama, Rikiya *Gendai Nihon Eiga no Kantoku Tachi* (Tokyo: Gendai Kyōyō Bunko, 1991).

Treat, John Whittier 'Yoshimoto Banana Writes Home: Shōjo Culture and the Nostalgic Subject' in *Journal of Japanese Studies* Vol. 19, No. 2 (1993) pp. 353–89.

Tsuboi, Hideto '"Tassha" o Motomete' in Katsumi Tōgō et al. (eds) *Shōwa Bungakushi: Nichijō to Hinichijō* Vol. 4 (Tokyo: Yūseidō, 1989) pp. 260–70.

Tsuboi, Hideto 'Itō Hiromi Ron (Jō)—Teritorii Ron II' in *Nihon Bungaku* Vol. 38, No. 12 (Dec. 1989a) pp. 24–35.

Tsuboi, Hideto 'Itō Hiromi Ron (Chū)—Teritorii Ron I (Sono 1)' in *Nihon Bungaku* Vol. 39, No. 2 (Feb. 1990) pp. 48–57.

Tsuboi, Hideto 'Kōdo Shōhi Shakai to Shi no Genzai' in Wada, Hirofumi (ed.) *Kingendaishi o Manabu Hito no Tame ni* (Kyoto: Sekai Shisōsha, 1998) pp. 264–77.

Tsuchiya Yoshio Interview 'Kurosawa san to Sugoshita Hibi no Subete ga Boku no Kate ni Natte iru' in *Kinema Junpō*, Rinji Zōkan (Aug. 1998) No. 1262, pp. 118–21.

Tsuge, Teruhiko 'Hichijō to Hinichijō no Hazama' in Katsumi, Tōyō et al. (eds) *Kōza Shōwa Bungaku Shi* Vol. 4 (Tokyo: Yūseidō, 1989) pp. 3–17.

Tsunazawa, Mitsuaki 'Yanagita Kunio no Teikō Seishin: Nōhon Shugi Hihan o Chūshin ni' in Nihon Bungaku Kenkyū Shiryō Sōsho (ed.) *Yanagita Kunio* (Tokyo: Yūseidō, 1976) pp. 185–97.

Tsurumi, Kazuko 'Warera no Uchinaru Genshijin—Yanagita Kunio wo Jiku ni Shite Kindaikaron wo Kangaenaosu' in Nihon Bungaku Kenkyū Shiryō Sōsho (ed.) *Yanagita Kunio* (Tokyo: Yūseidō, 1976) pp. 152–69.

Tsurumi, Shunsuke *An Intellectual History of Wartime Japan 1931–1945* (London: Kegan Paul International, 1986).

Tsutsui, Kiyotada *Jidaigeki Eiga no Shisō: Nosutarujii no Yukue* (Tokyo: PNP Shinsho, 2000).

Uchida, Shungicu *Maboroshi no Futsū Shōjo* (Tokyo: Futabasha, 1988).

Uchida, Shungicu *Mimamotte Kudasai* (Tokyo: Kawade Bunko, 1995).

Uchida, Shungicu *Fāzā Fakkā* (Tokyo: Bunshun Bunko, 1996).

Uchida, Shungicu *Watashitachi wa Hanshoku Shite Iru* (Tokyo: Bunkasha, 1996a).

Uchida, Shungicu *Ai no Sei Kashira* (Tokyo: Bunshun Bunko, 1998).

Ueda, Shizuteru *Nishida Kitarō: Ningen no Shōgai to iu Koto* (Tokyo: Iwanami Shoten [Dōjidai Raiburarii], 1996).

Ueno, Chizuko *Hatsujōsochi: Erosu no Shinario* (Tokyo: Chikuma Shobō, 1998).

Ueno, Yūko 'Yoshimoto Banana no Sekai: Hinshutsu suru Kotoba o Tegakari to shite' in *[Kanazawa Joshi Daigaku] Nihon Bungaku Kenkyū Nenshi* No. 4 (1995) pp. 69–80.

Ueyama, Shinpei 'Zettai Mu no Tankyū' in *Nihon no Meicho: Nishida Kitarō* (Tokyo: Chūō Kōronsha, 1970) pp. 7–85.

Umehara, Takeshi *Ama to Tennō* 2 Vols (Tokyo: Asahi Shinbunsha, 1991).

Umehara, Takeshi *Kūkai no Shisō ni Tsuite* (Tokyo: Kōdansha Gakujutsu Bunko, 1980, repr. 1996).

Watanabe, Makoto et al. (eds) *Yoshimoto Takaaki Variant: Genzai no Chijiku* (Tokyo: Hokusōsha, 1985).

Watanabe, Naomi '"Sekai Shisen" aruiwa Kenshikan no Honfuku' in *Kokubungaku: Kaishaku to Kyōzai no Kenkyū* 33:3 (1988) pp. 90–7.

Watsuji, Tetsurō *Fūdo* (Tokyo: Iwanami Shoten, 1935, repr. 1973).

Welleck, René & Warren, Austin *Theory of Literature* (Harmondsworth, Middlesex: Penguin Books, 1973).

Williams, Raymond *Keywords: A Vocabulary of Culture and Society* (London: Flamingo, 1985).

Wilson, Michiko N. *The Marginal World of Ōe Kenzaburō: A Study in Themes and Techniques* (New York: M. E. Sharpe, Inc., 1986).

Yamada, Amy *Beddo Taimu Aizu* (Tokyo: Kawade Shobō Shinsha, 1987).

Yamada, Amy *Trash* trans. Sonya L. Johnson (Harmondsworth, Middlesex: Penguin Books, 1996).

Yamaguchi, Masao '"Center" and "periphery" in Japanese culture—in light of Tartu semiotics' in Henri Broms and Rebecca Kaufman (eds) *Semiotics of Culture* (Helsinki, Finland: Aratov, Inc., 1988) pp. 199–219.

Yamamoto, Tetsuji 'Towards a Theory of *Pratique*: philosophical fields in social theories' in *Iichiko Intercultural* No. 1 (1989) pp. 14–67.

Yamamoto, Tetsuji et al. *On the Pre-Asian Pratique/Yoshimoto Takaaki no Bunkagaku* (Tokyo: Bunkagaku Kōtō Kenkyūin Shuppan Kyoku, 1996).

Yanagita, Kunio 'Gendai Kagaku to iu Koto' in *Yanagita Kunio Zenshū* Vol. 26 [Chikuma Bunko] (Tokyo: Chikuma Shobō, 1990, 2nd ed. 1996) pp. 567–84.

Yanagita, Kunio 'Sanjin Gaiden Shiryō' (1913) in *Yanagita Kunio Zenshū* Vol. 4 [Chikuma Bunko] (Tokyo: Chikuma Shobō, 1994) pp. 385–418.

Yanagita, Kunio 'Yamabito Kō' (1917) in *Yanagita Kunio Zenshū* Vol. 4 [Chikuma Bunko] (Tokyo: Chikuma Shobō, 1994) pp. 235–54.

Yanagita, Kunio *Kainan Shōki* (1925) in *Yanagita Kunio Zenshū* Vol. 1 [Chikuma Bunko] (Tokyo: Chikuma Shobō, 1994) pp. 297–525.

Yanagita, Kunio *Jidai to Nōsei* (1948) in *Yanagita Kunio Zenshū* Vol. 29 [Chikuma Bunko] (Tokyo: Chikuma Shobō, 1991) pp. 7–227.

Yanagita, Kunio *Kaijō no Michi* (1961) in *Yanagita Kunio Zenshū* Vol. 1 [Chikuma Bunko] (Tokyo: Chikuma Shobō, 1994) pp. 7–297.

Yanagita, Kunio *Kyōdō Seikatsu no Kenkyū Hō* (1935) in *Yanagita Kunio Zenshū* Vol. 28 [Chikuma Bunko] (Tokyo: Chikuma Shobō, 1996) pp. 7–245.

Yanagita, Kunio *Minkan Denshō Ron* (1934) in *Yanagita Kunio Zenshū* Vol. 28 [Chikuma Bunko] (Tokyo: Chikuma Shobō, 1996) pp. 245–507.

Yanagita, Kunio *The Legends of Tōno* trans. Morse, Ronald, A. (Tokyo: The Japan Foundation, 1975)

Yanagita, Kunio *Tōno Monogatari* (1910) in *Yanagita Kunio Zenshū* Vol. 2 (Tokyo: Chikuma Shobō, 1997).

Yanagita, Kunio *Tōno Monogatari* in *Yanagita Kunio Zenshū* Vol. 4 [Chikuma Bunko] (Tokyo: Chikuma Shobō, 1994).

Yomota, Inuhiko *Nihon Eiga Shi Hyakunen* (Tokyo: Shūeisha Shinsho, 2000).

Yoneyama, Toshinao 'Yanagita and His Works' in Koschmann, J. Victor et al. *International Perspectives on Yanagita Kunio and Japanese Folklore Studies* (Ithaca, New York: East Asia Program, Cornell University [Cornell East Asia Papers No. 37], 1988) pp. 29–52.

Yoshida, Fuminori 'Shi to iu Kōi—60 Nendai Shi ni tsuite' in *Kokubungaku: Kaishaku to Kyōzai no Kenkyū* 41:13 (Nov. 1996) pp. 119–26.

Yoshida, Issui *[Teihon] Yoshida Issui Zenshū* Vol. 1 (Tokyo: Ozawa Shoten, 1982).

Yoshimasu, Gōzō *Osiris, the God of Stone* trans. Hiroaki Sato (Laurinberg, North Carolina: St. Andrew's Press, 1989).

Yoshimoto, Banana *Kitchin* (Tokyo: Fukutake Shoten, 1988).

Yoshimoto, Banana *Painatsu Purin* (Tokyo: Kadokawa Bunko, 1992).

Yoshimoto, Banana *Kitchen* trans. Megan Backus (London, Boston: Faber and Faber, 1993).

Yoshimoto, Banana *N.P.* trans. Ann Sherif (New York: Grove Press, 1994).

Yoshimoto, Banana *B Kyū Banana: Yoshimoto Banana Tokuhon* (Tokyo: Fukutake Bunko, 1995).

Yoshimoto, Banana *Amurita* 2 Vols (Tokyo: Kadokawa Bunko, 1997).

Yoshimoto, Banana *Amrita* trans. F. Wasden (New York: Washington Square Press, 1998).

Yoshimoto, Takaaki 'Machū Shō Shiron—Hangyaku no Ronri' in *Yoshimoto Takaaki Zenchosakushū* Vol. 4 (Tokyo: Keisei Shobō, 1969) pp. 42–106.

Yoshimoto, Takaaki *Yoshimoto Takaaki Zenchosakushū* Vol. 5 (Tokyo: Keisei Shobō, 1970).

Yoshimoto, Takaaki *Yoshimoto Takaaki Zenchosakushū* Vol. 6 (Tokyo: Keisei Shobō, 1972).

Yoshimoto, Takaaki *Yoshimoto Takaaki Zenchosakushū* Vol. 11 (Tokyo: Keisei Shobō, 1972a).

Yoshimoto, Takaaki *Yoshimoto Takaaki Zenchosakushū* Vol. 13 (Tokyo: Keisei Shobō, 1972b).

Yoshimoto, Takaaki *Yoshimoto Takaaki Zenchosakushū* Vol. 10 (Tokyo: Keisei Shobō, 1973).

Yoshimoto, Takaaki *Shomotsu no Kaitaigaku* (Tokyo: Chūō Kōron, [Chūkō Bunko], 1981).

Yoshimoto, Takaaki *[Zōho] Sengoshiron* (Tokyo: Yamato Shobō, 1983).

Yoshimoto, Takaaki *Yoshimoto Takaaki Shishū* (Tokyo: Shinchōsha Gendaishi Bunko, 1986).

Yoshimoto, Takaaki *Hai Imēji Ron I* (Tokyo: Fukutake Shoten, 1989).

Yoshimoto, Takaaki *[Teihon]Gengo no Bi to wa Nanika I* (Tokyo: Kadokawa Shoten [Kadokawa Sensho 200], 1990).

Yoshimoto, Takaaki *[Teihon]Gengo no Bi to wa Nanika II* (Tokyo: Kadokawa Shoten [Kadokawa Sensho 200], 1990a).

Yoshimoto, Takaaki *Hai Imēji Ron II* (Tokyo: Fukutake Shoten, 1990b).

Yoshimoto, Takaaki *Masu Imēji Ron* (Tokyo: Fukutake Bunko, 1994).

Yoshimoto, Takaaki *Katari no Umi: Gengo to iu Shisō* (Tokyo: Chūō Kōron, 1995).

Yoshimoto, Takaaki *Jōkyō to Shite no Gazō: Kōdo Shihonshugika no 'Terebi'* (Tokyo: Kawade Shobō Shinsha, 1995a).

Yoshimoto, Takaaki *[Teihon] Yanagita Kunio Ron* (Tokyo: Yōsensha, 1995b).

Yoshimoto, Takaaki '*Dansu Dansu Dansu* no Miryoku' in *[Gunzō Nihon no Sakka] Murakami Haruki* (Tokyo: Shōgakukan, 1997) pp. 215–30.

Yoshioka, Minoru *Yoshioka Minoru* [Gendai no Shijin 1] (ed.) Mutsuo Takahashi (Tokyo: Chūō Kōronsha, 1983).

Yoshioka, Minoru *Celebration in Darkness: Selected Poems of Yoshioka Minoru* trans. Christopher Drake (Rochester, Michigan: Katydid Books/Oakland University, 1985).

Yusa, Michiko 'Philosophy and Inflation: Miki Kiyoshi in Weimar Germany, 1922–1924' in *Monumenta Nipponica* 53:1 (Spring 1998) pp. 45–71.

INDEX